Macmillan: A Publishing Tradition

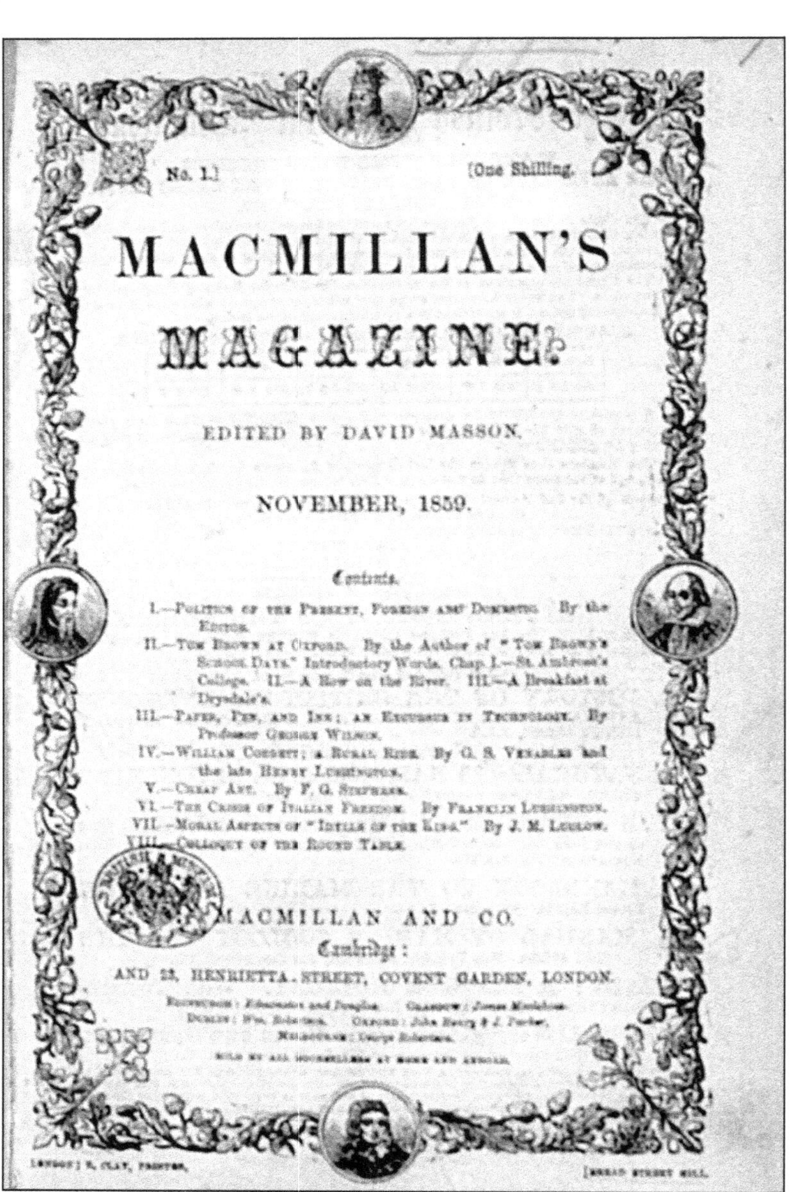

No. 1.] [One Shilling.

MACMILLAN'S

MAGAZINE.

EDITED BY DAVID MASSON.

NOVEMBER, 1859.

Contents.

I.—Politics of the Present, Foreign and Domestic. By the Editor.

II.—Tom Brown at Oxford. By the Author of "Tom Brown's School Days." Introductory Words. Chap. I.—St. Ambrose's College. II.—A Row on the River. III.—A Breakfast at Drysdale's.

III.—Paper, Pen, and Ink; an Excursus in Technology. By Professor George Wilson.

IV.—William Cobbett; a Rural Ride. By G. S. Venables and the late Henry Lushington.

V.—Cheap Art. By F. G. Stephens.

VI.—The Crisis of Italian Freedom. By Franklin Lushington.

VII.—Moral Aspects of "Idylls of the King." By J. M. Ludlow.

VIII.—Colloquy of the Round Table.

MACMILLAN AND CO.

Cambridge:

AND 23, HENRIETTA-STREET, COVENT GARDEN, LONDON.

Edinburgh: Edmonston and Douglas. Glasgow: James Maclehose.
Dublin: Wm. Robertson. Oxford: John Henry & J. Parker.
Melbourne: George Robertson.

SOLD BY ALL BOOKSELLERS AT HOME AND ABROAD.

[London:] R. Clay, Printer, [Bread Street Hill.

The first issue of *Macmillan's Magazine*, November 1859.

Macmillan: A Publishing Tradition

Edited by

Elizabeth James
Curator of British Collections, 1801–1914
The British Library

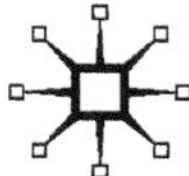

Published by
PALGRAVE MACMILLAN
Houndmills, Basingstoke, Hampshire RG21 6XS and
175 Fifth Avenue, New York, N. Y. 10010
Companies and representatives throughout the world

PALGRAVE MACMILLAN is the global academic imprint of the Palgrave Macmillan division of St. Martin's Press, LLC and of Palgrave Macmillan Ltd. Macmillan® is a registered trademark in the United States, United Kingdom and other countries. Palgrave is a registered trademark in the European Union and other countries.

ISBN-13: 978–0–333–73517–6

This book is printed on paper suitable for recycling and made from fully managed and sustained forest sources. Logging, pulping and manufacturing processes are expected to conform to the environmental regulations of the country of origin.

A catalogue record for this book is available from the British Library.

A catalogue record for this book is available from the Library of Congress.

Contents

List of Plates

List of Tables

List of Figures

Notes on the Contributors

Nicolas Barker is Editor of *The Book Collector*, and author of many works on bibliography and the history of books; his *Hortus Eystettensis: the Bishop's garden and Besler's great botanical book* (1994) was awarded the Premio Felice Feliciano. He was, until 1995, Deputy Keeper in the British Library.

Bill Bell is Co-director of the Centre for the History of the Book and Lecturer in English at the University of Edinburgh. He has published widely on nineteenth-century culture and is General Editor of *A History of the Book in Scotland*, to be published in four volumes by Edinburgh University Press.

Michael Bott is Keeper of Archives and Manuscripts at the University of Reading Library, where he has been much involved with the growth of the archive of British Publishers, the *Location Register of British Book Trade Archives*, and the recent establishment of the Centre for Writing, Publishing and Printing History, of which he is Deputy Director.

Rimi B. Chatterjee is Assistant Professor in English Language and Literature at the Indian Institute of Technology, Kharagpur. She recently completed a doctoral thesis at Oxford on the trade to India of Macmillan and OUP between 1875 and 1900, and has extended this research to 1947 with a view to publication. In February 2000 her English translation of Mahasweta Devi's *Titu Mir* was published by Seagull in Calcutta.

Simon Eliot is Professor of Publishing and Printing History at the University of Reading, and Director of the History of the Book MA at the School of Advanced Study, University of London. He is a specialist in the quantitative history of the book, author/publisher relations and in the history of reading, and is joint editor (with David McKitterick) of *The Cambridge History of the Book in Britain, Volume 6: 1800–1900.*

Warwick Gould is Professor of English in the University of London, where he teaches at Royal Holloway and is Director of the Institute of English Studies in the School of Advanced Study. He is co-author (with Marjorie

Reeves) of *Joachim of Fiore and the Myth of the Eternal Evangel in the Nineteenth Century* (1987), co-editor of *The Collected Letters of W. B. Yeats,* Volume II 1896–1900 (Clarendon, 1997), and editor of *Yeats Annual.* He is working on editions of Yeats's *Early Essays* and *Mythologies* for the Macmillan *Collected Edition of the Works of W. B. Yeats,* and of *Yeats's Occult Diaries (1898–1901).*

John Handford is a graduate of Cambridge and honorary DLitt at Plymouth, where he was instrumental in setting up the course in publishing. Before his retirement in 1999, he worked for Macmillan for 36 years, for the last 11 of them as Archivist and Librarian.

Elizabeth James is Curator of British Collections, 1801–1914, at the British Library, where she has been responsible for a number of exhibitions relating to nineteenth-century authorship and publishing. She is an Associate Fellow of the Institute of English Studies, University of London, and co-author (with Helen Smith) of *Penny Dreadfuls and Boys' Adventures* (1998).

Michael Millgate is a University Professor of English Emeritus of the University of Toronto. He has written and published extensively on Thomas Hardy, in particular *The Collected Letters of Thomas Hardy* (7 vols, co-edited, 1978–88), *Thomas Hardy: a Biography* (1982), and *The Letters of Emma and Florence Hardy* (edited, 1996). His editing for Macmillan of Hardy's ghost-written *The Life and Work of Thomas Hardy* (1984) led to the wider exploration of authorial deaths and literary estates which provided the basis for his *Testamentary Acts: Browning, Tennyson, James, Hardy* (1992).

Donald E. Moggridge is Professor of Economics at the University of Toronto. He has served as joint managing editor of the Royal Economic Society's edition of *The Collected Writings of John Maynard Keynes,* and with Susan Howson has also edited the diaries of James Meade and Lionel Robbins. He is currently engaged in editing the correspondence of D. H. Robertson and in writing a biography of Harry Johnson.

Frances Spalding is an art historian, critic and biographer. She is the author of *British Art since 1900* and *The Tate: a History,* and has written biographies of the artists Roger Fry, Vanessa Bell, John Minton and Duncan Grant, and of the poet Stevie Smith.

Michael Wace worked in publishing for over 40 years, most of them with Macmillan, publishing both books for schools and general children's books. He retired in 1994.

George Worth is Professor Emeritus of English at the University of Kansas. His publications include books on James Hannay, Harrison Ainsworth, Thomas Hughes, and Charles Dickens, and he is completing another, on *Macmillan's Magazine*.

Acknowledgements

This volume owes its existence to Macmillan Press Ltd, whose important and extensive archive, so carefully maintained for over a century, has become an invaluable source for the study of modern British literary and publishing history. In particular, the contributors represented here, and many others who have used the archive, would like to express their sincere gratitude to the firm's archivist John Handford, and his successor Robert Machesney, for their advice, encouragement and unfailing patience in answering countless queries. A further debt is owed to Tim Farmiloe, who as a director of Macmillan was instrumental in achieving the sale of the archive to the British (Museum) Library, and in commissioning this publication. Special thanks are also due to the libraries and their staff who now share the custodianship of the Macmillan archive: the British Library, University of Reading Library, and New York Public Library. For permission to quote from material in all these collections we are indebted to Macmillan Ltd, the British Library Board, the University of Reading, Simon & Schuster, and the Manuscripts and Archives Division, New York Public Library, Astor, Lenox and Tilden Foundations. Other material is reproduced with the kind permission of the Tennyson Research Centre, Lincoln, David H. Baker, Professor John Kelly and Oxford University Press, Christopher Johnson and the Provost and Fellows of King's College, Cambridge.

The portrait of Frederick Macmillan (Plate 1) is reproduced with the permission of Christopher Hatch, who very kindly made available a number of photographs from his family collection. The photographs of the headquarters of The Macmillan Company of New York and the portrait of George Platt Brett (Plates 8 and 9) are reproduced by courtesy of Simon & Schuster, and with the kind assistance of James D. Birchfield, University of Kentucky Library. Plates 11 to 13 are reproduced by courtesy of the University of London Library. The illustrations from *The Runaway* in Chapter 11 are reproduced with grateful thanks to Gwen Raverat's daughter, Mrs Sophie Gurney; and Charles Dodgson's illustrated letter to Macmillan (Chapter 12) by permission of A. P. Watt Ltd on behalf of the Trustees of the C. L. Dodgson Estate.

This volume has been long in the making, and I should like to express my personal thanks to the contributors for their patience and understanding. I am particularly grateful to Ken Price and Oliver Pickering for their help and advice during the preparation of the typescript; Laurence Pordes and Peter Carey for photographs of items in the British Library's collections; Helen Smith for preparing the index; and to Eleanor Birne and her colleagues at Palgrave for their care in seeing the volume through the press.

E.J.

Abbreviations

Except where stated otherwise, all references are to the Macmillan Archive in the British Library.

BL	British Library
KC	King's College, Cambridge
NYPL	New York Public Library
Reading	University of Reading Library
SRC	Stratford Record Centre
TRC	Tennyson Research Centre, Lincoln
ULL	University of London Library

Foreword

John Sutherland

Publishing history is one of the newer academic specialisms. There is, as yet, no fully-fledged department but a vigorous undergrowth thrives in the traditional areas of university English, History and Sociology. Outside the academy, among librarians, booksellers, bibliophiles and collectors there is a pool of longer-standing expertise which valuably enriches the new discipline. (The conference which inspired this book was sponsored by senior members of the British Library, and largely attended by non-professional book lovers. As is their wont, academics did most of the spouting from the platform.)

In disciplinary terms, publishing history ('material bibliography', as the French call it) is very demanding. Dauntingly so. There are vast continents of data for the ambitious publishing historian to digest. There are, by latest count, some 12 million British books in the BL. Behind each book there can be yards of pre-publication manuscript, office materials and other trade peripherals. Publishing History suffers (the term is appropriate) from a surplus of what is often lacking elsewhere – primary materials.

The term itself is a misnomer. To say that books are 'published' is convenient shorthand for the creative and mechanical apparatus involved in: composition, judicious acceptance, investment, manufacture (typesetting, printing, binding), wholesale distribution, advertising and review, retail sale (or library circulation), consumption. The circuit that connects the author's brainwaves with the reader's eye movements is immensely complex. And it changes all the time. Publishing is a fast-evolving industry.

To be done well, publishing history requires infrastructural investments long before any publishing historians come on the scene. More than most scholars, they stand on the shoulders of others. It is necessary, in the first instance, that books are comprehensively collected and catalogued. This is something best done in national copyright libraries. It is also necessary that a wealth of preliminary materials be available: from authors' manuscripts, through business correspondence, to proofs and ledgers. It is seldom that such materials are comprehensively kept, after the relevant publication has passed out of the backlist into oblivion. Even where office materials survive, it is advantageous that they be re-catalogued and arranged by the library. The needs of commerce are different from those of scholarship.

As is asserted in this volume and demonstrated by the contributors, the Macmillan Archive is unusually intact – uniquely so, some would say. The intricate diplomacy, and subsequent purchases, which have lodged the nuclei of the collection in London and Reading are chronicled in Elizabeth James's introduction. And, having acquired this vast archive, the BL has – over the last 30 years – put it in apple-pie order for the publishing historians to do their superstructural work.

I have been privileged to work on the archive for three separate projects: an essay on the (near) publication of Thomas Hardy's first novel; an essay on the extraordinary collaboration between the founding Macmillan brothers and Charles Kingsley which produced the firm's first fiction best-seller, *Westward Ho!*; and an essay on the firm's dealings with Mrs Humphry Ward, on the publication of her first novel, *Miss Bretherton* (it sold wretchedly: to their later chagrin the firm declined her next novel, the super-selling *Robert Elsmere*).

What struck me, working on these minor projects, was the sensitivity with which the matching runs of incoming and outgoing correspondence had been preserved (by Macmillan), sorted and conserved (by the BL). Unusually, Macmillan preserved readers' reports from its earliest period of operation. There are full ledger accountings. Moreover, as they approached their half-century, the firm itself put together an invaluable resource: James Foster's *A Bibliographical Catalogue of Macmillan and Co.'s Publications from 1843 to 1889*. Would that all British publishers had done the same.

The contributors to this volume have dug much deeper than I into the Macmillan Archive. And their approaches valuably indicate the range of tools and diversity of materials available to the publishing historian. Elizabeth James (whose other scholarly interest is the Routledge Archive) offers – by way of introduction – an account of how the firm's office materials became the library collection, together with a skeletal history; John Handford (until recently archivist to the Macmillan Company) provides a *dramatis personae*; while Michael Bott's chapter adds a postscript to the 'Letters to Macmillan' story.

Simon Eliot (one of whose other scholarly interests is the Chatto Archive) has undertaken a strenuously bibliometric analysis of the firm's output in its first, massively expansionist, phase. His interim conclusion (p. 21), that 'within 20 years of its founding, the firm's production pattern had settled down into a form which paralleled, without slavishly copying, the general pattern of production' strikes me as both convincing and well substantiated. Eliot's formulation allows room for that most tricky of aspects of publishing history, 'house style'. Macmillan books are, to the experienced eye, as distinctive as those of Cape, Faber, or Gollancz. What makes them so is often hard to say.

Among its other virtues, the essays in this collection are intelligently assembled. Eliot's chapter, with its panoptic view of the firm's product, reminds us that Macmillan published many other kinds of book than the famous landmarks, dutifully commemorated in the Chronology. And they published books in more markets than any other British house of their time (Elizabeth James's chapter on the New York branch, Rimi B. Chatterjee's chapter on 'Macmillan in India' cover two of these overseas presences).

Macmillan have the glory of being Hardy's, Arnold's, Tennyson's and Yeats's publishers (as Michael Millgate, Bill Bell and Warwick Gould attest). But Macmillan also had, from the first, a strong interest in children's books, as Michael Wace records. The variety of the firm's activities is further indicated in the chapters by George Worth (on the pioneering *Macmillan's Magazine*); D. E. Moggridge (on Maynard Keynes as Macmillan author) and Frances Spalding (on the publication of Gwen Raverat's illustrated edition of *The Runaway*).

In an ideal world, I would have liked some other chapters, to complete the small picture of what became a very big firm. Specifically, a discussion on Macmillan as a leader in the evolution of the British booktrade (the Net Book Agreement was, famously, Frederick Macmillan's invention), and something on Macmillan as the publisher of scientific material (notably in *Nature*). The volume ends, however, with Nicolas Barker's extraordinarily evocative account of the personnel and procedures at Macmillan, in the period that he had dealings with the firm. This tends to be the material that is lost forever to the publishing historian.

The timeliness of this volume, *Macmillan: a Publishing Tradition,* is enhanced by the announcement, in autumn 2000, that Macmillan's UK academic publishing and St Martin's Press (Scholarly and Reference) in the US have combined to form a new imprint, 'Palgrave'. To commemorate the event, on 5 October 2000, Palgrave reissued one of the most famous Macmillan books (first published in 1861), *The Golden Treasury*, with a new foreword by poet laureate, Andrew Motion – the first 'Palgrave author'.

London, 2000

Macmillan Biographies, 1843–1965

John Handford

Daniel Macmillan (1813–57), son of an Arran crofter, was apprenticed to a bookseller in Irvine, Ayrshire, at the age of ten. He moved to Glasgow and, in 1833, to England. He worked for booksellers in London and Cambridge until he opened his own business in Aldersgate Street, London, and Trinity Street, Cambridge, in 1843. In poor health from an early age, he lived to publish works by Archdeacon Hare and F. D. Maurice as well as the first best-selling Macmillan book, *Westward Ho!* by Charles Kingsley.

Alexander Macmillan (1818–96), younger brother of Daniel and co-founder of the company, joined Daniel in London in 1839 to form the partnership that set the Macmillan company on the road to success. He identified opportunities in the field of education both at home and in other English-speaking countries. *Nature* and *The Statesman's Year-Book*, both of which flourish today, were founded by him, as was *Macmillan's Magazine*. He was publisher to the University of Oxford from 1863 to 1881. The crowning achievement of his career came in 1884 when he contracted to publish all the works of Tennyson.

Sir Frederick Orridge Macmillan (1851–1936) was the elder son of Daniel. After spending five years with the fledgling New York house, he returned to London in 1876, and took a leading role in the establishment of branches in India, Canada and Australia. He campaigned for the Net Book Agreement of 1899, and was one of the founders of the Publishers Association, of which he was twice president. He was knighted in 1909.

Maurice Crawford Macmillan (1853–1936), younger son of Daniel, spent six years as a schoolmaster before becoming a partner in 1883. In 1884–85 he toured India, Australia and New Zealand, where he initiated the development of the business. A direct result of this tour was the establishment of the Colonial Library, the most successful such venture by any British publisher.

Malcolm Kingsley Macmillan (1852–89) was Alexander's eldest son. He was working for the firm as early as 1871, but he spent much of his time in study and travel. He wrote a story, *Dagonet the Jester*, published in 1886. He disappeared during an ascent of Mount Olympus in 1889, and his fate has remained a mystery.

George Augustin Macmillan (1855–1936), Alexander's second son, joined the firm on leaving school, and remained for the rest of his life. His love of music, and of the art, archaeology and literature of ancient civilisations, are reflected in the publications of the period, notably Grove's *Dictionary of Music and Musicians*, Frazer's *The Golden Bough* and Sir Arthur Evans's *The Palace of Minos*.

George Lillie Craik (1837–1905) became a partner in 1865. His role is described by Charles Morgan as 'Chancellor of the Exchequer', and he had Alexander's complete trust. He was married to the novelist Dinah Maria Mulock.

Daniel de Mendi Macmillan (1886–1965), classical scholar and friend of Keynes, was the eldest of Maurice's three sons. His entire working life was devoted to publishing; he became chairman on the death of the three second-generation directors in 1936, and remained active almost until his death.

Maurice Harold Macmillan, 1st Earl of Stockton (1894–1986), youngest son of Maurice, entered the firm in 1920, and was elected a member of parliament in 1924. He divided his time between publishing and politics, serving in Churchill's war government from 1940 to 1945, in Conservative administrations from 1951 to 1957, then as prime minister until 1963. He then returned to publishing, and presided over the company's rapid expansion worldwide. He became Earl of Stockton in 1984.

Sir Richard Gregory (1864–1952) had assisted Sir Norman Lockyer in his astronomical research before joining the staff of *Nature* in 1893. He succeeded as editor in 1919, and was also the company's publisher of scientific books. He continued in both roles until his retirement in 1938. Macmillan published his biography by W. H. G. Armytage in 1957.

G. J. Heath (1864–1939) joined as a boy in 1877 and never retired. He was general manager, later director, and had special responsibility for overseas business, especially in India. He was closely associated with the work of Enid Blyton. He was succeeded as general manager by his son **Roland J. Heath** (1892–1970), who served the company from 1914 to 1959.

Thomas Mark (1890–1963) joined in 1914. Until his appointment as a director in 1944, he is described in the records as 'Reader'. He was known for his acute literary judgement and his meticulous correction of proofs. A trusted friend and ally of many authors, notably Hugh Walpole and W. B. Yeats, he retired in 1962.

Horatio Henry ('Rache') Lovat Dickson (1902–87) ran a publishing business under his own name in the 1930s before joining Macmillan in 1938. He was mainly concerned with fiction and general publishing, and became the confidant and publisher of Richard Hillary in 1941. He was the author of a number of books, including lives of Wells, Hillary and 'Grey Owl', and two volumes of autobiography. He retired in 1964.

Alfred B. ('John') Brooks (1903–90) joined in 1919, became office manager in the 1930s, and company secretary during the war. He succeeded Roland Heath as general manager, then took charge of Indian publishing and the overseas schools list. He retired in 1967.

L. J. F. ('Jack') Brimble (1904–65) was recruited in 1931 to assist Sir Richard Gregory both as editor of *Nature* and in his schools publishing role. A botanist, he wrote and illustrated several books in the schools list. On Sir Richard's retirement in 1938, he became joint editor of *Nature* with **A. J. V. Gale**, and from the latter's retirement in 1961 until his death he was sole editor.

Harry A. Evans (1906–86), whose service spanned the years 1921–65, was referred to as publishing manager in the pre-war years, and production manager thereafter. The latter title is a more accurate description of his role in today's terms.

R. C. ('Bob') Rowland Clark (1909–78) joined the accounts department in 1927. He served in the army throughout the war, then became company secretary. He was appointed a director in 1954, and in the 1960s he took charge of the home schools list. He retired in 1970.

Frank H. Whitehead (1918–88) was the chief executive of Macmillan during Harold Macmillan's chairmanship in the 1960s. He joined the company in 1937, served in the army during the war, and, apart from a short break, continued in Macmillan's service until his retirement in 1983. A director from 1963, he masterminded the transfer of the warehouse from London to Basingstoke in 1964.

R. F. ('Rex') Allen (1919–) joined on demobilisation from war service in 1946, first as assistant to Thomas Mark, and later to Daniel Macmillan. He was appointed a director of Macmillan & Co. Ltd in 1963. He worked mainly on academic publishing, and on the schools classics list. He left in 1974 to take up a position with David & Charles.

Maurice Victor Macmillan, Viscount Macmillan of Ovenden (1921–84) was the son of the first earl. He joined the firm in 1946, and remained a director (except when in government) until his death. He was closely associated with Macmillan's participation in the fledgling Pan Books in the early post-war years. He was a member of parliament from 1955, except for the years 1964–66, and he had ministerial appointments under Douglas-Home and Heath. The Macmillan family members of the present generation, **Alexander, 2nd Earl, David** and **Adam** are his sons.

Alan D. Maclean (1924–) became Lovat Dickson's assistant in 1954 and a director of Macmillan & Co. Ltd in 1963 with special responsibility for fiction. He retired in 1984 and, in 1997, published a volume of reminiscences, *No, I Tell a Lie, It Was the Tuesday ...*

All these were partners, directors, or employees, but there are a number of others whose letters are to be found in the Macmillan archives, though they may not have worked full time for the company, or even had an office on the premises. These include the founding editor of *Nature*, Sir Norman Lockyer, the founding editor of *The Statesman's Year-Book*, Frederick Martin (and his successors), John Morley (later Viscount Morley of Blackburn), David Masson, Sir George Grove, Mowbray Morris, Charles Whibley and Sir John Squire.

Macmillan Chronology, 1843–1970

John Handford

1843	Daniel and Alexander Macmillan trading at 57 Aldersgate Street, London
1843	First Macmillan book: *The Philosophy of Training* by A. R. Craig
1844	Business transferred to 17 Trinity Street, Cambridge
1855	Charles Kingsley *Westward Ho!*
1857	Thomas Hughes *Tom Brown's School Days*
1857	Death of Daniel Macmillan
1858	Business moved to 23 Henrietta Street, Covent Garden, London
1859	First issue of *Macmillan's Magazine* (published monthly to 1907)
1861	F. T. Palgrave *The Golden Treasury*
1862	Christina Rossetti *Goblin Market and other Poems*
1863	Business moved to 16 Bedford Street
1863	Alexander Macmillan appointed publisher to Oxford University (to 1881)
1864	First edition of *The Statesman's Year-Book*
1864	Globe Shakespeare, edited by W. G. Clark and W. A. Wright
1865	George Lillie Craik taken into partnership
1865	Lewis Carroll *Alice's Adventures in Wonderland*
1865	Matthew Arnold *Essays in Criticism. First series*
1866	Samuel Baker *The Albert Nyanza*
1867	Alexander Macmillan visited USA
1869	First issue of *Nature*
1869	New York office opened under George Brett
1874	J. R. Green *A Short History of the English People*
1874	George Augustin Macmillan joined the firm
1875	First books for Indian schools
1877–89	First edition of Sir George Grove's *Dictionary of Music and Musicians*
1878	English Men of Letters series launched
1879	Macmillan first published Henry James
1883	*English Illustrated Magazine* published (to 1892)
1883	Maurice Crawford Macmillan joins the firm

1884	Tennyson's works transferred to Macmillan
1885	H. S. Hall and S. R. Knight *Elementary Algebra for Schools*
1886	Macmillan declined to publish George Bernard Shaw
1886	Colonial Library launched
1887	Thomas Hardy *The Woodlanders* published in book form
1887	English Classics series launched
1890	Alfred Marshall *Principles of Economics* – the first net book
1890	Sir J. G. Frazer *The Golden Bough*
1890	Rudyard Kipling *Plain Tales from the Hills.* First Macmillan edition
1895	First Australian representative employed
1896	Macmillan & Co. registered, Frederick Macmillan chairman
1896	New York company incorporated
1896	Death of Alexander Macmillan
1897	Move to new premises in St Martin's Street
1898	Macmillan acquired the business of Richard Bentley
1899	R. H. Inglis Palgrave *Dictionary of Political Economy* completed
1899	Net Book Agreement came into force
1900	Frederick Macmillan president of the Publishers Association (to 1902, and again 1911–13)
1901	Bombay branch opened
1902	Thomas Hardy's works transferred to Macmillan
1905	Weekly publication of *Nursing Times* began
1905	Melbourne branch opened
1906	Macmillan Company of Canada formed
1907	Calcutta branch opened
1908	Macmillan decline H. G. Wells *Anna Veronica*
1909	Frederick Macmillan knighted
1909	H. G. Wells *Tono-Bungay*
1912	James Stephens *The Crock of Gold*
1912	Macmillan first published Rabindranath Tagore
1913	Madras branch opened
1916	W. B. Yeats' works transferred to Macmillan
1919	J. M. Keynes *The Economic Consequences of the Peace*
1920	(Maurice) Harold Macmillan joined
1925	Sean O'Casey *Juno and the Paycock*
1930	Hugh Walpole *Rogue Herries*
1933	James Hilton *Lost Horizon*
1936	Margaret Mitchell *Gone with the Wind*
1936	J. M. Keynes *The General Theory of Employment, Interest and Money*

1936 Sir Frederick, Maurice and George Macmillan died; Daniel de Mendi Macmillan chairman
1938 Lovat Dickson joined as director
1941 Richard Hillary *The Last Enemy*
1942 Charles Morgan *The House of Macmillan, 1843–1943*
1944 Hardy copyrights purchased
1944–55 Enid Blyton's Adventure series
1945–50 Osbert Sitwell *Left Hand, Right Hand*
1946 Macmillan a partner in Pan Books
1947 Hugh Trevor-Roper *The Last Days of Hitler*
1951 Macmillan Company of New York sold
1951 C. P. Snow *The Masters*
1951 Rumer Godden first published by Macmillan
1952 St Martin's Press incorporated
1953 *Nature* published Crick and Watson's paper on DNA
1954 Pan's first million-copy bestseller: Paul Brickhill *The Dam Busters*
1957–63 Harold Macmillan prime minister
1961 Muriel Spark *The Prime of Miss Jean Brodie*
1964 Warehouse and administrative departments opened in Basingstoke
1965 Publishing departments move to 4 Little Essex Street
1965 Nicholas Byam Shaw, later chief executive, appointed director
1965 Daniel de Mendi Macmillan died
1966 Harold Macmillan's first volume of memoirs *The Winds of Change*
1967 Simon Nowell-Smith (ed.) *Letters to Macmillan*
1968 Gill & Macmillan formed in partnership with M. H. Gill & Son Ltd, Dublin
1972 Macmillan Company of Canada sold to Maclean Hunter

Macmillan: A Publishing Tradition

Introduction

Elizabeth James

In February 1843 Daniel Macmillan and his brother Alexander opened their first bookshop at 57 Aldersgate Street in the City of London; by the end of the year they had published their first title, A. R. Craig's *The Philosophy of Training,* a 93-page treatise on the importance of training teachers for the wealthier classes. The younger sons of a Scottish farmer, the brothers had been brought up in the small Ayrshire town of Irvine, where their mother instilled in them a love of literature and education. Daniel in particular, was a devout, sensitive man who made a lasting impression on those who came to know him. 'I can see him now,' recalled one customer, 'with his thoughtful face, and a certain attractive gentle power, as he stood and had a few words, now with one, now with another, as they came in'. Alexander, a more resilient character, had drifted from teaching, to employment in a chemist's shop, and a brief interlude as a seaman, before following his brother into an apprenticeship in the booktrade, and eventual partnership in their own enterprise.

In 1844 the Macmillans moved their business to larger premises at Cambridge, where they quickly found a place in the academic and literary community, attracting a distinguished circle of teachers and Christian socialists to their shop in Trinity Street. Wordsworth's visit later that year was a source of immense pride and delight: 'He came upstairs and stayed with me an hour and a half,' Daniel recalled, 'and discoursed with the greatest simplicity on all manner of subjects'. Within 18 months he was able to write to his childhood companion, the missionary David Watt, 'We are just in the middle of term; & are pressed with business from early morning till late at night.' Theology and sermons, classical literature and educational guides (mostly with a Cambridge connection) characterised their early lists until the astonishing success of Charles Kingsley's *Westward Ho!* (1855), a rollicking adventure story deliberately designed to lift the nation's spirits during the horrors of the Crimean War, and Thomas Hughes' *Tom Brown's School Days* (1857) laid the foundations of a strong line in fiction.

Daniel, never a strong man, died of tuberculosis in 1857. His young family, and the rapidly expanding business, were left to the care of Alexander, who rose enthusiastically to the challenge. He lost no time in transferring the firm's operations back to London, which was, by this time, the centre of a vibrant publishing industry. *Macmillan's Magazine*, his venture into the important, but extremely competitive, mid-Victorian market for literary periodicals, was launched in 1859; Palgrave's *The Golden Treasury* appeared in 1861; *The Statesman's Year-Book*, one of a number of long-lived and influential reference works, began in 1864; Lewis Carroll's *Alice's Adventures in Wonderland* was published in 1866; the first issue of *Nature*, an ambitious response to the growing interest in science, appeared in 1869. Also in 1869, the firm was one of the first English publishing houses to recognise the importance of overseas markets when it opened a branch in New York. Gradually the catalogue diversified to include poetry, science, history and travel; while the Education Act of 1870 led to an expansion in the production of carefully edited school texts, both at home and abroad. During the 1880s George Macmillan, a long-standing officer of the Hellenic Society, was responsible for a renewed emphasis on ancient Greek texts, which he justified in commercial terms by pointing to the expense and difficulty of obtaining permission to reprint copyright works.

By the 1890s, although described, rather disparagingly, by H. G. Wells as 'solid, sound and sane', Macmillan was the chosen patron and publisher of a galaxy of established writers – including Matthew Arnold, Alfred Tennyson, Rudyard Kipling and Henry James – with valuable reputations to protect and promote. Thomas Hardy became a Macmillan author for the first time in 1886, when, with *The Woodlanders* appearing in instalments in *Macmillan's Magazine*, he was invited to support their latest enterprise, the Colonial Library. This series of standard works and popular fiction, intended for publication only in India and the colonies, was one of the most successful of its kind, extending to more than 600 titles before it was relaunched in 1913 as the Empire Library. In 1898 Macmillan purchased the flourishing business of Richard Bentley, also noted for its fiction list, which brought a host of valuable copyrights and stock, together with steel and copper plates by artists such as Cruikshank, Tenniel and Du Maurier. At about this time, too, the firm was negotiating with contemporary artists such as Walter Crane, Laurence

Housman, Thomas Sturge Moore and Hugh Thomson to produce a number of attractively bound and illustrated editions of literary works.

The company entered the twentieth century as a senior member of the booktrade, having pioneered under Daniel's son, Frederick, the founding of the Publishers Association and the Net Book Agreement. It acquired many new authors, particularly from Ireland – W. B. Yeats, James Stephens, Sean O'Casey – and most significantly in the field of politics and economics – Alfred Marshall, J. M. Keynes, Roy Harrod, and Joan Robinson, granddaughter of one of the firm's earliest celebrities, the theologian F. D. Maurice. Other important figures associated with Macmillan at this time included James Hilton, Vera Brittain, Osbert Sitwell, the prolific and popular but often demanding, Hugh Walpole, and from Canada, the novelist Mazo de la Roche.

The years immediately preceding the outbreak of the Second World War were difficult financially and personally for the family, with the deaths in 1936 of George, Frederick and Maurice Macmillan. Yet the triumphant success of the New York company, and Margaret Mitchell's *Gone with the Wind,* raised the firm's fortunes and spirits so that it was able to face the hardships of wartime London with confidence – not to say bravado – proudly advertising its intention to remain in the substantial Victorian office building in St Martin's Street until 'taxed, insured, ARPd or bombed out of existence'. Restrictions and shortages, import quotas and censorship became familiar obstacles as the 1940s progressed; there was little newspaper space for advertising, and the many authors who begged to be allowed to contribute to the war effort were advised that there was no better way than 'by continuing with your work as writers'. The circumstances were not ideal for centenary celebrations in 1943, but two prizes of £500 each were offered for a novel and a work of non-fiction, and Charles Morgan, one of the best-selling authors of the day, was commissioned to write a history of the firm's first hundred years.

The end of the war saw the third generation of the family in control and overseeing a period of reconstruction and rapid expansion into serious academic and literary publishing, as well as the setting-up of new branches overseas. Every effort was put into reissuing the many important works which had fallen out of print, as well as reviving lapsed rights and pursuing new ones in film and radio. There was particular emphasis on educational publishing, both for the home market and on behalf of government agencies in Africa, India and the Far East; and in the revitalised children's department a succession of talented editors advised and encouraged new authors such as Jill Paton Walsh, Rumer

Godden and Enid Blyton. In 1947, anxious to break into the increasingly powerful paperback market, Macmillan joined with Collins and Hodder & Stoughton in purchasing a share in Pan Books, the two-year-old subsidiary of the Book Society. Despite their eye-catching covers (the distinctive logo was based on an original design by Mervyn Peake), and later emphasis on crime and adventure stories, Pan Books were intended as pocket editions of 'works of ... reputation'. The first title, Rudyard Kipling's *Ten Stories,* appeared in 1947, followed closely by James Hilton's *Lost Horizon,* Agatha Christie's *Ten Little Niggers,* and J. B. Priestley's *Three Time-Plays.* Like the Tauchnitz editions of 50 years earlier, Pan books were designed to conform to a preferred length, which even well-established authors such as Mazo de la Roche and Hugh Trevor-Roper were advised to accept for the sake of their enormous sales. Print runs were set at about 25,000 copies, and within a year total sales had reached two million.

By 1964 the firm had outgrown its premises in St Martin's Street, which it had occupied since 1897, and was preparing to transfer the supply and distribution operations to new offices at Basingstoke, about 40 miles south-west of London. The vast accumulation of old files and papers, documenting 120 years of negotiations with many of the country's greatest writers, scholars and artists, inevitably came under close scrutiny as the time of the move came closer. The successful sale in 1957 of Lewis Carroll's letters had already drawn attention to the financial value of some of this material, and now the possibility of a lucrative and space-saving sale of the bulk of the archive seemed doubly attractive. Early in 1964 negotiations were opened with Sotheby's, but after some initial sorting it was concluded that 'winnowing the wheat from the chaff' would be a long and exacting task.

This was the situation in October, when Simon Nowell-Smith tentatively approached Macmillan for permission to consult the archives in preparing his Lyell lectures on international copyright law. Within a short time he had been commissioned both to prepare the material for auction, and edit a 'scrapbook' of authors' letters. With the help of an assistant provided by Reading University – already keenly interested in publishers' archives – he sorted thousands of letters, ledgers and other documents into categories to keep, to sell, to destroy, or to give to the British Museum Library. By November 1965 his painstaking work was sufficiently far advanced for Macmillan to agree to present the correspondence of less significant authors to Reading. But by then the impending sale 'of a kind to warm the cockles of American bibliographical hearts', as Harold Macmillan famously described it to *The Sunday*

Telegraph, had aroused considerable attention, especially amongst literary historians concerned by the imminent dispersal of such a unique resource. The British Museum now began to express an interest in the whole archive, and, after protracted discussions largely concerned with the extent and nature of the material on offer, it was finally announced on 20 October 1967 that the correspondence and papers of the publishing house of Macmillan had been acquired for the nation. This original tranche of material, described in detail in *The British Library Catalogue of Additions to the Manuscripts ... 1966–1970* (British Library, 1998), documented the firm's activities up to 1939; a second instalment, acquired in 1990, covered the period 1940–70.

The estimated 2,200 volumes of the British Library's Macmillan archive chart the history of the firm primarily through its correspondence, beginning with Daniel's earnest letters to F. D. Maurice and Archdeacon Julius Hare, in which he sought moral and financial support for his ambitious plans. The backbone of this vast mass of material is the outstanding sequence of general letter books, containing pressed and carbon copies of over 300,000 outgoing letters, the vast majority written by members of the Macmillan family. These document not only negotiations with individual authors over specific books, but every aspect of the business of publishing: there are requests for paper samples, printing estimates, readers' reports and reviews, complaints about unfulfilled orders and the cost of advertising, discussions on binding styles and illustration, and on the pricing of books. Separate sequences are devoted to the Macmillan Company of New York, St Martin's Press, the Macmillan Company of Canada, and printers such as Richard Clay and R. & R. Clark, with whom Macmillan was closely involved and communicated in the form of frequent (usually weekly) memoranda. Beyond these 'open' letter books are the private ledgers, recording confidential discussions between Macmillan family members, certain financial matters (especially relating to important authors like Tennyson or Hardy), staffing difficulties (particularly in the troubled Canadian company of the early 1920s), or bold new ventures and developments.

The other side of this correspondence is contained in approximately 650 volumes of incoming letters from over 1,000 authors and editors, readers and literary agents, printers and fellow publishers. About a quarter of these are from the Macmillan Company of New York and other overseas branches, and a small but significant number from the literary agents A. P. Watt, Pearn, Pollinger & Higham and Curtis Brown, but the great majority are written by authors (or their families) representing every discipline of Macmillan's publishing activity. The novelists range from Charles Kingsley in 1849 to Vera Brittain in 1966, taking in a host of famous names along the way – Thomas Hardy, Henry James, Charlotte M. Yonge, F. Marion Crawford, Rudyard Kipling, H. G. Wells, Hugh Walpole, Charles Morgan, James Stephens and James Hilton. The roll-call of poets is shorter but equally impressive, including two poets laureate (Lord Tennyson, whose correspondence was handled by his son, Hallam, and Alfred Austin), Matthew Arnold, W. B. Yeats, Edmund Blunden and Edith Sitwell, and not forgetting F. T. Palgrave. Representing Macmillan's academic strengths are most of the major economists of the nineteenth and twentieth centuries, from W. S. Jevons in 1866 to Roy Harrod in 1963, together with historians such as John Morley and J. R. Green, the socialist G. D. H. Cole, the anthropologist James Frazer and archaeologist Aurel Stein. And amongst all these are smaller, but fascinating caches of letters from *Punch* editors Mark Lemon and F. C. Burnand, the critic Walter Pater, artists C. E. Brock and Arthur Rackham, children's authors Richard Crompton and the redoubtable Enid Blyton, to name only a few.

Large though it is, the British Library Macmillan archive is not complete. In 1965 and again in 1990, the University of Reading received many thousands of residual letters, extracted from the main archive primarily because their authors were considered less important, but occasionally perhaps because they were represented by too few items to merit inclusion in a commercial sale. Such decisions are bound to be subjective, and many eminent authors – Max Beerbohm, Hilaire Belloc, Laurence Binyon, André Gide, Herbert Read and George Russell among them – slipped through the net. So, too, did many of the firm's advisers, editors, readers, and collaborators such as Stanley Morison, whose letter revealing his part in the design of the Sussex Edition of Kipling's works is to be found at Reading. Indeed, the Reading letters are especially relevant for the history of publishing, and particularly the development of overseas markets for English books.

Advising Macmillan in the 1960s, Simon Nowell-Smith recommended the retention of all files necessary for present and future publishing activities. Those documents, now held in the firm's archives at Basingstoke, include the contracts and accompanying letters, and the correspondence of living authors. They also include the first Editions Book, a large folio of 946 pages compiled by James Foster, author of *A Bibliographical Catalogue of Macmillan and Co.'s Publications from 1843 to 1889*, recording print orders for most of the books issued during this period. As the volume filled up, new information was entered on cards, and from 1911 to 1938 these supplement not only the first Editions

Book at Basingstoke, but also the later Editions Books in the British Library. Then there are the books themselves, the company's library of its own publications, mainly dating from 1962 but including some 7,500 earlier titles.

The Lewis Carroll letters, sold by the firm in 1957, are now to be found in the Rosenbach Museum and Library, Philadelphia. In his influential essay 'The Bibliographical Significance of a Publisher's Archive: the Macmillan Papers', *Studies in Bibliography*, 23 (1970), William E. Fredeman drew particular attention to the transatlantic dispersal of these and other Macmillan materials. He mentioned a 'large cache' of letters from important authors of the 1850s and 1860s, now in the Berg Collection, New York Public Library, and referred to the correspondence files of the Macmillan Company of New York, also in New York Public Library. This archive, although not as comprehensive as Fredeman suggests, provides important documentary evidence of the American firm's activities from 1890 to 1960. Much of its publishing was conducted independently of London, but George Platt Brett, the company President from 1896 to 1931, maintained separate sequences of letter books for communications with the parent house, and for his own letters written during business visits to London, as well as 'foreign' files of correspondence with other British publishers. Many of the authors represented – Henry James, Margaret Mitchell, Vera Brittain and W. B. Yeats, for example – had experience of Macmillan on both sides of the Atlantic, which often makes for an illuminating, if not always good-tempered, exchange of views.

Since 1979 there has been a further archive of Macmillan materials, in the form of the papers of the Macmillan Company of Canada, at McMaster University. Based in Toronto, the Canadian branch was established in 1905 as a distributor for both New York and London titles, but went on to become one of the most important publishing houses in the country before increasingly difficult financial circumstances during the 1960s led to its eventual sale to Maclean Hunter in 1972. The archive includes correspondence with the London and New York offices, details of printing and production arrangements, as well as files relating to authors such as Mazo de la Roche, Hugh MacLennan and 'Grey Owl', many of whom were personal friends of successive company Presidents Hugh Eayrs and John Gray, or their staff.

These brief descriptions scarcely do justice to the inexhaustible interest and variety of the collective Macmillan archives, described most compellingly by Warwick Gould in *The Times Literary Supplement* (6–12 July 1990) 'as the finest publisher's archive in the world'. The British Library material was called into use almost as soon as it arrived in the Department of Manuscripts, and has never had time to gather dust on the shelves; even the letter books, originally thought too fragile for routine consultation, were found to be in such demand that there was no alternative but to set up an immediate and painstaking programme of conservation. Inevitably, attention focused first upon Macmillan's galaxy of literary figures, resulting in a steady flow of important biographies and textual works, with a fresh emphasis on bibliography and publishing history. More recently, and especially with the development of postgraduate courses in the History of the Book, the archive has become an invaluable resource for research into the British and colonial booktrade, the role of the publisher's reader, and the business of publishing itself, as well as an ever-widening range of biographical studies.

This volume of essays, which had its origins in a conference held at the University of London in 1997, draws on some of this research to explore aspects of the first 130 years of Macmillan's history, the period from 1843 to the 1970s covered by these archives. In the first chapter, '"To You in Your Vast Business": some features of the quantitative history of Macmillan 1843–1891', Simon Eliot sets the scene with a statistical account of the firm's steadily increasing activity during the nineteenth century. Using data compiled from contemporary trade literature and Macmillan's own *Bibliographical Catalogue*, he is able to confirm the overwhelming predominance of Religion, Science and Literature in the catalogue, and the Macmillan gift for spotting best-sellers. Together, these attributes – indicating a certain conservatism as well as a keen eye for a good book – were partly responsible for the reputation which attracted many established authors to the Macmillan imprint.

One of the earliest of these relationships was formed with Matthew Arnold, a close contemporary of Alexander Macmillan and a frequent guest at his Thursday evening 'tobacco parliaments'. Bill Bell's 'From Parnassus to Grub Street: Matthew Arnold and the House of Macmillan' follows the Oxford Professor of Poetry's transition from a 'gentleman-scholar' to celebrity writer, and examines both author and publisher's increasingly confident handling of the popular market. In contrast, Thomas Hardy's first encounters with Macmillan were far less assured. Michael Millgate's 'Thomas Hardy and the House of Macmillan. A comedy in chapters' catalogues a long succession of missed opportunities and missed connections before their Memorandum of Agreement was signed in 1902. By then Hardy was one of the most eminent writers of the day, but – like Arnold – his first experience of direct publishing with Macmillan had been as a contributor to *Macmillan's Magazine.* George Worth traces the history of the first of the great shilling monthlies of the mid-nineteenth century, from Alexander's original idea in 1855 until its quiet death a half-century later. Throughout this time, Margaret Oliphant contributed some of her most characteristic writing to the *Magazine*, using it to finance family holidays in Italy and, during the early 1880s, to bring her close to achieving a long-term aim of a regular income.

The celebrated explorer and administrator, Sir Samuel Baker, entered the Macmillan lists in 1866 with the publication of *The Albert Nyanza*, a best-selling account of his ambitious expedition to the source of the Nile. This led to a succession of books about his African life and adventures, and a remarkable correspondence with Alexander Macmillan which reveals Baker still very much preoccupied, even in retirement, with developments in Egypt and the Sudan. Michael Bott's selection from these important and characteristically outspoken letters begins in 1875, shortly after publication of the relatively disappointing *Ismailia.* Alexander was also the prime instigator of the firm's celebrated contract with Tennyson in 1884, which provided the Poet Laureate with a secure outlet for his later work, while effectively establishing Macmillan as the leading literary publisher of the day. Long before the expiration of the ten-year term, Tennyson was dead and the future of his texts entrusted to his surviving son, Hallam. In his second contribution, '"And Sacred is the Latest Word": Macmillan and Tennyson's "final" text', Michael Millgate discusses the complex negotiations which developed as Hallam (prompted by his mother) struggled to fulfil these responsibilities with the publication of an annotated edition of his father's works.

Distinguished authors such as these found in Macmillan not only a publisher able to foster their reputations at home, but one well-positioned to promote their work throughout the English-speaking world. Rimi Chatterjee charts the firm's determination to develop its early informal trading links with India into a full-scale publishing programme for the sub-continent, and demonstrates the essential role textbooks had to play in this transformation. By 1885, when Maurice Macmillan visited both India and Australia, the Company had experimented with a number of specially prepared educational and literary series, and by the First World War it was recognised as one of the major suppliers of books to the subcontinent, with branches in Calcutta, Bombay and Madras. Trade with America began on a similarly *ad hoc* basis, but was formalised in 1869 with the opening of an agency in New York under the management of George Brett. Drawing on the thousands of letters written by three generations of Bretts between 1869 and 1951, Elizabeth James traces the history of the New York business as it grew from these modest beginnings into an incorporated company, eventually emerging as an independent publishing house far larger than its parent.

W. B. Yeats was one of many authors who came to Macmillan through the American company. Warwick Gould's essay 'W. B. Yeats on the Road to St Martin's Street, 1900–1917' takes a closer look at transatlantic publishing as operated by Brett and experienced by one, increasingly important, author. The implications for Yeats's texts were far-reaching, especially as he, too, reassessed his work for a Collected Edition. The American market was also a significant factor in J. M. Keynes's unusual publishing career, the subject of Donald Moggridge's chapter, 'A Risk-bearing Author. Maynard Keynes and his publishers'. Most of Keynes's works were published on commission, a fairly common practice in the nineteenth century, but increasingly unusual in the twentieth. Joint editions with American publishers allowed Keynes to reduce his costs, but he took a calculated risk in thus deliberately forgoing copyright protection in the United States.

Macmillan is perhaps not generally identified with fine illustrated books, but over the years it has been associated with many talented artists. One of these was Gwen Raverat (like Keynes, born and educated in Cambridge), whose illustrated edition of a favourite childhood book, *The Runaway,* is discussed by Frances Spalding. By 1935, when Raverat first proposed the project, her reputation was sufficiently well established for Macmillan to encourage her participation in every aspect of the production, from the choice of format and type, to the colour of binding cloth, and even the printer. Michael Wace looks more closely at Macmillan's record as a publisher of children's books. He traces the role of the children's editor from the mid-nineteenth century through to his own experience in that position at the end of the twentieth century, though pointing out that there was no specific title or person devoted to that work until the 1950s.

The final chapter, by Nicholas Barker, provides an insider's view of the history of Macmillan, and is a welcome reminder that the writing and publishing of books is still going on with as much energy and enjoyment as ever – and that the History of the Book is not yet complete. It is to be hoped that this volume will stimulate further research in the field of publishers' archives, and those of Macmillan in particular.

1
'To You in Your Vast Business'[1]

Some features of the quantitative history of Macmillan 1843–91

Simon Eliot

In 1843 two brothers from an impoverished Scottish background published the first titles to appear under the Macmillan imprint from their bookshop at 57 Aldersgate Street. By 1891 the company that they had founded so modestly ranked, in terms of title production, backlist, status and influence, with the great publishing houses of Longmans and Rivington which had been established more than a century earlier. How had so much been achieved, and what precisely had been achieved, in the generation and a half between these two dates? Bibliometrics cannot provide complete answers to both these questions, but it can go a long way to answer the latter and, by doing so, suggest an outline response to the former.

The quantitative historian of Macmillan is fortunate in having two very rich sources of information covering this period, one printed and one in manuscript. In 1891 the firm published *A Bibliographical Catalogue of Macmillan and Co.'s Publications from 1843 to 1889* which had been compiled by a member of the firm, James Foster. This remarkable and highly unusual book listed by year, and then in alphabetical order, each Macmillan publication, with details not only of the author and title, but also imprint, pagination and format. For books that were reprinted (either as new impressions or new editions), reprint dates and additions to the text were included; for texts that were plated, the *Bibliographical*

Catalogue gave the date and even indicated the process (stereotype or electrotype) employed. It is a thorough, comprehensive and meticulous publication that reflects well on both the seriousness of the publisher and the conscientiousness of its compiler.

Inevitably the *Bibliographical Catalogue* had its limitations: it did not indicate the month of publication, it did not record the price, and it provided no information on the size of print runs. Fortunately, we also have recourse to the extensive Macmillan archives housed in the British Library, Reading University and at Macmillan's Basingstoke office. These include the Editions Books, a sequence of production ledgers that provides most of the information missing from the *Bibliographical Catalogue*, of which the volume covering the period up to 1892 is held at Basingstoke, and subsequent volumes are to be found in the British Library.[2]

All this material will provide us with a sense of the internal dynamics of the publishing house. What it will not do is help us place Macmillan in the broader context of British publishing during the middle and later part of the nineteenth century. This gap can be filled by a project currently under way at Reading University, which is intended to provide an account of trends in British publishing through the close quantitative study of a series of sample years between 1843 and 1926.[3] The main source of information for this project is the fortnightly lists (weekly from 1891) of new titles and selected reprints published by one of the two major book trade journals of the period, *The Publishers' Circular*. These lists have been converted to machine-readable form so that annual and monthly production, price, format and authorship can be analysed relatively easily. To reinforce this current project I have used a broader study of quantitative patterns and trends published in 1994.[4] Together these sources allow us to place developments within the firm of Macmillan into a series of broader contexts.

Annual production of titles 1843–89

Figure 1.1 illustrates the number of new titles published by Macmillan and listed in the *Bibliographical Catalogue*. It takes the form of a histogram, with an imposed five-year moving average line intended to illustrate a clearer trend than the inevitably very variable counts for individual years.

As one might expect, Macmillan's annual production of titles was very modest in the early years. 1843 and 1844 saw 2 titles in each year, and 1845 recorded 7. However, in 1846 production more than doubled to 16, and from then on until 1852 numbers varied from 11 to 19. The early

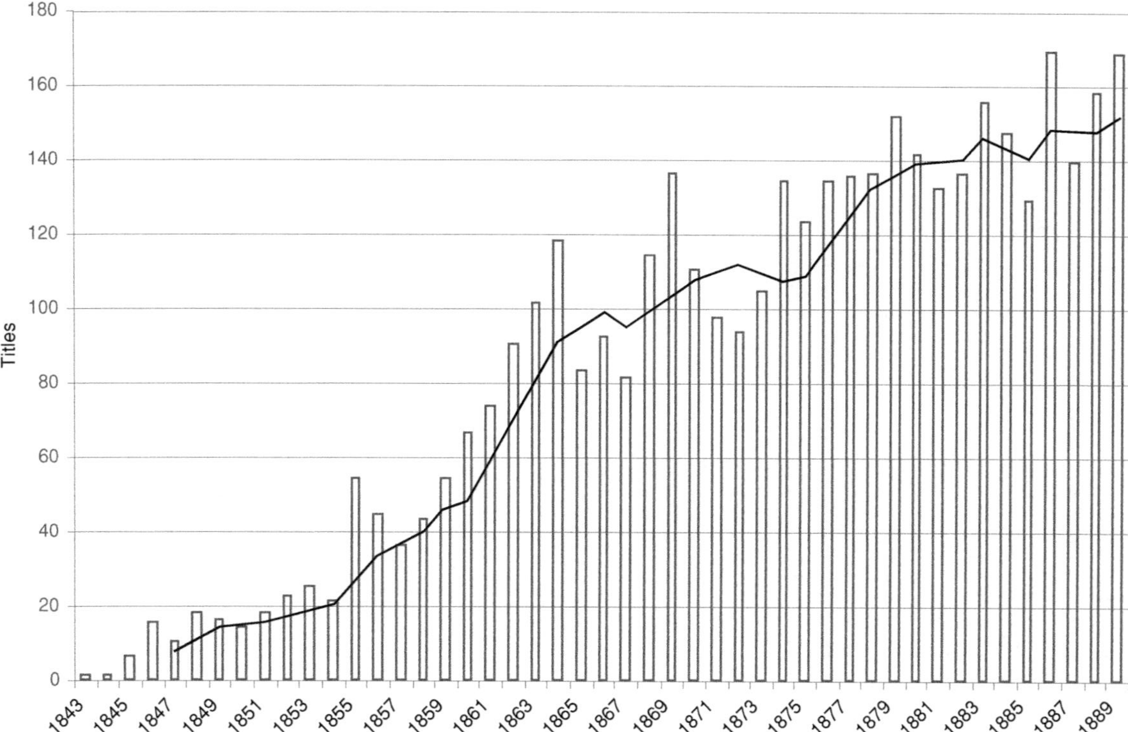

Figure 1.1 Title production 1843–89 and five-year moving average

1850s saw a distinctly rising trend, peaking in 1855 with 55 titles; 1856–57 saw a decline, but from 1858 onwards there was a steep rise from 44 to 119 in 1864. In some ways this pattern of production was not unlike the overall trend exhibited by the publishing trade as a whole during the 1840s and 1850s. The 1840s had seen a slow year-by-year rise in the number of titles published, whereas the 1850s had witnessed a dramatic increase in production.[5] Output had peaked early in the 1850s (roughly 1851–54), inflated by a general rise in publications aimed at the railway traveller, the pamphlet war associated with the re-establishment of the Roman Catholic hierarchy in England in 1850, and the burst of print activity encouraged by the Great Exhibition of 1851, the death of Wellington in 1852 and the start of the Crimean War in 1854.

However, one would not expect a new, almost embryonic, publisher to follow slavishly the trends set by established houses, and Macmillan did not. Most of the subjects that had inflated the overall figures left the Macmillan list undisturbed. The publishing of religious texts was always a significant feature of Macmillan, certainly in its earliest decades, but there is hardly a trace of the controversies of 1850 among its many collections of sermons, charges and Bible studies. Wellington was the subject of two titles published in 1852 (two sermons and a collection of sonnets), and the Crystal Palace sneaks in belatedly as the subject of a pamphlet by C. J. Vaughan, also published in 1852. New publishers commonly work to their own rhythm, either through necessity or innocence, and Macmillan was no exception to this rule.

As the general trend in production of titles slowly declined from its peak in the early 1850s, Macmillan's annual title production moved in the opposite direction. The surge in the firm's output during 1855 was in part due to a single, exceptional event: the publication of no fewer than 15 titles by F. D. Maurice, most of which had been bought from the firm of J. W. Parker and were now being reissued under the Macmillan imprint. Although exceptional, this occurrence highlights a significant and recurrent feature of Macmillan's early years – its dependence on religious works, and its reliance on Cambridge-based or Cambridge-educated authors. In 1846, the first year in which Macmillan published more than 10 titles, 12 of the 16 produced were written by Cambridge men or had Cambridge in their titles (two were scholarly journals). Similarly in 1855, of the 55 titles published, 42 had similar Cambridge associations (including Maurice himself, of course).

The pattern of rising production that began in 1858 was particularly important to Macmillan. On 15 September 1858 *The Publishers' Circular* announced that 'Messrs. Macmillan & Co., of Cambridge, have opened an establishment in London, in Henrietta Street, Covent Garden, in the house that was formerly the long-celebrated Offley's tavern, and in which more recently the Fielding Club held its meetings.'[6]

Although the headquarters of Macmillan was to remain in Cambridge for another five years,[7] this move marked a significant shift in both Macmillan's publishing culture and production pattern: the first full year of the London branch saw title production rival the most productive year (1855) in Cambridge, and from then on output rose steeply until the mid-1860s.

The main trade journal of the time also acknowledged the significance of this move. Prior to 1858 *The Publishers' Circular*, in its fortnightly lists of books, rarely if ever listed Macmillan as the publisher of its own books. Invariably Cambridge-published Macmillan books, if they were acknowledged at all by the *Circular*, were commonly listed under the imprint of 'Bell' or 'J. W. Parker', and occasionally under other publishers' names. It was not unusual for out-of-London publishers to use firms with a London base as agents in this way, and these agents were frequently listed as the publisher by trade journals.[8] In this case, George Bell had been a close associate of the Macmillan brothers since their early days as London booksellers, and became their representative in London when they moved their bookselling business to Cambridge in 1843. J. W. Parker, on the other hand, shared Cambridge associations with the Macmillans (the first J. W. Parker had been elected as official printer to the University of Cambridge in 1836) and, under his son, J. W. Parker junior, the firm had published writers such as F. D. Maurice and Charles Kingsley, who were later to become Macmillan authors.

As a result, 9 of the 16 titles listed in the *Bibliographical Catalogue* for 1846 were not recorded at all in the *Circular*, 4 were listed under Parker, 2 under Bell and 1 under Rivington's imprint. By 1856 when the *Bibliographical Catalogue* was listing 45 titles, 21 were omitted from the *Circular*, 23 were listed under Bell, and 1 under Hatchard. In 1858 the same pattern seems to have been repeated, with Bell and J. W. Parker credited with many of the Macmillan titles produced earlier in the year. Then, in the *Circular* lists covering the period 14–30 September 1858, the Macmillan imprint suddenly became visible almost exactly at the same time as the London office was opened.[9] From then on Macmillan was a consistent and increasingly important imprint within the *Circular's* listings.

Macmillan's annual production peaked in 1864 but then declined over the next three years, rising once more in 1869, only to fall again until 1874. Such variations do not make for clear trends, so it might be worth looking at the five-year average line in Figure 1.1. This shows that following a steep increase in the years up to 1863, the upward trend rose more gently, and did not sharpen again until the mid-1870s – a pattern which closely mirrored the general trend in title production during the 1860s and 1870s. Similarly, the steepening rise in the later 1870s, followed by a more gradual increase in the 1880s, echoes the trends visible in the overall production figures derived from *The Publishers' Circular* and the British Museum Copyright Receipt Books for the same period.[10] As Macmillan expanded its title production and settled down as a publisher, the firm seems to have become, as one might have expected, increasingly subject to the influences under which the rest of the publishing trade was operating. Thus from the mid-1860s onwards the trends in Macmillan's annual title production began to parallel those of the industry as a whole.

The monthly production pattern

The Macmillan Editions Book for this period usually included information about the dates of editions and impressions, frequently mentioning not only the year but also the month and, occasionally, even the day. This information is more common and more consistent, as one might expect, in those parts of the Editions Book covering the later decades of the century.

There is some ambiguity about the nature of these dates. Mostly they will indicate the dates on which the production was ordered rather than the date on which the book was issued. However, the process of print production in the nineteenth century was somewhat faster than it has become in the early twenty-first, so that the interval between placing the order and the time of issue was much shorter. Also in practice, as we shall see when we look at the histograms for the sample years, the periods of greatest production as indicated by the Editions Book seem to match well with the general seasonal patterns of publication of the later nineteenth century.

Ideally this survey should have recorded all the production data for all years covered by the *Bibliographical Catalogue*, but in practice this would have been an impossibly huge task. Entries in the Editions Book are not in a simple chronological order, and each title in the *Bibliographical Catalogue* has to be cross-referenced against an index to the relevant pages in the Editions Book. For these purely practical reasons a sample year was taken for each decade between 1843 and 1889. A number of current research projects involving the analysis of nineteenth-century book production data have selected years ending in '6' so, for consistency and to allow the possibility of comparison, the sample years selected were 1846, 1856, 1866, 1876 and 1886.[11] The data available for 1846 was so thin that it was excluded from this survey. Similarly, not all titles in the later years had the specific month information attached; those that did not were also excluded from the count in Table 1.1.

Table 1.1 Monthly distribution of titles 1856, 1866, 1876, 1886

	Jan	Feb	Mar	Apr	May	Jun	Jly	Aug	Sep	Oct	Nov	Dec	Total
1856	7	6	0	3	0	2	1	2	4	1	0	4	30
% share	23.3	20.0	0.0	10.0	0.0	6.7	3.3	6.7	13.3	3.3	0.0	13.3	100
1866	4	7	6	11	5	5	1	4	1	5	7	8	64
% share	6.3	10.9	9.4	17.2	7.8	7.8	1.6	6.3	1.6	7.8	10.9	12.5	100
1876	9	9	10	8	10	6	7	6	6	19	19	7	116
% share	7.8	7.8	8.6	6.9	8.6	5.2	6.0	5.2	5.2	16.4	16.4	6.0	100
1886	9	14	21	19	17	9	6	7	10	17	16	11	156
% share	5.8	9.0	13.5	12.2	10.9	5.8	3.8	4.5	6.4	10.9	10.3	7.1	100
1886 non-colonial	9	9	13	9	14	8	4	5	9	15	16	11	122
% share	7.4	7.4	10.7	7.4	11.5	6.6	3.3	4.1	7.4	12.3	13.1	9.0	100

The numbers we are dealing with are quite small. In 1856 Macmillan issued just 30 titles; by 1886 this annual number had risen to 156 titles but even this, in statistical terms, is still quite modest. One should not, therefore, expect the patterns produced by these numbers to parallel exactly those described in *Patterns and Trends in British Publishing 1800–1919*, for example, which are derived from 10,000s of titles. Moreover, *Patterns and Trends* generalises over a range of publishers and genres, whereas Macmillan was a very individual publisher with a list that exhibits specific biases to particular subjects (most notably religion, science, education and literature). With these caveats in mind let us look at the histograms in Figures 1.2–1.6.

The monthly distribution of titles in 1856 was unusual (see Figure 1.2). The firm had been running for just 13 years and its average title production was little more than two and a half per month. January and February were the months of highest production with seven and six titles respectively, followed by September and December with four titles each. The traditional book production season of Spring was hardly in evidence, with no titles in either March or May, and only three in April. The Christmas season, well developed in the publishing trade as a whole by the 1850s, was represented by just four titles in December, October having only one and November not registering at all. If this

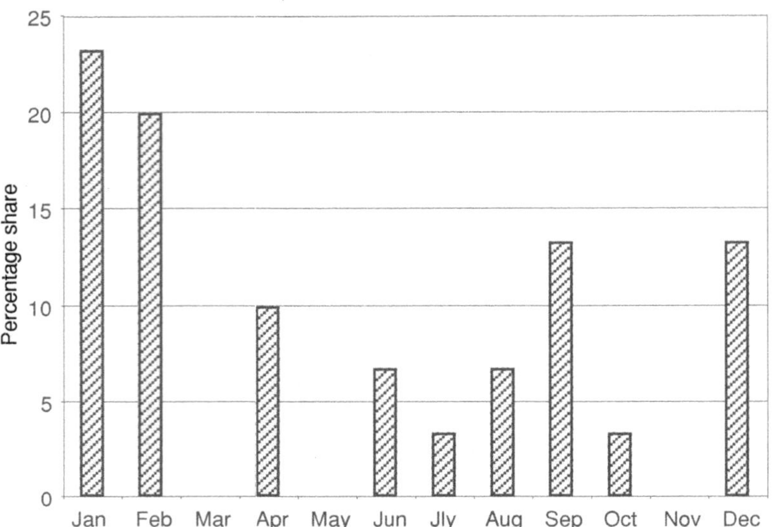

Figure 1.2 Distribution of title production 1856

pattern had persisted in later decades we would be obliged to regard Macmillan as a highly unconventional publisher, bucking the trend in which most other book producers concentrated their production in two well-defined seasons, namely Spring (March–May) and Christmas (October–December).

In order to establish whether this is the case or not, we should turn to the later decades. Figure 1.3 illustrates the monthly title production pattern for 1866. This represents a sample of 64 titles, more than double that of 1856, and the state of Macmillan after 23 years of activity. The histogram shows a much more recognisable pattern that parallels the general title production profile of the 1860s.[12] The two distinct seasons are visible: March to May with the peak in April, October to December with the peak in December. The parallel between general production patterns and Macmillan is not exact, of course – Spring is still, for Macmillan, the more important season in terms of number of titles, with the peak in April rather than May – but one would expect individual firms, with their particular interests and priorities, to vary from the norm to some degree.

Figure 1.4 shows the monthly distribution by percentage of the 116 accurately datable titles produced in 1876. This is a very different pattern from the earlier sample years. General publishing trends would lead one

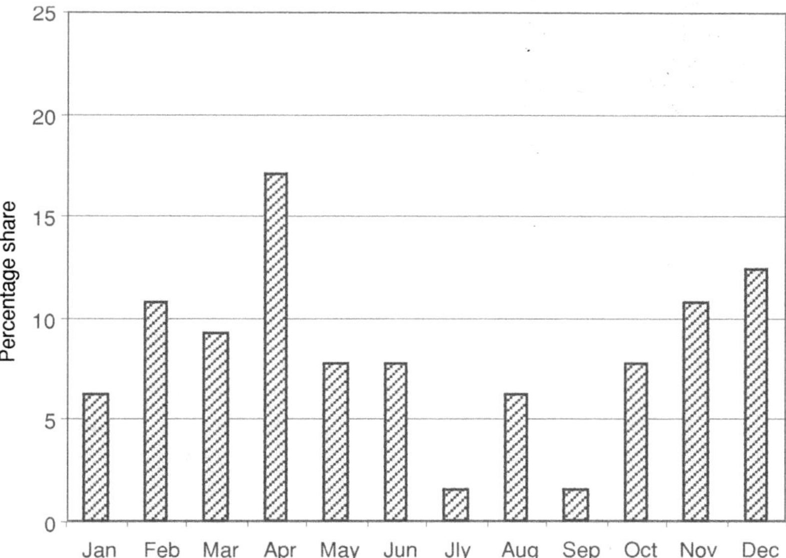

Figure 1.3 Distribution of title production 1866

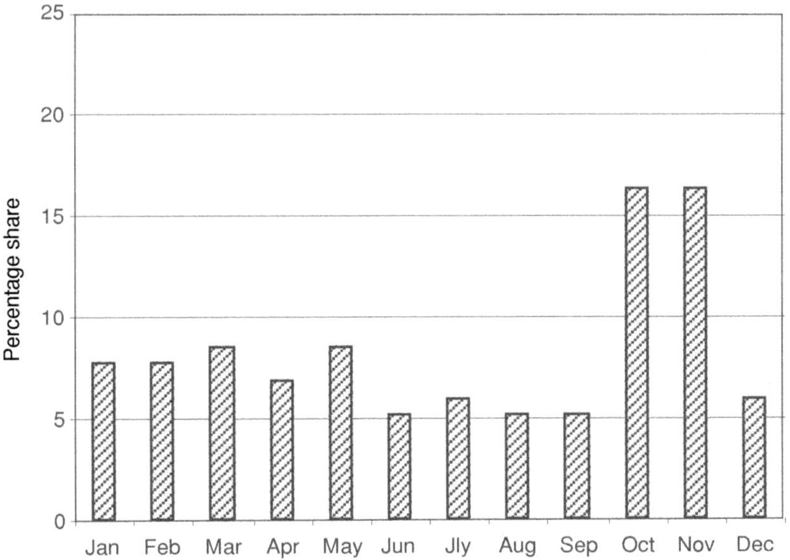

Figure 1.4 Distribution of title production 1876

to expect that by this time the Spring season would be present, though diminished, and that the Christmas season would dominate. Yet Figure 1.4 shows such a predominant Christmas, and such a diminished Spring, that one suspects 1876 of being, for Macmillan, an untypical year. Looking at the individual entries in the Editions Book for October and November 1876 it is difficult to see a pattern that would fully explain this anomaly. However, two features are worth comment. Firstly, the Editions Book indicates the existence of a number of titles not originally published by Macmillan with phrases such as 'Received' or 'Originally published elsewhere', and in 1876, of the 20 titles so distinguished, no fewer than 11 are dated either October or November. The second feature needs more explanation. The Editions Book usually gives not only the initial print-run, but also subsequent print-runs. It is therefore possible to assess the relative success of titles. As a crude measure, all titles with accumulated print-runs of more than 10,000 copies were regarded as unambiguous successes (assuming, that is, that their initial runs had been smaller – and all were, indeed, smaller). Twenty-eight titles originally published in 1876 ultimately achieved accumulated print-runs of over 10,000, including 12 of the 38 titles published in October and November, and 16 of the 78 titles published during the remainder of the year. Thus 31.6 per cent of titles published in October and November 1876 were unambiguous successes in terms of print-run, whereas, for the rest of the year, only 20.5 per cent could be so described. This is hardly a full explanation of the anomaly visible in the figures for 1876, but it does suggest that the titles produced in the first two months of the Christmas season were not quite typical.

Figure 1.5 illustrates the production pattern for our final sample year, 1886. This represents a more normal distribution than 1876, with both the Spring and Christmas seasons visible. Nevertheless, it still looks more like the pattern for a mid- rather than a later Victorian publisher, with Spring more productive of titles than Christmas. Certainly the production pattern derived from all the titles listed in both *The Publishers' Circular* and *The Bookseller* in the 1880s would suggest a predominant Christmas season.[13] However, here again the distribution has been somewhat skewed by a particular feature of Macmillan's output. 1886 saw the beginning of the 'Colonial Library' with no fewer than 34 titles issued in this series during the year. Since 156 countable (for this exercise) titles were published in 1886, this represents a significant portion of the total. Nor were the Colonial titles issued regularly or evenly throughout the year. Disproportionately, they were dated by the Editions Book to the earlier months (5 in February, 8 in March, 10 in

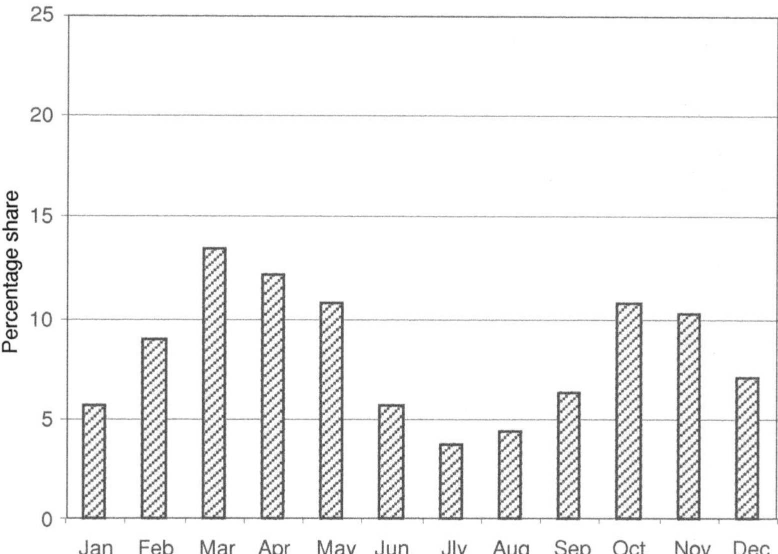

Figure 1.5 Distribution of title production 1886

April and so on[14]), whereas only 1 was issued in September and 2 in October. In order, therefore, to see the more usual trends underlying the surge in Colonial editions, Figure 1.6 illustrates the 'non-Colonial Library' titles. Here we can see the two-season pattern more clearly, with Christmas now just ahead of Spring as a season of highest production.

In summary, what can we say of the monthly production pattern of Macmillan as revealed by these rather limited sample years? Discounting 1846 and 1856 as being too early and too limited in production to act as sample years, we can say that within 20 years of its founding, the firm's production pattern had settled down into a form which paralleled, without slavishly copying, the general pattern of production. Between the 1860s and the 1880s the Spring season was usually somewhat more important to Macmillan, in terms of titles produced, than the general run of the publishing trade; and the Christmas season, although it grew in significance within Macmillan (as it was doing everywhere), did so at a less dramatic pace. Given the fact that we are looking at one, very distinctive, publisher, the differences between Macmillan and the general pattern should not surprise us. The reasons for the firm producing such a sparkling season as the Christmas of 1876 are certainly worthy of further investigation.

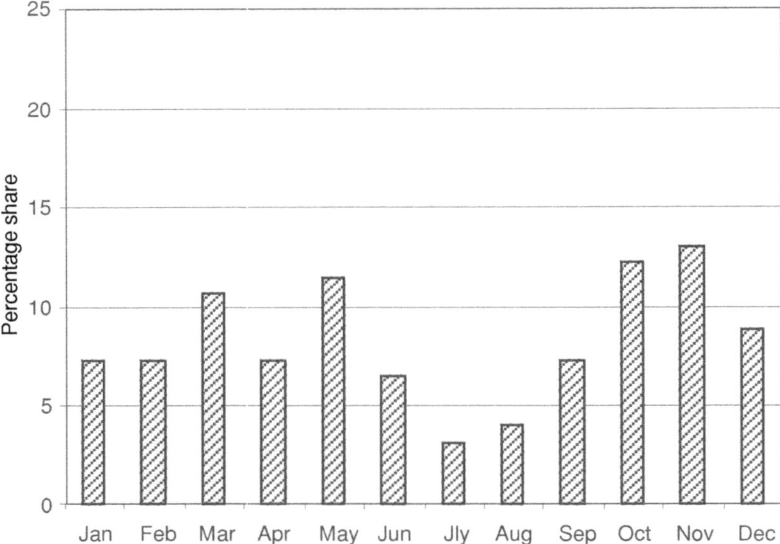

Figure 1.6 Distribution of non-colonial title production 1886

Print-runs in 1856, 1866, 1876, 1886

Relatively little large-scale statistical work has been carried out on print-runs in the nineteenth century for the simple reason that the information is often hard to come by. Some publishers' archives contain the necessary data, but many do not. In such a situation those that do may not be typical, so any conclusions drawn may be seriously skewed because the sample was so unbalanced. Work is currently being undertaken in this area, and Reading University's Nineteenth-Century Book Production Database, now with over 6,000 discrete records, should provide a broader base than is currently available. However, at present we have no reliable overall figures with which to compare the Macmillan data. For this reason the following section will not discuss trends, but merely content itself with describing what the Macmillan figures reveal of the four sample years.

As we have seen, details of both the initial and subsequent print-runs are included in the Editions Book, although this information was not available for every title in the sample years, and was hardly available at all for 1846. In this exercise, therefore, 1846 has been excluded. Table 1.2, Rows 1–3 include a comparison of total titles listed in the Editions

Book with those that provided print-run data, and expresses this as a percentage. In practice the usable title percentage for all four sample years was high: running from 75.6 per cent (1856) at the lowest to 89.5 per cent (1886) at the highest.

Table 1.2 Summary of non-reprint and reprint titles 1856, 1866, 1876, 1886

		1856	1866	1876	1886
1	Total titles listed in Editions Book	45	93	135	171
2	Total titles used	34	73	114	153
3	Total titles used as percentage of titles listed	75.6	78.5	84.4	89.5
4	Total of print-runs in year	29450	138150	336200	372350
5	Total of print-runs over life of title	111450	2400245	1950862	2143182
6	Average print-run per title in year	866	1892	2949	2434
7	Average print-run per title over life	3278	32880	17113	14008
8	Unreprinted titles	26	39	63	61
9	Unreprinted % of total titles used	76.5	53.4	55.3	39.9
10	Average print-run per unreprinted title	729	738	1257	1902
11	Reprinted titles	8	34	51	92
12	Reprinted % of total titles used	23.5	46.6	44.7	60.1
13	Average print-run of reprinted titles	1313	3228	5039	2786
14	Average total print-run of reprinted titles	11563	69525	36699	21993
15	Titles with over 10,000 total print-run	3	19	28	33
16	% of titles with over 10,000 total print-run	8.8	26.0	24.6	21.6

Given the complexities and time-consuming nature of extracting data from the Editions Book, the following figures refer only to titles first published in the sample year. For example, in 1856 the figure of 29,450 as the 'Total of print-runs in year' (Table 1.2, Row 4) refers only to titles newly published in that year, and does not include the reprinting of backlisted titles. However, this figure does not necessarily include only a first print-run; if a title were popular enough to justify a reprinting in the same year as it was first published, that print-run would be included in the figures.

Between 1856 and 1886 there was virtually a four-fold increase in the number of titles produced per annum, from 45 to 171 (see Table 1.2, Row 1). There was an even greater increase in countable output of copies: from 29,450 for first-published titles in 1856 to 372,350 in 1886, a more than twelve-fold increase (see Table 1.2, Row 4). This meant that the average print-run for new titles in the sample tended to rise, particularly in the earlier decades: from 866 in 1856, through to 1,892 in 1866, to 2,949 by 1876. However, in 1886 the average fell back to 2,434 (Table 1.2, Row 6).

This pattern of rapidly rising numbers between 1856 and 1866 or 1876, with a slight correction in 1886, is common among many of the categories in Table 1.2. If one looks at 'Total of print-runs over life of title' (Table 1.2, Row 5), a category which examines each title first published in the sample year and follows its publishing history by totalling all print-runs to the end of its life, then one will see that there was a dramatic rise between 1856 and 1866, from 111,450 copies to 2,400,245 copies. 'Life of title' print-runs in 1876 totalled fewer (1,950,862) but then rose again in 1886 (to 2,143,182) but not high enough to rival 1866. In fact, 1866 seems to have been a particularly successful year in that it saw the first publication of a number of titles that were to go on selling in high volume over a number of years. Here we see the firm establishing itself and beginning the process of creating a strongly-rooted backlist. This point is reinforced if one looks at the 'Titles with over 10,000 total print-run' (Table 1.2, Rows 15 and 16). In 1866 there were 19 titles that went on to achieve at least this level of print-run. This is fewer than in 1876 (28) or 1886 (33), but, in proportion to the total number of titles first published in the year, 1866 was certainly the most successful, with 26 per cent of its titles going on to be printed in more than 10,000 copies.

Some of these highly successful titles were religious in nature, such as Rev. G. F. Maclear's *A Class-book of New Testament History* (total 56,500), and *A Shilling Book of Old Testament History* (total 495,900); or B. F. Westcott's *The Gospel of the Resurrection* (total 20,500). Some were literary, such as C.M. Yonge's *The Dove in the Eagle's Nest* (total 38,250), Charles Kingsley's *Hereward the Wake* (total 119,000), *The Poetical Works of Sir Walter Scott*, edited by F. T. Palgrave for the Globe Edition (total 50,530), or *Words from the Poets selected for the use of Parochial Schools and Libraries* (total 155,570).

Overwhelmingly, however, in terms of both numbers of titles and very large print-runs, the greatest successes of 1866 were educational and scientific titles. Among these were Rev. T. Dalton *Arithmetical Examples* (total 55,000), T. H. Huxley *Lessons in Elementary Physiology* (total 199,845), H. E. Roscoe *Lessons in Elementary Chemistry* (total 430,000), Barnard Smith *A Shilling Book of Arithmetic* (total 430,000) and *Answers to Examples in Barnard Smith's Shilling Book of Arithmetic* (total 104,500), and I. Todhunter *Trigonometry for Beginners* (total 108,500). Perhaps not surprisingly, the titles, in whatever subject, that carried some reference to their likely educational market tended to do best of all. Phrases such as 'for national and elementary schools', or 'for beginners' or 'for the use of Parochial Schools and Libraries' indicated the successful targeting of a very specific market.

A striking characteristic shared by many of these best-sellers of 1866 was longevity. Although published in the mid-Victorian period, many were still on sale, albeit in new and cheaper editions, well into the twentieth century. *Hereward the Wake* was still on sale in May 1909; Westcott's *The Gospel of the Resurrection* had its final edition issued in May 1913; *Trigonometry for Beginners* was still in print in June 1921; *Words from the Poets* was still on sale in October 1923; *A Class-book of New Testament History* had its final edition printed in April 1932; and, finally, Palgrave's edition of *The Poetical Works of Sir Walter Scott* saw its last impression roll off the press in March 1935.

These great successes meant that the average print-run for a reprinted title first published in 1866 was 69,525 (Table 1.2, Row 14). This astonishing figure was not matched by any other sample year. More typically the average total print-run for a reprinted book was between 21,993 (1886) and 36,699 (1876).

If we now examine the differences between titles that were reprinted and those that were not, we find another means of measuring Macmillan's performance. We have looked at titles which, by any definition, could be regarded as very successful. In a period when average initial print-runs were usually small (commonly 250–2,000), anything over 10,000 could be regarded as a success. One might, indeed, argue that any title that did better than was originally anticipated could be thought of as a success, albeit on many occasions a rather modest one. Even a title whose initial print-run of 250 or 500 was augmented by a reprint of another 250 or 500 had clearly exceeded the publisher's original expectations.

In Table 1.2, Rows 8 and 11 give the total number of titles un-reprinted and reprinted respectively. Rows 9 and 12 express these totals as a percentage of the 'total titles used'. In 1856 more than three-quarters (76.5 per cent) of the total titles remained un-reprinted: they achieved, or did less well than, their expected sale. Only 8 titles (23.5 per cent) were successful enough to be reprinted at least once. The un-reprinted to reprinted ratio again suggests that the sample year of 1866 was outstanding: although 39 of its titles remained un-reprinted, no fewer than 34 titles had one or more additional impressions or editions. This represented 46.6 per cent of the total, double the reprint percentage of just ten years previously.

The sample year of 1876 did not quite sustain the reprint percentage of 1866, but at 44.7 per cent it was still high, and a 2 per cent fluctuation is well within the statistical margin of error. The evidence from the reprint percentages of both 1866 and 1876 suggests that Macmillan was becoming spectacularly more successful in identifying potential winners, and thus in building a sustained and profitable backlist. It is a publisher's backlist, of course, that guarantees financial stability and growth in the long term. Dramatic, short-lived best-sellers are always welcome, but by their very nature cannot be planned or budgeted for, whereas a healthy and growing backlist will guarantee a continued and growing income over the medium to long term. It will also help to define and stabilise the character and traditions of a publishing house.

In this context it is worth looking at Rows 13 and 14 of Table 1.2. Row 13 tabulates the average print-run of the first printing of all titles that were later to be reprinted at least once. Row 14 tabulates the average 'over the life of the book' print-run (from now on called 'total print-run') of all titles that were later reprinted. In 1856 the average first print-run of reprinted titles was 1,313; by 1866 it had risen to 3,228, and by 1876 it had reached 5,039. Roughly speaking, the 1866 figures were two and a half times the 1856 rate, and those for 1876 were four times the same rate.[15] Average Macmillan first-year print-runs were also increasing over the period 1856–76 (see Table 1.2, Row 6), if less quickly. In other words, reprint first-year print-runs reflect the firm's growing confidence in its ability to detect a popular book, and its willingness to risk longer initial print-runs with such titles.

Table 1.2, Row 14 tells us a little more about whether that confidence was justified in terms of a given reprinted title's total sales. In 1856, for example, the average total print-run for reprinted titles was 11,563. Just ten years later it had shot up to 69,525. All the statistics we have looked at so far have suggested that 1866 was an exceptional year, and this is confirmed by the average total reprint print-run for 1876, which dropped back to a still high but relatively modest 36,699. More surprisingly, this drop was not simply a correction to the exceptional sample year of 1866, because the average total run dropped again in 1886 to 21,993. There were 34 reprinted titles in 1866, but an almost three-fold increase to 92 in 1886; however, the average total print-run for these titles in 1886 was less than one-third of what it had been in 1866. Such a neat switch is likely to be no more than coincidental, but there is obviously a trend in which, although the number of titles reprinted goes up, and their proportion in terms of all titles also goes up,[16] most of these titles were doing less well in terms of total print-run. Macmillan was spreading its success widely but more thinly. It was a safer strategy for a maturing publisher.

This development is reinforced by a comparison of the longevity of reprinted titles published in 1866 with those published in 1886. As outlined above, a significant number of the 1866 titles were still being published many years later – six after 40 years, four after 50 years, and two after 60 years. The 1886 titles, though there were almost three times the number of reprints, had fewer Methuselahs – eleven after 40 years, four after 50 years, none after 60 years. Too much should not be read into a limited number of sample years, but what we may be detecting here are the first tentative signs of a shift to a characteristic twentieth-century pattern of book production, in which the range of titles continues to expand while the total print-runs contract and the backlist becomes somewhat more unstable. However, even if the trends are genuine they are very mild and relative. In relation to late twentieth-century publishing, Victorian publishers such as Macmillan had a highly stable identity, based on a long backlist of a significant number of medium- and long-term steady sellers that remained in print for decades – and, on occasions, for more than half a century.

The subject profile of Macmillan titles 1846–86

For the purposes of this exercise all the titles listed in the *Bibliographical Catalogue* for the sample years were classified, on evidence from the catalogue alone, using the ten classes of the Dewey decimal classification system. Admittedly, this is not a wholly satisfactory method for a set of obvious reasons: (1) although most titles or their attached descriptions in the *Bibliographical Catalogue* make classification easy, there are always some books whose titles are ambiguous or misleading; (2) restricting classification to ten classes means that significant subject distinctions are obscured: Latin classical texts and a contemporary novel will both find themselves in the 800s; books on history and books on travel will both inhabit the 900s; (3) books that are concerned with one subject may well be designed for a use which might justify classification in a different Dewey class (for example, an edition of Cicero's letters classified as a text in the 800s might be used as a textbook and therefore ought also to be found among Education texts in the 300s). Indeed, the problem of obscuring educational texts by classifying them under their ostensible subject is an important and tricky one. This is a particularly pressing matter in Pure Science (500s), Literature (800s) and History (900s). Some attempt will be made to correct this at the end of the section, but for the time being it is worth noting that a reclassification of these three classes in terms of a title's educational function would result in a reduction of the size of the 500s, 800s, and 900s, and a dramatic increase in Education within the Social Sciences (300s).

Despite these problems, a rough classification can help to point out a distinctive production profile that might be obscured by subtler methods, particularly when the samples are, in absolute terms, rather small. Nevertheless, these caveats should be born in mind as the discussion develops.

Table 1.3 Dewey subject classification of Macmillan titles 1846–86

	000s	100s	200s	300s	400s	500s	600s	700s	800s	900s	Total
1846	0	0	8	1	0	2	0	0	5	0	16
% 1846	0.00	0.00	50.00	6.25	0.00	12.50	0.00	0.00	31.25	0.00	100
1856	0	2	26	1	2	3	0	0	8	3	45
% 1856	0.00	4.44	57.78	2.22	4.44	6.67	0.00	0.00	17.78	6.67	100
1866	1	6	23	8	3	16	6	2	22	5	92
% 1866	1.09	6.52	25.00	8.70	3.26	17.39	6.52	2.17	23.91	5.43	100
1876	0	3	23	3	5	21	16	6	24	28	129
% 1876	0.00	2.33	17.83	2.33	3.88	16.28	12.40	4.65	18.60	21.71	100
1886	1	6	19	4	8	24	6	1	80	21	170
% 1886	0.59	3.53	11.18	2.35	4.71	14.12	3.53	0.59	47.06	12.35	100
1886 without the Macmillan Colonial Library titles											
1886	1	3	19	4	8	24	6	1	54	16	136
% 1886 -col	0.74	2.21	13.97	2.94	5.88	17.65	4.41	0.74	39.71	11.76	100

Table 1.3 and Figure 1.7 illustrate the results of this crude subject classification. By now we are familiar with the small numbers in the sample years of 1846 and 1856 producing rather odd results. Nevertheless it is worth observing that, although the coverage of the classes is poor in these sample years (as one might expect in a new and small publisher just getting under way), even as early as 1846 a characteristically Macmillan preoccupation with certain subjects is evident. Thus, though only four out of the ten Dewey classes are covered by the 16 titles produced in 1846, three of those four – Religion, Science and Literature (200s, 500s and 800s) – were to become the mainstay of the Macmillan list. The fourth, Social Sciences (300s) which included Education, was to represent another major theme of the firm's publishing enterprise. By 1856 Macmillan had expanded to cover seven of the ten Dewey classes, but still the 200s, 500s, and 800s dominated, though now joined by a further class that was to be another marker in the firm's subject profile, History, Biography, Geography and Travel (900s). Macmillan would

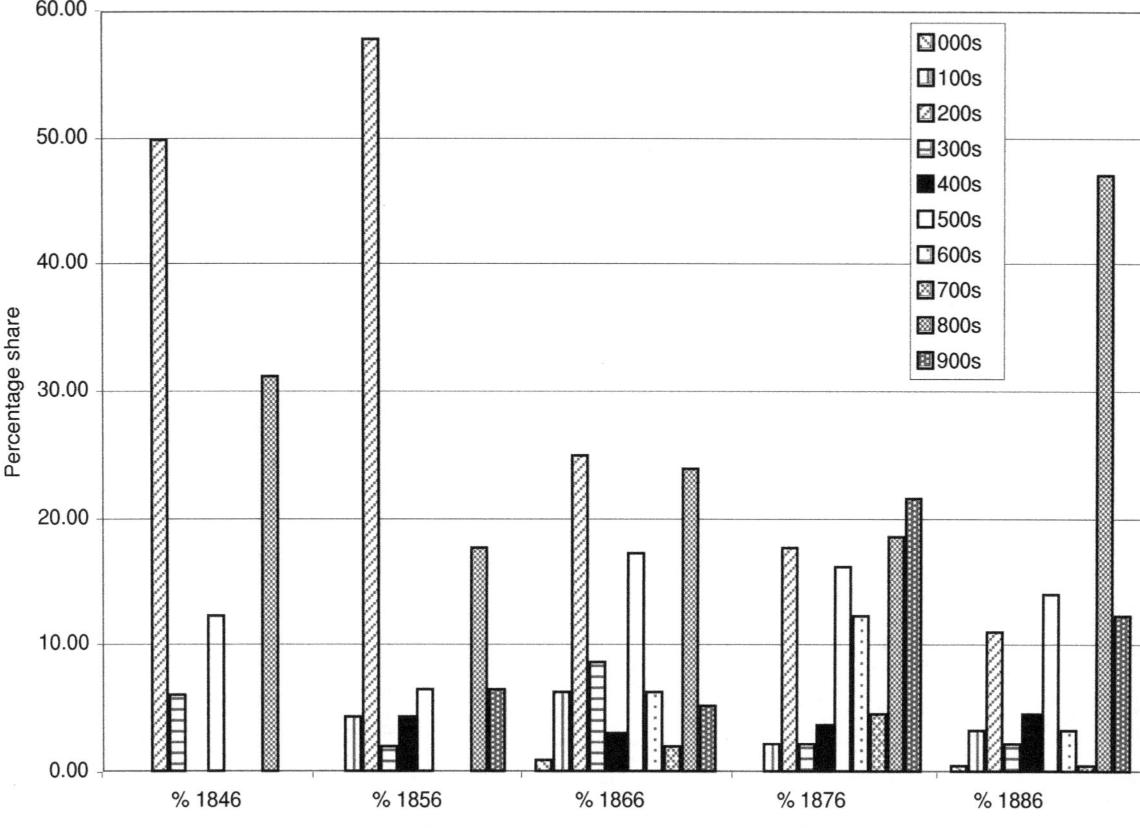

Figure 1.7 Dewey subject classification 1846–86

diversify and elaborate its functions as a general publisher, but it seems to have known from the outset where its production priorities would lie.

If one subject dominated the early sample years, that subject was Religion. Half the titles in 1846 were religious in nature, and by 1856 this share of the total output had actually risen to nearly 58 per cent. Literature, at 31 per cent and 18 per cent (these fluctuations are due to the small absolute numbers involved, and represent five and eight titles respectively), remained firmly in second place but a long way behind. Most of these titles in the Religion class were books on theology, books of prayers, individual sermons and collections of sermons, and included a string of 'Charges' issued by J. C. Hare to the clergy of the Archdeaconry of Lewes in the 1840s and 1850s. Indeed, Hare's output in 1856, with no fewer than eight titles published in that year alone, probably explained the marked rise in the proportion of religious books during the year.

However, if we follow Religion through into the period 1866–86 we will see a marked change. From a high of 58 per cent in 1856 the 200 class slipped dramatically to less than half that figure (25 per cent) by 1866. By 1876 Religion's share of the annual production of titles was down to 17.83 per cent and by the final sample year of 1886 it had been reduced to just over 11 per cent. This decline, though it was from a high that was peculiar to Macmillan, parallels the general trade contraction seen in the percentage share of titles in the Dewey 200s. For instance, in the decade 1870–79 *The Publishers' Circular* recorded Religion taking a 16 per cent share, while *The Bookseller* suggested an 11.2 per cent share for Religion between 1884–86.[17]

The overall figures from *The Publishers' Circular* and *The Bookseller* indicated that, from the 1870s onwards, if not before, Literature's proportional share was increasing as Religion's declined.[18] On the whole, Table 1.3 and Figure 1.7 confirm that this is a trend also visible in the Macmillan profile. If we discount 1846 where the figures are so small that the slightest change would have a dramatic effect on the percentages, the 800s gradually gained a greater significance in Macmillan's production. There was a rise from 17.78 per cent in 1856 to 23.91 per cent in 1866. This was checked in 1876 when the proportion contracted to 18.6 per cent, but it rose again dramatically in 1886, apparently, to 47.06 per cent. The 1886 figure includes, of course, the first tranche of Macmillan's Colonial Library with no fewer than 34 Colonial Library titles listed in the *Bibliographical Catalogue*, of which the overwhelming majority were literary works. The real trend might be more accurately discovered by removing all 34 Colonial Library titles from the count, as shown in the final two lines of Table 1.3 and the last set of histograms in Figure 1.7. This reduces the 800s share to 39.71 per cent. Nevertheless, this proportion is still higher than that recorded by the more general production trends in the later nineteenth century, where Literature was running at between 25 and 29 per cent.[19] The adjustment of the 1886 titles also results in Religion increasing to nearly 14 per cent, which matches well with the figure of 14.4 per cent from *The Publishers' Circular*.[20] By the last sample year, then, Macmillan, which had started off as a publisher of predominantly religious works, had altered course and was producing no more than an average proportion of titles in the 200 class. On the other hand, the proportion of titles occupied by the 800s was substantially in excess of the overall trends, and this must be regarded as a significant and distinctive feature of the publisher's subject profile.

Another defining characteristic of the Macmillan subject profile is illustrated in Figure 1.7. Even as early as 1846 Pure Science (500s) was making its mark, and although its share fell back in 1856, its presence was consistently strong in 1866, 1876 and 1886 at 17.39 per cent, 14.12 per cent and 17.65 per cent respectively (the latter using the non-Colonial Library figures). The percentages from *The Publishers' Circular* for this class, on the other hand, were never more than 8 per cent over the period 1870–99. As with the 800s and 900s, a proportion of the 500s could be redefined as educational texts, but, even so, a publisher producing a mixture of pure science books and science textbooks which accounted for between 14 per cent and 17 per cent of total titles – at least double the proportion in the general trade – is giving compelling evidence of a very individual subject profile.

In order to illustrate the strong educational element in the subject profile the sample years were reassessed by educational function rather than ostensible subject-matter. For instance, a title in Mathematics (in the 500s), or an anthology of poetry (normally classified in the 800s), if clearly aimed at a school or undergraduate audience, was reclassified as an educational work. This gave the following revised percentage share for educational works and textbooks: 1846, 6.25 per cent; 1856, 11.11 per cent; 1866, 32.26 per cent; 1876, 27.13 per cent; 1886, 28.68 per cent (see Table 1.4). This was accompanied, of course, by a corresponding reduction in the percentage share of those classes most likely to contain titles that could be regarded as textbooks (in particular, 400s, 500s and 800s). Thus another distinctive feature of the Macmillan subject profile in the later nineteenth century, and one that set it apart from the general publishing trends, emerged: this was the substantial production of textbooks, most notably in the pure sciences. It is no coincidence that the percentage share taken by textbooks was at its highest in 1866, the year in which a number of remarkably long-lived titles had first appeared. As was remarked in the third section, some of the best-sellers and most enduring titles first produced in 1866 were educational texts.

Table 1.4 Dewey subject classification of titles (textbook-related classified in the 300s)

	000s	100s	200s	300s	400s	500s	600s	700s	800s	900s	Total
1846	0	0	8	1	0	2	0	0	5	0	16
% 1846	0.00	0.00	50.00	6.25	0.00	12.50	0.00	0.00	31.25	0.00	100
1856	0	1	26	5	2	1	0	0	7	3	45
% 1856	0.00	2.22	57.78	11.11	4.44	2.22	0.00	0.00	15.56	6.67	100
1866	1	6	23	30	2	2	3	2	21	3	93
% 1866	1.08	6.45	24.73	32.26	2.15	2.15	3.23	2.15	22.58	3.23	100
1876	0	2	21	35	2	6	13	6	19	25	129
% 1876	0.00	1.55	16.28	27.13	1.55	4.65	10.08	4.65	14.73	19.38	100
1886	1	5	19	39	2	6	5	1	71	21	170
% 1886	0.59	2.94	11.18	22.94	1.18	3.53	2.94	0.59	41.76	12.35	100
1886 without the Macmillan Colonial Library titles											
1886	1	2	19	39	2	6	5	1	45	16	136
% 1886	0.74	1.47	13.97	28.68	1.47	4.41	3.68	0.74	33.09	11.76	100

Literature (800s), as we have seen, was always an important part of Macmillan's subject profile. As befits a serious educational publisher, however, Literature was not exclusively synonymous with novels and other forms of prose fiction. Turning to Table 1.5 we can see that in the first two sample years not one novel was listed: literature for Macmillan in these years consisted mostly of classical texts or poetry and drama. This is not to say that novels did not feature at all in Macmillan's output in this earlier period, merely that they were infrequent and sufficiently randomly scattered to avoid capture in the sample years. Charles Kingsley's *Westward Ho!* (1855) and Thomas Hughes's *Tom Brown's School-Days* (1857) were examples of Macmillan's earliest experiments with that most characteristic of Victorian genres, neither of which was published in the early sample years.

1866 marked a turning point in the composition of the Macmillan Literature list, as in so much else. Novels entered the sample and took a 36.6 per cent share, although Poetry and Drama still dominated with over 40 per cent. By 1876 novels and general fiction was the largest single category, but only just – for the share taken by Literature textbooks (under Education) and Poetry and Drama was not much smaller. Even when novels and fiction became predominant in Literature, which happened in 1886, they still represented less than 50 per cent of the total output of Literature titles. Macmillan was clearly responding to the huge demand for novels by the 1860s, but this response was always set within a broader context. This restraint should be compared with the general trend in the 1870s and 1880s. Between 1880 and 1889, for instance, *The Publishers' Circular* was suggesting that around 26 per cent of all titles were adult fiction and literature for juveniles, while only 3 per cent was devoted to Poetry and Drama. The distinctive tone and texture of Macmillan's backlist and current publications can be seen as clearly in Literature as it could in Science and Education.

Table 1.5 Macmillan titles: Literature 1846–86 (excluding Colonial Library)

	Classics	Poetry/Drama	Essays/BL	Education	Novels/Fiction	Total
1846	3	2	0	0	0	5
% 1846	60.00	40.00	0.00	0.00	0.00	100
1856	2	4	2	0	0	8
% 1856	25.00	50.00	25.00	0.00	0.00	100
1866	3	9	1	1	8	22
% 1866	13.64	40.91	4.55	4.55	36.36	100
1876	3	6	3	5	7	24
% 1876	12.50	25.00	12.50	20.83	29.17	100
1886	7	9	4	9	25	54
% 1886	12.96	16.67	7.41	16.67	46.30	100

The price structure of Macmillan titles 1846–86

The Macmillan Editions Book included information about the retail price of most titles. Price is a difficult issue because printed materials can be set at any given point along a very extended range from a halfpenny at one extreme to many guineas at the other. In practice, by the nineteenth century at least, the overwhelming majority of titles were priced somewhere in the range 1d. to 42s. As in quantum theory there are various discrete states with no intermediate positions, so in book prices in the nineteenth century there were distinct points which marked traditional book prices. For instance, both 2s. and 2s. 6d. were common book prices, but it was very rare to find a book priced between these two – at, say, 2s. 4d. Table 1.6 and Figures 1.8 – 1.12, which illustrate the distribution of Macmillan book prices in the sample years 1846–1886, use the range of book prices common in the Victorian period.

Table 1.6 Prices and their percentage share 1846, 1856, 1866, 1876, 1886

	3d	6d	1s	1s6d	2s	2s6d	3s	3s6d	4s	4s6d	5s	5s6d	6s	6s6d	7s	7s6d	8s	8s6d
1846	1		3			4		1			2							
	7.14	0.00	21.43	0.00	0.00	28.57	0.00	7.14	0.00	0.00	14.29	0.00	0.00	0.00	0.00	0.00	0.00	0.00
1856		3	6	2	2	3	4	4	2		1	2			1			1
	0.00	7.50	15.00	5.00	5.00	7.50	10.00	10.00	5.00	0.00	2.50	5.00	0.00	0.00	2.50	0.00	0.00	2.50
1866		9	14	2	3	5	1	5		9	2	3	5	2	1	7		2
	0.00	10.59	16.47	2.35	3.53	5.88	1.18	5.88	0.00	10.59	2.35	3.53	5.88	2.35	1.18	8.24	0.00	2.35
1876		5	13	6	6	8		8		5	2		13	1	2	5	1	6
	0.00	4.20	10.92	5.04	5.04	6.72	0.00	6.72	0.00	4.20	1.68	0.00	10.92	0.84	1.68	4.20	0.84	5.04
1886			4	7	5	7	2	11	1	16	6		17	3		10	1	
	0.00	0.00	3.01	5.26	3.76	5.26	1.50	8.27	0.75	12.03	4.51	0.00	12.78	2.26	0.00	7.52	0.75	0.00

	9s	10s	10s6d	12s	12s6d	14s	15s	16s	18s	21s	24s	28s	31s6d	32s	36s	42s	Total
1846	1	1		1													14
	7.14	7.14	0.00	7.14	0.00	0.00	0.00	0.00	0.00	0.00	0.00	0.00	0.00	0.00	0.00	0.00	100
1856			5	1	2								1				40
	0.00	0.00	12.50	2.50	5.00	0.00	0.00	0.00	0.00	0.00	0.00	0.00	2.50	0.00	0.00	0.00	100
1866			6	1	1				1	5		1					85
	0.00	0.00	7.06	1.18	1.18	0.00	0.00	0.00	1.18	5.88	0.00	1.18	0.00	0.00	0.00	0.00	100
1876	3		8	2	3	3	1	3		5		2	4	1		3	119
	2.52	0.00	6.72	1.68	2.52	2.52	0.84	2.52	0.00	4.20	0.00	1.68	3.36	0.84	0.00	2.52	100
1886	1		9	7	5	3		3	2	5	1		6		1		133
	0.75	0.00	6.77	5.26	3.76	2.26	0.00	2.26	1.50	3.76	0.75	0.00	4.51	0.00	0.75	0.00	100

These diagrams show that Macmillan favoured particular prices in particular decades, but also that, at one point or another over the five sample years, Macmillan tried out most of the standard prices. Some were much less favoured than others, however: 3d., 10s., 15s., 24s., 32s. and 36s., for instance, were experimented with just once. It may be that future research will find that individual publishers at specified times have their own characteristic price structure which could identify them, as a finger print would identify an individual.

Turning briefly to Figures 1.8 to 1.12 we should concentrate on two features: the four most frequent prices in each sample year, and the overall distribution of prices over each sample year. For instance, the 1846 prices (see Figure 1.8) were heavily skewed towards the cheap end with 1s., 2s. 6d., 3s. 6d., and 5s. predominating. The price slots occupied were few (8 out of a possible 34) and the range was relatively narrow (3d. to 12s.). In Figure 1.9, which illustrates Macmillan's price structure in 1856, more price slots were being used (16) and the range now ran from 6d. to 31s. 6d. However, the overwhelming weight of prices remained at the lower end between 6d. and 5s. 6d. (with 1s., 3s. and 3s. 6d. being the most popular) despite the fact that the half guinea was becoming significant (12.5 per cent share). By 1866 (Figure 1.10), with many more titles being produced, the distribution of prices was spreading out: 21 slots out of 34 were now occupied. Lower prices, most notably 6d., 1s. and 4s. 6d. were still predominant, but 7s. 6d. had joined 10s. 6d. as a common higher price. The weight of prices, compared with 1846 and 1856, had begun to shift towards the higher price zones. By the sample year of 1876 (Figure 1.11), this shift was vividly apparent: 26 price slots were occupied and although 1s., 2s. 6d. and 3s. 6d. were still popular, 6s. now rivalled 1s. as the most common price. Many more titles were being priced between 10s. 6d. and 31s. 6d. By 1886 (Figure 1.12) the price structure had been pared down with slightly fewer slots occupied than in 1876 (24 as opposed to 26). The most striking difference was that there was a noticeable further shift toward higher prices: the range 1s. to 3s. diminished in significance, and 4s. 6d., 6s. and 7s. 6d. rose in importance, 6s. alone taking over 12 per cent of the total.

To make the data in Figures 1.8 to 1.12 more manageable, we will employ the same crude classification as was used in *Patterns and Trends*.[21] That is, all titles at or below 3s. 6d. will be regarded as low priced, all titles between 4s. and 10s. as medium priced, and all titles above 10s. as high priced. As with all crude systems this will involve some inaccuracies but at least it will allow some useful distinctions to be made. Table 1.7 summarises the classification of Macmillan prices into low, medium and high, and Figure 1.13 illustrates the result.

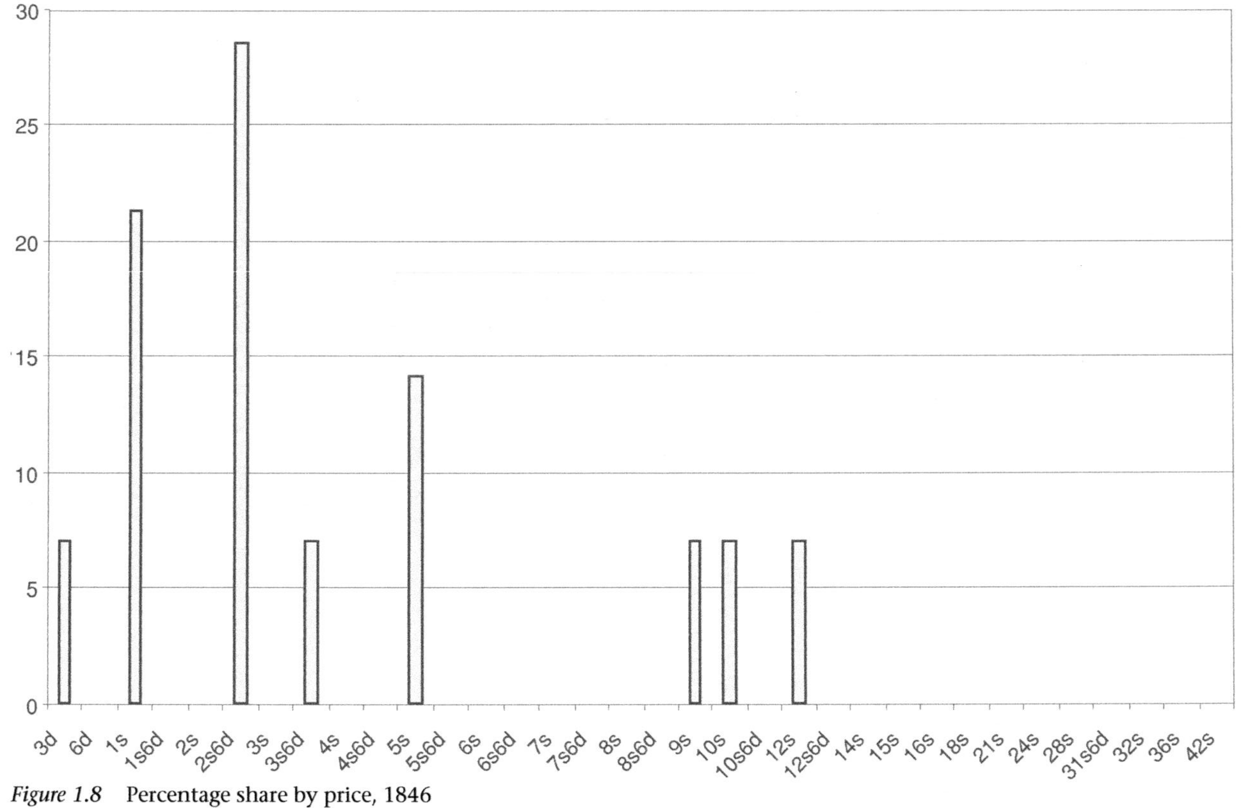

Figure 1.8 Percentage share by price, 1846

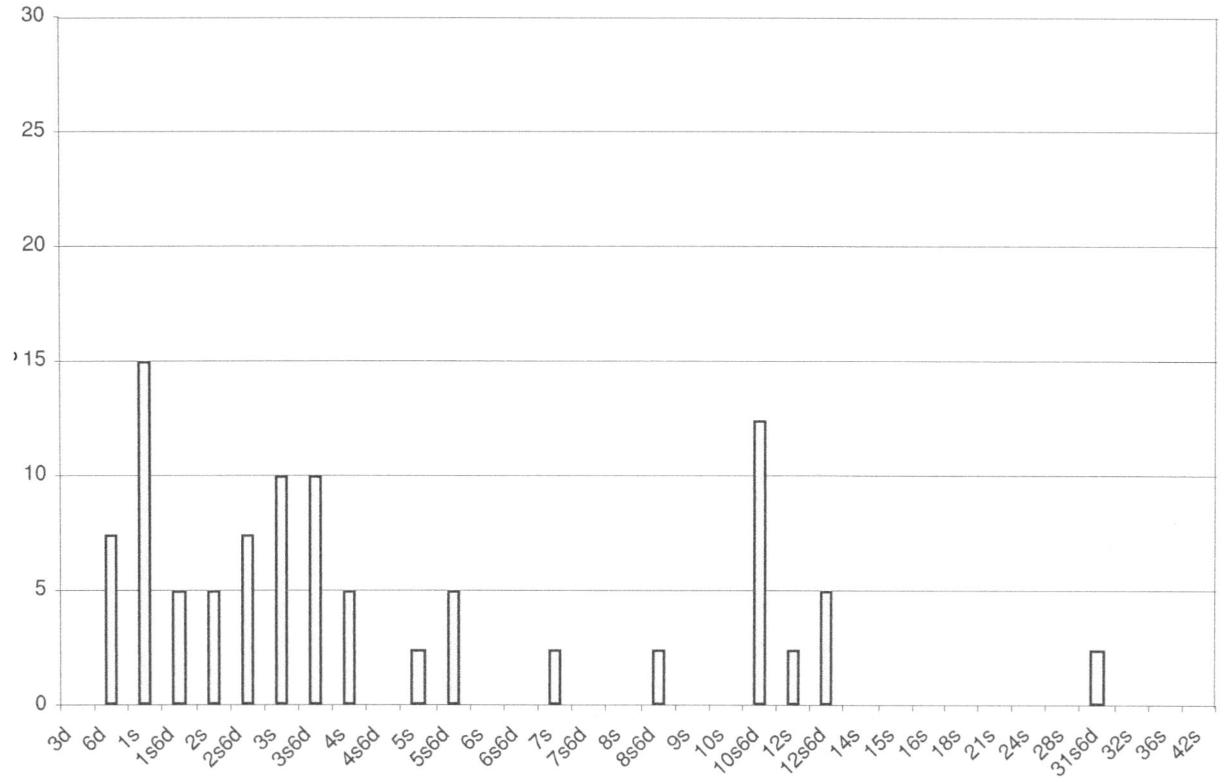

Figure 1.9 Percentage share by price, 1856

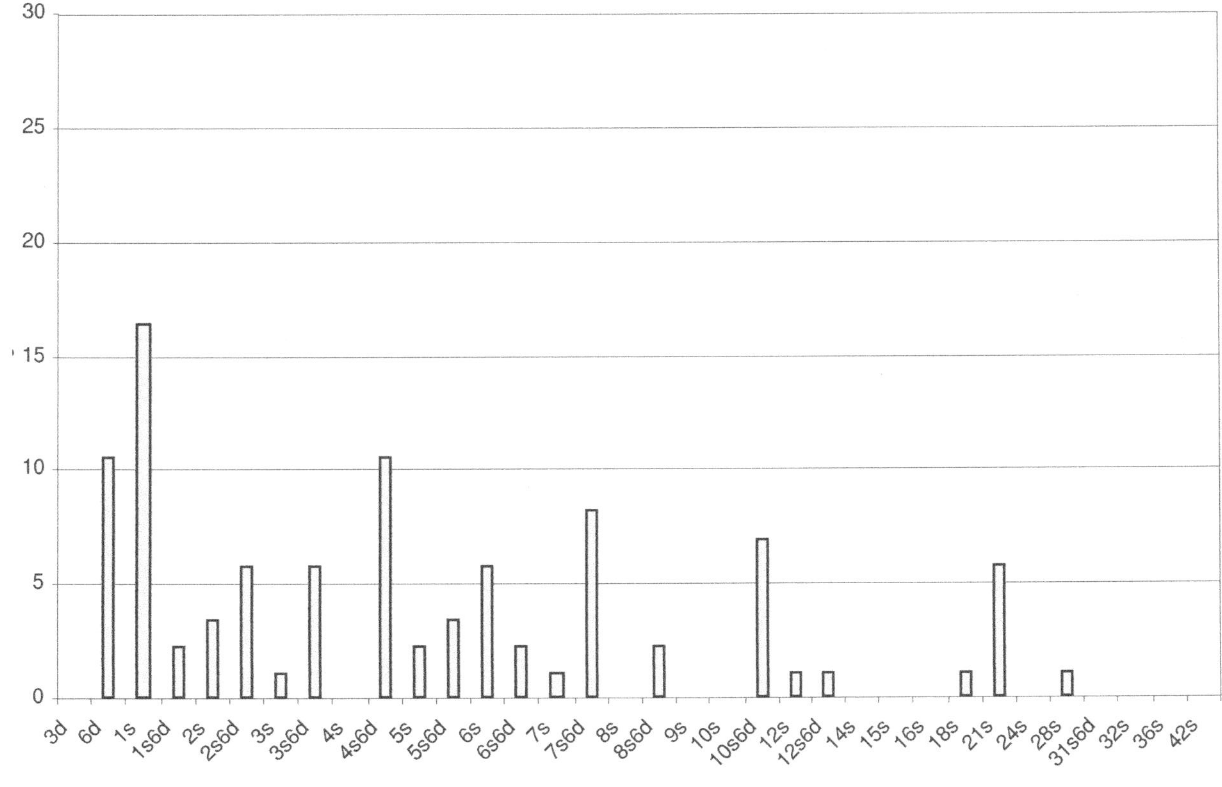

Figure 1.10 Percentage share by price, 1866

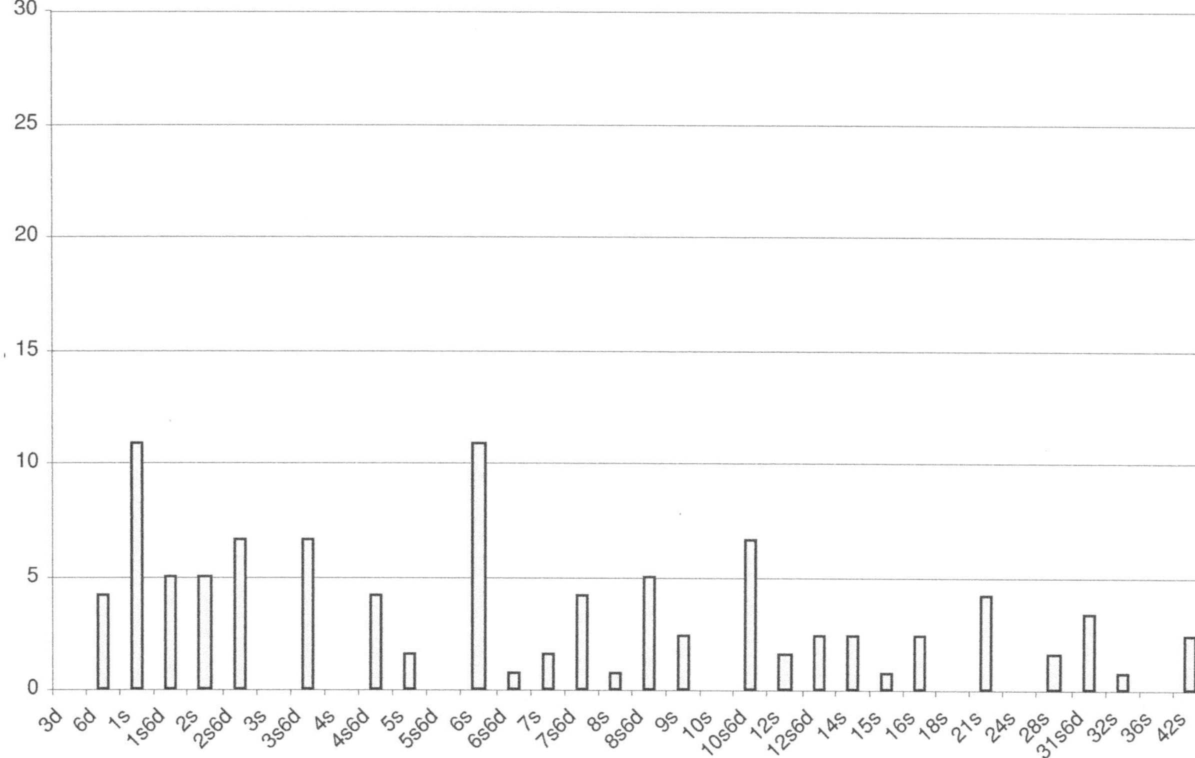

Figure 1.11 Percentage share by price, 1876

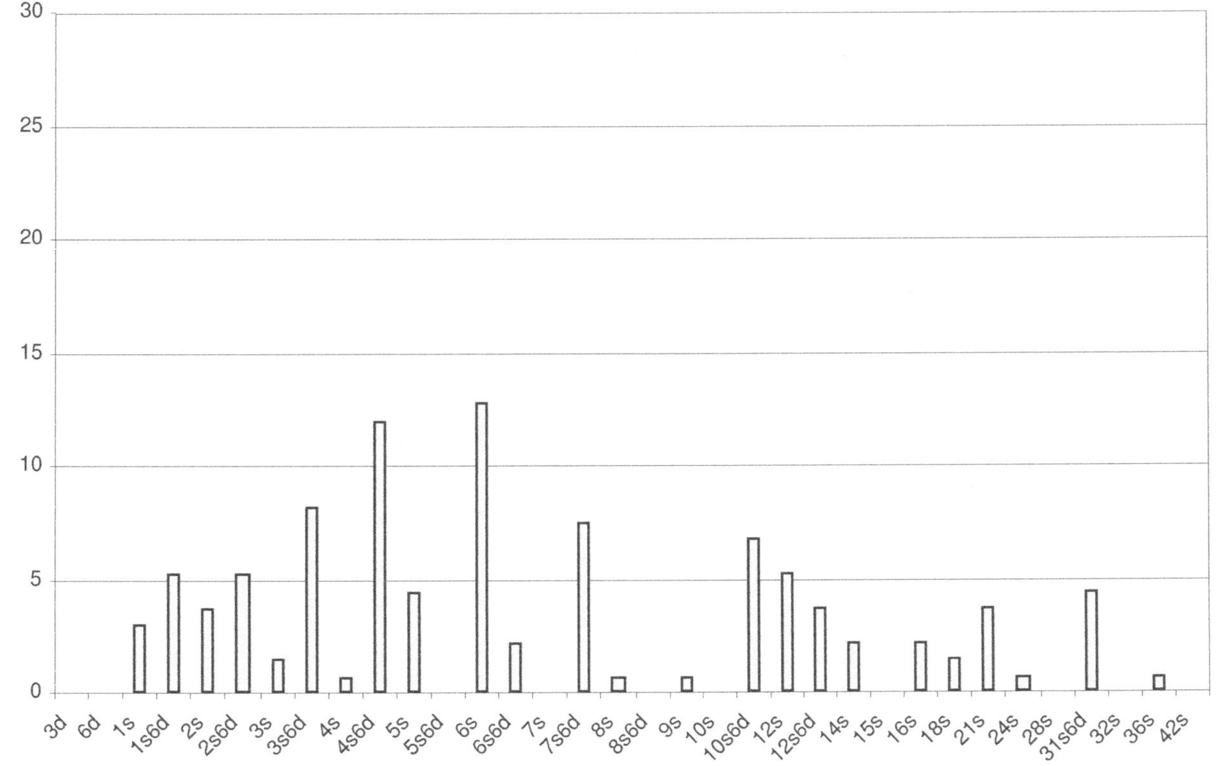

Figure 1.12 Percentage share by price, 1886

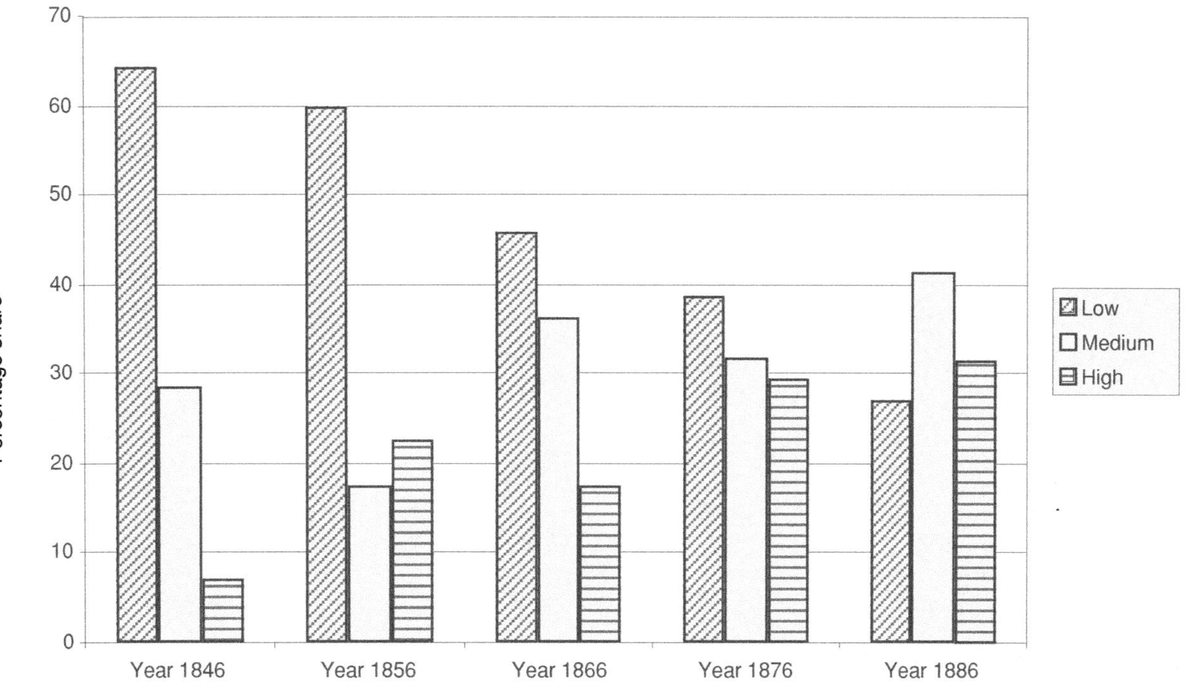

Figure 1.13 Prices: low, medium and high

Once again, 1846 had so few titles and marked a year so early in the life of Macmillan as a company as to be highly untypical. However, along with the figures for 1856, it illustrates most clearly an important point that emerged in Figures 1.7 and 1.8. In the first two decades of its existence Macmillan was overwhelmingly a publisher of low-price books. In 1846 64 per cent of titles, and in 1856 60 per cent of titles, were priced at or below 3s. 6d. As Table 1.7 makes clear, these percentages represent very small numbers (nine in the case of 1846 and 24 in 1856) but, nevertheless, the contrast between the early years and the period 1866–86 is sufficiently striking to need comment. As we have seen in the fourth section, Macmillan's production in the first two sample years was strongly biased towards religious publications; this class of book tended to be characterised by lower than average prices geared to the market at which they were commonly aimed. More general trends confirm this. Figures given in *The Bookseller* in 1858, 1865 and 1875 show that between 60 and 70 per cent of all religious titles were priced at 3s. 6d. or below.[22]

Table 1.7 Price structure: low, medium and high

	Low	Medium	High	Total
Year 1846	9	4	1	14
Year 1846	64.29	28.57	7.14	100
Year 1856	24	7	9	40
Year 1856	60.00	17.50	22.50	100
Year 1866	39	31	15	85
Year 1866	45.88	36.47	17.65	100
Year 1876	46	38	35	119
Year 1876	38.66	31.93	29.41	100
Year 1886	36	55	42	133
Year 1886	27.07	41.35	31.58	100

By 1866 the price structure of Macmillan titles had begun to change. Low-price books dropped for the first time to less than half the total (45.88 per cent), and medium-price titles more than doubled their percentage share, from 17.5 per cent in 1856 to 36.47 per cent. The price structure of 1876 was even more striking: low-price books were now under 40 per cent (38.66 per cent), medium-price books accounted for 31.93 per cent, with an almost equal proportion of high-price books (29.41 per cent). There was no more than 10 per cent between the three price levels, a dramatic change from just 20 years earlier when the difference between the largest share and the smallest had been more than 40 per cent. The price structure for the final sample year, 1886, was even more remarkable. For the first time, low-price titles were less numerous at 27.07 per cent than either medium-price titles (41.35 per cent) or high-price titles (31.58 per cent).

This is quite astonishing. All the general price trends so far observed in British publishing in the later nineteenth century suggested a steady and considerable reduction in prices. By 1885, excluding government publications (which always tended towards lower prices), titles at 3s. 6d. or below accounted for between 60 per cent and 70 per cent of the total; medium price for about 25 per cent of the total; and high price for between 5 per cent and 15 per cent of the total.[23] The Macmillan price structure, at least in the sample years of 1876 and 1886, was, in both form and tendency, quite contrary to more general price movements.

This is the more surprising when one considers a feature that is the subject of current research. Put briefly, between the 1860s and the 1890s Britain was undergoing a period of severe price disinflation. That is, prices generally were falling and thus the purchasing power of money was increasing. One might at least expect prices to remain constant, if not fall. Any price that did remain constant was actually higher in real terms in 1886 than it had been in 1866. Publishers who had kept their price structures relatively stable over these years would have been earning more in real terms by the early 1890s even if they had not sold a single extra book. That Macmillan was actually increasing its average price, and shifting its whole price structure towards higher prices at a time of deflation is quite extraordinary. If any publisher could have withstood underselling and discounting it would have been Macmillan, and yet it was Macmillan that was at the forefront of resale price maintenance in the form of the Net Book Agreement as it developed during the 1890s.

Macmillan in the 1890s

Although the *Bibliographical Catalogue* ends in 1889 there are other sources that allow us to take the quantitative history of Macmillan through to the end of the nineteenth century. Beyond the Macmillan archive (and the later Editions Books in particular), these include the production details derived from a systematic survey of *The Publishers' Circular* currently being undertaken by this writer. The information, which relates to the UK publishing trade as a whole, is still incomplete but is available for the months January to August 1891.

An additional surviving feature of the Macmillan archive for this period is the 'Terms Book' that lists the contractual terms offered to authors and others for their work.[24] This allows us to look at the relative use of different agreements in relation to literary property. As such information does not seem to have survived from an earlier period, it is not possible to produce a dynamic survey; however, in selecting three sample years from the 1890s (1893, 1896, 1899) we are able to gain a fair impression of the relative importance to Macmillan of different literary contracts in the last decade of the nineteenth century.

The Terms Book is concerned with potential, rather than actual deals, that is, offers to authors and other publishers. The material is therefore a reflection of Macmillan's intentions rather than its achievements, although one guesses that, as far as most individual authors were concerned, offer and acceptance were not significantly different. However, these books also occasionally document Macmillan attempting to sell literary property to other publishers, and such deals, one suspects, were subject to much more haggling.

In Table 1.8 it will be noticed that there are two sets of figures: the first including 'Others' (Table 1.8A), that is, deals that did not fall into the defined types, or for which the information was uncertain or non-existent, and the second (Table 1.8B) excluding that category. Table 1.8A is included to give some idea of the size of the unknown contracts (high at over 30 per cent, for instance, in 1899) but the discussion that follows and Figure 1.14 are both based upon Table 1.8B.

The 'Bought in' category was commonly used for texts that were to appear in the Colonial Library. With this exception, the overwhelming majority of terms offered by Macmillan in 1899 were of four types: royalties, half-profits, commission and outright sale. It should be noted that outright sale in the 1890s was often associated, not with original material, but with payment for revisions, editorial matter or illustrations which, being part rather than the whole of a text, could not be calculated easily within the terms of a royalty or half-profits arrangement. Over the three sample years, outright sale accounted for an average of roughly 13 per cent of the known offers.

Offers to publish on commission grew over the sample years, and by 1899 accounted for 18.44 per cent of the known offers. Nowadays we tend to regard commission publishing as synonymous with vanity publishing of the sort undertaken by undistinguished, and sometimes dubious, publishers on the margins of the trade. In the nineteenth century, however, it was a very much more respectable and normal form of contract.[25]

The two forms of contract which feature most strongly in the three sample years are half-profits and royalties. Despite the short span of only six years, we can still observe that there was a distinct dynamic relationship between these two types of agreement: royalty's share of the

Table 1.8 Term Books 1893, 1896, 1899

Table 1.8A: (including 'Others')

	Royalty	Half-Profits	Commission	Outright Sale	Bought in	2/3 to author	Others	Total
1893	65	91	29	42	13	6	35	281
% 1893	23.13	32.38	10.32	14.95	4.63	2.14	12.46	100
1896	74	59	24	18	9	3	43	230
% 1896	32.17	25.65	10.43	7.83	3.91	1.30	18.70	100
1899	79.00	23	33	23	21	0	80	259
% 1899	30.50	8.88	12.74	8.88	8.11	0.00	30.89	100

Table 1.8B: (excluding 'Others')

	Royalty	Half-Profits	Commission	Outright Sale	Bought in	2/3 to author	Total
1893	65	91	29	42	13	6	246
% 1893	26.42	36.99	11.79	17.07	5.28	2.44	100
1896	74	59	24	18	9	3	187
% 1896	39.57	31.55	12.83	9.63	4.81	1.60	100
1899	79.00	23	33	23	21	0	179
% 1899	44.13	12.85	18.44	12.85	11.73	0.00	100

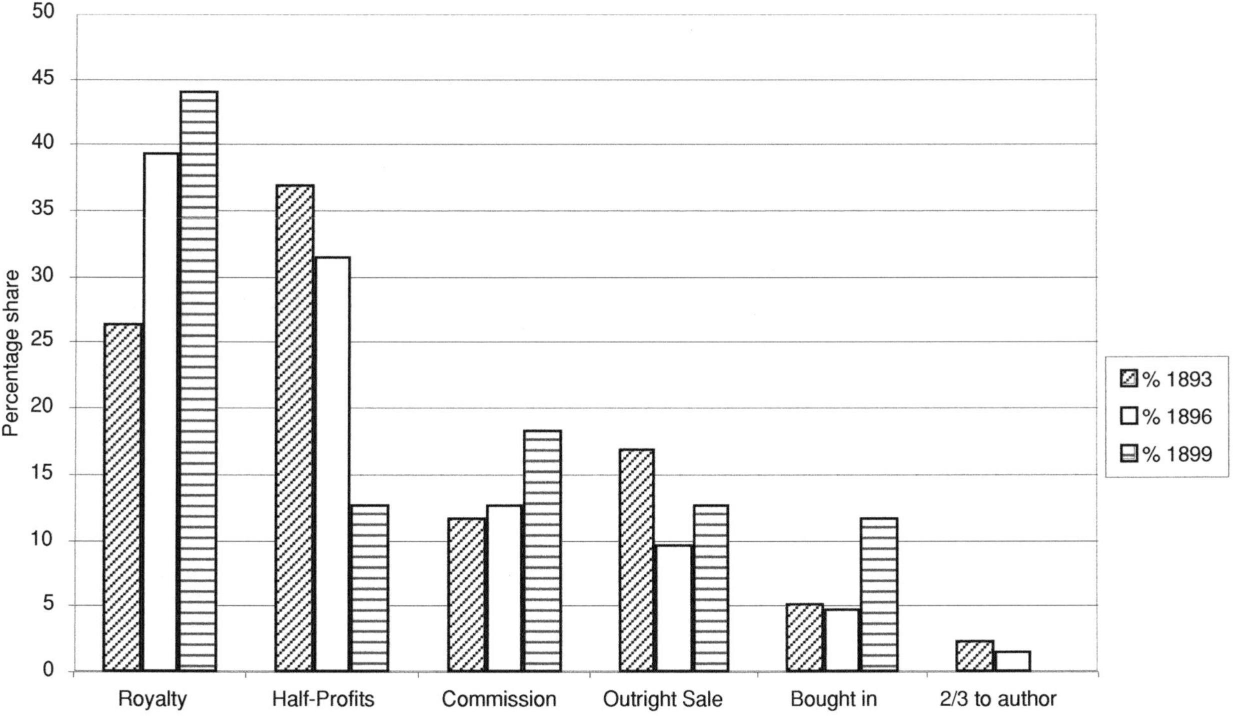

Figure 1.14 Negotiating literary property 1893, 1896, 1899

offered contracts went up as half-profits went down. In 1893 nearly 37 per cent of the known offers were being made on the basis of half-profits; by 1896 this percentage share was down to 31.55 per cent, and by the end of the century it was claiming just under 13 per cent of the contracts offered. This is an extreme contraction and is probably the result of too limited a sample. However, even if the 1899 figure was uncharacteristically low, the trend was almost certainly genuine, if more modest than this would suggest. Along with outright sale, half-profits and elegant variations on it had probably been the dominant form of author–publisher contract for much of the nineteenth century. The royalty arrangement, which had been the most favoured form of contract in the USA for some time, was gradually making its way into the British literary property market. It was, however, a slow process, if the letterbooks of the Society of Authors (founded in 1883) are anything to go by. The correspondence in the Society's archives suggests that half-profits was still the most popular form of contract, although this may be a false impression created by the fact that half-profits were notoriously difficult to calculate and gave unscrupulous publishers much scope for sharp practice – and authors many reasons to complain to the Society of Authors. Nevertheless, other sources also suggest that, even at the end of the nineteenth century, the majority of authors still either sold their works outright (or for a specified time, say five years), or entered into a half-profits agreement.

In this context the fact that, even as early as 1893, over 26 per cent of Macmillan's offers were based on royalty arrangements is quite striking. Even more so is the speed with which this proportion increased: 39.6 per cent by 1896 and over 44 per cent by 1899. How can we explain this trend which, although it was probably happening generally, appears to have been at a higher level and moving more quickly in Macmillan than elsewhere?

There are two factors that go some way to explain this. Macmillan had taken the lead in introducing the Net Book system in 1890.[26] This was to be formalised in 1899 as the Net Book Agreement but it was already having a considerable impact by the mid-1890s. The Net Book system, basically a device of resale price maintenance, reduced the scope for discounts and thus stabilised prices. As royalty rates were usually calculated as a percentage of retail prices, this stability was naturally important for the royalty system in Britain. The development of the Net Book arrangement, and the increase in the share of royalty agreements, were thus the two sides of one coin.

The second reason for the very high number of royalty-based offers was almost certainly the growing American influence channelled through Macmillan's very active participation in the US book market. In 1891 the New York office had been established as an independent partnership and by 1896 the Macmillan Company of New York was an entirely separate business.[27] As the royalty system was the standard means by which authors were paid in the USA, it would have been surprising if that practice had not filtered back into the parent company in Britain.

The American publishing system had other effects on the practices of Macmillan. Until 1891 copyright relations between Britain and the USA were legally unregulated. In that year the Chace Act granted American copyright protection to non-resident authors as long as the book in question was published in the USA at the same time as it was published in the author's home country, and provided the American edition was produced from type set in the USA. These were tough conditions, and Macmillan was wise to maintain a sister company in New York through which such arrangements could be secured. From evidence in the Editions Book it is clear that on at least one occasion even this system was not enough. Lewis Carroll's *The Hunting of the Snark* was first published on 29 March 1876 in an edition of 10,000 copies. The type was plated by the electrotype process and subsequent impressions printed from the electrotype plates.[28] There were impressions in May 1876 (print-run of 5,000), December (3,000) and then two short runs of 250 each in July and December 1890. In January 1891 the Editions Book recorded a further impression of 1,000 copies, indicating that this was for the American market. As this impression was taken from the existing electros it could not satisfy all the conditions of the Chace Act. Some sleight of hand was necessary to give the *Snark* US copyright protection, and this was provided by a comment written into the Editions Book next to the details of this impression: 'Not to be printed in the Bibliography: to be treated as printed in N.Y.' James Foster was the admirable and meticulous compiler of the early Editions Book, and he was also responsible for the *Bibliographical Catalogue*. As the *Catalogue* extends only to 1889 this written warning seems to have been redundant. Perhaps a new and more extensive edition of the *Catalogue* was planned, perhaps the original edition, published in the summer of 1891, was originally designed to cover the printings of 1890 and early 1891. Whatever the reasons, the motives for confusing the origin of the American edition of *The Hunting of the Snark* are clear.

As Macmillan was successfully, if with mild deviousness, adjusting to the challenges of the new market in the USA, what was its standing in the British book market? What was the significance of all the trends in production that we have been observing? As a result of the current research project referred to earlier, we are able to look at the monthly totals of titles produced by all the publishing firms covered by *The Publishers' Circular* in 1891. So far this project has surveyed the period January to August 1891.

In January 1891 Simpkin Marshall, commonly the most frequently listed publisher (not surprisingly, as Simpkin was by this time also the major book wholesaler and agent for small provincial publishers), had 36 titles listed. Longmans came next with 19, Sampson Low with 18, and then Macmillan with 17. In February Longmans topped the list (31), Simpkin was second (22) and Macmillan third (18). In March Simpkin was back on top with 34 titles, but this time Macmillan was second with 31 titles.[29] Overall, between January and August 1891 in *The Publishers' Circular* list of new editions and impressions, Simpkin Marshall predominated with 305; in second place, with 177 mentions, was Macmillan, pushing Longmans, Routledge, Cassell and Sampson Low into third, fourth, fifth and sixth places respectively.

In 1843 Daniel Macmillan wrote, 'We have commenced in a small way ... If the business should prosper, we shall, both of us, do our best to realise some of our ideals ...'.[30] The processes and structures that we have observed in this chapter had, by 1891, gained for them a place among the front rank of British publishers. From this position the second generation of Macmillans could not only realise personal ideals but also, through the Net Book system, reform the publishing system of which they were such a significant part.

Notes

1. In a letter to Alexander Macmillan on 4 August 1881, Thomas Woolner, with the over-confidence of an enthusiastic poet, argued for a large print-run for his poem *Pygmalion*; an important issue for Woolner 'whereas to you in your vast business it is a mere trifle' (Add.MS. 55230, f. 28).
2. The information varies slightly over the years, but usually includes the number of copies ordered and the date, the name of the printer, type and date of paper order, and details of illustrations, jackets or wrappers as appropriate.
3. The sample years selected are: 1843, 1846, 1853, 1861, 1866, 1871, 1876, 1881, 1886, 1891, 1896, 1901, 1906, 1911, 1916, 1921, 1926. (It is a happy coincidence that *The Publishers' Circular*, which began in 1837, first issued clear and unambiguous lists of new publications in the year the Macmillan brothers established their firm.) The work is still in progress so as yet not all

sample years are represented, and not all years that are represented are fully converted into machine-readable form. However, there is already sufficient data to point to trends, many of which can be confirmed from other sources.

4. Simon Eliot, *Some Patterns and Trends in British Publishing 1800–1919* (London: Bibliographical Society, 1994).
5. *Patterns and Trends*, pp. 7–10.
6. *The Publishers' Circular*, 15 September 1858, p. 397.
7. Charles Morgan, *The House of Macmillan (1843–1943)* (London: Macmillan, 1943), p. 50.
8. For instance, the wholesaling and publishing firm of Simpkin Marshall was the company most frequently listed by *The Publishers' Circular* in the 1880s and 1890s; this high frequency was caused by Simpkin Marshall issuing a multitude of titles in their capacity as an agent for provincial publishers.
9. The first titles were: Charles Kingsley *Shore Wonders Companion*, 12 mo, 3s. 6d.; G. B. Sowerby *Companion to Mr. Kingsley's 'Glaucus'*, Fscap, 8vo, 6s. 6d. (carrying the imprint 'Cambridge: Macmillan and Co. and 23 Henrietta Street, Covent Garden'); E. Thring *Sermons Delivered at Uppingham School*, Cr. 8vo, 5s.
10. *Patterns and Trends*, pp. 7, 12.
11. Some catalogues, and particularly the *Nineteenth Century Short Title Catalogue (NSTC)*, allocate undated material to the nearest decade or half-decade, thus artificially swelling the figures for years ending in either '0' or '5'. More reliable figures can be obtained by choosing two years per decade that avoid this false inflation of numbers. The years ending in '1' after 1841 have an advantage for bibliometry, namely that they are census years. Once census years have been chosen, an equal, two-years-per-decade, sampling policy requires that the second years in each decade should end with '6'.
12. *Patterns and Trends*, pp. 33–5.
13. *Patterns and Trends*, pp. 36–7.
14. The other months that saw Colonial Editions were May (3), June (1), July (2) and August (2).
15. Using 1856's 1,313 as a baseline, 1866 was 245.85, 1876 was 383.78 and 1886 was 212.19.
16. By 1886 60 per cent of all countable titles were reprinted. See Table 1.2, Row 12.
17. *Patterns and Trends*, pp. 47, 54.
18. *Patterns and Trends*, pp. 46–55.
19. *Patterns and Trends*, pp. 49, 54.
20. *Patterns and Trends*, Table C3, p.128. The figure is, however, higher than that derived from *The Bookseller*, which suggested an average of 11.2 per cent for Religion over the period 1884–86.
21. *Patterns and Trends*, p. 60.
22. *Patterns and Trends*, pp. 70–1.
23. *Patterns and Trends*, p. 71.
24. This is held alongside the firm's contracts at Basingstoke.
25. Leslie Howsam, *Kegan Paul. A Victorian Imprint. Publishers, books and cultural history* (London: Kegan Paul International; Toronto: University of Toronto Press, 1998) has estimated (p. 131) that over half the firm's publications were 'sponsored directly by their authors in this way'. Some of Macmillan's most

notable commission arrangements, with the economist J. M. Keynes, are discussed in Chapter 10.

26. Sixteen titles were issued as net books by Macmillan in 1890; by 1897 136 titles were issued as net books (see Morgan, p. 180).
27. Morgan, p. 163.
28. One of the striking features of Macmillan production is its strong inclination to electrotype, as oppose to stereotype, when producing plates. The former is more expensive and technically trickier, but frequently gives finer results as well as producing many more copies. Stereotyping, as the older, cheaper and better known of the techniques, dominated the earlier sample years. In 1846 there was just one plated book listed in the *Bibliographical Catalogue*, and that was produced as a stereoplate. In 1856 there were seven stereos and one stereo later replaced by electroplate. As ever, the 1860s seem to have marked a turning point: in the sample year of 1866, 8 stereos were recorded, 4 platings that were initially stereo and later electrotyped, and no fewer than 15 electros, some of which were the arithmetical textbooks of Barnard Smith. In 1876, stereos and electros were roughly balanced with 24 of the former and 22 of the latter. In 1886 there were 31 stereos and 25 electros. Some of the electros could be justified by the fact that the books they reproduced needed clearly and finely printed mathematical symbols and formulae, but not all of Macmillan's mathematical books were produced in electrotype – and some novels were reproduced by means of electrotype. Clearly the right technology had to be used, and Macmillan's commitment to educational texts would frequently require it to use electrotype for clarity. One suspects however, that the extensive use of electrotype is above all a reflection of Macmillan's interest in producing good-quality texts. It is no coincidence that that most fastidious of men, Charles Dodgson, chose Macmillan to produce his books.
29. The top three firms between April and August 1891 were as follows: April: Simpkin (53), Macmillan (19), Longmans (18); May: Simpkin (42), Macmillan (26), Routledge (23); June: Simpkin (49), Macmillan (24), Longmans (19); July: Simpkin (38), Longmans (24), Macmillan (20); August: Simpkin (33), Routledge (24), Macmillan (19).
30. Quoted in Morgan, p. 4.

2
From Parnassus to Grub Street
Matthew Arnold and the House of Macmillan

Bill Bell

> Just understand the difference between a man like Reardon and a man like me. He is the old type of unpractical artist: I am the literary man of 1882. He won't make concessions, or rather, he can't make them; he can't supply the market ... Literature nowadays is a trade ... your successful man of letters is your skilful tradesman ... our Grub Street of today ... knows what literary fare is in demand in every part of the world, its inhabitants are men of business ...
>
> George Gissing *New Grub Street* (1891)

Jasper Milvain's distinction between the servant of commerce and the man of culture is one that Matthew Arnold, had he survived to read it, would have recognised immediately. Arnold's own position in the emerging debate about literary culture and publishing practice was pivotal in the mid- and late-nineteenth century, owing to the changing positions which he himself came to occupy throughout the period. As he negotiated the literary field over three decades Arnold can be seen to have manoeuvred the transition from a traditional kind of 'gentleman-scholar' early in his career, eventually becoming, towards the end of his life, the kind of celebrity writer described by Milvain as 'the literary man of 1882'.

The production of most of Arnold's British books was divided during his lifetime between two publishing companies. Macmillan was responsible for several editions of poetry and literary criticism, including *Essays in Criticism* (1865), *New Poems* (1867), *Poems* (2 vols, 1869), *Selected Poems* (1878), *Mixed Essays* (1879), *Poems* (3 vols, 1885), *Discourses in America* (1885), and, posthumously, *Essays in Criticism, Second Series* (1888). For Macmillan Arnold also prepared a number of popular editions of other writers, including *Johnson's Lives of the Poets* (1878), *Poems of Wordsworth* (1879), and *Poetry of Byron* (1881). Several of Arnold's essays also made their first appearance in *Macmillan's Magazine.* Smith, Elder, under its proprietor George Smith, had responsibility for much of Arnold's social criticism and theology, including *On the Study of Celtic Literature* (1867), *Culture and Anarchy* (1869), *St Paul and Protestantism* (1870), *Friendship's Garland* (1871) and *Literature and Dogma* (1873). Arnold was also a regular contributor to Smith's periodicals, the *Cornhill Magazine* and *Pall Mall Gazette.* Arnold's relations with these publishers beg larger structural questions about the operation of the literary field in general, revealing much about the way in which an increasingly organised and commercial book trade was coming to operate throughout the second half of the nineteenth century.

'The most unpopular of authors'

Arnold's business with Macmillan & Company began early in 1862, when he first wrote to Alexander to compliment him on the appearance of Palgrave's *Golden Treasury,* then fast becoming a staple of the firm's list.

> My dear Arnold
> I am very glad you like the look of the 'Garland' so far. I hope that you will see that the inner stuff corresponds there to[o]. Palgrave told me that you had been kind enough to send his book to a distinguished French critic. I wish I could read French easily enough to enjoy the writings of one whom you call the Prince of Critics. The stuff that passes for criticism in our common English press is, as a rule, at present the dreariest stuff – barren platitudes or stupid and impertinent witticisms. I don't read all of course but I see none that have an approach to the honest pains which Brimley used to take with his work. Now and then a *Saturday* article is good & honest, and as a whole allowing for Saturdayism, there is really thought always present. But too often it is thought about how to say a clever thing, not how really to make clear the character of the book they are handling.

> Could you give me the pleasure of your company on Thursday next week Jan 30, to dinner, Hour 6, and we don't dress. Palgrave is coming.[1]

Macmillan's response, in which a new author is effectively reeled in for the first time, demonstrates the kind of tact and skill that Alexander would routinely come to deploy in his handling of Arnold. Through the use of highly nuanced language Macmillan subtly insinuates himself, first flattering Arnold by registering an interest in his beloved Sainte-Beuve ('the Prince of Critics'), then going on to echo his correspondent's own high-handed view of English criticism. The disavowal of the vulgar literary marketplace was calculated to appeal to the Oxford Professor of Poetry who, as Macmillan knew, was becoming increasingly outspoken in his condemnation of the *Saturday Review* and the general Philistinism of the English newspapers. You and I are not part of the 'Common English press', Macmillan effectively tells him, because, like Brimley (Macmillan's father-in-law), we both understand what honest criticism is.

For years Arnold had been making himself a reputation as a scornful critic of English audiences. In the recent essay on Heine he had characterised Britain as a land of Philistines, a country in which 'the born lover of ideas, the born hater of commonplaces, must feel ... that the sky over his head is of brass and iron'.[2] It was to the European – particularly the French – literary milieu, with its rejection of mass culture and its advocacy of minority values that Arnold was increasingly turning throughout the 1860s. For some time his writing had been full of references to his own necessary obscurity. 'You – Froude – Shairp,' he once told his sister, 'I believe the list of those whose reading of me I anticipate with any pleasure stops there'.[3] To his friend Arthur Clough he had said that he harboured such a 'bitter feeling' towards his contemporaries that he felt he could 'if need be, dispense with them all'.[4] This fugitive aesthetic was never articulated more clearly than in the poem to 'Obermann' in which he writes:

> Some secrets may the poet tell,
> For the world loves new ways;
> To tell too deep ones is not well –
> It knows not what he says.

Although he was gradually to temper his views, Arnold appears still to have been harbouring contempt for popular reading audiences on the publication of the 1865 *Essays in Criticism* which, he told his mother, would 'reach and influence the writing and literary class, not the great reading class whom the *Country Parson*, for instance, reaches: for reputation this is all very well, but for sale and profit it is, of course, not so well'.[5] Shortly before its publication Arnold had candidly admitted to Alexander Macmillan, the book's publisher, that he was 'the most unpopular of authors', and that if the volume failed to pay its expenses he would 'try this infernal English public no more'.[6]

In its presentation as well as its content the *Essays* was deliberately unconventional. Informing a surprised Macmillan of his intention 'to inaugurate a most desirable novelty in English publishing', Arnold proposed in August 1864 that the book should be bound not in 'those odious boards', but in 'yellow paper – neatly lettered'. The calculated seriousness of the enterprise is evident in Arnold's desire to avoid all appearance of self-publicity. Prior to its publication he had requested of his publisher, 'Pray do not, in advertising my book, put the newspaper panegyrics at the bottom. I have an inexpressible dislike to it.'[7] Hedging his bets between conventional commercial practice and tasteful literary standards, Macmillan replied three days later: 'Surely your will on such a point is law to a conscientious and tender hearted publisher. I have given strict injunctions to my advertising clerk to avoid any appearance of puff. Indeed I only half like it myself – perhaps not quite half.'[8]

Yet, such 'an aura of indifference and rejection towards the buying and reading public', as Pierre Bourdieu reminds us, can very often represent little more than a means of securing the long-term exchange value of a text or an author as a reproduceable commodity. While he might have rejected the vulgarity of overt forms of self-publicity, Arnold's ambivalent relationship with fame surfaces time and again, not least in the careful detail with which he regards the general reviewing establishment. For someone who had formerly insisted to his friends and family that reviews of his work meant nothing to him, Arnold had begun to take a remarkable interest in his reception by the mainstream press. In February of 1865 he wrote to Macmillan with instructions to add the *Illustrated London News* – which he admitted to reading regularly – along with the *Athenaeum, Church and State Gazette*, and the *London Review* to the list of those who should receive review copies of *Essays in Criticism*.[9] In their subject-matter also, the essays that make up the collection take as one of their recurrent themes the often difficult relationship between fame and literary value. The essay on Maurice de Guérin, which portrays its subject as the epitome of the underrated writer 'careless of fame', provides a case in point. A poet who never sought publication in his own lifetime, Guérin is presented as the quintessential romantic quietist, someone who 'lived like a man possessed', Arnold tells us, 'with his eye uplifted'.[10] An account of the same writer's posthumous rise to fame is presented in the companion essay on his sister's heroic struggle to win recognition for her Guérin's literary genius:

> She was very different from her brother; but she too, like him, had that in her which preserves a reputation. Her soul had the same characteristic quality as his talent, – *distinction*. Of this quality the world is impatient; it chafes against it, rails at it, insults it, hates it; – it ends by receiving its influence, and by undergoing its law. This quality at last inexorably corrects the world's blunders, and fixes the world's ideals. It procures that the popular poet shall not finally pass for a Pindar, nor the popular historian for a Tacitus, nor the popular preacher for a Bossuet. To the circle of spirits marked by this rare quality, Maurice and Eugenie de Guérin belong; they will take their place in the sky which these inhabit, and shine close to one another, *lucida sidera*.[11]

Such a preoccupation with literary reputation might, among other things, be read as an unwitting allusion to Arnold's own ambivalent desire for recognition at this time. The necessary deferral of worldly fame in the present, in the interests of securing long-term canonisation in what Bourdieu calls 'the sub-field of restricted production' was also becoming a central theme in much of the publishing correspondence. While emphasis is frequently laid on the scrupulous distinction between reputation and mere popularity, there is increasingly detectable in Arnold's use of language a significant elision between the otherwise mutually exclusive categories of literary culture and market forces. Such internal contradiction is more than evident in the conclusion of Arnold's argument in 'The Literary Influence of Academies' for the inferiority of British reference works to their European counterparts. Those who set high standards in such matters, we are told, 'are isolated, they form no powerful body of opinion, they are not strong enough to set a standard, up to which even the journeyman work of literature must be brought, if it is to be vendible'.[12]

'A poor inhabitant of Grub Street'

> If I am to do any work of my own besides school inspecting I find I must lead the life of a galley slave.
>
> Arnold to Macmillan, 13 July 1875

In 'The Function of Criticism' Arnold had famously characterised the nineteenth century as an 'epoch of expansion', with the promised land of a cultural renaissance a generation away. While at the end of the essay he takes encouragement from the belief that the age of criticism is imminent, he nevertheless concludes with a fatalistic reference to 'the promised land it will not be ours to enter, and we shall die in the wilderness'.[13] A year later, he was writing again to Macmillan:

> Confucius says: The Sage is afflicted at his insufficiency, not at his obscurity (of reputation). But a certain curiosity is slowly awakening, I think, about the things I publish; a suspicion that the way I am going, at any rate, we all must go if we are to get forward. Still, I shall no doubt die in the wilderness.[14]

Almost from the moment that they enter into business relations, the letters exchanged between author and publisher are full of such speculation about the relationship that was developing between Arnold's texts and a changing public. As this comment and others show, although he continued throughout to maintain a clear distinction between popular reputation and purer intellectual pursuits, Arnold was by this time clearly beginning to derive pleasure from the prospect of the reading public's growing 'curiosity'.[15]

While much of his correspondence with publishers is characterised by modest restraint, in the letters to his mother Arnold is more forthright, commenting freely on his financial position and the literary labour in which he is increasingly engaged. In November 1867 he writes:

> I constantly hear of the way my things are making, and people say to me that I am 'a power'; I am sure there is great need of a power in our present troubled condition, if the power can but make or keep itself a good one. I have just sold a sort of school-book on Greek poetry to Macmillan for £300 for 3 years: £150 down now, before the book is begun, the other £150 when the book is published. This is the first money of any importance I have made by literature, and I hope it will help to set us straight.[16]

Two years later he writes again to his mother on the publication of the two-volume edition of his verse:

> My book was out yesterday and the day before I got from Macmillan the note I enclose ... He sent a cheque for £200 with it, having paid the first £100 at Lady Day, when the bargain was first made. This makes £500 my poems have brought me in within the last two years, so that they are beginning to make amends for their long unprofitableness ... I expect the present edition will be sold out in about a year. Macmillan tells me the booksellers are subscribing very well for it. My poems represent, on the whole, the main movement of mind of the last quarter of a century, and thus they will probably have their day as people become conscious ... of what that movement of mind is, and interested in the literary productions which reflect it.[17]

It is curious to note the extent to which Arnold's commentators, while often citing the famous sentence on 'the main movement of mind', have failed to connect this statement with its financial context. In both of these passages, Arnold moves, unproblematically, between the language of the business account and assertions of aesthetic value.

It was indeed under Macmillan's guidance that several moderately successful editions of the poetry were produced, beginning with the *New Poems* of 1867:

> My dear Arnold
> The book is actually published. We sent you a copy by post last Saturday. Hutton had one the same day. I sent it the moment I had your note. The other review copies, of which I enclose a list, were sent early this week.
>
> Could you conveniently come tomorrow to write the names in your presentation copies? Any time from 10 till 5 will suit us. On Saturday I am giving my people a holiday.
>
> I have read the greater part of your volume through, with care & great admiration. Empedocles is a noble poem. I had only a dim remembrance of it, and thought of it as obscure. I did not find it so this reading. I really think you should succeed.
>
> I hope you like Henry Sidgwick's article. Of course he does not agree with you, but he is full of admiration in general. I am sure these discussions do great good & the country owes you much. Your critics and opponents increase your influence for good.
>
> Yours ever faithfully,
> Alexr Macmillan[18]

Here we can see the original terms subtly shifting as Arnold moves from the position of a worthy, but unremunerative labourer in the field of restricted literary production, to becoming a 'successful' writer and valuable literary property. Highly euphemistic in the veiled references he makes to the economics of literary labour, Macmillan is nevertheless here recognising Arnold's transition in the late 1860s from a previously obscure economic position towards one of increased financial success. From now on, both men will begin to tell each other that economic and aesthetic value might, after all, no longer occupy opposing positions in relation to a market in which 'influence' and 'goodness' were not only compatible, but mutually contingent. Always an attentive reader of Arnold, Alexander Macmillan wrote to him on the appearance of *St Paul and Protestantism* under the Smith, Elder imprint in 1870 that he would be curious 'to see the effect on the public mind – if there is such an entity, or at least on the feelings & prejudices which serve the purposes of a thinking faculty'.[19] Three years later he would write, 'I have read through carefully your "Literature & Dogma". It sure[ly] ought to make a stir and do good ... when I was in Cambridge last week ... I urged people to read & consider it – as it certainly deserves.'[20]

Such comments, helpful as they are, might be regarded as anecdotal, were it not for their frequency and subtle modulation over the years. For all their high-minded language, it is apparent that Arnold and Macmillan were gradually becoming less reticent in their attitudes towards the popular market. Thanks in part to the steady sales of his poetry, and the public attention brought by the political and theological controversies surrounding works such as *Culture and Anarchy* and *Literature and Dogma*, Arnold had found by the early 1870s that he had moved from a position of minority appeal to moderate fame. Since 1862, he had been learning how to maximise his income by selling books chapter by chapter to the monthlies. Engaging in popular controversies in periodicals like the *Cornhill*, he had also come to understand, generated the kind of publicity that sold books. As he confessed to his other publisher George Smith in 1869, shortly before publication of his essay on 'The Modern Element in Literature', the appearance of an article in *Macmillan's Magazine* would 'prepare people's minds for value of the commodity laid before them'.[21]

Although his reputation was in the ascendant, financial returns from his books were still far from lavish. As one commentator has observed, the publication of *Literature and Dogma*, by far his most popular book to date, 'made him notorious but not rich'.[22] Over the years Arnold had become increasingly reliant on his literary income in order to keep himself solvent. By the late 1860s, he was discovering that the salary of a School Inspector was not in itself sufficient to sustain a domestic economy involving a houseful of children, a manservant, a cook, and two housemaids. In 1867 he found himself applying to George Smith for a loan of £200: 'I make literature put my boys to school,' he wrote, 'and literature is failing me'.[23] A year later he was again writing to Smith to request a year's forbearance, offering to pay the interest in the meantime and blaming his situation on 'the incorrigible laxity of Grub Street in money matters'.[24]

Despite the family's removal to Harrow in the following year, and the fact that their lifestyle was in consequence now 'plainer than it was in London', Arnold's letters to his mother continue to display anxiety over the extent of his personal expenses:

> The bills of all kinds for getting into this house seem, both for number and bigness, as if they would never end, and this ... seems to adjourn still to the future the prospect of our getting clear, and to condemn one to struggle on perpetually, never having any money to spend and yet never free ... I seriously think of getting rid of Mrs. Tuffin and Price, and being with three servants, which would be quite possible with our present family ... But I look at the small boxlike houses about this hill, with no stables and hardly more than a yard for a garden, and think that we might really do very well in one of them and might cut off half our expenses there ... I expect my decline of life will very likely be spent in one of these 'boxes' which when young I thought so odious and intolerable. The only intolerable thing, as one gets older, is the harass and bondage of worldly cares and money difficulties.

Matters were probably not helped throughout this period by the fact that Arnold was proving to be one of the most sociable of companions, dining regularly and expensively with the most notable literary and political figures of the day. The same letter concludes,

> This is a rather melancholy subject, so I will leave it. I am just going to be elected a member of a club called the Literary Club ... It is of very old standing, has only 40 members, and all of them interesting people. Lord Salisbury is just going to become a member too, and that will shew you from what different sorts of people the club is recruited.[25]

Adversaries in collusion

> The makers and marketers of works of art are adversaries in collusion, who each abide by the same law which demands the repression of direct manifestations of personal interest, at least in its overtly 'economic' form, and which has every appearance of transcendence although it is only the product of the cross-censorship weighing more or less equally on each of those who impose it on all the others.
>
> Bourdieu *The Production of Belief*

Only half-joking Arnold had written to Macmillan from Mentone in March of 1873: 'travelling is terribly expensive, but to you succubusses of the publishing trade that does not matter. In a few years, however, the Continent will be absolutely closed to the poor inhabitants of Grub Street, who will have to stay the rest of their lives at home.'[26] Two years later, and under increasing financial pressure, Arnold informed Macmillan that he had now to 'attend a little more to my literary profits than I have hitherto done'. Becoming increasingly desperate, he wrote in March 1875 to say that he was unsatisfied by recent accounts that he had received from Macmillan, adding that he had been dining with three literary men ('all of them friends or acquaintances' of Macmillan) who had told him that he 'ought to be extremely dissatisfied' with what he was receiving for the *Essays in Criticism*, and informing Macmillan that, before a new edition appeared, he intended to transfer the book to Smith, Elder.[27] Immediately there ensued an uncustomarily formal exchange, concluding with Macmillan reminding Arnold: 'It is ten years since the first edition of the *Essays* was published [and] it was not so apparent then as it is now that your audience was of a kind not to be materially increased by a lower price.'[28] Several days later Arnold wrote a letter of reconciliation, agreeing finally to allow Macmillan to continue to publish the *Essays in Criticism* under new terms, and admitting that 'the whole business of haggling about the profits of my works is distasteful to me'. On receipt of the letter the now cautious Macmillan appended an instruction to his clerk across the top of the document, 'This should be kept as an agreement.'[29] Thereafter, all references to terms of agreement become detailed and officious. Laying out his understanding of the new situation on October 25, the publisher wrote in the following unambiguous terms:

> I mean this: we have promised to pay you a fixed sum for an edition of 1500 copies for the Essays. What we propose is to have leave to

> print 2000, paying you something more for these, but in proportion to what we can make in [the American] market ... The result as regards the Essays will be this:- we pay you £175 for an edition of 2000 copies. The book will sell in England at 9s. But we will send 500 copies to America at 2s. each ... [30]

The depth of Macmillan's lingering disquiet is detectable in the note of highly charged irony with which the letter concludes: 'If sweetness & light are what we ought to strive after they must be real and attainable. Don't you think so?' To Macmillan's mind, Arnold had quite clearly overplayed his hand, and it would be another eight years before the publisher would consent to reissue the *Essays*. The impugnity on his character Macmillan had taken hard, and on this occasion a wayward author would be made to kiss the rod.

While the acrimony of 1875 was soon to pass, the rupture with Macmillan would considerably weaken Arnold's hand for some time to come. For all of his apparent success, the income generated by his literary labour remained at best irregular and, even combined with a modest School Inspector's salary, continued to be insufficient to maintain the kind of lifestyle to which he was accustomed. By early 1876, Arnold's financial situation had become critical, it having recently come to light that his son had incurred gambling debts at Oxford to the tune of £1,000. His personal situation now almost intolerable, Arnold wrote to Smith in January, 'it makes a difference to me, particularly as I get older and feel the grind of school-inspecting more oppressive, what my books bring me'.[31] On 4 June, he also wrote to Macmillan, saying that he required £500 'for a special purpose', though having cleared his debts several years earlier with a legacy, he was now reluctant, as he put it, 'to become a borrower again'. Preferring instead to raise the money from the sale of his works, he offered Macmillan the rights for the *Poems*, *Essays in Criticism*, and *Isaiah* for the next five years, assuring him that 'for the next five or ten years the sale of my books is likely to increase rather than to diminish; that is my great [pride] as an author, my only one – a growth in circulation which though it has been slow seems steady'.[32] Two days later, Macmillan replied coolly that 'So far as we see the Poems is the only book on which an advance could well be made without having in it some at least of the elements of borrowing because the Essays & Isaiah have so recently been advanced on. Would £200, or £250 from us meet your needs?[33]

Thereafter Arnold was to enter into a series of contracts to undertake what in less desperate times he had dismissed as 'the journeyman work of literature'. It was in the preparation of popular classics that Arnold and his publisher found a way to cultivate two very different kinds of market simultaneously, allowing the author to continue with his civilising mission while giving Macmillan the opportunity to appeal to a wider audience. Writing in September 1872 after the initial success of *A Bible-reading for Schools*, Macmillan had informed Arnold that it was his intention to produce in future two kinds of edition, 'one dearer & finer in type & print for general readers, and a quite cheap one without the preface for the schools'.[34] This is not to suggest that Arnold was at this time entirely comfortable with his role as populariser of the classics. In 1877, when he was preparing his edition of Johnson's *Lives of the Poets* for the press, he wrote to Macmillan remarking, 'I am against having many notes. Let us not aim at a *school-book*, but rather at a literary book which schools can and will use.'[35] As he explained in March 1878, 'My notion is that the book should be read by all young students of literature ... But not a library book, nor yet a cheap book for the general public (there is already, I believe, a cheap Johnson's Lives at 1s. 6d.), is what I design; I design a book to hit the needs of the young student of English literature.'[36]

Arnold's most popular success was to come with the Golden Treasury *Poems of Wordsworth*, which sold no fewer than 17,000 copies in the decade after its appearance in 1879. Just how far his projected audience had changed by this time is evident from Macmillan's proposal for an edition which 'should be done & annotated only to the extent of common intelligence – if only one knew what that is – and not for scholastic purposes'. Even more revealing is the publisher's advice that '"Bottles" touched with emotion is the sort of audience you seek to reach – and create. I am sure your interest in "Bottles" will greatly help you in such a work.'[37] In alluding to the fictional Mr Bottles, the satiric epitome of middle-class Philistinism who had appeared in Arnold's *Friendship's Garland*, Macmillan was admitting, for the first time, that Arnold's readers were, in fact, the very middle classes he was so fond of castigating. The ambivalence involved in 'the audience you seek to reach, and create' shows that Macmillan understood clearly the delicate position in which Arnold now found himself. As Stephen Gill observes, 'his publishers knew exactly what market they served and there is more than a touch of cynicism in Macmillan's remark to Arnold'.[38]

Yet it is also clear from the correspondence and from the Preface itself that Arnold was not now himself above a little fiscal realism when it came to tailoring his critical voice to the literary market. Whereas in *Essays in Criticism* he had famously criticised the English romantics,

Wordsworth and Byron included, as constituting only *'minor currents'* in European writing, when he came to write the Preface to *Wordsworth* he was to present the reading public with quite a different estimate. Going so far as to call himself a 'Wordsworthian', Arnold now admitted that, while he had failed to achieve due recognition, Wordsworth was in fact 'one of the very chief glories of English poetry'. Critics can change their minds, and it is certainly possible that Arnold's views on the significance of Wordsworth's poetry had shifted in the intervening years. It is just as likely that such a complete volte-face was prompted in part by the commercial necessities of popular preface writing.

Throughout their subsequent transactions there seems to have been a tacit understanding between author and publisher that these editions would go a considerable way to offsetting Arnold's standing debt. Shortly before the appearance of the Wordsworth volume, George Craik wrote on Macmillan's behalf to say that he had every hope that the collection would 'do well', and that, although he was loath to make any additional commitments, the firm would now at least be in a position to cancel the loan.[39] In terms of the labour involved, the edition would be the easiest money that Arnold would ever earn, its preparation requiring little more than the marking-up of an 1832 edition, provided by the publisher himself, and the composition of a brief preface to appear as an appetising article in *Macmillan's Magazine* shortly before the book's publication. In return, Arnold was eventually to receive '£100 for the first edition of 3500 copies & a royalty of 9d. a copy on all beyond sold in England': on copies sold in America he was to receive half the English royalty.[40] Prior to its publication Macmillan asked Arnold if he had any objection to stereotyping, a process 'that would enable us to print 1000 at a time, which has certain advantages, when a book has a steady sale that can be calculated on'. Whatever his earlier misgivings about the relationship between aesthetic value and popular appeal, Macmillan had the pleasure of informing Arnold that the result would be 'a beautiful and successful book'.[41] Moreover, the book's publisher was now not alone in allowing for the unproblematic association of aesthetic superiority with financial return. Anxious to capitalise on the success of Palgrave's *Golden Treasury*, Arnold insisted that the *Wordsworth* should be set in identical type in order to create an association with the famous anthology in the public mind.[42] A close reading of Arnold's Preface also indicates an intimate connection between literary value and economic possibility. In his early years, we are told, Wordsworth's poetry 'had never brought him in enough to buy his shoe-strings'. Because the poet was not now 'so accepted and popular' as he once was, the task that lay ahead of his devoted followers, begins the Preface, was 'getting him recognised' and in doing so, win him readers among 'the public [which] has remained cold'.[43]

When two years later he came to prepare his popular edition of Byron for Macmillan, Arnold was to establish the connection between publishing practice and canonical value once and for all:

> When at last I held in my hand the volume of poems which I had chosen from Wordsworth, and begun to turn over its pages, there arose in me almost immediately the desire to see beside it, as a companion volume, a like collection of the best poetry of Byron. Alone amongst our poets of the earlier part of this century, Byron and Wordsworth not only furnished material enough for a volume of this kind, but, also, as it seems to me, they both gain considerably by being thus exhibited.[44]

Not for the first time in his career had Arnold overturned a critical estimate for the sake of personal income. Presenting the edition as the result of spontaneous critical judgement, all indications of its more pragmatic origins (as a book commissioned to capitalise on the increasing market value of a well-known romantic poet) were obscured as critic and publisher once again conspired to create a 'disinterested' critical context in which a writer's work could once again find a popular audience. If Bourdieu is correct in his assertion that all prefatory writing is, to some extent, a euphemistic attempt to legitimise symbolic capital, then it is hardly surprising that Arnold should conclude his argument on behalf of Byron with the remark that 'the critic who does most for his author is the critic who gains readers for his author himself'.[45]

As well as preparing cheap editions of other writers, Macmillan and Arnold had been turning their minds for several years towards the popularisation of his own works. In response to a growing demand for the poetry, Macmillan issued in 1878 a one-volume edition of 3,000 copies of *Selected Poems* at the cheaper price of 4s. 6d. So popular did the experiment prove that two years later the publisher was proposing a new printing, informing its author that the success of the selections had not, to his mind, damaged its author's appeal among more serious readers of the authoritative two-volume edition. Arnold, Macmillan assured him, now had a 'large enough public of the kind who do not grudge possessing – which means from a publishers point – purchasing you in two or more forms'. Becoming more explicit about the operation of the market, Macmillan then went on to translate earlier statements about an intellectually improving audience into the more explicitly economic terms of supply and demand: 'the livelier quarter is coming and we wish to have food for the improved appetite of the public, which grows by what it feeds on. May it grow still more.'[46]

The presentation of the Arnold canon in terms of a lightweight volume of selections provides just one more example of how, in collusion with his publishers, Arnold was increasingly experimenting with ever more popular modes of production. In the Preface to the popular 2s. 6d. edition of *Literature and Dogma*, one of a number of cheap editions which Smith, Elder began issuing in the 1880s, Arnold's apology for such modes of publication begins, revealingly, by speculating on two very different classes of reader:

> The argument of the work is more readily followed, and for the general reader it probably gains in force, by the suppression of a good deal of the apparatus of citation and illustration from Scripture which originally accompanied it. The public to which the book was in the first instance addressed was one which expects, with a work of this kind, such an apparatus. But to the general public its fullness is not so well suited, and, for them, its reduction probably improves the book at the same time that it shortens it.[47]

While an ostensible distinction between the scholarly community and the general reader is maintained throughout the Preface, what Arnold neglects to mention here is that 'the public to which the book was first addressed' was not in fact an academic one at all, but the solid middle-class readership of the *Cornhill Magazine*. To privilege such an audience over the new 'general reader' reveals much about how for himself, and the book trade in general, the centre of gravity had actually shifted since the 1860s.

For all of his posturing, Arnold had apparently come to see the irresistible benefits of the new publicity machine, culminating in his agreement, in 1883, to a lecture tour of the United States conducted by the impresario Richard D'Oyly Carte. The idea of an American tour, as Clinton Machann has observed, 'did not arise primarily from intellectual curiosity ... Arnold made the calculated decision to take on an exhausting schedule ... in order to pay off his debts.'[48] Before his departure Arnold had written to tell George Craik that if his American trip was a success it 'would make people buy the books'.[49] Although not as remunerative as he might have hoped, the enterprise proved reasonably profitable: owing to the issue of several popular reprints produced for the American market it would be the most prolific year ever in the production of his works.

The conditions under which were composed the pieces that made up Arnold's last volume, the posthumously published *Essays in Criticism, second series,* show a remarkable shift from the *bon mots* of an obscure poet speaking to an Oxford audience about Celtic literature and little-known French authors in the 1860s, to the writer of popular verse and introductions to Byron, Shelley and Wordsworth of the 1880s. It is significant, too, that several of the essays had been composed for middlebrow magazines like *The Century* and *Macmillan's,* all, according to Park Honan, 'meant for fairly wide audiences'.[50] Here, if it were required, is final evidence of the extent to which by the end of his career Arnold had come to recognise the impossibility of an unambiguous distinction between high culture and mass production. While it would perhaps be going too far to say that he ever became Milvain's 'literary man of 1882', throughout his career we see him moving closer by degrees to just such a position, learning to play the market more effectively while capitalising on his reputation for occupying a position above such a vulgar pursuit. In this contest for legitimation and disavowal, as Macmillan understood, Arnold's aesthetic aloofness and his desire for pecuniary success provided a deadly combination.

Between his first encounter with Alexander Macmillan in 1862 and his death in 1888, Arnold was, with the assistance of two shrewd and well-placed publishers, to develop a highly marketable voice. By the time that Charles Morgan came to write *The House of Macmillan (1843–1943)* over half a century later, he was able to tell the story of a self-confident, established company, legitimated in large part through its associations with the Great and the Good, of which Matthew Arnold was surely one of the greatest and the best. Over the years, Macmillan had self-consciously distanced himself from what he had called in his first approach to Arnold 'the common English press', deliberately building up an impressive portfolio of 'serious' writers that would continue to remunerate the company conveniently well. In the creation of this distinct market identity the acquisition and nurturing of the Prophet of Culture had been, to say the least, strategically important. Through their purchase of Arnold, Macmillan & Company had brought themselves nothing less than the classical tradition, high seriousness and literary authority.

Notes

1. Quoted in William Buckler, *Matthew Arnold's Books: towards a publishing diary* (Geneva: Librairie Droz, 1958), p. 16. While Arnold's business dealings with

Macmillan might be said to have started in the 1860s, there has been a brief correspondence over the publication of Stanley's *Life of Thomas Arnold* which Macmillan had hoped, in 1857, to issue in a cheaper edition. (See *The Letters of Matthew Arnold*, edited by Cecil Lang. University Press of Virginia, 1996. I, pp. 365–6.)

2. *Complete Works of Matthew Arnold*, edited by R. H. Super, Volume 3, *Lectures and Essays in Criticism* (Ann Arbor, University of Michigan Press, 1962), p. 113.
3. *Letters* I, 277.
4. *Letters* I, 126.
5. *Letters* II, 398.
6. *Letters* II, 333.
7. *Letters* II, 387.
8. Buckler, p. 70.
9. *Letters* II, 380.
10. *Complete Works* III, 34.
11. *Complete Works* III, 106.
12. *Complete Works* III, 257.
13. *Complete Works* III, 285.
14. *Letters* III, 25–6.
15. Writing to his mother in May 1866 regarding the critical success of his lectures on *Celtic Literature*, Arnold remarked that it had produced 'an effect beyond what I had ventured to hope; this is a great pleasure to me' (*Letters* III, 44).
16. *Letters* III, 194.
17. *Letters* III, 346–7.
18. Alexander Macmillan to Matthew Arnold, 25 July 1867 (Add.MS. 55387, f. 386).
19. Buckler, p. 101.
20. Buckler, p. 96.
21. Buckler, p. 154.
22. Park Honan, *Matthew Arnold: a life* (London: Weidenfeld & Nicolson, 1981), p. 368.
23. *Letters* III, 118.
24. *Letters* III, 280.
25. *Letters* III, 308.
26. Add.MS. 54978, f. 67.
27. Buckler, p. 71.
28. Buckler, p. 72.
29. Add.MS. 54978, f. 71.
30. Add.MS. 55398, f. 222.
31. Buckler, p. 30.
32. Matthew Arnold to Alexander Macmillan, 4 June 1876 (Add.MS. 54978, ff. 83–4).
33. Buckler, p. 40.
34. Buckler, p. 121.
35. Buckler, p. 126.
36. Buckler, p. 126.
37. Buckler, p. 133.

38. Stephen Gill, *Wordsworth and the Victorians* (Oxford: Clarendon Press, 1998), p. 107.
39. Add.MS. 55405, f. 695.
40. Buckler, p. 133.
41. Add.MS. 55405, f. 563.
42. Buckler, p. 134.
43. *Poems of Wordsworth* (London: Macmillan, 1879), p. v.
44. *Poems of Byron* (London: Macmillan, 1881), p. vii.
45. *Poems of Byron*, p. xxix.
46. Buckler, p. 53.
47. *Literature and Dogma*, popular ed. (London: Smith, Elder, 1883), pp. v–vi.
48. Clinton Machann, *Matthew Arnold: a literary life* (London: Macmillan, 1998), pp. 59–60.
49. Add.MS. 54978, f. 177.
50. Honan, p. 385.

3
Thomas Hardy and the House of Macmillan

A comedy in chapters

Michael Millgate

Let me confess at once that my subtitle is essentially an attempt to cast a thin aura of novelty over familiar materials. Charles Morgan's centenary history, *The House of Macmillan,* published in 1943,[1] devoted no less than ten per cent of its space to Hardy's association with the firm – a proportion or, rather, disproportion doubtless explicable in part by Morgan's having staged, in 1919, an Oxford production of *The Dynasts* that stirred a reluctant university, once stigmatised as Christminster, into giving Hardy a belated honorary degree. But the Hardy–Macmillan story also figured largely, if disconnectedly, in the essentially autobiographical 'life' of Hardy that Macmillan published over the name of Florence Hardy in 1928 and 1930, and various aspects of the relationship have been treated in more recent writings on Hardy and on publishing history by Simon Gatrell, John Sutherland, Dale Kramer and others. As co-editor of the *Collected Letters of Thomas Hardy* I have myself put on public record all of Hardy's letters to Macmillan – supplemented of course by annotations and quotations derived from the Macmillan side of the correspondence – and encountered in the process the customary miseries and occasional splendours of documentary research.

Especially memorable was my brief experience of working at Birch Grove, the former Macmillan estate in Sussex, on what subsequently became the first great instalment of the archive now in the British

Library. Conditions in that dark and dusty space over an old stable were scarcely ideal, but it was exciting to be alone amid the room's infinite riches, and very pleasant to enjoy the refreshing hospitality of the house itself. I was escorted by the first Lord Stockton himself through the gallery of Frederick Sandys' crayon portraits of nineteenth-century Macmillan authors – among them John Morley, who figures in the present narrative as Macmillan's principal reader throughout much of the high Victorian period. 'Yes, that's John Morley', said Lord Stockton, as we paused before the portrait. 'He was a Liberal politician. He looks like a butler. All Liberal politicians look like butlers.'

But I would not have the 'comedy' in my subtitle understood as promising a laugh a minute. I claim the Hardy–Macmillan story as a comedy chiefly in the sense that it has a happy ending and only a minor villain. And I call it a comedy in chapters because its various missed opportunities and missed connections serve to break it quite naturally into a sequence of distinct units. The phrase 'A Comedy in Chapters' is of course taken from the subtitle to Hardy's novel *The Hand of Ethelberta*, which can at one level be read as a kind of allegory of the compromises and self-suppressions endured by the literary artist (Ethelberta in the novel, Hardy himself by implication) in the pursuit of personal affluence and possibilities of self-expression as a poet. Alas, *The Hand of Ethelberta* was originally published by Smith, Elder, not by Macmillan, but had Hardy and Macmillan got together earlier there would of course be less of a story to tell.

Despite its inconclusiveness, Hardy's first encounter with the house of Macmillan was sufficiently remarkable to demand treatment at some length. Though Hardy trained as an architect and worked as an assistant to leading architects both in Dorset and in London, he seems always to have cherished literary and, indeed, specifically poetic ambitions. By the late summer of 1867, when he was 27 years old and returning to Dorset after five years in London, he had decided that he wanted to live by writing but could hope to do so only by putting poetry aside and pursuing a career as a professional novelist. Over the next several months he wrote and then recopied a long first-person novel called 'The Poor Man and the Lady', and on 25 July 1868 he sent the manuscript to Macmillan – along with a letter of introduction from his much-admired friend Horace Moule, whose Hulsean Prize dissertation, *Christian Oratory: an inquiry into its history during the first five centuries*, had been published by Macmillan in Cambridge in 1859.

The Macmillan Record of Manuscripts attests to the arrival of Hardy's manuscript on 27 July and its transmission to Alexander Macmillan at his house in Tooting in two parts, comprising 440 pages in all, the first part on 6 August and the second on 8 August.[2] Before being sent to Tooting the manuscript had already gone to John Morley (of the Sandys portrait) and been received with a mixture of admiration ('A very curious and original performance') and distaste ('a certain rawness of absurdity that is very displeasing, and makes it read like some clever lad's dream'). Morley's final blended judgement was that 'If the man is young there is stuff and promise in him; but he must study form and composition, in such writers as Balzac and Thackeray.'

Morley's report is entered in the first volume of Macmillan Readers' Reports,[3] but a copy also went to Alexander Macmillan who in turn forwarded it to Hardy on 10 August 1868 together with a long, detailed, and deeply engaged letter of his own (the original is now in the Dorset County Museum).[4] Alexander had, of course, been running the firm alone since his brother Daniel's death in 1857, as well as bringing up Daniel's children as his own, and although he had recently taken George Lillie Craik into partnership it is still impressive to find him devoting so much time and attention to an unsolicited first novel. In his letter Macmillan praised Hardy's writing and addressed him in encouraging terms as an author 'at least potentially, of considerable mark, of power and purpose'. At the same time, he found difficulty in accepting the bleakness of the novel's portrayal of contemporary class-conflict and concluded by asking Hardy if he would be willing to consider modifications to this aspect of the book.

Beyond this point the survival of correspondence is incomplete, although the Macmillan files do preserve the letter to Alexander Macmillan of 10 September 1868 in which Hardy expressed anxiety at not having heard from him again and added the plaintive and, as Morgan says,[5] deeply moving postscript: 'Would you mind suggesting the sort of story you think I could do best, or any literary work I should do well to go on upon?'[6] Macmillan evidently responded to this appeal, asked Hardy to call on him in London in December of 1868, and while finally rejecting 'The Poor Man and the Lady' (as 'a class of book' the firm could not publish) he did give its author a letter of recommendation to another publisher, Chapman and Hall, who might take it on.[7]

They didn't, nor did anyone else, but Hardy's interview with Chapman and Hall's reader, who proved to be George Meredith, famously resulted in the composition of the sensation-novel he called *Desperate Remedies*. Macmillan, on Morley's recommendation, declined *Desperate Remedies* also, four weeks after Hardy submitted it early in March 1870.[8] On the other hand, Morley did write positively of *Under the*

Greenwood Tree when it arrived in August 1871,[9] but the manuscript was inconveniently short for publication in that heyday of the three-decker, and Malcolm Macmillan (Alexander's elder son) and then Alexander himself wrote temporising letters. Hardy, rightly or wrongly, read delay as rejection, and took the book – as he had already taken *Desperate Remedies* – to the less prestigious but more immediately welcoming house of Tinsley Brothers.

Tinsley's welcome to *Desperate Remedies*, however, had been conditional upon its author sharing in the production costs, and since Hardy had failed to recoup all of the £75 he had invested in that first book, he perhaps felt in no position to refuse the £30 Tinsley now offered him for the copyright of *Under the Greenwood Tree*. Morgan says that Hardy later bought back the copyright for £300,[10] but although that was indeed the price named by Tinsley in 1875 (after the success of *Far from the Madding Crowd*) Hardy declined to pay so much and never in fact recovered control of the copyright – which passed to Chatto & Windus following Tinsley's failure in 1878. *Under the Greenwood Tree* thus became, years later, the only work of Hardy's of which Macmillan did not control the British and colonial rights. The punishment, if it can be so called, was long-lasting, if not excessively severe, and it was deserved only in the minimal sense that Alexander Macmillan, though so sympathetically responsive to Hardy's work, did not and could not imagine how delays that were for him merely trivial and prudential might affect the urgently creative but unsettled, impecunious, and no longer quite so young man in the Dorset cottage.

And so ends the first chapter, which I'll perhaps call – borrowing Hardy's abandoned title for *Tess of the d'Urbervilles* – 'Too Late, Beloved'. The second chapter, which might be called 'Skirmishing', covers the somewhat desultory exchanges between Hardy and the Macmillans that occurred between the misunderstanding over *Under the Greenwood Tree* in 1871, and the agreement of March 1885 for serialisation of a Hardy novel in *Macmillan's Magazine*. Hardy during these years published mostly with Smith, Elder and Sampson Low, but it was Frederick Macmillan, in New York in the early 1870s, who first drew *Under the Greenwood Tree* to the attention not only of his own fiancée – as she recalled to Hardy some 50 years later[11] – but also of the New York publisher Henry Holt.[12] Holt brought the novel out in his Leisure Hour series in 1873 and remained Hardy's principal American publisher for the next 13 years.

There were also more direct exchanges. For three years between 1878 and 1881 Hardy and his first wife, Emma, rented a house in Trinity Road,

Upper Tooting, not far from Knapdale, where Alexander Macmillan and his double family had long been established. Richard Davenport-Hines considers it snobbishly inaccurate of Hardy to have claimed to be Alexander's neighbour,[13] but Knapdale was within easy walking distance of the Trinity Road house and Hardy, as a country boy, probably thought that neighbourly enough. The Hardys seem to have visited the Macmillans with some frequency and when Hardy fell seriously ill in October 1880 it was the Macmillans who summoned their doctor to his assistance and Margaret Macmillan, Alexander's daughter by his first wife, who visited his sickbed during the ensuing months.[14]

As publishers, however, the Macmillans continued to keep their distance. They promptly returned the specimen chapter or so of *The Trumpet-Major* Hardy sent them in early June of 1879, and can scarcely have been charmed by his later novel, *Two on a Tower*, in which the abandoned heroine marries an unsuspecting bishop in order to obtain a father for her unborn child – prompting the editor of the magazine that was running the serial to complain that he had been promised a family story but given one in the family way. And Hardy, for his part, may have had some doubts about the financial terms Macmillan would be willing to offer. Henry James, early established as a Macmillan author, took his novel *Confidence* to Chatto & Windus in 1879 out of dissatisfaction with Macmillan's 'half-profits' contracts, explaining to his brother that 'The Macmillans are everything that's friendly – caressing – old Macmillan physically *hugs* me; but the delicious ring of the sovereign is conspicuous in our intercourse by its absence.'[15] By 1885, however, the Macmillans were prepared to offer contracts involving at least some element of royalty, and while they may have found Hardy less huggable than James, it seems somehow suggestive of mutual good feeling and trust that when Hardy called in person on Alexander Macmillan and George Lillie Craik to arrange for serialisation of *The Woodlanders* neither Macmillan nor Craik made an accurate note of what was decided – so that Hardy had to be asked what he had written down in *his* diary.[16]

This of course takes us into chapter 3, or 'Two Steps Forward, One Step Back', and Hardy's first direct experience of publishing with the house of Macmillan.[17] *The Woodlanders* ran in *Macmillan's Magazine* from May 1886 to April 1887, the final instalments being anticipated, in the customary manner, by Macmillan's publication of the three-volume first edition in March 1887. A cheaper one-volume edition appeared six months later. Mowbray Morris, however, the actual editor of *Macmillan's Magazine,* may never have been consulted about the serialisation of *The Woodlanders*, and he was soon complaining to Hardy about improprieties in its language and plot, and insisting that the sexual relationship between Fitzpiers and Suke Damson be handled with greater discretion: 'Let the human frailty be construed mild.' Morris's attribution of blame for such interference to the 'pious Scottish souls' who read the magazine and took offence 'wondrous easily'[18] has been interpreted as a veiled allusion to the puritanical views of Alexander Macmillan himself, but Morris's later dealings with Hardy seem indicative of a more personal agenda. In November 1889 Morris rejected *Tess of the d'Urbervilles* as a serial for the *Magazine* on the grounds of its excessive sexual 'succulence',[19] not only obliging Hardy to seek elsewhere for a publisher, but prompting him to excise for separate publication the two episodes – 'Saturday Night in Arcady' and 'The Midnight Baptism' – that seemed likeliest to give offence to the squeamish. Later on, Morris wrote an anonymous review of the published novel, savagely attacking both its sensuality and the 'hole-in-the-corner' publication of the omitted episodes. It was this review, whose authorship Hardy may never have discovered, that prompted him to declare: 'Well, if this sort of thing continues no more novel-writing for me. A man must be a fool to deliberately stand up to be shot at.'[20]

Macmillan in 1888 brought out Hardy's first short-story collection, *Wessex Tales*,[21] but, thanks to Mowbray Morris, *The Woodlanders* remained the only Hardy novel to make its first appearance over the firm's imprint. *Tess* went to the London-based but American-owned house of Osgood, McIlvaine, and chapter 4 of my narrative, 'One Step Back, Two Steps Forward', finds its unpromising beginning in Hardy's agreement with Osgood, McIlvaine for the publication of a first collected edition of his works and in Macmillan's reluctance to release *The Woodlanders* and *Wessex Tales* for such a purpose. There was an elaborately polite – which is to say mildly acrimonious – exchange of letters in June 1893, Hardy maintaining that the rights he had granted were 'revocable at will',[22] Macmillan responding that so long as they paid the royalties due they had every right to continue to sell the two titles during the term of copyright – and that, in any case, they were still £200 short of recovering their initial publication costs.[23] Hardy went so far as to question the validity of Macmillan's figures in a letter to Maurice Colles, a literary agent operating under the aegis of the Society of Authors,[24] and the impasse was only broken, so he told Colles on 13 July, by his 'accidentally' meeting some members of the Macmillan firm and reaching a gentlemanly compromise by which they released the books but he did not insist upon their technical obligation to do so.[25]

Warmer relations evidently ensued, and in the spring of the following year, 1894, Hardy agreed to the comprehensive inclusion of his works in Macmillan's Colonial Library, intended, so the standard formula went, 'for circulation only in India and the British Colonies'.[26] *The Mayor of Casterbridge, The Woodlanders,* and *Wessex Tales* had already appeared in the Colonial format in exchange for single cash payments to the author of £25 for the *Mayor* and £50 each for *The Woodlanders* and *Wessex Tales,*[27] but these were nonetheless included in the memorandum of agreement between Hardy and Macmillan dated 21 May 1894[28] which covered all of Hardy's Colonial Library titles and specified payment of the fourpence a copy royalty then apparently standard for colonial editions.[29]

In producing their Colonial volumes Macmillan drew variously upon plates of the titles they already had in the series, on line-for-line resettings of existing Osgood, McIlvaine titles (for example, the one-volume edition of *Tess of the d'Urbervilles*), and on either plates or resettings of the volumes Osgood, McIlvaine had prepared (often well ahead of publication) specifically for inclusion in their 'Wessex Novels' collected edition. Whenever resetting was involved Macmillan insisted upon R. & R. Clark's compositors following the layout of the Osgood, McIlvaine volumes in every possible detail, and after Hardy himself had pointed out inconsistencies in the page numbers and running heads for the Colonial *Far from the Madding Crowd* a stern rebuke was sent north to Edinburgh on 19 September 1894: 'We thought it had been made clear that the page in every way was to be the same as "Tess": on July 23 we said "style and type of Tess" and on August 1, when you suggested something else we said "follow the style of McIlvaines edition of Tess exactly". Please see that we are not charged for the correction.'[30]

Because the Colonial editions, by intention and in fact, were often only minimally distinguishable from the corresponding Osgood, McIlvaine volumes, they possess among textual editors a somewhat nightmarish reputation that is further intensified by the difficulty of locating copies. The first Macmillan Colonial printings of Hardy titles in the 1890s ran mostly to 3,000 copies, rising to 10,000 copies in the case of the newly published *Jude the Obscure*[31] – figures well ahead of the 500 or 1,000 copies said by Simon Nowell-Smith to have been customary in such circumstances.[32] But they were essentially cheap editions, issued in wrappers as well as in cloth, and they were widely distributed throughout the world, often to places where the heat and humidity were by no means stabilised at the levels now deemed appropriate to rare book libraries. Macmillan and Co. did not keep copies, and by the time anyone thought to collect them the vast majority had disappeared. The British Library, however, is now gathering in whatever volumes it can, and a few years ago the Beinecke Library at Yale purchased from the Australian dealer, James Dally, a significant collection of more than 400 Macmillan Colonial volumes – though it proved to include only half-a-dozen or so Hardy titles.

It is understandable that some editors should seek to work around the problem by arguing that colonial editions were not in the direct line of textual transmission. But such a policy may not be risk-free. Hardy was sent proofs of the Colonial volumes,[33] and while he undertook to insert in those proofs the same corrections as he would be making for the Osgood, McIlvaine edition,[34] it seems highly unlikely that he could have completed such a process without errors, omissions, or changes of mind. It also appears that Macmillan made duplicate plates for the Hardy titles issued in the Colonial format and may occasionally have used such plates for some impressions of the collected Hardy they first issued on the domestic market in 1902–03.[35]

But I am anticipating the crucial act in my narrative, the marriage that confirms its generic status as a comedy. I'll call the chapter 'Home at Last'. With the death of James Ripley Osgood in 1892 the house of Osgood, McIlvaine lost its principal driving force, and before the end of the century it had ceased to be the London agent for Harper and Brothers of New York and become absorbed completely into Harper's as its London branch. Hardy found it irksome, and indeed inappropriate, that his English editions should be brought out by an American publisher – especially after Harper's itself had gone temporarily into receivership in 1899 – and when in early 1902 the date approached for renewal of the agreement he had originally made with Osgood he decided instead to approach Frederick Macmillan with the suggestion that the house of Macmillan might become the British publisher of all his books – including by this time the first two volumes of verse.[36] Harper's, informed that they would in future be his American publishers only, claimed that they would be unfairly damaged by such a defection, and Hardy, agonising over the propriety of his planned move, sought and received reassurance on the point from the Society of Authors and its solicitor, and from Anthony Hope (*Prisoner of Zenda*) Hawkins, one of the Society's most active members.[37]

When Hardy formally made his proposal to Frederick Macmillan on 18 March 1902,[38] it was of course greeted with as prompt and warm a welcome as the generation of Macmillans then running the firm was capable of extending – a hugging at least figurative and financial. Rache

Lovat Dickson, who knew and admired Frederick, Maurice, and George in their last years, used in conversation to speak of them as Forsytes to a man. His autobiographical volume, *The House of Words*, however, describes them indeed as 'fine bluff Christian gentlemen dispensing good and making a satisfactory profit out of it', but adds that they were 'larger than Galsworthy's Soames Forsyte' because altogether stronger, in their private as well as their public lives, and absolutely confident in the rightness of all their actions and decisions.[39]

The final Hardy–Macmillan union was consecrated, or at any rate inscribed, in a memorandum of agreement signed on 2 April 1902.[40] Technically, the agreement was renewable every seven years, but Hardy made it clear from the first that he intended it to be permanent – to borrow the Thomas Campbell quotation he used as his chapter title for the wedding in *Under the Greenwood Tree*, 'A knot there's no untying.' Nor did he have much motivation to unravel an assignment of royalties of 25 per cent on books retailing at six shillings, 20 per cent on those retailing at between four and five shillings, and just under 17 per cent (the agreement says one-sixth) on those sold at less than four shillings. The fourpenny royalty remained payable on each Colonial Library volume sold.

Percentages such as these make it easy to understand Hardy's having attained by his death in 1928 a degree of affluence unimaginable at the time of his birth in the Dorset cottage, the more so when they are collated with the totals of Hardy volumes ordered from the printers – figures available in the Macmillan Editions Books in the archive[41] and supplemented, sometimes corrected, by the records of the copies actually received that are still in the possession of the firm. Hardy was never in his lifetime a hugely-selling author, but Macmillan after 1902 brought out his works in many different formats, and while some of these – such as the Wessex Edition and the signed Mellstock Edition – were directed at limited markets, others were issued and repeatedly reissued within and beyond Hardy's lifetime – notably the initial Uniform Edition of 1902–03 and, from 1906 onwards, the highly popular Pocket Edition, available in both cloth and leather.

A Pair of Blue Eyes, for example, standing somewhere in the middle rank of Hardy's novels in terms of its popularity, was a steady but unspectacular Pocket Edition seller during the Edition's early years, with seven separate printings of 2,000 copies each between 1906 and 1919, but despite a post-war rise in Pocket Edition prices (to four shillings, later four and sixpence, in cloth, six shillings in leather) there were five printings of *A Pair of Blue Eyes* amounting to 33,000 copies in all between

1920 and 1926 and a further printing of 10,000 copies in the year of Hardy's death.[42] It's perhaps worth noting that during the 1920s Macmillan's Globe Publishing subsidiary advertised all 26 volumes of the 'Famous Pocket Leather Edition' of Hardy's complete works as available on instalment terms: '7/6 as first payment brings the set to YOUR HOME IMMEDIATELY.' Hardy's royalty of 10½d. on copies sold by this route was slightly less than the shilling he received on copies in leather sold through the booksellers; for copies in cloth, sold only through booksellers, the royalty was 9d.[43]

The Hardy–Macmillan marriage did have its stressful moments. Hardy by the turn of the century had abandoned fiction in favour of poetry,[44] and poetry did not always sell especially well. Very early on the three separate volumes of *The Dynasts* became a burden that Frederick Macmillan had to bear, while George Brett, at Macmillan's New York branch, despaired altogether of selling the second part in the American market after the dismal showing of the first: 'The first volume has had almost no sale at all here and I should think the second volume might sell even worse than this.'[45] Even this little problem, however, was eased by Hardy's ever-increasing fame during his final years, and the three-volume limited signed edition of *The Dynasts* issued by Macmillan in 525 copies in November 1927, just a few weeks before Hardy's death, was sold out on publication.[46] No hint of complaint had in any case been allowed to intrude into the firm's correspondence with Hardy, variously conducted by Frederick Macmillan (Sir Frederick as he became in 1909), his brother Maurice, his cousin George, and, later on, his nephews, Maurice's sons, Daniel and Harold. It was on Frederick that Hardy chiefly depended for wise advice in publishing and related matters – valuing his judgement more highly, it would appear, than that of anyone else – but he knew all the Macmillans and dealt with them, and especially with those of the older generation, on terms of mutual friendship and respect.

Perhaps, indeed, I can find an appropriate coda for the comedy in an actual wedding, that of Harold Macmillan to Lady Dorothy Cavendish, daughter of the Duke and Duchess of Devonshire, at St Margaret's, Westminster, in April 1920, the occasion of Hardy's making his very last visit to London in order to join other Macmillan authors in lending literary fame and intellectual weight to the groom's side of a church that was on the bride's side thickly, not to say densely, populated by the uppermost echelons of the hereditary aristocracy. Also among the Macmillan contingent were James Bryce, the distinguished historian, jurist, and statesman, and John Morley – a Viscount himself by now but in his early eighties doubtless looking, and in such company perhaps even feeling, like a butler fast approaching superannuation. Morley glanced around at Bryce and Hardy, fellow members with himself of the Order of Merit, and then at the Duke of Devonshire and whispered in Florence Hardy's ear, 'Which weigh most, three O.M.'s or one Duke?'[47]

The anecdote has become well known through its inclusion in Hardy's self-ghosted official biography, and his having so recorded it encourages me to believe that even he, so often and so unjustly deemed the most melancholy of writers, might have accepted the term 'comedy' as a way of characterising his extended, generally happy, and in the long run mutually profitable relationship with the house of Macmillan and its sympathetic inhabitants.

Notes

1. Charles Morgan, *The House of Macmillan (1843–1943)* (London: Macmillan, 1943), pp. 87–100, 152–62, etc.
2. Add.MS. 56016, f. 7.
3. Add.MS. 55931, pp. 62–3.
4. It is published, with minor inaccuracies, in Morgan, pp. 88–91, and *Letters of Alexander Macmillan*, edited by George A. Macmillan (Glasgow: privately printed, 1908), pp. 245–8.
5. Morgan, p. 92.
6. *The Collected Letters of Thomas Hardy*, edited by Richard L. Purdy and Michael Millgate, 7 vols (Oxford: Clarendon Press, 1978–88), I, 8.
7. Thomas Hardy, *The Life and Work of Thomas Hardy*, edited by Michael Millgate (London: Macmillan, 1984), p. 60.
8. Macmillan & Co. (initialled F.M.) to Hardy, 4 April 1870 (Dorset County Museum). See also Add.MS. 56016, f. 15, and Add.MS. 55931, pp. 134–5.
9. Add.MS. 56016, f. 21; Add.MS. 55931, pp. 175–6.
10. Morgan, p. 99.
11. Lady Macmillan (née Georgiana Warrin) to Hardy, 18 April 1924 (DCM).
12. Holt to Hardy, 29 May 1873 (DCM).
13. Richard Davenport-Hines, *The Macmillans* (London: Heinemann, 1992), p. 87.
14. *The Life and Work of Thomas Hardy*, pp. 149, 152.
15. *The Correspondence of William James. Volume I: William and Henry 1861–1884*, edited by Ignas K. Skrupskelis and Elizabeth M. Berkeley (Charlottesville: University Press of Virginia, 1992), p. 315.
16. Frederick Macmillan to Hardy, 17 March 1885 (DCM); *Collected Letters*, I, 131–2.
17. He had, however, published a short story, 'Interlopers at the Knap', in the Macmillan-owned *English Illustrated Magazine* for May 1884.
18. Morris to Hardy, 19 September 1886 (DCM); see Michael Millgate *Thomas Hardy: a biography* (Oxford: Oxford University Press, 1982), pp. 273–4.
19. Quoted in Millgate, *Thomas Hardy: a biography*, pp. 300–1.

20. *Life and Work of Thomas Hardy*, p. 259; Morris's review, 'Culture and Anarchy', appeared in the *Quarterly Review* for April 1892.
21. Some references to the printing of this title may be found in the Macmillan and Co. letters to the printers R. & R. Clark copied in Add.MS. 55329.
22. *Collected Letters*, II, 12.
23. See Frederick Macmillan letter of 1 June 1893, and Macmillan and Co. letters of 9 and 14 June 1893 as copied in Add.MS. 55440.
24. *Collected Letters*, II, 13; although Hardy dated this letter 10 June 1893 its accompanying documents and the stamped date of receipt clearly indicate that it must have been written on 18 June.
25. *Collected Letters*, II, 22. See also Frederick Macmillan to Hardy, 16 April 1894. (Add.MS. 55843, ff. 472–3.)
26. Some titles, notably *Desperate Remedies*, *A Group of Noble Dames*, and *Tess of the d'Urbervilles*, seem to have continued to appear in the 'colonial' lists of George Bell & Sons and E. A. Petherick.
27. Hardy's receipts for these amounts are in Add.MS. 54923, ff. 19, 27, 31, and dated respectively 8 June 1886, 9 May 1887, and 5 May 1888.
28. Add.MS. 54923, f. 40; though Hardy's signature is also dated 21 May 1894, it would appear from Frederick Macmillan's letters to him of 24 and 25 May (Add.MS. 55444) that he must actually have signed it on the 24th or 25th.
29. Simon Nowell-Smith, *International Copyright Law and the Publisher in the Reign of Queen Victoria* (Oxford: Clarendon Press, 1968), pp. 100, 102.
30. Add.MS. 55332, f. 406; copies of other relevant letters to R. & R. Clark are also to be found in this MS. and in Add.MS. 55333. Hardy's letter to Frederick Macmillan is in *Collected Letters*, II, 63.
31. Add.MS. 55910: for example, double-page 69 (for *A Pair of Blue Eyes* and *Two on a Tower*) and double-page 136 (for *Jude*).
32. Nowell-Smith, p. 100.
33. Macmillan to R. & R. Clark, 3 August 1894 (Add.MS. 55332, f. 325).
34. *Collected Letters* , II, 63.
35. When Hardy spoke of purchasing duplicate sets of plates from Harper's (*Collected Letters*, III, 27, 28) Frederick Macmillan replied (15 July 1902, Add.MS. 55470, f. 471) that such duplicates were unnecessary 'as those we had in the Colonial Library are in very good condition and will last for a long time'.
36. *Under the Greenwood Tree* was published by Macmillan, as by Osgood, McIlvaine, under licence from Chatto and Windus.
37. G. Herbert Thring to Hardy, 5 March 1902, and Hawkins to Hardy, 7 March 1902 (both DCM).
38. *Collected Letters*, III, 11–12.
39. Lovat Dickson, *The House of Words* (London: Macmillan, 1963), pp. 204–5.
40. Add.MS. 54923, f. 60. A more elaborate codified agreement, specifying royalty rates for individual works and series, was signed in September 1923.
41. Add.MS. 55914, ff. 92–4, 110 and Add.MS. 55914–55927. Editions Books figures for numerous Hardy titles and editions are helpfully supplied in Simon Gatrell, *Hardy the Creator: a textual biography* (Oxford: Clarendon Press, 1988), pp. 246–53.
42. Figures kindly supplied by John Handford from the Macmillan archives at Basingstoke. The Pocket Edition of *Far from the Madding Crowd* was printed

in a total of 70,000 copies during the 1920s, with a further 30,000 copies delivered in January 1930.

43. Typescript 'Notes on correspondence with Macmillans', prepared by Irene Cooper Willis and sent to Sir Sydney Cockerell 6 October 1938 (copy, Purdy Papers, Beinecke Library).
44. The only prose volume originated by Macmillan after 1902 was the miscellaneous gathering of stories called *A Changed Man*, first published in 1913; *The Short Stories of Thomas Hardy*, published shortly after Hardy's death, was composed entirely of stories that had been previously collected.
45. G. Brett to F. Macmillan, 24 October 1905, quoted in Peter Selley, Catalogue 4 [1993], item 421.
46. *Collected Letters*, VII, 86 and n.
47. *Life and Work of Thomas Hardy*, p. 434.

4
Margaret Oliphant and *Macmillan's Magazine*

George Worth

A note on *Macmillan's Magazine*

There was a certain inevitability about the appearance of the first number of *Macmillan's Magazine* at the end of October 1859.

In the middle of the nineteenth century the British market for periodicals was being served not only by such august publications as the *Edinburgh Review*, the *Quarterly Review*, and *Blackwood's Edinburgh Magazine*, designed for an educated audience with plenty of leisure to peruse long and weighty articles, but also by a number of more recent arrivals that were much cheaper and made far fewer demands on their readers. But by the 1850s there had come into being a growing class of middlebrow readers whose needs were not being met by either the elite quarterlies and reviews or the popular weekly magazines. Sensing the emergence of a market for a new kind of periodical, publishers began to cater to it.

They were not always successful. *Bentley's Quarterly Review*, launched in April 1859 by Richard Bentley, lasted only four numbers, among other reasons because it cost too much. As the historian of Bentley's firm has written, '1859 was the time not for a six-shilling review but a one-shilling magazine: that much is clear from the brilliant successes of the *Cornhill Magazine* [whose first number came out at the end of the year] and *Macmillan's Magazine*.'[1] George Smith, publisher of the *Cornhill*, recalled that he 'conceived the idea of founding a new magazine' early in 1859, believing that 'a shilling magazine' containing, 'in addition to other first-class literary matter', a serial by an established novelist 'must command a large sale'.[2] That Bentley was wrong and Smith right – that the age was ready and waiting for periodicals like *Macmillan's* and the *Cornhill* – was proved by what Walter Houghton called an 'outburst of shilling magazines' following shortly behind them over the next few years.[3]

Alexander Macmillan, the sole head of the House of Macmillan after the death of his brother and partner Daniel in 1857, had actually 'conceived the idea of founding a new magazine' several years before Smith, as early as 1855. For various reasons he did not refine his concept of such a publication or take steps to act on it until after the firm, originally based in Cambridge, opened its London office in 1858. Prodded by two of his fellow-Christian Socialists, John Malcolm Ludlow and Thomas Hughes, and with the blessing of the 'Prophet' of that movement, Frederick Denison Maurice, Macmillan began approaching potential contributors in the summer of 1859 and appointed the 37-year-old David Masson, a respected Scottish man of letters, then serving as Professor of English Literature at University College London, as the first editor of what would soon become *Macmillan's Magazine*.

From its inception, *Macmillan's* was marked by deep moral earnestness. Many of its early contributors took principled stands of a distinctly liberal character on such public issues of the day as electoral, educational, and church reform, women's rights, the abolition of slavery in the United States, and the growing role of science in modern society. (The second issue carried T. H. Huxley's important review of *On the Origin of Species*, which had appeared shortly before.) Alexander Macmillan and his colleagues gave much latitude to those who wrote for the *Magazine*, and the results of this freedom of expression were not always happy: for instance, Maurice and especially Ludlow were incensed by the publication of Carlyle's pro-slavery 'Ilias (Americana) in Nuce' in the August 1863 number, and Macmillan's subsequent defence of that 'grand old man' did nothing to appease them.[4]

Alexander Macmillan had always conceived of a magazine with a belletristic as well as a polemical dimension, and that, too, was present from the outset. Thomas Hughes's *Tom Brown at Oxford*, a sequel to the hugely popular *Tom Brown's School Days* (published by Macmillan & Co. in 1857), which began its 21-month run in the initial number of the *Magazine*, was the first of dozens of novels to be serialised in its pages. Later ones included Charles Kingsley's *The Water-Babies*, Henry James's *The Portrait of a Lady*, Thomas Hardy's *The Woodlanders*, and a very young Winston Churchill's *Savrola*, as well as titles by such other writers of fiction as R. D. Blackmore, Frances Hodgson Burnett, F. Marion Crawford, Bret Harte, Henry Kingsley, Dinah Maria Mulock, Caroline Norton, Margaret Oliphant, Anne Ritchie, Anthony Trollope and Charlotte M. Yonge. Literary criticism – much of it by major figures like Arnold, Pater, and Saintsbury – and poetry – including work by Arnold, Eliot, Kipling, Meredith, Christina Rossetti, and Tennyson – were also to be found in *Macmillan's*, as were book reviews and essays on many, varied themes.

During the nearly five decades of its existence, four men successively bore the title of editor of *Macmillan's Magazine*: David Masson from November 1859 until December 1867, George Grove (January 1868–April 1883), John Morley (May 1883–October 1885), and Mowbray Morris (November 1885–October 1907). Each in his own way was accomplished and conscientious, but all of them worked under certain handicaps. They were, first of all, distracted by other tasks: Masson by his own writing and his academic responsibilities; Grove by his musicological and a wide range of other interests; Morley by his political career; and Morris – certainly the least remarkable member of this quartet, who also suffered from increasingly frail health – by his extensive duties as a reader for Macmillan & Co. Then there was the somewhat mixed blessing of Alexander Macmillan's active involvement, until his retreat into retirement beginning in the early 1880s: though he was personally fond of his editors and allowed them plenty of leeway, he made it quite clear that it was he who was really in charge of the *Magazine*, and did not hesitate to let them go when he thought that they were no longer able to function as he wished – Masson after he moved to Edinburgh to become a professor at the university there, and Grove when he was appointed director of the newly-founded Royal College of Music.[5]

Macmillan's gradual withdrawal was only one of several reasons why the fortunes of the monthly that bore his name, and that he had done more than anyone else to shape, declined after its first two decades of life. Though never strictly speaking a Christian-Socialist organ, *Macmillan's* lost much of its ideological thrust following the defection of Ludlow in the mid-1860s and the death of Maurice in 1872; Hughes, an early mainstay, fell away when Grove left the editor's chair. The market for periodicals changed further during the last third of the century, and Macmillan & Co. itself both recognised and contributed to that change with the establishment of *Nature* in 1869 and the *English Illustrated Magazine* in 1883. Not only did these new ventures syphon off some of the best writers who had contributed to *Macmillan's*, but they also reflected a growing demand for more specialised and more physically attractive magazines than their stodgily produced and increasingly unfocused predecessor.

Operating under the benign neglect of Alexander Macmillan's son George, nephews Frederick and Maurice, and long-time partner George Lillie Craik, Mowbray Morris did his best to keep the magazine alive into the new century, sprucing up its layout and halving its price from a shilling to sixpence, but to no avail. There was a marked falling-off in the quality of its contents, perhaps partly because contributors were now normally being paid only 15 shillings per page of copy rather than the £1 that had been standard from the beginning – and the new literary agencies, which had gained considerable power during Morris's editorship, were pocketing some of that.

Conceived with considerable passion in the late 1850s, *Macmillan's Magazine* died a quiet, unmourned death a half-century later. Almost nothing about its passing appears in the relevant letterbooks, though there are a few indications in correspondence from the early 1900s that Morris was not receiving enough contributions, especially fiction, that met his high standards.[6] By the summer of 1907 it was becoming clear that the current volume of *Macmillan's* would be its last: this is certainly the inference one must draw from a letter of 3 July in which Morris tells George Macmillan that 'one Mrs. Jamieson' has submitted a novel to the magazine but that 'were it the best novel ever written it would of course be useless to me'.[7] Writing to Maurice Macmillan on 15 September of that year, Morris announced tersely: 'Actum est – I have sent our last number to Clay', the printer.[8] Macmillan's reply, dated two days later, was equally matter-of-fact, but as kind as the Macmillans had unfailingly been to Morris: 'I got your letter about the Magazine. The way in which you have managed to come to an end, leaving practically nothing outstanding, moves my admiration.'[9]

Admiration is also what one must feel nearly a century later as one surveys the 48-year history, with all its ups and downs, of *Macmillan's Magazine*.

Though Margaret Oliphant's association with William Blackwood & Sons and their *Blackwood's Edinburgh Magazine* was exceptionally long, close, and productive, she also worked with a number of other publishers during a career that spanned five decades, from the 1840s to the 1890s. Chief among those firms was Macmillan & Co., which brought out 31 of Oliphant's books in England and issued a number of others in its Colonial Library, for sale in the empire but not at home. Her contributions to *Macmillan's Magazine* were not so astonishingly numerous as her appearances in *Blackwood's* but included some of her most characteristic writing: six serialised novels; some shorter fiction, including two of her famous (or notorious) 'Little Pilgrim' stories; six pieces published under the title *The Convent of San Marco* that ultimately went into one of her most successful Macmillan books, *The Makers of Florence*; and review articles and obituary essays appraising the work or life, or both, of three of her friends: the Scottish clergyman Robert Herbert Story, Thomas Carlyle, and Dinah Mulock Craik.

Interesting in its own right as much of this work in *Macmillan's Magazine* is, some acquaintance with the conditions under which it was conceived, produced, and paid for can teach us a good deal not only about Victorian publishing, of books as well as of periodicals, but also about the habits, character, and personality of one of the most remarkable figures on the Victorian literary scene. Because many of the relevant documents, chiefly letters, have survived in the British Library's Macmillan archive, it is possible, though not always easy a century after Oliphant's death, to trace the vicissitudes of her extensive and often stormy connection with Macmillan & Co. in general and *Macmillan's Magazine* in particular.

This task does entail some difficulties. Though much of Oliphant's copious correspondence with Macmillan & Co. has nothing to do with *Macmillan's Magazine* – and therefore no legitimate claim on space in this chapter – her work for the *Magazine* must be considered in the context of her complicated relations with the firm and those who guided its fortunes, and so we must from time to time go beyond those letters concerned specifically with her periodical contributions. But some crucial letters from Oliphant are missing, and the chronology of those that have been preserved is not always clear. She was rather cavalier about dating letters, often supplying only days of the week. On many, dates are entered, usually in pencil, in handwriting that is obviously not hers: frequently these are conjectural, and sometimes they are plainly wrong. Even worse, some of the outgoing letters preserved in the firm's letterbooks, particularly those from George Lillie Craik, have become so faded or smeared over the past hundred years and more as to be virtually or totally illegible. What we have to work with, therefore, is a record that is considerably short of perfect. Nevertheless, it is most revealing.

The first of Oliphant's Macmillan novels, *Agnes Hopetoun's Schools and Holidays*, was brought out for the Christmas trade in December 1858,[10] less than a year before the debut of *Macmillan's Magazine* the following November, and she had been personally acquainted with Alexander

Macmillan earlier than that. Nevertheless, as far as we know, Oliphant was not among those of his writer-friends from whom Macmillan solicited contributions to his fledgling periodical.

It was not until the spring of 1862 that *Macmillan's Magazine* was mentioned in their correspondence. When Macmillan, who had been much impressed by Oliphant's recently published *The Life of Edward Irving*, finally got around to asking her to write for his *Magazine*, she demurred, pleading her time-consuming commitments to *Blackwood's* and her objection to what she called Macmillan's '*nominal* principle' – that is, the idea that contributors to *Macmillan's Magazine* should ordinarily be identified rather than anonymous. But Oliphant wanted something else from Macmillan. She began the letter – one of 15 from Oliphant to Alexander Macmillan in the Berg Collection of the New York Public Library – in which she declined his invitation, with a request of her own. Could he oblige Henry Blackett, the publisher of *The Life of Edward Irving*, by finding a knowledgeable and sympathetic reviewer for her new book? And could she venture to recommend her friend Robert Herbert Story as that reviewer? Always eager to accommodate Oliphant, Macmillan recruited Story for this assignment, and Story's warmly favourable notice of *Edward Irving* duly appeared in *Macmillan's Magazine* in May 1862.

Oliphant had formed a kind of mutual admiration-and-aid society with Story, some of whose work she had persuaded both Alexander Macmillan and Henry Blackett to bring out.[11] A few weeks after Story's review of her book was published in *Macmillan's Magazine*, she volunteered to reciprocate by reviewing Story's new *Memoir* of his father in the same monthly. Alexander Macmillan declined her offer because, he explained, the book had already been assigned to J. Llewelyn Davies.[12] But for some reason Davies never wrote the review, and so Oliphant made her first appearance in *Macmillan's Magazine* in July 1863 with an article, 'Clerical Life in Scotland', which reviewed both Story's life of his father and a similar biography, A. M. Charteris's *Life of the Rev. James Robertson*. At her insistence, the *Magazine's* '*nominal* principle' was breached in the case of this piece: 'No *name* please – not even initials', she asked Macmillan. 'This I particularly desire in respect of this article and trust you will be good enough to secure that it shall be *quite anonymous*.'[13]

Once the ice was broken in July 1863 with this review essay, Oliphant became a frequent contributor to *Macmillan's Magazine* during the next 27 years, and went on turning out Macmillan books virtually until her death in 1897; a final volume of her fiction was published posthumously in 1898. And characteristically, it was Oliphant who took the initiative in maintaining the flow that had begun with 'Clerical Life in Scotland'.

In a typically forthright letter written on 27 August 1863, less than two months after the publication of this essay, Oliphant informed Alexander Macmillan that she was thinking of going 'to Rome for the winter with my children', and, she continued,

> I mean you to pay my expenses if you are so disposed – that is to say, I am willing if you wish it, to undertake for you *anonymously* a sketch of the story you once proposed to me ... something that would run through three or four numbers of your Magazine – for which you could give me a hundred pounds.[14]

Macmillan immediately agreed to Oliphant's proposition, and she in turn set to work, undeterred by the fact that she had another serial novel (*The Perpetual Curate*) coming out in another periodical (*Blackwood's*), but making it clear that she expected prompt payment. Writing to Macmillan a week before her departure, Oliphant told him, 'I want you to send me, please, *now,* the £100 which I told you I wanted for my journey and which is to stand against four numbers of the *Son of the Soil.*'[15]

The opening instalment of that novel, consisting of three chapters, appeared in the November 1863 number of the *Magazine,* as Macmillan had hoped. But matters did not proceed altogether smoothly after that promising start – something that was to be characteristic of most of Oliphant's serial contributions to *Macmillan's.* Instead of the projected 'three or four numbers' on which Macmillan and his editor, David Masson, had been planning, *A Son of the Soil* went on for 18 months – skipping April 1864, when Oliphant was incapacitated by a family tragedy, the unexpected death of her ten-year-old daughter Maggie. Macmillan and Masson were remarkably complaisant about the metamorphosis of this 'short sketch' into a full-blown novel, but other vexing issues kept coming up as the serial continued its run.

In accordance with Oliphant's wish, *A Son of the Soil* was published anonymously in *Macmillan's,* but when a reviewer of the fifteenth instalment rather casually identified Oliphant as the author she held Macmillan responsible.[16] He protested his innocence,[17] and subsequently denied that he was unwilling to bring out *A Son of the Soil* as a Macmillan book as Oliphant had alleged: he admitted that he had entered into negotiations with Henry Blackett about having the novel appear under the Hurst and Blackett imprint but maintained that he thought he was carrying out Oliphant's wish in so doing.[18] In the end,

Macmillan & Co. did publish the book version, anonymously. Not for the last time in her long association with the company, Oliphant had written her novel without any clear understanding, on her part or her publisher's, about the ultimate disposition of the serial version, or the exact amount she would be paid for her work – somewhere between £700 and £750 to judge by the still-available evidence.[19]

When it became necessary to think about converting the serial into a book, Alexander Macmillan ventured to propose some changes he thought Oliphant should make in her text. Could she, he asked, engage in some 'judicious compression', emphasising 'the permanent and eternal' features of her subject rather than the 'local'? And could she 'eliminate the *polemic* which is an artistic mistake, and dreadfully weakens the general interest'? 'Of course,' he added diffidently,

> you will only follow any hint I throw out so far, and no further than it becomes your *own way*. After the manner of my sex I am fond of seeing things done in my own way, but I am not masterful when its of no use. I tyrranize [sic] over my own household, of course, but this does not warrant me in attempting it elsewhere, particularly when I know I could not carry it out![20]

Oliphant stuck to her guns and did not hesitate to deploy some of her artillery in unamused service of the gender warfare to which Macmillan had playfully alluded.

> We will not go into argument about the laws of fiction, but I fear the local particulars are more in my way than grand universal principles of any description – and I am dreadfully addicted to having things my own way like as (you men say) [sic] most women.[21]

She did, however, agree to change Benjamin Jowett's name to Heward in the book version at Macmillan's request,[22] and removed the *Magazine* text's reference to him as 'the great heresiarch'.[23]

Though nothing by Oliphant appeared in *Macmillan's* for more than seven years after *A Son of the Soil* finished its run in April 1865, her prolonged absence from its pages was by no means the result of any lack of effort on her part. On the contrary, she made repeated overtures to Alexander Macmillan, which he gently but firmly turned aside, declining her offer to review *Felix Holt*, a novel he much admired, because he feared that she would be too hard on Eliot's new work,[24] and informing her on at least two occasions that there was already so much new fiction on hand that he could not accept any more from her.[25] Macmillan did, however, encourage Oliphant to keep in touch with the *Magazine*'s second editor, George Grove, who printed her four-part novella, *The Two Marys*, starting in September 1872.

Oliphant's continuing correspondence with Alexander Macmillan eventually led to her next *Magazine* project, one that was to have a significant effect on the rest of her career. Macmillan had become infatuated with Florence after a visit there with his new wife early in 1873 and suggested to Oliphant, who knew Italy well, that she undertake a book on 'the marvellous life of poetry, art, and deep human emotion' that pulses through the city. He realised that such a volume could not be completed quickly and proposed that parts of this work-in-progress be published in his *Magazine*.[26] Though *The Makers of Florence* did not come out until 1876, sections of the third part, collectively titled *The Convent of San Marco*, appeared in *Macmillan's* between July 1874 and September 1875.

The Convent of San Marco/The Makers of Florence turned into something of a cash cow for Oliphant. Not only did she persuade Macmillan to finance another trip to Italy so that she could conduct some on-site research, but she also managed to produce articles and books for other publishers based on her investigations: substantial essays in *Blackwood's* and the *Cornhill*, and a little book on Dante in the Foreign Classics for English Readers series that she was editing for Blackwood.[27] She enjoyed herself so much in Florence that she subsequently asked Macmillan to subsidise yet one more such Italian journey. 'You should give me a commission for a companion volume on Venice. This is my only way of giving my boys foreign trips ...'[28] And so she turned out not only *The Makers of Venice* (1887), but also such later, similar Macmillan books as *Royal Edinburgh* (1890), *Jerusalem* (1891), and *The Makers of Modern Rome* (1895).

The Convent of San Marco re-established Oliphant's connection with *Macmillan's*, and she went on to serialise five more novels in the magazine between 1875 and 1890: *The Curate in Charge* (August 1875–January 1876), *Young Musgrave* (January–December 1877), *He That Will Not When He May* (November 1879–November 1880), *The Wizard's Son* (November 1882–March 1884), and *Kirsteen* (August 1889–August 1890). There were usually difficulties and misunderstandings along the way to publication: about payment for her work (even though Oliphant was now normally working under written agreements), about advances and loans, about delivery of copy, about correcting and returning proofs, about her inability to get on with the *Magazine*'s last two editors, John

Morley and Mowbray Morris, and – more fundamentally – about the honesty and good-will that each party brought to the transactions between author and publisher.

It did not help matters that Oliphant's old friend Alexander Macmillan was gradually withdrawing from the business during these 15 years. Most of her correspondence with the firm was now handled by George Lillie Craik, Macmillan's partner, and husband of her fiction-writing colleague (and rival) Dinah Mulock Craik. Basically an accountant rather than a man of letters, he was less inclined to humour Oliphant than the more bookish Macmillan had been; and, though he tried to be civil to her, and generally succeeded, he did on occasion lose his temper.

The whole story yielded by these exchanges of letters is too long and intricate to be rehearsed in this space; a few representative examples, however, will serve to convey something of its flavour.

The serialisation of Oliphant's second *Macmillan's Magazine* novel, *The Curate in Charge*, proceeded relatively smoothly. But when, in October 1876, George Grove offered Oliphant £750 for 'the entire copyright' of the *Magazine* and three-volume versions of what was to become the third, *Young Musgrave*,[29] Oliphant asked for more. After consulting Craik, Grove added £250 to the amount he had proposed, stipulating that the novel would begin its run in *Macmillan's* in January, and that Oliphant's fee would be paid in two equal amounts, £500 on 1 January 1877 and £500 'on the delivery of the last portion of the MS'.[30]

That sounds straightforward enough, and Oliphant certainly kept her part of the bargain, at least as far as delivery of copy was concerned. *Young Musgrave* began in *Macmillan's* in January 1877 as planned, finished in December, and came out as a three-volume Macmillan novel before the end of that year. But the financial part of her arrangement with the firm, as often happened, turned out to be more complicated than it initially sounded. There was no problem about the first payment of £500: Craik deposited it into her bank account on 1 January,[31] and on the same day she signed a receipt for that amount 'on account of "Young Musgrave"'.[32] On 8 June, Oliphant received a further £200, in the form of a two-month bill, again 'on account of Young Musgrave';[33] but if this was a loan rather than an advance it was not repaid, for after she sent the rest of the manuscript in August, Frederick Macmillan wrote to her on the 23rd that he had paid into her account 'the £300 that remained due to you for "Young Musgrave"'.[34]

The three payments do add up to £1,000, and so it is tempting to regard the matter of Oliphant's remuneration for *Young Musgrave* as settled. But there seems to have been more to it than this exercise in simple arithmetic indicates. As late as 31 October 1878 – the year following the publication of *Young Musgrave* in *Macmillan's Magazine* and in book form, and shortly after Craik and Oliphant had negotiated an agreement for her next serial novel, *He That Will Not When He May* – he rather sheepishly wrote to her that one of his clerks had pointed out to him that she had inadvertently been overpaid by £100 for *Young Musgrave*. Craik apologised for the error and proposed that the amount be deducted from the next payment she was to receive for her new novel.[35] As he might have expected by this point in their relationship, Oliphant did not care for the suggestion. Confessing that she had thought her final payment for *Young Musgrave* to have been too high but never got around to mentioning it,[36] she pleaded with Craik '*not* to deduct [the £100] from my next payment ... as I really want the money badly' and requested that, instead, 'it represent the final hundred' for *He That Will Not When He May*, which would not be due until that novel was published as a book, 'or I will do my magazine work for it during the year'.[37] The fact that Craik and Oliphant agreed that her last £300 for *Young Musgrave* was an overpayment confuses our arithmetic, calls into question both Oliphant's honesty and Macmillan's efficiency, and raises the possibility that she received another, unrecorded, advance of £100 while working on that novel.

The publication of *He That Will Not When He May* occasioned a different set of issues from those that had surrounded its immediate predecessor. As Grove had done in opening negotiations for *Young Musgrave*, Craik offered Oliphant £750. 'We will gladly take your novel for the magazine or otherwise as we may decide', he wrote on 22 October 1878, proposing to divide her £750 into three parts; '£350 now[,] £200 when the manuscript is in our hands & the rest when the whole book is published'.[38] Again Oliphant objected, this time not to the amount of the total payment but rather to the size of the second instalment. The memorandum of agreement that she accepted on 24 October stipulated payments of £350 immediately, £300 'on delivery of the manuscript', and £100 'when the publication is completed'.[39]

Shifting £100 from the third instalment to the second was a minor adjustment, though it did bring to light the overpayment in this amount that Oliphant had received for *Young Musgrave*. The timing of that second £300, however, turned into a more serious issue. On 5 December 1878, a Thursday, Oliphant advised Craik that she would send off '[t]he rest of my novel ... either on Saturday or Monday' and asked him to 'do me the favour to have the three hundred pounds paid on Saturday to my bankers'.[40] Craik's answer, dated that Saturday, the 7th, consisted of one sentence: 'I will pay the three hundred pounds into your account when the rest of the manuscript comes.'[41] Offended by his curt reply and disregarding the previous advances she had received from Macmillan (most of them authorised by Craik himself), she was disturbed by his insistence on conforming to the letter of their agreement in this case and accused him of not trusting her. She replied immediately the same day, 'that you may see I had no intention of deceiving you, I send by this same post in a registered packet ... the second half of "He that will not when he may" – with the exception of the very end which shall be sent on Monday'.[42] Craik did not acknowledge receiving 'the last of the copy' until 11 December;[43] but before that, on the 9th, he apologised for his letter of the 7th, claiming that he had misunderstood hers of the 5th (which is hard to believe), sidestepping the matter of trust that she had raised, and expressing himself almost as tersely as he had done originally.[44]

Craik's letter of 11 December brought up another question that was to cause trouble between him and Oliphant: when to begin the serialisation of *He That Will Not When He May*. Craik was aware that two novels were then running in the *Magazine*: Annie Keary's *A Doubting Heart* and Frances Hodgson Burnett's *'Haworth's'*. 'I speak without referring to the magazine,' he told her, 'but I think Miss Keary's story ends about June [1879] & we should begin yours in July'. If Craik had consulted Grove before writing he might have been able to predict more accurately when *A Doubting Heart* would end, which turned out to be December, not June, 1879. Having finally spoken to his editor, Craik revealed to Oliphant on 27 January 1879 that Grove 'proposes to begin your story after Haworths, which will finish in October', going on to express his 'hope [that] this is satisfactory to you, for it will begin our new volume which dates from November'.[45] It all happened as Craik had predicted: Burnett's novel did indeed 'finish in October', and the first four chapters of Oliphant's were given prominence by leading off volume 41 of *Macmillan's Magazine* the following month.

But Oliphant was not appeased by this revised arrangement, believing that Craik had been taking advantage of her. On 15 February 1879 she frankly admitted that she would have preferred to have *He That Will Not When He May* start 'in July as you originally intended'. 'I should not have offered it to you at so cheap a rate,' she continued, 'had I had the slightest idea that you were likely to require it so soon!'[46] Disregarding the question of her fee, Craik replied two days later to thank her for the 'opportunity of publishing the story sooner, but we have now arranged for the later date & it would not be a convenience to us to change it'.[47]

Evidently Oliphant was unwilling to let the matter rest there, for Craik pointed out to her that they had agreed on a fair price for the novel and that, if she was having second thoughts, 'we are quite willing to give you it back for the £750 we paid you'.[48] Oliphant's resigned response to Craik's offer to return the copyright of *He That Will Not When He May* in exchange for that amount of money – which most probably she no longer had – was negative. She did not want to 'haggle', she wrote 'a thing that is done is done ... One must pay the penalty of one's weaknesses – of all kinds.'[49]

There are three noteworthy features associated with the publication of Oliphant's next *Macmillan's Magazine* serial novel, *The Wizard's Son*. First, it was part of a package deal that brought her very close to the goal of regular payment for her work at which she had been aiming for some time.[50] But, second, that same creative financial arrangement led to heightened misunderstanding and even ill-will between her and Macmillan. And, third, the serialisation of *The Wizard's Son* further poisoned her relations with the *Magazine*'s new editor, John Morley.

On 28 July 1881 Oliphant proposed to Craik that Macmillan pay her £1,000 per annum for two years in return for which she would produce 'three novels – one for use in the magazine[,] the others to be published in the usual way'. She suggested quarterly payments but preferred to view them as a consolidation of her 'earnings into regular income' rather than advances, and pledged 'to publish nothing else during the time that would in the least interfere with them'. Such a plan, she believed, would 'relieve me of the uncertainties and negotiations which always annoy me, and it would divide my money into regular payments'.[51]

There is no written record of the exchanges between Oliphant and Craik that must have ensued over the next few months, but it is clear that at some point the flourishing newspaper syndicate run by W. F. Tillotson in Bolton came into the picture, for on 25 November Oliphant and Craik agreed on a scheme that called for one novel (*The Wizard's Son*) to be serialised in *Macmillan*'s, a second (*Sir Tom*) to appear in several English and Welsh newspapers under the auspices of Tillotson's Fiction Bureau, and a third (*Hester*) to be published 'in library form' – that is, in three volumes. During the two years covered by this arrangement, Oliphant would receive the £2,000 for which she had asked, £300 from Tillotson and £1,700 from Macmillan, in quarterly payments of £250 each.[52]

Tillotson's entry into Oliphant's professional life confused still further her already tangled finances, for she took to borrowing from Macmillan against the payments she was to receive from Tillotson. On the one hand, Craik and his colleagues did what they could to help her monetarily (and there is no record of any missed payments from Tillotson via Oliphant to Macmillan), but, on the other hand, their willingness to yield to Oliphant's repeated pleas made them progressively less patient in the face of her periodic complaints that they had not been dealing honestly with her. In July 1884, and again in June and July 1894, Craik and Oliphant engaged in acrimonious correspondence about which party owed how much to the other, Oliphant maintaining that she had been cheated and Craik insisting that they had lost money on most of her books.[53]

When *The Wizard's Son* began appearing in *Macmillan's* in November 1882, the *Magazine*'s editor was still George Grove, with whom Oliphant's relations were correct if not exactly cordial. In May 1883, however, after 6 of the novel's 17 instalments had been published, Grove was succeeded by John Morley, who was decidedly no friend to Oliphant. They had crossed swords even before Morley assumed the editorship of *Macmillan's*. While Morley was at the helm of the *Pall Mall Gazette,* he had declined to accept Oliphant's proferred services as a reviewer – a slight that Oliphant continued to resent for years.[54] An additional source of strain between them was the awkward fact that Morley in his capacity as the initiator and first editor of Macmillan's English Men of Letters series had strong objections to Oliphant's contribution, a volume on Richard Brinsley Sheridan, which came to him in January 1883, four months before he became editor of *Macmillan's Magazine*. Craik played the thankless role of intermediary between Morley and Oliphant, managing to persuade Morley not to 'throw ... aside' her *Sheridan;*[55] Oliphant, however, was not appeased by Craik's attempts to mollify her and offered to withdraw the book and repay the £100 she had been paid for it – an offer that she made to Craik, for she refused to meet with Morley face-to-face, and one that was not accepted.[56]

Once installed in the editor's chair, the most visible change Morley introduced in the contents of the *Magazine* was the inclusion of a 'Review of the Month', written at first by W. T. Stead, but beginning in October 1883, by Morley himself. Brief though this new feature was, seldom running to more than ten pages at the end of each number, its inclusion meant that something else in *Macmillan's* had to go, and Oliphant's serial novel was an obvious target. To banish *The Wizard's Son* would have been impossible, but to shrink it was an option – one that Morley chose to exercise, with what feelings we can only imagine. Again it fell to Craik to serve as go-between;[57] and, though on this occasion it took Oliphant a few months to work up her anger, she finally let Craik know in no uncertain terms that she had been chafing under the space restrictions laid down by the new editor.[58]

Oliphant got on no better with Mowbray Morris, who succeeded Morley in November 1885.[59] Just as Oliphant seems not to have communicated directly with Morley, preferring to work through Craik, so there is no surviving correspondence with Morris. Again Craik was the rather hapless man in the middle. He could not persuade Morris to print Oliphant's 'The Land of Darkness' in *Macmillan's*, nor did Morris publish the excerpts from her *The Makers of Venice* or her article on Robert Henryson that Craik had urged on him.[60]

There were special circumstances surrounding the publication of the only essay by Oliphant to appear in the *Magazine* during Morris's editorship. Her old acquaintance Dinah Mulock Craik died unexpectedly on 12 October 1887. As a long-time Macmillan author and *Macmillan's Magazine* contributor, she was a natural subject for an obituary essay in the *Magazine*; she was also the wife of George Lillie Craik. And Oliphant, who had known her since both of them were young women, was its natural author. For understandable reasons, she approached Frederick Macmillan rather than Craik about this particular piece, and Macmillan had little difficulty in persuading Morris to give Oliphant '5 pages for the paper on Mrs. Craik',[61] which appeared in December 1887.

The last of Oliphant's novels to be serialised in *Macmillan's* – *Kirsteen* – was the source of more friction between her and her publisher. (Mowbray Morris seems not to have been directly involved.) In October 1888 she tried unsuccessfully to place it in *Blackwood's* for a fee of £400.[62] She then almost immediately offered it to Craik, who warned her that, because 'we fail to get the same result from the sale of your later [novels] than we once got', he would have to pay her significantly less for it 'than you have been used to'. 'I say this now,' his letter went on, 'for you might like to go elsewhere. I am sincerely anxious that you should do the best for yourself.'[63] Having already tried and failed to 'go elsewhere' and in need of money as usual, Oliphant did not take time to bargain but accepted £300 'for the entire copyright', and signed a receipt for a payment of that amount the day after Craik wrote to her.[64]

It came as something of a shock to Oliphant when Craik informed her on 15 April 1889 that 'We propose to begin "Kirstine" [sic] in the Magazine in July.'[65] Two days later she protested that their 'bargain was solely for its publication in book form', and complained of the 'dry and peremptory' tone of Craik's letter.[66] In his reply of 24 April, it was Craik's turn to protest. Insisting that there had been nothing 'dry or peremptory' about his letter, he reminded Oliphant that she had sold Macmillan the 'entire copyright' of *Kirsteen* six months earlier. 'It happens that we could have it in the Magazine, but rather than that you should feel that you have been wronged we will give this up & publish it in the regular form.' He then lapsed into the lecturing mode that he sometimes adopted in dealing with Oliphant:

> I must, however, say that you have no right to interfere & I feel the inconvenience of our right being questioned. Had I ever thought of this, I should have hesitated to buy a book which we did not see our way to publish at the time. We kept it waiting for such an opportunity as the Magazine offers. The terms of this agreement are so explicit that I could not conceive our right being stated in any more embracing way.[67]

By the time he contacted Oliphant again six days later on the same vexed question of *Kirsteen* and its possible appearance in *Macmillan's Magazine*, Craik – perhaps having had second thoughts – took a more conciliatory tone, giving voice to some hurt ('It is a pain to me to feel that you have any idea that our relations are not in every way satisfactory'), proclaiming his good intentions ('I have always striven to do the best I could for you & have no reflection that I forgot your interest at any time'), and, not least, offering an olive branch ('That there may be no feeling of dissatisfaction on your part I propose to pay you a further £100 for the book. Will this be in all ways satisfactory to you?').[68] In the end, *Kirsteen* was serialised in *Macmillan's*, beginning not in July but in August 1889, and running until August 1890; Macmillan brought out the three-volume version in September 1890.[69]

Nothing else by Margaret Oliphant appeared in *Macmillan's Magazine* during the last seven years of her life. But it is important to view the epistolary quarrels between her and Craik during the 1880s and 1890s in perspective. She went on producing Macmillan books until she died; though she never again earned even as much as £400 for any one novel, she did rather better with her non-fiction.[70] Most of the letters she exchanged with Craik and his associates were businesslike at worst and personally friendly at best. Like Alexander Macmillan before him, Craik continued to show his willingness to break or bend house rules in order to satisfy Oliphant's needs – usually for money. And there is no reason to doubt the sincerity of the solicitude he expressed in his letters regarding her family's troubles and her own health and well-being.

Within days after Oliphant's death on 25 June 1897 Craik initiated a movement to establish a public memorial to her, inducing a reluctant William Blackwood to assume the honorary secretaryship of the committee that raised the necessary funds and made the arrangements. All this took time, but on 16 July 1908 a handsome plaque bearing Oliphant's likeness and attesting to her 'genius and power as novelist, biographer, essayist and historian' was unveiled by J. M. Barrie in St Giles' Church, Edinburgh.[71] Shortly after Oliphant died, Craik was also instrumental, along with Blackwood, in securing a Civil List pension of £75 per annum for Oliphant's niece Denny, who had been financially and emotionally dependent on her aunt.[72]

On balance, it seems clear that Craik's admiration for Oliphant's many accomplishments powerfully outweighed and ultimately negated the irritation she had often caused him. As for Oliphant, she brought her voluminous and often tempestuous correspondence with Craik to a poignant close in a letter written just nine days before she died. From what she knew was her deathbed, she made one last effort to square both her financial account with Macmillan and her personal standing with Craik, concluding as follows: 'I am dying but not suffering much. I am sorry that there has been a cloud on the end of our long friendship – but no unkind feeling on my part. Goodbye.'[73]

Notes

1. Royal A. Gettmann, *A Victorian Publisher: a study of the Bentley papers* (Cambridge: Cambridge University Press, 1960), p. 147.
2. George Smith, 'Our Birth and Parentage', *Cornhill Magazine*, new series 10 (January 1901), 4–17 (p. 4).
3. Walter E. Houghton, 'Victorian Periodical Literature and the Articulate Classes', *Victorian Studies*, 22 (Summer 1979), 389–412 (p. 407).
4. Macmillan's reference to Carlyle is to be found in a letter to F. D. Maurice, 17 August 1863, in which he responds to Maurice's objections to the 'Ilias (Americana) in Nuce', published in the *Spectator* of 8 August (Add.MS. 55381, ff. 399–400).
5. Macmillan bade Masson farewell in a letter of 20 December 1867 (Add.MS. 55842, ff. 90–2); it fell to G. L. Craik to do the honours for Grove on 8 December 1882 because, so he told Grove, Macmillan was indisposed with a cold (Add.MS. 55843, ff. 49–51).
6. Evidence to support this conclusion appears, for example, in George Macmillan's letters to Morris of 4 and 5 January 1904 (Add.MS. 55475, ff. 422, 460).
7. Add.MS. 54794, f. 135.
8. Add.MS. 54794, f. 139.
9. Add.MS. 55488, f. 173.

10. *A Bibliographical Catalogue of Macmillan and Co.'s Publications from 1843 to 1889* (London: Macmillan, 1891), p. 59.
11. Vineta Colby and Robert A. Colby, *The Equivocal Virtue: Mrs Oliphant and the Victorian Literary Market Place* (Hamden , CT: Archon, 1966), p. 79.
12. Add.MS. 55380, f. 122.
13. Add.MS. 54919, f. 301.
14. Add.MS. 54919, ff. 313–14.
15. Add.MS. 54919, f. 299.
16. *The Spectator*, 38 (4 February 1865), 133.
17. Add.MS. 55384, f. 158.
18. Add.MS. 55384, ff. 363, 372.
19. Add.MS. 55842, f. 34; Add.MS. 55843, f. 504.
20. Add.MS. 55384, f. 532.
21. Add.MS. 54919, f. 322.
22. Add.MS. 55384, f. 135.
23. *Macmillan's Magazine*, 11 (February 1865), 293.
24. Add.MS. 55386, ff. 173, 189.
25. Add.MS. 55388, f. 582; Add.MS. 55390, f. 594.
26. Add.MS. 55394, ff. 88–9.
27. 'Michael Angelo', *Blackwood's Edinburgh Magazine*, 118 (October 1875), 461–82; 'The Early Years of Dante', *Cornhill Magazine*, 32 (October 1875), 471–89; 'Dante in Exile', *Cornhill Magazine*, 32 (December 1875), 670–90; *Dante* (Edinburgh: Blackwood, 1877).
28. Add.MS. 54919, f. 52.
29. Add.MS. 55400, f. 199.
30. Add.MS. 55400, f. 442.
31. Add.MS. 55401, f. 266.
32. Add.MS. 54919, f. 42.
33. Add.MS. 54919, f. 56.
34. Add.MS. 55403, f. 503.
35. Add.MS. 55407, f. 366.
36. In advising Craik on 20 August 1877 that the remainder of the manuscript of *Young Musgrave* was on its way, and asking him to pay the balance to her bankers, 'if possible on the 23rd', the amount she had stated was £200 rather than £300 (Add.MS. 54919, f. 150).
37. Add.MS. 54919, f. 93.
38. Add. MS. 55407, f. 292.
39. Add. MS. 54919, f. 91.
40. Add. MS. 54919, f. 96.
41. Add.MS. 55407, f. 745.
42. Add.MS. 54919, f. 98.
43. Add.MS. 55407, f. 790.
44. Add.MS. 55407, f. 757.
45. Add.MS. 55407, f. 1274.
46. Add.MS. 54919, ff. 102–3.
47. Add.MS. 55408, f. 53.
48. Add.MS. 55408, f. 1053.
49. Add. MS. 54919, ff. 108–9.

50. She first approached Craik with this idea in December 1879; see *The Autobiography and Letters of Mrs M. O. W. Oliphant*, edited by Mrs Harry Coghill (Edinburgh: Blackwood, 1899), pp. 291–2. (The letter as printed there is misdated 1880; I have been unable to find the original in the Macmillan archive.) The following month Oliphant also wrote to William Blackwood of her desire 'to get regular work which I can arrange beforehand and which will bring in regular payment' (Blackwood MS. 4410, quoted in Colby and Colby, p. 146).
51. Add.MS. 54919, ff. 125–6.
52. Add.MS. 55413, f. 353; Add.MS. 54919, f. 34. Each of these novels was ultimately published in three volumes by Macmillan: *Hester* (1883) was followed by *The Wizard's Son* and *Sir Tom* the next year. For a concise bibliographical overview see John Stock Clarke, *Margaret Oliphant (1828–1897): a bibliography* (St Lucia: University of Queensland, English Department, 1986), pp. 62–3. The terms of the agreement were spelled out more fully in a letter from Craik to Oliphant dated 19 December 1881 (Add.MS. 55413, ff. 528–9).
53. For Craik's side of the story, see Add.MS. 55843, ff. 84–5, 496–7, 504–5, 507–8; Add.MS. 55444, ff. 1055, 1103–4. The correspondence giving Oliphant's version unfortunately seems not to have survived.
54. Add.MS. 54919, ff. 160–1.
55. Add.MS. 55415, f. 485.
56. Add.MS. 55415, ff. 495–6; Add.MS. 54919, ff. 139–40, 141, 142–3.
57. Add.MS. 55415, ff. 1338–9.
58. Add.MS. 54919, ff. 142–3, 152, 153–4.
59. Add.MS. 55843, f. 97; Add.MS. 54794, f. 9.
60. Add.MS. 55422, f. 1069; Add.MS. 55421, ff. 167, 316, 375, 497, 1048; Add.MS. 55430, f. 1368.
61. Add.MS. 55425, f. 303.
62. Blackwood Ms. 4523, quoted in Colby and Colby, p. 145.
63. Add.MS. 55427, f. 212.
64. Add.MS. 54919, f. 197.
65. Add.MS. 55428, f. 528.
66. Add.MS. 54919, ff. 211–12.
67. Add.MS. 55428, f. 576–7.
68. Add.MS. 55428, f. 629.
69. Clarke, p. 71.
70. She received £250 each for the copyrights of *The Railway Man and his Children* (1891), *The Heir Presumptive and the Heir Apparent* (1892), *The Marriage of Elinor* (1892), and *Lady William* (1893) (Add.MS. 54919, ff. 251, 229, 250, 282). All these three-deckers, however, had been serialised in, and paid for, by periodicals and newspapers prior to their publication in book form by Macmillan. These figures should be compared with the more generous payments received for her Macmillan non-fiction during the 1890s: £600 for *Royal Edinburgh* (1890), £1,200 for *Jerusalem* (1891), and £800 for *The Makers of Modern Rome* (1895) (Add.MS. 54919, ff. 210, 226, 243–4, 249, 279–80, 284).
71. Colby and Colby, pp. 243–4.
72. Colby and Colby, p. 268.
73. Blackwood MS. 4664, quoted in Colby and Colby, p. 241.

5
Letters to Macmillan: an Addendum

Sir Samuel White Baker's letters to Macmillan[1]

Michael Bott

When Simon Nowell-Smith sorted out the Macmillan archives in the 1960s, both for his *Letters to Macmillan* (Macmillan, 1967) and for the saleroom, Sir Samuel Baker missed the cut. The Macmillan archive at Reading, therefore, contains 53 letters from Baker, 1875–90, while the British Library holds copies of letters to him, mainly from Alexander Macmillan, in the Macmillan letter books, and a small number of related items in other collections. There are relatively few letters from Baker in public collections – the *Location Register of English Literary Manuscripts and Letters* records fewer than 300 – and the letters at Reading were not used for either of Baker's recent biographies: Richard Hall's *Lovers on the Nile* (Collins, 1980) and Michael Brander's *The Perfect Victorian Hero* (Mainstream, 1982).

Both books, however, are to be recommended, and I am unable to improve on the blurb in the latter for a thumbnail biography:

> Samuel White Baker (1821–1893) – explorer, writer, administrator, soldier and hunter ... was born the son of a typical Victorian wealthy middle class family, but abandoned a comfortable life as a businessman in favour of travel and adventure ... He bought his second wife in a slave market on the lower Danube, and, with her, spent five years exploring Abyssinia and the sources of the Nile ... Later

1. These letters are reproduced here with the kind permission of David H. G. Baker.

he was, at the request of the Prince of Wales, to turn once more to Africa with a remit to work to bring about an end to slave trading.

The letters fall conveniently into two chronological groups, of which I have chosen to illustrate the earlier, those dated between 1875 and 1881. The later series, mainly 1888–90, is largely concerned with the publishing details of *Wild Beasts and their Ways: reminiscences* ... and is an excellent example of the author being involved in all the minutiae of production. He complains about high prices and textual corrections, and shares with Macmillan his rambling thoughts about illustrations. He gets very angry about the photographic work of William Friese-Greene, whose mind must have been on pioneering cinematography rather than on Baker's animals. He comments on what he is reading and recommends material for publication. Above all he expounds upon the iniquities of reviewers and journalists. The earlier sequence highlights the author's interests too, but also demonstrates more graphically the relationship between author and publisher beyond purely bookish concerns.

Baker's glory days of explorations and expeditions were over by 1875, though his travels were by no means finished. One of the most interesting aspects of these letters is the close attention he paid to the exploits and difficulties of his successor in Egypt and the Sudan: Colonel, later General, Gordon. A mutual respect seems to have been established between the two men, though the true situation is probably best expressed by Richard Hall in his biography of Baker and his wife, *Lovers on the Nile*: 'Although Baker and Gordon were ultimately lavish in their praise of one another, the former was bitterly critical of his successor in letters to [John Thaddeus] Delane of *The Times*. Gordon was likewise withering about Baker while writing to [James] Grant.' In the Abou Saood affair Baker exhibits very much of a 'told you so' attitude, though he is quick to point out, 'I have no wish to *triumph* but simply to see fair play' – but of course!

Abou Saood was a notorious slave trader and a significant thorn in Baker's side, but Gordon employed him in an attempt to foster a softly-softly approach in the fight against slavery, in contrast to Baker's confrontational strategy. Abou Saood wielded considerable power as the son-in-law of Sheik Agad who had the official exclusive right of trading, ostensibly in ivory but actually in slaves, in the Sudan. From all accounts he was vicious, furtive and oleaginous, a thoroughly bad lot who might have emerged from the pages of an E. Phillips Oppenheim novel. 'A forthright man himself, Sam preferred an outright scoundrel and swashbuckling rogue rather than the Uriah Heep type of fawning snake represented by Abou Saood' (Michael Brander). His downfall was only temporary as Gordon's successor reinstated him in 1881. In typical fashion he sat back and presided over the massacre of his troops by the Mahdi, who was just then emerging as leader of the Sudanese rebellion, and who would go on to be Gordon's nemesis four years later.

Macmillan published eight books by Sir Samuel Baker:

The Albert N'yanza, Great Basin of the Nile, and Explorations of the Nile Sources, 1866.
The Nile Tributaries of Abyssinia: and the sword hunters of the Hamran Arabs, 1867.
Cast up by the Sea, 1868.
Ismailia: a narrative of the expedition to Central Africa for the suppression of the slave trade organized by Ismail, Khedive of Egypt, 1874.
Cyprus As I Saw It in 1879, 1879.
True Tales for my Grandsons, 1883.
The Egyptian Question: being letters to The Times *and* Pall Mall Gazette, 1884.
Wild beasts and their Ways: reminiscences of Europe, Asia, Africa and America, 1890.

The earlier books about Baker's expeditions were very successful; Macmillan printed some 25,000 copies of *The Albert N'yanza* and 18,500 of *The Nile Tributaries*. The story was rather different for *Ismailia* – the first edition of 6,000 copies proved difficult to shift, as Macmillan's letters to Baker show, and the cheap edition, which also ran eventually to 6,000 copies, moved sluggishly. J. B. Lippincott of Philadelphia picked up a few thousand of the first two titles for sale in America, and Harper & Brothers of New York published an edition of *Ismailia*. Various French and German translations of these three books appeared; significantly perhaps, several of them were also abridgements.

The letters reveal a man who is not content to sit at home in Newton Abbot, who is trying to come to terms with Progress, proud of his humanitarian achievements, trying to be ecologically sound while remaining deeply conservative, and who at times can be deliciously non-p.c. Perhaps the best example comes from a letter of 29 June 1885:

> We left England 2 Febry and went up the Brahmaputra to Assam. It was an interesting trip which exhibited the immense results of steam

transport in the development of agricultural industry. All the flat but rich alluvial deposits of the Brahmaputra which only a few years ago were grass jungles swarming with tigers, are now being rapidly cultivated, as the produce can be sent cheaply to market by the large steamers upon the river, and by rail. The tigers are so much diminished that I only shot six, and three leopards – all that I fired at.

Unless otherwise noted, all letters later than May 1875 bear an embossed letterhead: Sandford Orleigh, Newton Abbot.

Teignmouth
2 Jany 1875

My dear Mr Craik

Very many happy years to you! – & to yours –

I enclose you an extract from the New York Times of 11 Dec1874 – which I think may be made useful respecting 'Ismailia'. Mr Southworth* the writer of the article is the Secretary of the American Geographical Socty and he went to the Sudan in the hopes of joining me in 1871. The terrible state of the Nile which was blocked with vegetation rendered his advance impossible, and after a residence of five months in the country during which time he gained all information he was forced to return.

His evidence is valuable as he was behind the scenes.

We are now rejoicing in soft mild weather.

The purchase of Sandford Orleigh is completed; – the conveyance made, and the money paid. I hope we shall get it furnished and take possession about 1. April.

I little thought that I should become the proprietor when you first pointed it out to me in the 'Times' advertisements.

I hope that 'Ismailia' is going off satisfactorily.

Very sincerely yours
Sam W Baker

Please take care of slip from 'New York Times'.

* Alvan S. Southworth, author of *Four Thousand Miles of African Travel: a personal record of a journey up the Nile and through the Soudan to the confines of Central Africa, embracing a discussion on the sources of the Nile, and an examination of the slave trade* (Sampson Low, 1875).

Teignmouth
14 Jany 1875

My dear Mr Macmillan

I received last evening a letter from Colonel Gordon dated 18 Novr 1874 Gondokoro*

He has found out Abou Saood's real character, and he has removed him! – He has discovered that he is a brigand, and a great liar, therefore he is dismissed.

At the same time that it is most satisfactory to see this corroboration of my opinions of this man's character, I cannot help regretting that Colonel Gordon should ever have employed a man who had behaved in so scandalous a manner towards myself.

This rascal Abou Saood has been the cause of much unpleasant correspondence. As you are well aware I was blamed by certain correspondents of the 'Times' for having misrepresented Abou Saood's character; in fact I had been harsh and hasty – towards a man who should have been regarded with leniency. Colonel Gordon was to be well served by this useful man to whom I had shown un-necessary severity.

Abu Saood is now discovered to be a despicable character, a brigand like all the rest of the White Nile Arabs, and a consummate liar – he is therefore removed by Gordon as a failure.

I cannot send you Gordon's letter to me as it is marked 'private', but I dare say you will know how to circulate the main fact.**

I knew that the truth must come out, and that Gordon would soon repent of his charitable view respecting his protegé Abou Saood. He is well quit of the fellow who would have given him trouble, and I prophesy he will even yet endeavour to undermine him from a distance.

Very sincerely yours
Sam W Baker

* 'Gondokoro was a perfect hell. It is utterly ignored by the Egyptian authorities, although well known to be a colony of cut-throats ... my presence at Gondokoro was considered as an unwarrantable intrusion upon a locality sacred to slavery and iniquity.' *The Albert N'yanza*, chapter 2.

** Alexander Macmillan wrote on 19 January 1875 that he had passed on the information to Mr Greenwood, editor of the *Pall Mall Gazette* who 'has found opportunity of putting the matter in a clear & impartial light. It is indeed satisfactory to have this rascal found out & exposed' (Add.MS. 55396, f. 787).

Stover
21 Jany 1875

My dear Mr Macmillan

I enclose receipt with thanks for your cheque which followed me here where we are staying for a few days (Duke of Somerset's) as this lovely spot is only 1½ miles from our new home Sandford Orleigh – It ought to be called 'Craik Hall' for it was our friend Mr Craik who first pointed it out to me by an advertisement in the Times.

The notice in the Pall Mall about Abou Saood was quite sufficient – as I have no wish to triumph but simply to see fair play.

Very sincerely yours
Sam W Baker

Teignmouth
19 Feby 1875

My dear Macmillan

I am truly obliged for your letter of 17th and for the kind interest you have shewn in your communication with Mr Greenwood. By all means let Abou Saood be buried as deep as possible, or subjected to cremation, and let him end in smoke and dust rather than disturb us by again appearing in print.

The public are like school-boys who delight in holding two otherwise friendly cocks face to face in the hope of inciting them to fight – thus some journals insist in regarding Gordon and myself as rivals, and continue to draw invidious distinctions – in the hope of causing a row.*

I have no doubt that 99 out of a 100 of my critics who are jealous of my salary (which they repeatedly parade in print as £10,000 a year) would have refused it if offered to themselves?

They forget at the same time, that my first expedition of 4 years and 8 months in Africa to solve the Nile sources was entirely voluntary, and was paid for by myself without one farthing of extraneous aid.

In recent African history the only independent expeditions have been those of Mdlle. Tinne;** – Baron van der Decker; and my own. Both of the former adventurous explorers were cut to pieces – by the natives – thus we are the only survivors, and nevertheless there are envious spirits who begrudge me a pecuniary indemnity for the risks of African toil. This is all very wrong, but as the world is unfortunately constituted it is very natural – 'Envy, hatred, malice, and all uncharitableness' must be common complaints otherwise we should not pray against them.

For my own part I uphold Gordon upon every opportunity in public and private as a man who will persevere in doing what he considers right, but in spite of his good work he will I fear discover that he will eventually suffer trouble and annoyance from detractors.

I am sorry to hear that the very unfair review in the Times had so bad an effect – but I hope a cheaper edition will be more successful.*** I think the American edition is admirable, and the binding is very superior. The leaves are smoothly cut, and the book lays open without straining the back.

If ever you can get time for a little change of air, both Lady Baker and myself shall be delighted to welcome you here.

Very sincerely yours
Sam W Baker

* In a letter to Gordon dated 10 October 1878 (Add.MS. 52388) Baker writes: 'It ... appeared that the British public were to believe that you and I were unfriendly rivals – Why? or upon what grounds God knows, except that a change of Ministry had taken place about that time and the English are in the habit of an Opposition. Gladstone went out, and Disraeli came into office. I suppose I was Gladstone, and you were Disraeli in Central Africa, therefore the British world regarded us as political rivals – with a proper amount of personal frigidity.'

** presumably Alexine Tinne.

*** In his letter of 17 February 1875 (Add.MS. 55396, f. 971) Alexander Macmillan discussed the effects of the review in *The Times* and went on to say: 'I have refrained from telling you exactly how the sale stood till we could be quite sure about it. Of course four thousand copies is a considerable sale, but you know we looked for a good many more, and if that Times article had been in a different key I am sure we might have nearly doubled it.'

Teignmouth
3 March [1875]

Did your clerk forward a copy of Macmillan's Magazine February to Alvan S. Southworth Esq American Geographical Socty, Coopers Institute, New York

My dear Macmillan

You will have seen by young Russell's communication to the Times from Berber on the Soudan Nile, that the slave trade is going on as usual across the deserts under the eyes of the Egyptian officials. In fact both my interference and that of Gordon becomes a mockery if the authorities are determined to connive at the traffic; therefore the best way is to cease to trouble our heads in England about slavery. The Pall Mall had an article yesterday on the subject in which they quote Dr. Schweinfurth.*

Now as I know everything connected with the Soudan I am convinced that Schweinfurth is right in his accusations against the Egyptian authorities – but I am disgusted at hearing that the trade is still going on – in Upper Egypt.

The position is clearly this – accepting the sincerity of the Khedive – He has given orders to suppress the slave trade. His authorities connive at it – but they will excuse themselves by declaring that the Soudan is so extensive that they cannot watch the movements of slave caravans.

If this excuse is accepted (and it will be) how can we believe that an enormous extension of territory will secure the desired end?

If the authorities cannot watch the Soudan, how will they guard Central Africa?

The only way to stop slave hunting is to declare it piracy.

If Abou Saood had been imprisoned for life or for 21 years – the slave trade would have ceased – but his pardon and promotion was an encouragement to others.

I enclose a few lines on the recent news from Gordon's people who met the slaves – perhaps Mr Greenwood would not object to accept it, for the Pall Mall – not as coming from me, but pro bono &c as I do not wish my name to appear, although I am disgusted with the Egyptian authorities who evidently ridicule the efforts of both Gordon & myself.

Ever sincerely yrs
Sam W Baker

* Georg August Schweinfurth, 1836–1925, author of *Im Herzen von Afrika ...* translated as *The Heart of Africa. Three years' travels and adventures in the unexplored regions of Central Africa from 1868 to 1871* (Sampson Low, 1873).

Teignmouth
21 Mar [1875]

My dear Mr Macmillan

I never heard of Mr M'Coan* in Egypt – neither have I the least idea who he is – but there are many business people and contractors &c &c in that country whom I never knew, and possibly he may have been engaged in some works – public or otherwise. At all events I shall be happy to give you my opinion if you send me the sheets in print.

The weather has much improved here lately, but the winter has been a series of chilly gales.

I envy you your trip to Italy but I regret to hear that you still suffer from rheumatism as such a complaint is a sad enemy if chronic.

I do not think I shall remain in England next winter – the long dreary months from Novr to April render existence a misery.

We hope to get into our new home about 15 April when the blossoms will make everything cheerful.

Lady Baker begs me to give her kind remembrances to you and hopes that some day we may have the pleasure of seeing you when we shall be fairly settled.

Very sincerely yrs
Sam W Baker

* *The Times* of 1 January 1875 published a somewhat sycophantic letter from J. C. M'Coan about the current state of Egypt. He had submitted to Macmillan a portion of and an outline of a book entitled *Egypt and its Future* which Alexander Macmillan asked Baker to look at (Add.MS. 55397, f. 157). Macmillan did not publish it, but in 1877 Cassell, Petter & Galpin published M'Coan's *Egypt As It Is*.

2 May 1875

My dear Mr Macmillan

A friend of mine Mr. Willcocks [sic]* the author of a book called 'The Sea Fisherman' has asked me to introduce him to you.

The 'Sea Fisherman' is the best book on sea-fishing that I have ever read, and it has gone through three editions published by Longmans & Co.

Such a book will always be a standard work, as the subject is so generally and permanently interesting. The hottest sale would always be during the summer months when everybody takes to the sea for yachting and fishing.

Mr Willcocks wishes to sell the copyright – and if you have no objection I should offer to go halves with you should you purchase it, as I feel confident that the book will be always saleable.

Should you prefer to buy the copyright as the sole monopoly of Macmillan & Co of course I should not have the slightest objection: I only offer to share the purchase as a proof of my opinion of the book.

Mr Willcocks has been connected with 'The Field' since 1863 as a regular correspondent.

Mr Willcocks' address is No 1 Powderham Terrace Teignmouth. Will you kindly address a note to him in reply to this.

I may mention that the last edition of the Sea Fisherman was issued (1000) this spring therefore Longmans & Co have some copies on hand

Very truly yours
Sam W Baker

We moved into our new home yesterday 1 May.

* James Carrall Wilcocks, *The Sea Fisherman.* Second edition published 1 June 1868, third edition published 13 March 1875. The first edition had been published, probably in 1865, for the author by S. Barbet in Guernsey. Longman went on to publish a fourth edition on 5 April 1884.

George Craik replied to Baker on 4 May, thanking him for the offer but declining: 'Our practice is not to take another publisher's books. It is a matter of courtesy & honor, & I must not depart from the rule in this case ...' (Add.MS. 55397, f. 335).

18 July 1875

My dear Mr Macmillan

About this time last year when some unpleasant opinions were expressed relating to the conduct of the Khedive's expedition under my command – we frequently said that 'our time would arrive when the real truth would come out'.

Of course every one now knows that I was just towards Abou Saood who has only met with merited disgrace at the hands of Colonel Gordon; but I think you will be interested to learn the opinion that my successor has expressed in a very long and gratifying letter addressed to myself which I received last week.

Colonel Gordon writing from the country of the Bari about eighteen miles south of Gondokoro in which he has now had long experience – says

'I do not credit you with cruelty to the natives ... The necessity that induced you personally to fire upon the natives I agree to, for had you not done so, what with the bad shooting of the soldiers and their newness to war, you would perhaps have been all massacred ...

You may rest assured that whatever may be said to the disparagement of your proceedings, there will remain the fact that you have done more for these countries than any living man can or will do hereafter, and history will never put my puny efforts in any way near your own.'

This generous appreciation of the results of my labors expressed by so honorable and capable a man as Colonel Gordon who is actually now in the heart of the country and among my former enemies, is a great reward to me for all the hard work and anxiety that I suffered in the earnest endeavour to do good during our long sojourn in Africa.

I always felt sure that the waspish cavilling that appeared in print from time to time could never emanate from so chivalrous a man as Gordon.

Of course you cannot publish any extracts from Col. Gordon's letter, but as you were in communication with Mr Greenwood – I feel sure it would be gratifying to him to know the real truth as it were from Colonel Gordon's lips.

To me it is a great pleasure that no paltry spirit of rivalry can exist between Gordon and myself and I feel sure that we both work with one spirit for the same end, trying to do 'our duty in that state of life in which it has pleased God to call us' – If ever you publish a 2nd edition of Ismailia omit everything in Appendix reflecting upon the appointment of Abou Saood.

Believe me sincerely yrs
Sam W Baker

10 Decr 1875

My dear Mr Macmillan

I returned here from a visit in Cornwall this evening and found your note with many others waiting for me.

You must really take great care of yourself this trying weather as such a severe attack of bronchitis as you have suffered will make you very susceptible of a return of the complaint – I suffered in many ways for quite twelve-months after the attack of pneumonia that got hold of me when I arrived from Africa. It left in addition to physical weakness, a wretched depression of the nervous system that magnified trifles into cares of great importance. Since I left London I have been as strong as ever. I wish you would take a run down here for change of air. I think it would do you good if you like quiet, and Lady Baker and I will do all we can to make you comfortable – but I am afraid you will feel dull after the daily excitement of London. If you can come, I hope you will drop us a line to say you can arrive about 20 Inst and spend Xmas with us.

I can fully understand your scruples in publishing anything of Col. V. Baker's* at the present moment. From your silence I concluded that you declined – therefore when I ran up to town for a day or two to attend the Geographical meeting I saw Col V. Baker – and I also met Capt Barton who said perhaps Chatto & Windus would do it. They have arranged with Col Baker to publish his travels in the Perso Indian frontier – as I hear this day from him.

'Entre nous' I am afraid that it will serve to bring his name before the Press again and subject him to remarks that will be galling – I should have preferred to wait until I were once more independent.

I have today received a long letter from Colonel Gordon dated October 1. It is written in so chivalrous a spirit and altogether it is so painfully expressive of his deep appreciation of all my difficulties which he by sad experience now fully understands, that I felt bound to send it to Sir Henry Rawlinson. When he returns it, I will send it to you, or shew it to you if you will give us the pleasure of a visit here.

Poor Gordon seems quite broken-hearted at the impossibility of doing good – : speaking of the natives he repeats these miserable words 'hopeless, hopeless !'

With kind regards to Mr Craik
Very sincerely yrs
Sam W Baker

* Valentine Baker, 1827–1887, Sir Samuel's brother and author of *Clouds in the East: travels and adventures on the Perso-Turkoman frontier* (Chatto & Windus, 1876).

26 Decr 1875

My dear Mr McMillan [sic]

It was very kind of you to send me Monteiro's* new book on West Coast – Congo which I have quickly read straight through.

It gives a great amount of useful information and is no doubt thoroughly trustworthy as there is a fearless independence of expression ...

My last letter from Gordon dated 2 October is very strong on this subject.

I hope we shall be able to persuade him to write a book and that you will publish it.

Lady Baker and I are very sorry that your visit is sine die.

We are so distressed to-day at hearing of the death of poor Lord Stanhope – he was a dear old friend of ours.

Pray accept from us both every kind wish of the season – with the same coupled with best remembrances to Mr Craik

Very sincerely yrs
Sam W Baker

* Joachim John Monteiro, *Angola and the River Congo* (Macmillan, 1875).

20 Jany 1876

My dear Mr Craik

I return you the enclosed receipt which you forwarded together with the balance, for which pray accept my acknowledgements.

I wish you could fix some time that would suit your own convenience to pay us a visit here – as <u>you</u> were the mentor who first discovered this place in the 'Times' and so kindly took me to Stanford's to look it out on the map. The reason that it was not to be found was simple, as it <u>was not built</u> when the map was made.

Lady Baker and I shall be very glad if you can find time to visit us. Of course we look best in summer – but if your leisure is greater in winter pray select your own opportunity.

I tried to tempt Mr Macmillan but he was too much engaged.

What do you think of doing respecting 'Ismailia'?

I think from what I hear from outsiders that it was too expensive for any general circulation on an extended scale.

<u>Numbers</u> of my friends <u>have not yet read it</u>, as they get tired of useless applications to circulating libraries which had a very limited number owing to the high price.

Bickers & Son told me it was much too dear for a popular work. Several booksellers said the same when the work was announced.

I cannot help thinking that a cheap edition would sell well.

When Colonel Gordon comes home I feel sure that he will decline to publish a book – but in a letter to me he has expressed a very chivalrous wish to publish the difficulties that <u>I</u> had to overcome. I think it might be arranged that he might bring out a work as a third volume to Ismailia – he and Macmillan & Co taking all profits until the first edition balanced; – when I might come in as a shareholder.

With best wishes for the new Year
Very Sincerely yrs
Sam W Baker

18 Feby 1876

Messrs Macmillan & Co.

My dear Sirs

I enclose you a letter that I have received from Messrs Cassell & Co which please return. I wrote in reply that I could not give an answer as it would require consideration &c.

Nothing would induce me to write for any publisher than yourselves without first communicating with you and giving you the option of priority.

I could not write such a work on Egypt as is now required without again visiting the country and obtaining information from headquarters which could not be procured secondhand.

I should not like to go there in the summer – but I have written to enquire whether a work on Egypt would be agreeable to the Khedive?

If so, I could obtain most valuable information and the work might be made exhaustive as a standard book of reference. There is no doubt that England is destined to occupy the position of a protectorate in Egypt although we should not assume it without urgent reasons.

A dependable work upon the country is much required, as nothing except tourist twaddle has been written since Lane's* incomparable old work 'Modern Egyptians' – It would take me quite twelve months to prepare and write such an important work.

Very faithfully yours
Sam W Baker

* Edward William Lane, 1801–1876, *An Account of the Manners and Customs of the Modern Egyptians* (Charles Knight, 1836). Alexander Macmillan wrote in a letter of 22 February: 'I think there is no doubt that a good book from you on Egypt & her resources would have a considerable sale. Lane's book was excellent for its time & indeed remains a standard work. But of course your personal & recent knowledge must give great & fresh interest to such a book ... If you were inclined to undertake such a book for us we would of course be delighted to give you two thirds of profits as they accrue. But I fancy what Cassells want is a large pictorial work such as one sees advertised on all hoardings. I don't know if you would care to undertake that ... (Add.MS. 55398, f. 925).

16 July 1876

Messrs Macmillan & Co

Dear Sirs

Pray accept my best thanks for the interesting volume you have kindly forwarded to me – 'Journal of Augustus Margary'.* Poor fellow, he has added one to the list of many who have been sacrificed in opening a new route through wild countries!

I am glad to see that the geography of the 'Albert N'yanza' is proved.

You will also see by the enclosed telegram I have received from the Revd Horace Waller** that in all probability my theory is correct that a communication exists between the Albert and Tanganyika.

With kind regards to your Mr Macmillan & Mr Craik
Sincerely Yours
Sam W Baker

* Augustus Raymond Margary, 1846–1875, *The Journey of Augustus Raymond Margary from Shanghae to Bhamo, and Back to Manwyne* (Macmillan, 1876).
** Horace Waller, 1833–1896, author of pamphlets on Central and East Africa, and of an account of David Livingstone's death added to his *Last Journals*.

22 July 1876

My dear Mr Macmillan

I much regret to see in the Pall Mall list of deaths that you have lost a nephew – and I am also very very sorry to see by your note that you have been suffering so severely from sciatica and I also regret that when you were so near us as Bath you did not let us have a line of notice to be followed directly by yourself – I should much enjoy a visit from you.

I think you are quite right to bring out a cheap edition of Ismailia as I believe the high price of the first was against an extended sale.

I should alter the appendix and there are many little alterations that might be made with advantage by curtailing the book.

In reply to Messrs Cassell & Co's letters I left the Egyptian book <u>open</u> – as I did not feel justified in coming to any decision until I had myself been to Egypt.

I would rather remain free and if I can obtain the information that I require – the manuscript would be valuable; – but <u>without</u> special information it would be merely the historical pudding that any literary cook could produce.

Very Sincerely Yours
Sam W Baker

6 Novr 1876

My dear Mr Macmillan

I enclose a note from Miss Channells who wishes me to introduce her to your firm. This will explain her object without preface from me.

I have advised her <u>not</u> to publish a journal – as it would offend the Khedive – but I think such a title as

'The Court of Egypt
and
Life and Death of Princess Zeneb
Daughter of H.H. the Khedive[']

would sell well.

I knew poor little Princess Zeneb when she was a child. She was brought up strictly as European by Miss Maclean – daughter of General Maclean who educated at the same time Ibrahim Pasha – her brother.

She afterwards married at far too early an age – and I believe died of grief at some separation from her husband and brother of whom she was devotedly fond. I do not know Miss Channell's [sic] powers, but she should produce a nice little book from such materials – as she had the advantage of being Zeneb's governess.

I have advised Miss Channell [sic] to call upon you.

With kind regards to Mr Craik
very Sincerely yours
Sam W Baker

If you were to write her to fix a time for an interview – I am sure she would feel obliged. Her address Miss Channells 29 Hereford Square South Kensington.

26 Decr 1876

My dear Mr Macmillan

All the happiness that you may wish for! is my Xmas ejaculation.

I send you by book Post some printed matter that you may perhaps think worthy of a place in your Magazine – 'First Instincts of Adoration in Primitive Man'.*

The idea is not common and it will form a lecture that I have to give on 4 Jany at the Exeter Lity Socy. It was put off from 23 Decr as I was engaged.

I quite dropped the idea of an Egyptian book for Cassell, Petter, & Galpin as I am a bad hand at Mill-work, and can only write when I am in the humour – I also believe that a man cannot serve two masters – or even Publishers.

If the winter should prove wintry I think we shall take a run to Egypt and then go to Constple. in the spring and home through Italy to arrive in end of May.

Lady Baker joins me in kind regards to you, and pray give all the best wishes of the season from me to Mr Craik.

Very Sincerely Yours
Sam W Baker

* On 30 December 1876 George Craik wrote to Baker a masterpiece of the polite brush-off: 'Mr Macmillan has given me your lecture which I have read carefully, and I hope you will not think I undervalue your work when I say that I would prefer at present not to have an article on that subject. It is at all times a risky one for a magazine of general miscellaneous character like mine; and one ought to have some excuse for publishing it, such as some new or original research or discovery – to which your lecture with all its merits does not make claim ...' (Add.MS. 55401, f. 264).

Many happy New Years!
30 Decr 1876

My dear Mr Macmillan

When I wrote to you a very long time ago on the subject of Colonel Gordon I suggested that on his return <u>if</u> he should write a book it might possibly be arranged to combine an abridged edition of Ismailia with it. This was entirely a suggestion or idea of my own, but from letters I received from him subsequent to that idea (which I never mentioned to him) I should not think he would <u>publish anything</u>.

Some time ago he wrote to me expressing his opinion that I should not have exposed the weaknesses of the Egyptians by 'Ismailia'.

If any work upon an expedition is published – either the whole narrative or nothing should see daylight – I wrote all exactly as it happened, and I believe it was most distasteful to the Egyptn. authorities. If you read 'Naked Truths of Naked People'* written by Colonel Long who formed part of Col. Gordon's staff you will see that everyone thought the employment of Abou Saood a mistake.

The best men must make mistakes sometimes, and it does not matter now – But, if the whole history of the late expedition were written with the perhaps foolish honesty of 'Ismailia' you would find quite as many or more wars & bloodshed (all necessary I am sure) in the Gordon expedition as in the Baker ... Thirty six of the poor 40 Thieves** together with the French officer Linant de Bellefords were killed by the Moogi – (Baris). Then the Moogis had to be subdued by Gordon.

All these have been without doubt the necessary steps in the enterprise, but according to the tendencies of penny-a-liners in the English Press such things had better not be published as they invite hostile criticism. The Times correspondent at Alexandria says that Gordon cut through the obstacles of the White Nile 'as graphically described by Baker'.

The Nile had been opened by Ismail Ayoob Pasha through my instructions! and was perfectly clear before Gordon arrived at Khartoum or that he steamed up to Gondokoro in a wonderfully short time (I think 19 days) in one of the steamers I had sent up from Cairo –!

The fact is that the man who plants the tree seldom eats the fruit – Gordon has done this work very ably and very well but the whole of the material was organised and carried up by myself including all the steamers, iron magazines – boats – merchandize &c &c – He found the Nile open and navigable with seven steamers all at work on the river – one of which I constructed at Gondokoro and the other six I had sent from Cairo up all the cataracts to Khartoum.

He found my garrisoned stations

1. Gondokoro – Lat N 4°.54' 350 men
2. Fatiko – Lat 3° 300 men
3. Fabbo – " 3° – 22 miles East of Fatiko – 150 men
4. Foweera – Lat. 2° 5' – 250 men
5. Farragalla " 3°.20' – 60 "

I am sure Colonel Gordon would be the last man to endorse erroneous statements in the Press as to his cutting the Nile open &c but no one can possibly reply to or contradict one half the gushing twaddle of newspapers.

He has done all that could be done and still the thing is not half done yet. This shews what I had to do as the <u>beginner</u> – I don't think he will write a book and I think he will be wise, as he would raise up a host of ignorant critics whom he might despise, but they would nevertheless bother him like vermin.

Gordon very manfully accepted the whole responsibility and stuck to his work after the entire European Staff either died or returned to England – and he will fully deserve all the Kudos he will receive.

Very truly yours
Sam W Baker

* Charles Chaille-Long, 1842–1917, *Central Africa: naked truths of naked people* (Sampson Low, 1876).
** Baker's personal bodyguard of Egyptian and Sudanese soldiers.

16 Jany 1878

Dear Mr Grove

I shall be very happy to write anything for your Magazine – but I think in re Stanley it would be better to wait until he shall have arrived in England.

The Geographical Socy are going to give him a great welcome and I shall come up for the occasion.

Last year it was touch and go that they did not pass a vote of censure upon him at the invidious instance of a Mr Hyndman who attacked him in the Pall Mall Gazette.

There was a great row raised at the time, and I think Stanley will most likely request Mr Hyndman who is F.R.G.S. to explain his reasons publicly.

I thought the attack most unfair in Stanley's absence and I did all I could sub rosa to assist by writing in his cause to the President.

There are always such venomous characters in English society whose literary ability would be un-noticed unless the pen is dipped in scandal.

Ever Sincerely Yours
Sam W Baker

23 Jany 1878

Many thanks for the cheque
I enclose official receipt

My dear Mr Macmillan

I was glad to see your handwriting again, and I will send you the revised edition of Ismailia when I shall have had a talk with Mr Stanley about the South end of the Albert N'yanza; as I want to write a new preface.

You sent me a copy (an inter-leaved copy) last year, and I completed the revision for a small edition. I see by the papers that many boat-loads of slaves have been coming down the Nile lately! where is Colonel Gordon?

I shall come to Town next week to meet Stanley. Cannot you become his Publisher?

I wish you had published my brother Jem's book 'Turkey in Europe'*as I believe it has been a success. It is very clever and painstaking. My brother Valentine Baker Pasha ought to write a book after the war and I am sure it would have a large sale. I hope you will do it for him. It is curious that two Pashas should be in one English family. The poor Turks are utterly crumpled up – but although I sympathise with their suffering I am not in the least surprised. They are so jealous and stubborn that they invariably neglect to do the right thing. If they had paid England the compliment to invite her to assume the temporary protection of the Suez Canal, and Gallipoli, they would have enlisted British sympathy at once by showing a regard for British Interests; but they expect us to be a sacrifice for them at the same time that they refuse all confidence.

I think the general row has yet to begin when the true Eastern Question will be exhibited in the terms of peace between Turkey and Russia.

Lady Baker begs me to add her very kind regards to you. With kind remembrance to Mr Craik.

Very truly yrs
Sam W Baker

* James Baker, *Turkey in Europe* (Cassell, Petter & Galpin, 1877).

14 March 1878
[embossed letterhead
Athenæum Club
Pall Mall S.W.]

Dear Mr Macmillan

I called yesterday and unfortunately you were out; but I mentioned to your son that General V. Baker is going to write a book upon the war and the political situation in Turkey. I have recommended him to confine it to two rather small volumes of 320 pages each in good type <u>without any illustrations</u> but only his maps.

I believe the literary world is seeking for his pen, therefore I mention the fact to you in case you would wish to communicate with him. His address I left at your office (92 Jermyn St)

Sincerely Yours
Sam W Baker

Alexander Macmillan replied to Baker the same day (Add.MS. 55405, f. 478) '... we are shrinking from undertaking any book on this Eastern question at present, as we fear that the public will be soon tired of the subject, or get as much as they want in the newspapers. The Daily Newsbook which we published on the Prussian-Frankish war sold four or five times as much as the book we have just issued on this, and yet the writing is as good as it can be ...'

30 May 1878

My dear MacMillan [sic]

Lady Baker has an idea of submitting to me her journals (which were very carefully kept throughout many years in Africa) in order that I might arrange them for publication under the title of 'Our Huts and Homes in Africa'.* There are a thousand little homely scenes and incidents – many connected with the native children and women which in the rougher sphere of my own career were never noted by me.

I will not edit her journals unless I know that you would like to have them, so I shall await your reply.

I heard from Gordon a few weeks ago – dated from Berbera on the Red Sea. My nephew Julian who is first lieutenant of the flag-ship 'Undaunted' had been travelling with Gordon in the interior for a few days and they both took a mutual fancy to each other.

It appears that Gordon who must be a very chivalrous character has taken a pleasure in unearthing and demolishing those who were my secret enemies during the difficult task I had undertaken in laying the foundations for freedom and demolishing the slave hunter's business in Central Africa ...

Gordon's experience of four years of my old territory is very satisfactory to me; and from time to time I receive letters from old officers and servants who served under me which shew that some seeds fell upon good ground even upon the wilderness of Central Africa.

I am sufficiently weak to enjoy and appreciate these simple tributes to 'auld lang syne' more than worldly honours. If you can spare time to come and see us here in our lovely home both my wife and I shall be very happy.

Sincerely yours
Sam W Baker

* Macmillan was keen on the idea but the book was never published in this form. Some of her journals were edited by Anne Baker and published as *Morning Star: Florence Baker's diary of the expedition to put down the slave trade on the Nile, 1870–1873* (Kimber, 1972).

[summer 1878]

My dear Mr Macmillan

Some months ago your firm sent the interleaved copies of Ismailia and I carefully revised them, cutting out several things, and especially the Appendix. I will now write a new preface and then forward the books to you.

Gordon's work will of course render the new preface interesting as it will form a sequel to the original. We are rather lazy here with regard to 'Huts and Homes in Central Africa' as the summer is lovely, the house full of friends, and life is passed out of doors. Wet weather and winter are the times for writing – when in the country.

I have to write a review for the 'Quarterly' upon a very nice book 'Thirteen Years with the Wild Beasts of India' by Sanderson.* This is published by Allen & Co.

I suggested to Mr Sanderson that he should submit his manuscript to you; and he had the intention of doing so, but the friend to whom he dedicated his work (Colonel Malleson) had already arranged the matter for him with Allen & Co. It is the best book on elephants that I have ever read.

My nephew Julian will return home in Septr from the M ... [?] station. Gordon has taken an immense fancy to him. It is very curious now to see the actors who were behind the scenes opposing the expedition in my time, brought forward and un-masked by Gordon.

Very Sincerely Yours
Sam W Baker

* George P. Sanderson, *Thirteen Years among the Wild Beasts of India: their haunts and habits from personal observations; with an account of the modes of capturing and taming elephants* (W.H. Allen, 1878). Baker's review, entitled 'Elephant-catching' appeared in *The Quarterly Review*, 292 (October 1878), pp. 361–84.

Brook Hill
Dartmouth
1 Septr 1878

My dear MacMillan [sic]

I send you by Book Post the Preface for new edition of '<u>Ismailia</u>'. It will make the fresh volume interesting as I have shown in a very few pages the immense changes and progress that have taken place in Egypt since I first started the project of an expedition to open the Nile Basin and to suppress the slave trade.

I firmly believe that English influence in Egypt dates from that period, and that my appointment to a supreme command under that Government was the thin edge of the wedge which has since broken up the power of the local Pashas and administrators of the old school.

I shall run home for a day next week and will then forward to you the volumes of Ismailia corrected & revised for new edition, which are completed.

We intend to make rather an extensive Eastern journey and shall leave England towards the end of October. I shall see you before this.

With kind regards from Lady Baker.
Very Sincerely Yours
Sam W Baker

Sandford Orleigh
Newton Abbot
2 Octr 1878

My dear Mr Macmillan

I sent off today by train the parcel of revised 'Ismailia', and I hope the new edition will be a success. There is a dearth of 'Africa' in the market just at present, so it may come in at a good time.

I think the 'Times' will be courteous if you can get them to review it. Mr MacDonald wrote to me a short time ago asking me if the editor might make use of some information I had given, for Editorial remarks. I declined to have my name referred to – but I gave him privately a resumé of the progress since I first established English influence in the interior – and I referred to the wanton and utterly groundless attacks made upon me some years ago in the columns of the Times by a drunken scoundrel of a mechanical fitter or engineer of steam engines whose liquor I had stopped in Africa owing to repeated attacks of delirium tremens.

Of course I have been proved to be right in the policy I adopted when employed to suppress the slave-trade; this was unflinching in the suppression of the traffic. Colonel Gordon has persisted in the same course, and British influence is supreme.

When I regard the weakness and vacillation of our Government in foreign policy I confess to a pride in watching the results of our individual efforts.

With kind regards from Lady Baker
Ever yours
Samuel W Baker

We are off to Cyprus next month and I will write a little book that will be a guide.

Sandford Orleigh
Newton Abbot
10 Octr 1878

My dear Mr MacMillan [sic]

Pray accept my thanks for the book on Cyprus, but I was much shocked to see in the advertisement of publications at the end of the volume an extract from a private letter to me from Colonel Gordon! – heading the advertisement of 'Ismailia'.

I shall feel so humiliated and ashamed at this breach of confidence that I must immediately explain my innocence to him.* His letters to me are strictly private, and you will remember that when I confided his letter to you nearly three years ago authorizing you to shew it privately to the Editor of the Pall Mall Gazette, it was with the express stipulation that it was not to be published.

If Colonel Gordon were to publish any extract from a private letter of mine laudatory of himself I should lose all respect for his character and accuse him of the worst possible taste – but he never would condescend to such a false step.

I can assure you I never felt so humiliated or ashamed of myself. Pray take every means to suppress the unauthorized publication of such an extract which will lose me many friends, as although innocent I shall be charged with a gross breach of confidence.

Very truly yours
Sam W Baker

* Baker wrote to Gordon the same day – the letter is in the British Library (Add.MS. 52388, ff. 14–15). He huffed and puffed at some length, and the irony is that he got it completely wrong. In a letter dated October 11, Alexander Macmillan explained 'The extract from Colonel Gordon was not taken from a private letter, but from the "Proceedings of the Royal Geographical Society" published Dec. 31 1875. You are in no sense responsible for our action in this matter ... If you wish it we will destroy all the catalogues containing the extract and never use it again.'

13 Octr 1878

My dear Mr Macmillan

I was very glad to receive your note and I really do not like to ask you to destroy anything that would entail trouble and expense. I have no idea for how long? this extract from Colonel Gordon's letter has been published? – but a great friend of mine expressed a horror equal to my own when he heard of the circumstances of its publication as an advertisement for the book!!

I wrote to Colonel Gordon immediately and enclosed him a copy of the note I had addressed to you together with the slip of advertising sheet which I cut out of the book in Cyprus. He may not think as much of it as I do, but I think he will.

I have read Mr Hamilton Lang's 'Cyprus'* and some friends who are staying with me knew him while in Egypt.

If you ask my opinion of his book I should say it gave him some trouble to compile but there is too much extracted matter in the way of Ancient History &c which you can obtain in any Cyclopaedia and there is a great lack of descriptive power and brightness. I cannot understand the features of the country in the least degree – he gives no information regarding the natural history of the island birds, beasts, fishes, nor of the general appearance of the surface.

I am having gipsy vans built by Fison in Cambridge which will be a new and interesting way of travelling in the East.

Very truly yours
Sam W Baker

* Robert Hamilton Lang, *Cyprus: its history, its present resources, and future prospects* (Macmillan, 1878).

Octr 18 – 1878

My dear Mr MacMillan [sic]

I return proof of Preface corrected. If you will please send one two or three copies of it I will send one to Mr MacDonald of the Times, as it will give him a very clear and concise resumé of the work that has been accomplished, and will be good material for a review. I will also send one to Colonel Gordon. I heard from him the day before yesterday.

You will I feel sure adopt whatever steps you may think right to suppress any further publication of the extract from his private letter to me. From the contents of his long and interesting communications to me he places the most thorough confidence, and I should indeed feel distressed if this reliance should be misplaced.

I wrote a review in the Quarterly Review for this month upon Mr Sanderson's work 'Thirteen years with the Wild Beasts of India'. It is titled 'Elephant Catching'. I do not think the Quarterly noticed 'Ismailia'. Do you think they would review the new Edition?

Sincerely yours
Sam W Baker

Trooditissa Monastery Cyprus
11 August 1879

My dear Mr Macmillan

I have finished 'Cyprus as I saw it in 1879' and I will send you the manuscript either by mail or by General Biddulph* when he goes to England next month. I think it will be better to trust it to the mail 'registered' so that you may receive it quickly.

According to my calculation it will make 400 Pages of 34 lines to the page and 10 words to the line including the Introduction. This will be just the right size.

Now that the Afghan and Zulu wars are over, I think we shall have a favorable season if the book is published in November.

I shall enclose with manuscript a photograph of the Van and our start from Larnaca which will make a good print for the outside cover if the artist will reverse the positions and place the Gipsy-van in front – the covered no 2 van, second, and the native cart third – in rear. It will be something new – and will be attractive. The oxen are admirable in the Photograph.

As it will be quite impossible for me to receive and correct proofs unless I could receive them here complete by the 25 September, I must leave all revision to yourselves. I have read carefully through it, and there will not be much to alter except the printer's errors which are sure to occur.

Although there are no stirring incidents in this tame country I have endeavoured to make easy reading by amalgamating all necessary information with the data of daily life instead of jamming it into a compressed form.

What price do you propose to place upon the book? I think it should be arranged so as not to be a bulky volume, as heavy books are generally disliked; perhaps there are sufficient words for two vols. but you will arrange these details according to your own judgment. I think it would be well to advertise it quickly for November so as to obtain early orders from booksellers, and perhaps you could make some arrangement with Harper & Co. of New York.

We are in a Paradise of climate here – with the original old Monks as companions. When you get the Manuscript turn to Chapter 15 which will amuse you as it describes the domestic troubles of the Monks and Monastic life.

Sincerely yours
Sam W Baker

* Sir Michael Anthony Shrapnel Biddulph, 1823–1904, who commanded the Quetta field force during the Afghan war of 1878–79.

Yokohama
28 February 1881

My dear Mr Macmillan

It is long since I have heard from, or written to you. I bought a copy of 'Cyprus' here the other day for a friend, and his first exclamation was 'What? no Map?[']

I do not think that any book on Japan would be worth writing at present as so many books upon the same topic have recently been published.

Miss Isabella Bird's book 'Unbeaten Tracks in Japan'* must nevertheless have sold well. I have read it here, and it is a far better book than Sir E. J. Reed's. **

We shall leave in May for San Francisco, and shall spend late summer and early autumn in a tour through the Rocky Mountains on our way to New York, where we should arrive in October.

Will you please let Harper & Co know that we are coming there, as it may assist in the sale of Ismailia.

We have now been here nine months, and my great amusement has been the study of Japanese art-industry, and forming a very choice collection.

It is a pity that Miss Bird took no interest in what is the chief characteristic of the Japanese – i.e. the peculiar talent of the people for all that appertains to artistic taste.

Her book is good in its way, but there is too much about the 'hairy Chins', and naked people &c, while nothing is said about the artistic productions of the country.

We are going to Tokyo (Jedo)*** this evening to be ready for the opening of the Exhibition tomorrow, which will be by the Mikado in person.

The Exhibition of all the manufactures and productions of Japan will be very interesting. In my opinion the resources of this country have been over-estimated. There are few wealth producing natural advantages. The country is exceedingly mountainous and utterly devoid of any natural pasturage. The soil is poor, and only the level places can be cultivated – but the extreme industry of [the] people, and the careful collection of all that will create manure, supplies the food for 33 millions of inhabitants.

Mineral wealth may possibly be developed when it may suit the Japanese to open their country to foreigners.

At present the imports are in excess of exports, therefore the coin drains away from the country, and the want of confidence in Govt. finance has depreciated the Govt paper money 75 per cent! in the exchange for silver.

Lady Baker begs me to give you her very kind regards. Also please remember me to Mr Craik and Mr Grove. I am quite distressed to hear that my friend Frank Buckland is dead!

Very Sincerely Yours
Sam W Baker

* Isabella Lucy Bird, 1831–1904, *Unbeaten Tracks in Japan: an account of travels in the interior, including visits to the aborigines of Yezo and the shrines of Nikko and Ise* (John Murray, 1880).
** Sir Edward James Reed, 1830–1906, *Japan: its history, traditions, and religions: with the narrative of a visit in 1879* (John Murray, 1880).
*** 'Tokyo founded in 12th cent. as small village called Yedo ...' *Columbia Lippincott Gazetteer of the World*

6
'And Sacred is the Latest Word'
Macmillan and Tennyson's 'final' text

Michael Millgate

Tennyson's first and only publishing contract with the house of Macmillan came into effect in January 1884, when he was already in his seventy-sixth year, and he died in October 1892, before that ten-year agreement had run its course. To speak of Tennyson as a Macmillan author is therefore to speak of him in his old age, a period of his life that I have already to some extent addressed in *Testamentary Acts: Browning, Tennyson, James, Hardy*,[1] a book chiefly dedicated to exploring the (mostly unsuccessful) attempts of writers in late career to ensure that posterity will receive positive impressions of their works and lives. But if some aspects of this present chapter have been anticipated by parts of the Tennyson chapter in *Testamentary Acts* – the quotation in my title (from 'To the Marquis of Dufferin and Ava') is invoked there – the focus here is specifically upon the relationships between the Macmillan publishing house and its representatives on the one side and the poet and his representatives on the other. And it narrows further – in contrast to the broad survey already available in June Steffensen Hagen's *Tennyson and his Publishers*[2] – into an exploration of the vexed question of where, if anywhere, is to be found that final text to which both the poet himself and Hallam Tennyson, his intensely loyal son and heir, attached so much importance.

Something must first be said, however, about Alexander Macmillan, whose name occurs with a disappointing infrequency in the standard accounts of Tennyson's life and work. Sir Charles Tennyson evokes the first meeting between the two men in 1859 and speaks of their later 'intimate and happy relations'.[3] Robert Bernard Martin says of the move to Macmillan that Tennyson, while not altogether pleased with the terms of the contract itself, was always on excellent terms with Alexander Macmillan and 'content to have a publisher he could trust and also respect intellectually'.[4] Neither biography, however, documents the bases of that intimacy and mutual trust the two men are said to have enjoyed. Charles Morgan's references to Tennyson are, for once, unhelpful,[5] while Hallam Tennyson, in *Alfred Lord Tennyson: a memoir*, alludes to the relationship in terms ostensibly positive but at the same time somewhat distant and patronising:

> With none of the publishers into whose hands circumstances had thrown my father, was the connection so uninterruptedly pleasant as with Messrs Macmillan, unless perhaps that with Mr Henry King. Alexander Macmillan's genuine enthusiasm for his authors was especially remarkable.[6]

It is not easy to think of Tennyson, notoriously a hard bargainer, as being thrown helplessly by 'circumstances' into the hands of his successive publishers, and while there had been genuine difficulties with Moxon and Kegan Paul,[7] Hallam's remark was perhaps tinged by the standard contemporary categorisation of publishing as 'trade'. Of Macmillan's enthusiasm for Tennyson's works, on the other hand, there can be no doubt. He had devotedly followed the successive titles from the two-volume *Poems* of 1842 onwards, published in the second issue of *Macmillan's Magazine* a defence of *Maud* written (under a pseudonym) by himself,[8] and seems always to have nursed the hope of one day adding the name of Alfred Tennyson to the Macmillan list.[9] He published volumes by Tennyson's elder brother Charles in 1864 and 1868, and when the contract with Tennyson himself came into effect in January 1884 he told Emily Tennyson:

> It is just forty years since I first read 'Poems by Alfred Tennyson', and got bitten by a healthy mania from which I have not recovered – and don't want to recover. I then tried to bite others, with some success. I have now other, I cannot say deeper motives for continuing the process. How much I owe to Alfred Tennyson for the increase of ennobling thought & feeling, no one can tell. Now our closer connection will not lessen my desire to repay the debt.[10]

It was with obvious satisfaction that he passed on to Emily Tennyson six months later a 'beautiful' remark of Dante Gabriel Rossetti's: 'You never can open Tennyson at the wrong place.'[11]

Macmillan's relations with the Tennysons were of course intensified by the business arrangement begun in 1884, but he had in fact been on friendly terms with the family for some 25 years. Tennyson dined with the Macmillans in Cambridge in 1859 and, later, at Tooting,[12] and sometimes attended the Thursday evening 'Tobacco parliaments' that Alexander hosted during the firm's first few years in London, once staying on in the unimaginably smoke-filled room until half-past-one in the morning.[13] Macmillan for his part visited the Tennysons at Farringford and Aldworth on several occasions, and correspondence surviving from the years prior to 1884 testifies to a continuing connection, at once professional and personal, between the two families.[14]

The relationship was perhaps not uniformly easy. Macmillan's long self-introductory letter to Emily Tennyson of September 1859, though clearly sincere, now seems embarrassingly fulsome,[15] and a few years later, in June 1864, she suspected him of persuading her husband, over dinner, to adopt for his next volume a title of which she herself disapproved.[16] A month after that, in July 1864, William Allingham recorded Macmillan as declaring that he and his brother Daniel and their sister 'used to have better conversations together on literature than he [had] ever heard since "from Tennyson and all the rest of them"'.[17] Much more recently the editors of *The Letters of Alfred Lord Tennyson* have commented negatively on Alexander Macmillan's prudishness over the text of 'Lucretius', the long poem about the power of sexual passion that Tennyson published in *Macmillan's Magazine* for May 1868. But if Macmillan does not emerge especially well from the episode when judged by present-day standards, it can at least be said that Tennyson himself acceded – temporarily at least – to the modest bowdlerisation involved, and that the crucial issue, as so often in that period, seems to have been not so much the personal responses of the magazine's owner and editors as their fearful and perhaps exaggerated sensitivity to what their readers would and would not accept.[18]

Tennyson certainly contributed to *Macmillan's Magazine* on a number of occasions before and after 'Lucretius' – his 'Sea Dreams: an idyll' had appeared there as early as the third issue, in January 1860 – and the overall impression that emerges from the limited evidence available is of a friendship warmly if not very intensively kept up on both sides and reinforced from time to time by mutually satisfactory business dealings – among them, presumably, the £300 that Macmillan & Co. paid for the

280 lines of 'Lucretius'.[19] It was, in any case, a friendship that provided the basis for a congenial and highly successful author–publisher relationship. With the ten-year Macmillan contract, signed in September 1883, operative as of 15 January 1884, Tennyson effectively arrived – rather as Hardy would do some 18 years later – at a secure and comfortable anchorage for his creatively active final years.

The contract provided, specifically, for a guaranteed (that is, non-returnable) annual advance of £1,500 against royalties of one-third on the published price of all titles.[20] At the end of 1892 – a year made exceptional not only by Tennyson's death but by the publication of two new titles – the total remitted by Macmillan was an astonishing £10,390, although a comparable figure (£10,328) was subsequently reached only in 1897, the year of publication of Hallam's *Memoir* of his father, and the overall tendency of the royalties was persistently downwards.[21] To Alexander Macmillan, Tennyson's long-sought accession brought much personal satisfaction.[22] For the Macmillan house Tennyson's name translated into higher revenues and, no less importantly, into enhanced prestige, to the point that the firm's increasingly confident rise to the position of leading literary publisher of the day might be said to have culminated in its triumphant organisation of the national event that was Tennyson's funeral on 12 October 1892. Still preserved in the British Library's Macmillan archive is the mass of letters received from those seeking tickets of admission to the Westminster Abbey service.[23]

Part of the difficulty of 'reading' the later stages of the Alfred Tennyson–Alexander Macmillan relationship is that it was so largely conducted by proxy. As early as 1874 Hallam Tennyson, the older of the Tennysons' sons, had been summoned home from Cambridge, without completing his degree, in order to share with – and largely take over from – his ailing mother those secretarial and other practical roles she had always played in her husband's life, but to which she no longer felt equal.[24] From that time onwards, and despite the persistence of Emily Tennyson's active interest in such matters, the bulk of the specifically business correspondence emanating from Farringford and Aldworth was written in Hallam's contorted hand and, for the most part, over his signature. Several of his letters to the Macmillan house in the mid-1880s are addressed to Alexander Macmillan – with whom he had, of course, been acquainted since childhood – but as the Macmillan empire expanded during the century's final decades its affairs increasingly shifted into younger hands. Daniel Macmillan's sons, Frederick and Maurice, moved into leading positions, as did Alexander's own son George, and the firm also depended on such able employees as David

Masson (later Professor of Rhetoric and English Literature at Edinburgh University) and George Grove (of the *Dictionary of Music and Musicians*), Masson's successor as editor of *Macmillan's Magazine*. During the exchanges over 'Lucretius' Tennyson began one of his letters 'My dear Grove, or Macmillan'.[25]

Especially important during the latter decades of the century was George Lillie Craik, son of a Scottish man of letters, husband of the novelist Dinah Mulock, and a partner in the Macmillan firm from 1865. Until his death in 1905 it was Craik who conducted most of the firm's dealings with Tennyson and with Tennyson's representatives. He worked directly with Tennyson himself on numerous occasions[26] – Emily Tennyson evidently trusting his judgement rather than her husband's when revisions were in question[27] – but seems to have corresponded almost exclusively with Hallam. Letters did, of course, pass between Craik and Emily Tennyson, and between Hallam Tennyson and one or other of the Macmillans, but from 1887 until Craik's death much of the publication history of Tennyson's works can best be traced by collating Hallam's letters to Craik in the Macmillan archive with Craik's side of the correspondence – as represented thinly by surviving letters in the Tennyson Research Centre, and more comprehensively (if not always legibly) by the copies entered into successive volumes of the Macmillan 'General' and 'Private' letterbooks.

Hallam's tone in these letters is sometimes brisk – in September 1890 he announces that '[t]he alterations given to you have been printed wrong again'[28] – and Craik is on occasion addressed almost as if he were the family's London agent and asked to supply copies of specific books and magazines, order bottles of a special Apollinaris water for Aldworth, or notify *The Times* and the *Morning Post* of the family's annual moves between Farringford and Aldworth.[29] Irritation, too, creeps in when Hallam is forced to deal, after his father's death, with such distracting trivia as hard-to-ignore requests for contributions toward the cost of memorials of which he was sure his father would have disapproved.[30] But it remained an amicable correspondence, overwhelmingly concerned with publishing matters – occasionally, indeed, with items published by Hallam himself [31]– and increasing in intensity from late 1892 onwards as Hallam dedicated himself to the preservation of his dead father's memory and literary fame.

By the terms of his father's will Hallam inherited all surviving 'manuscripts Literary Works and Copyrights',[32] and thus became directly responsible both for the disposition of Tennyson's literary remains and for the future publication of his poetical works. He also succeeded to the peerage his father had accepted late in 1883 – nicely coincident with his move to Macmillan – took his seat in the House of Lords as the 2nd Baron Tennyson, and later spent four years in Australia, as Governor-General first of South Australia and then of the newly federated Commonwealth. But though from time to time preoccupied by these public duties, Hallam always remained profoundly committed to the fulfilment of his formal obligations to his father's estate and his emotional obligations to his father's memory.

In the aftermath of Tennyson's death Hallam saw his most immediate responsibility as the completion of the *Memoir* of his father's life that he had long had in contemplation, and much of the correspondence with Craik during the mid-1890s was necessarily devoted to the planning and preparation of the *Memoir*, to its publication by Macmillan in 1897,[33] and to Hallam's nervousness as to its reception.[34] But kept always in view was Hallam's long-term ambition to prepare and publish an eventual collected edition of Tennyson's works in which the individual poems and plays would be accompanied by the 'authorial notes' which he had himself first elicited during his father's lifetime and subsequently expanded and revised. No other 'critical or annotated edition' would be sanctioned, he told Craik on 23 November 1900, adding, with heavy underlining: 'My Father left me his poems as a sacred trust – to bring out an Annotated Edition myself.'[35]

Hallam's enthusiasm for an annotated edition was always centred upon the annotations rather than upon the texts themselves. He seems to have taken absolutely for granted that what had been left to him as 'a sacred trust' was the text embodied in his father's last-dated acts of publication, modifiable only by changes that Tennyson might at an even later hour have inscribed or voiced. And in fiercely defending the inviolability of that final text he was able to invoke his father's many denunciations of the publication of an author's abandoned readings. He quoted some of those denunciations in the *Memoir*, insisted to Craik in 1895 that Churton Collins, then diligently disinterring the discarded versions of Tennyson's early poems, was someone to be stopped 'at all costs',[36] and subsequently imposed severe restrictions, not lifted until 1969, upon access to Tennyson manuscripts (especially those he had himself given to Trinity College, Cambridge) from which abandoned variants might otherwise have been readily recovered.[37] Curiously, he seems not to have recognised any conflict between these attempts at suppression and his own quotation of rejected passages in the *Memoir*.[38]

Tennyson's immense fame, as reflected in a long series of collective editions and single-volume reissues, had provided many opportunities for textual revision, and the extensive presence of Hallam's own hand in surviving – often multiple – proofs and working copies of his father's successive volumes provides ample evidence of his intimate involvement in those same revisionary processes. He was sharply aware, therefore, of the impermanence of so many of his father's textual choices – the way in which a word, a line, or an entire stanza would be altered once, twice or several times, only to be returned, as often as not, to the original reading. He noted in the *Memoir*, indeed, that 'very often what is published as the latest edition has been the original version in his first manuscript, so that there is no possibility of really tracing the history of what may seem to be a new word or a new passage'.[39] Such habits of persistent reconsideration and long-term provisionality call into question the stability of Tennyson's text as of any given moment.[40] The surviving sets of marked proofs of the posthumously published *The Death of Oenone and Other Poems* show that Tennyson was actively revising, resequencing, and even eliminating poems until just a few days before he died,[41] and I have suggested in *Testamentary Acts* that the onset of illness and death were at least as important as authorial intention in determining the precise moment at which – hence the precise form in which – the Tennysonian text might be said to have become permanently frozen.

It would require far more space than I have here – and a greater research investment than I have yet been able to make – to reconstruct, in detail and through time, the processes by which Tennyson, variously assisted by his wife as well as by Craik and Hallam, corrected multiple proofs of new volumes, transferred his finally endorsed corrections to the various collective editions, and kept those editions more or less textually parallel. Broadly trackable even so, and certainly identifiable as being of special textual importance, are the two editions envisaged (though not specifically named) in Macmillan's original proposal to Tennyson of 27 September 1883: the one-volume *Works* (Wise's 'Collected Edition'), published at seven shillings and six pence in 1884, and the grander ten-volume *Works* (Wise's 'New Collected Edition'), of which the first seven volumes were sold as a set, price thirty-five shillings, in 1884, and the final three added in 1893.[42] Constantly extended and adapted, closely parallel in their texts and structures yet always significantly distinctive, these two editions and their direct, if sometimes disguised, successors – what might crudely be called the one-volume sequence and the multi-volume sequence – provided the principal means by which the Macmillan house conducted its progressive integration of the accumulating Tennyson canon during the poet's lifetime and its remarkably successful, if not entirely consistent, projection of the poet's final textual choices well into the twentieth century.

As originally published in January 1884, the Macmillan one-volume edition included everything that Tennyson wished to retain from what he had published up to that point. It greatly resembled its Kegan Paul one-volume predecessor in size, binding, and double-column layout, but shrewdly got 50 lines to each of those columns as against Kegan Paul's 43. And since Tennyson had published little since *Ballads and Other Poems* of 1880, the contents of the two editions were almost identical, although the addition of a few poems not previously reprinted and the elimination of Kegan Paul's duplication of 'The Golden Supper' serve to confirm that the Macmillan text had indeed been reviewed with some care by the poet himself.[43] In his letter to Emily Tennyson of 16 January 1884, the effective date of the Tennyson contract, Alexander Macmillan wrote: 'I am sending you by this post a copy of our first book as Lord Tennyson's publisher. We have striven to keep it simple & as beautiful as the narrow conditions will allow. We hope by & bye to do worthier editions.'[44]

Macmillan's 'worthier' looked forward to the initial seven-volume set of the 'New Collected' edition, published later that same year, but the one-volume 'Collected' was itself, as he claimed, a handsome and extremely serviceable book in its own right. It was also to prove exceptionally popular and long-lived. There were nine impressions totalling 77,000 copies between January 1884 and November 1888,[45] with minor changes to the second and sixth impressions. 'To Alfred Tennyson My Grandson', for example, the dedication to *Ballads and Other Poems*, was unintentionally omitted from the first impression but squeezed into the second, awkwardly and in a reduced font, between the end of 'The Lover's Tale' and the beginning of 'The First Quarrel', remaining thus throughout the subsequent history of the edition.[46] Somewhat perversely, the title of the seven-line poem appeared – and continued to appear – in the Contents entirely in capitals, as if it were a volume in itself.

The original plates – or possibly duplicate plates[47] – used throughout these early printings also provided the bulk of the text for the considerably expanded version of the one-volume edition brought out in February 1889 to accommodate the poems and plays published since the beginning of the Macmillan contract. Incorporation of the contents of *Tiresias and Other Poems* was in itself a straightforward matter of setting up additional pages in the same font. Much of the existing text, however, had to be disrupted and repaginated to permit the insertion of 'The Marriage of Geraint' and 'Balin and Balan' into the (thus completed) structure of *Idylls of the King*, and the opportunity was taken to group together the four new plays and the two existing plays at the end of the volume. As a result the newly set *Tiresias* poems were followed by the existing but now renumbered settings of *Queen Mary* and *Harold*, and then by the new settings of *Becket*, *The Cup*, *The Falcon*, and *The Promise of May*.

This 1889 redaction of the one-volume 'Collected' – enlarged and restructured but still retaining much of the original 1884 setting – went through ten more impressions over the next five years, three of them in 1892, the year of Tennyson's death.[48] In September 1894 it re-emerged, still further enlarged, as the first one-volume 'Complete' edition, so described on its half-title though not on the title-page itself. The first 803 pages of the 1894 volume (up to the end of *The Promise of May*) reproduced the entire text of 1889 as modified by subsequent minor revisions – many of them anticipated in an authorially corrected copy of the 1889 text now in the Berg collection – and the quiet insertion of the sonnet 'To W. C. Macready' into what had been a vacant space following the last of the poems from the *Tiresias* volume. Added from page 804 onwards, and of course newly set, were the contents of Tennyson's last volumes, beginning with *Demeter and Other Poems*, of December 1889, continuing with *The Death of Oenone and Other Poems*, published posthumously in late October 1892, and concluding with *The Foresters*, of March 1892. 'Crossing the Bar' was inserted, in accordance with Tennyson's expressed wish, at the very end of the volume, but the placement of *The Foresters* caused grave distress to Hallam and his mother, who valued *The Death of Oenone* volume highly and regarded *The Foresters* neither as the poet's final work nor as in any sense his culminating achievement.

The family's shock upon receiving a copy of the published volume was conveyed to Craik in an extravagant letter of Hallam's that began with an angry abruptness emphasised by the absence of any salutation:

> This is a terrible mistake of yours – How can it have happened that you thought of not placing 'Oenone' his last will & testament at the end? It has made my mother very ill – I fear that she is fading away gradually – I have summoned Dr Dabbs.[49] He will move her to the Island, I think.

Having thus accused Craik of driving Emily Tennyson to an early death by his dastardly act of editorial malfeasance, Hallam went on to enumerate his secondary sins:

(1) You promised to put for her To E.T. at the top of 'June Bracken'
(2) also this note to 'Crossing the Bar' [My father asked me always to print 'Crossing the Bar' at the end of his collected works. T.]
(3) Don't you remember that my mother wrote herself actually to you to put as a note to De Profundis (To H.T. Begun Aug 11th 1852)
You really must send me the proofs of all new Editions. I promised him always to take the same care of his proofs as I had always done. In consequence, because he trusted me, he made me his sole literary executor. We thought that you would at all accounts be sure to send proofs of this his complete works, and that they wd be published for a Xmas book.

I am sorry, Craik, after all your kindness, I should have to write thus about what you must see to be carelessness. We cannot in the least understand it except that you must have been away for your holidays.
Yours in deep anguish of spirit

Tennyson[50]

Some of the complexities of Hallam's position emerge very clearly here, not least among them his relationships on the one hand with his strongly emotional and gently authoritarian mother (evidently the source of much of the letter's energy and urgency)[51] and on the other with the experienced, businesslike, and normally co-operative Craik. He seems also to have felt a deep sense of guilt at having betrayed his father's trust and specific testamentary instructions by failing, for whatever reason, to keep a sufficiently close check on the final stages of the new collective volume.

In the event Craik apologised, promised appropriate corrections, and sought an early restoration of good relations between the Tennysons and the house of Macmillan. Hallam, writing on 11 October, reported his mother as thanking Craik for his 'kind message' but grieving at his inability to recognise his 'blunder with respect to [Tennyson's] feeling & all feeling of art'. He added: 'Of course we thought that your single volume edition would follow the ten volume edition in having the last published volume last before "Crossing the Bar".'[52] On 14 October Craik wrote to Lady Tennyson directly, addressing Hallam's criticisms one by one in conciliatory fashion but gently insisting that he had not been given 'specific instructions' on these points.[53] Lady Tennyson replied next day that she and Hallam 'could not bear that even the semblance of a shadow should come between us and you who have been so true a friend in your kindness & sympathy'.[54]

The responsiveness of Craik and the Macmillan house to the Tennysons' complaints about the 1894 volume was prompted, of course, by good will but also by a clear-eyed recognition of both the short-term profitability and likely long-term importance of an edition that gathered within a moderately priced and attractively produced (if double-columned) single volume all of the poems and plays that Tennyson had publicly chosen to preserve. Craik was therefore prepared to make the relatively modest changes requested by the poet's family in order to regain their approval and establish the claim that the edition fully embodied Tennyson's final wishes. In the revised 'complete' edition of 1895 the first 803 pages, up to the conclusion of *The Promise of May*, appeared, at a first glance, unchanged from the edition of 1894. In fact, a dedication to Hallam had been added to 'De Profundis' on page 532 and the text of 'Kate' (an early poem of 31 lines that Hallam seems particularly to have admired) inserted on page 24, the disruption to the setting of type and the page numbering being made good by adjusting the spacing on the next ten pages. Following *The Promise of May* an altogether more obvious rearrangement of texts, plates and page numbers pushed *The Foresters* back with the other plays and assigned the two final places in the volume to the contents of, respectively, *Demeter and Other Poems* and *The Death of Oenone and Other Poems*. The dedication to 'June Bracken and Heather' now became 'TO E.T.' instead of merely 'TO -', and although Hallam had evidently been persuaded that the note to 'Crossing the Bar' might better be reserved for his projected annotated edition,[55] the poem itself appeared, as required, on the final page of text, immediately following 'The Death of the Duke of Clarence and Avondale'.

The question as to which redaction of the one-volume edition – which stage in the ongoing one-volume sequence – came closest to representing Tennyson's 'final intentions' is difficult, perhaps impossible, to answer with confidence. The 1894 text constituted the first substantial revision of the edition since 1889, and the last that Tennyson could have influenced.[56] A textual purist, however, might advance instead the theoretical claims – so far as the poems included by the time of the 1889 revision were concerned – of the December 1892 impression, as being the last in which Tennyson could conceivably have had a direct hand prior to his death on 6 October of that year. The 1895 redaction might similarly be disqualified on the grounds that Tennyson's 'final intentions' had been displaced by the interventions of his family; on the other hand, it could reasonably be asserted that Tennyson's widow and son were well qualified to interpret the wishes of the deceased and that, so far as the important critical issue of the organisation of collected works was concerned,[57] the 1895 volume represented his discoverable preferences more fully than any of its predecessors.

The 1895 text proved in any case to be the form in which Tennyson's work was most persistently and prolifically, if not most prestigiously, projected forwards over the succeeding decades. Nearly a quarter of a million copies were printed of the 1895 one-volume *Works* itself by the time of its last impression in 1932,[58] and the plates for the poems only – divorced from the plays – were also used to produce the cheaper one-volume 'Globe' edition of the *Poetical Works of Alfred Lord Tennyson,* published in 1899 in a first impression of 100,000 copies and much reprinted thereafter, to a total of 293,520 copies by 1935.[59] Even so, the edition most respected and quoted by subsequent scholars and critics has unquestionably been the nine-volume Eversley edition of 1907–08. Handsomely produced, containing the first comprehensive set of authorial annotations,[60] and bearing the ostensibly authenticating name of Hallam Tennyson as editor, the Eversley has been long and widely accepted as the canonical embodiment of Tennyson's final intentions: Hallam himself suggested to Maurice Macmillan that it be advertised at Christmas 1908 as the Centenary Edition, 'the only text authorized/sanctioned' – Hallam wrote these words one above the other – 'by the Author'.[61] But the presence of Hallam's name on the title-pages had a more limited significance than at first appeared: the claim, 'Edited by Hallam Lord Tennyson', is printed below the statement 'Annotated by Alfred Lord Tennyson', and it is necessary to understand Hallam's editorial activity as having been primarily and indeed almost exclusively directed towards selecting, elaborating, and supplementing his father's annotations and adding to the volumes their respective appendices.

The texts included in the Eversley volumes are not in any case new but traceable directly back through the 'multi-volume sequence' to that 'New Collected Edition' which had been launched by Macmillan in 1884 as a seven-volume set containing – like the one-volume 'Collected' edition of that year – all the poems and plays that Tennyson wished to preserve from what he had written up to that date. The 'New Collected' itself, printed in 5,000 copies of each volume, seems never to have gone to a second impression, but electrotype plates were made and subsequently re-used, in 1888, to produce the first seven volumes of the eight-volume 'New Library Edition', which was offered for sale not as a set but as individually purchasable volumes numbered only on the half-titles.[62] Essentially, therefore, the first seven volumes of the 'New Library' constituted a reprinting of the 'New Collected', and most of those volumes made the transition unaltered. Two, however, were expanded in order to accommodate, respectively, the completed text of *Idylls of the King* and the recently published *Tiresias and Other Poems*, and a slight alteration in sequencing allowed the volume containing the existing texts of *Queen Mary* and *Harold* to be moved from sixth position in the 'New Collected' format to seventh position in the 'New Library', to be grouped there with an entirely new eighth volume devoted to the added plays: *Becket, The Cup, The Falcon*, and *The Promise of May*.

Both the multi-volume collective editions were completed after Tennyson's death and the publication of his last works. The 'New Collected', not expanded since 1884, was in 1893 rounded off by the addition of two volumes devoted to the later plays – *Becket* and *The Cup* in one, *The Foresters, The Falcon*, and *The Promise of May* in the other – and a tenth and final volume containing, in sequence, the *Tiresias, Demeter*, and *Death of Oenone* poems. It was to that final volume that Hallam appealed when insisting to Craik, on 11 October 1894, that he and his mother had 'of course' taken it for granted that the new one-volume complete edition would follow the precedent of 'the ten-volume edition' in placing *The Death of Oenone and Other Poems* last, save only for 'Crossing the Bar'. It was also in 1893 that Macmillan decided to complete the 'New Library' edition, which was already more up to date than the 'New Collected' had been and lacked only the same rather mismatched group of late works as was subsequently added to that 1894 'Complete' edition printing of which the Tennyson family so much disapproved. But in 1893 – probably in the interests of juxtaposing the one new play to the plays already gathered into the existing 'New Library' volumes 7 and 8 – *The Foresters* was placed first in the new volume 9, unobjectionably followed by *Demeter and Other Poems* and, finally, *The Death of Oenone and Other Poems*.[63]

A dozen years later, when the 'New Library' edition was in its turn mutated into the Eversley edition – a process again involving a readily traceable and for the most part perfectly straightforward transfer of settings and plates[64] – the separation of the plays from the poems became the central organising principle, with somewhat unfortunate results. To what extent Hallam Tennyson participated in that decision – or, indeed, in the fundamental choice of the edition's base text – is unclear. The resulting sequencing of texts perhaps simplified the arrangement of the edition's annotations, but that convenience was achieved at a significant cost to those overall organisational values on which Hallam and his mother had so strongly insisted in 1894: the contents of the once-precious *Death of Oenone* volume and even

'Crossing the Bar' itself were left somewhat obscurely stranded, just ahead of *The Cup* and *The Promise of May*, in the middle of the seventh volume – itself unhelpfully identified, on both spine and title-page, only as *Demeter and Other Poems*, and it was once again *The Foresters*, placed at the end of the ninth volume, that brought the entire edition to a close. It is true that 'Crossing the Bar' reappeared, as a manuscript reproduced in facsimile, at the very end of that final volume, following the notes to *The Foresters*, and that Hallam seems by this point to have acknowledged *The Foresters* itself as a genuinely late text and accepted its placement as a necessary consequence of the division between the poems and the plays.[65] But other of the deficiencies protested against in 1894 also persisted: 'De Profundis' lacks the dedication to Hallam, the dedication to 'June Bracken and Heather' remains blank, and as late as 7 July 1908 Hallam was evidently surprised and indeed concerned to discover that 'Kate', though present in the one-volume 'Complete' edition, was not in the Eversley.[66]

It seems possible to wonder, indeed – especially in the light of his not very practical suggestion of a few days later that 'Kate' might be added to 'Timbuctoo' and 'The Hesperides' in the appendix to the edition's already published initial volume[67] – whether Hallam ever fully appreciated the long-standing distinctiveness of the two editions. Even George Macmillan seems to have been temporarily puzzled by the disappearance from the Eversley proofs of 'To W. C. Macready': added at the end of the *Tiresias* poems in both the one-volume sequence and the final 'New Collected' volume of 1893, it had in fact been slid into 'New Library' volume 9 between the end of *The Foresters* and the beginning of the *Demeter* poems, only to be somehow lost sight of when the major contents of that volume were being dispersed among Eversley volumes VII and IX. It was eventually agreed to reinsert the sonnet into space made available towards the end of Eversley IX by removing the 'Dean Milman' note from the end of 'Happy' and placing it among the authorial notes at the back of the book.[68] Despite this rare intervention, it remains true of the Eversley edition that – annotations and appendices apart – responsibility for the presence or absence of any particular poem or textual detail lay, almost without exception, not with Hallam Tennyson's sometimes shifting interpretations of his father's testamentary wishes but with the transmission history of the texts themselves.

The Eversley edition, of course, will always be important for its annotations and appendices, and its texts, when all is said and done, differ only very occasionally from those of the one-volume sequence as it had developed by 1894. But any claim the edition might have to embody Tennyson's final text would appear to rest, not upon the appearance of Hallam's name as editor on its title-pages, but rather upon the almost total absence of textual intrusion on his part – upon the directness of the connection back to the 'New Library' and even 'New Collected' volumes published while Tennyson was still alive. That very connection, however, preserved a number of readings that Tennyson had himself discarded,[69] and perhaps brought with it the worn plates that seem likely to have been responsible for those occasional absences of end-line punctuation to which Christopher Ricks has drawn attention.[70]

The edition's arrangement is similarly problematic. It is true that the Eversley volumes (like those of the 'New Library' edition) were designed for separate purchase and bore only their individual titles on the title-page itself. It also seems likely that when, in 1894, Hallam and his mother expressed such concern over the placement of *The Death of Oenone and Other Poems*, they were reflecting their own profound emotional investment in the volume, its dedication, and its recently deceased author rather than any disposition preferred, requested, or perhaps even considered by Tennyson himself. Even so, the arrangement of collective editions is a significant editorial and indeed critical issue, and while the Eversley cannot properly be faulted for reproducing a separation of the plays from the poems that had more than once been effected during Tennyson's lifetime, it does seem appropriate to challenge its apparently undiscriminated re-use of existing settings from different dates, to criticise the resulting inelegance of volume VII, and even to raise a quizzical ideological eyebrow at Hallam's inclusion in the appendices of several complete poems that were by then in the public domain but had not in fact been chosen for reprinting by Tennyson himself.

In 1913 Macmillan published, in one volume, *The Works of Tennyson. With notes by the author*, edited, with a Memoir, by Hallam, Lord Tennyson. The volume, awkwardly bulky at more than a thousand pages, did not have a large sale,[71] and seems most often to have been regarded, at the time of its publication and since, as essentially a hand-me-down version of the grander nine-volume Eversley.[72] The 1913 volume, indeed, is sometimes referred to as the one-volume Eversley, although that description inadequately registers the substantial differences between the two editions. The annotations, for example, are far from identical, the edition of 1913 omitting some of those that were present in the Eversley but adding others that were not – it was of the 1913 edition that Hallam was speaking when he said that he had written more than half of the notes himself[73] – and correcting a few that were initially erroneous.[74] More significantly still, the actual text of the poems and plays in the 1913 edition is not that of the Eversley, nor even in the same line of transmission, but printed from the plates of the one-volume 'Complete' edition as reorganised in 1895.[75] 'Kate', the dedication to 'De Profundis', and the full dedication to 'June Bracken and Heather' are back, therefore; 'To W. C. Macready' returns to the end of the *Tiresias* poems, and the contents of *The Death of Oenone* volume once more occupy last place – not through any specific intervention of Hallam's, it again seems necessary to insist, but simply because of the shift back to the other major line of textual transmission imposed by the one-volume format itself.

'And sacred is the latest word', wrote Tennyson of his dead son Lionel's last letter home, and Tennyson's own last textual inscriptions were clearly regarded by his other son, Hallam, with a passionate sense of their sacredness that was doubtless intensified by a direct, vivid, and indeed unforgettable association of them with his father's actual dying and death. For Hallam, therefore, the 1913 volume was a distinct, distinctive, and centrally important publication, the realisation of his father's – and hence his own – ambitions for a single reasonably-priced volume in which the works of Alfred Tennyson would be comprehensively represented by their final texts and elaborated annotations. And the edition, even though published more than 20 years after Tennyson's death, does possess special claims to authenticity by virtue of its uniquely combining significant aspects of both the textual sequences this chapter has attempted to trace. Its texts are precisely those of the one-volume 'Complete' edition, revised by Tennyson not long before his death: its organisation, for good or ill, is that approved by Hallam and his mother in 1895. As in the Eversley edition, much authorial and post-authorial annotation is supplied, and although the back-of-the-volume apparatus is less opulent than the Eversley's, it is rendered in a sense 'purer' by the absence of the appendices and thus of the poems not selected for republication by Tennyson himself.

But such discriminations can seem not so much fine as forced, and while it seems worthwhile to call attention to the interest and importance of an edition too often ignored, it would be quite another thing to claim to have found in that edition the true textual grail, the final or at any rate ultimate Tennysonian text. It has surely become clear, indeed, that no such single text existed, or was ever likely to exist. Many writers in old age systematically collect and revise their past works and reissue them, newly prefaced and uniformly bound, in so-called 'definitive' editions that scholarly editors unavoidably and, in a sense, automatically confront. That Tennyson produced no edition of that kind is in part a consequence of his long-continued creativity, interrupted as it was only by his death. But the absence is also, and more crucially, reflective of a scrupulous and almost obsessive attention to his texts, before, during, and after publication, that moved their potential finality – what I earlier and perhaps less kindly called their long-term provisionality – persistently forward through time and so ensured that death itself would find those texts, and to that extent their creator, amply prepared for the more absolute permanence thus thrust upon them.

Tennyson remained for many years after his death a highly visible and highly profitable Macmillan 'property', and the firm's representatives worked patiently and on the whole effectively with Hallam Tennyson as he sought to be loyal to his father's memory and creative legacy. The one-volume *Works* and its off-shoot, the 'Globe' one-volume *Poetical Works* remained in print well into the 1930s, and although no volumes of the Eversley edition seem to have been reprinted later than 1920, the multi-volume sequence might be said to have been definitively terminated only with the destruction of the Eversley plates in 1937[76] – just a year after the deaths, one after the other, of the three Macmillan partners, George Macmillan and his cousins Maurice and Frederick, whose careers with the firm went back to Tennyson's time. But there is a sense in which both the one-volume and multi-volume sequences initiated in 1884 remain unreplaced and actively present even today: Christopher Ricks uses the Eversley texts, collated against the one-volume text of 1894, in his magnificent 'variorium' edition of the poems. The two editions displayed, indeed, from the moment of their publication, a resilient capacity for self-perpetuation, taking on a powerful life of their own, deeply rooted in the unignorable realities of commercial publishing, that the Macmillans themselves, with all their personal and professional respect for Tennyson's works, and even for his specific textual decisions, were virtually powerless to limit or control.

Notes

1. Michael Millgate, *Testamentary Acts: Browning, Tennyson, James, Hardy* (Oxford: Clarendon Press, 1992), especially pp. 38–72.
2. June Steffensen Hagen, *Tennyson and his Publishers* (London: Macmillan, 1979).
3. Charles Tennyson, *Alfred Tennyson* (London: Macmillan, 1950), p. 320.
4. Robert Bernard Martin, *Tennyson: the unquiet heart* (Oxford: Clarendon Press, 1980), p. 549.
5. Charles Morgan, *The House of Macmillan (1843–1943)* (London: Macmillan, 1943). Morgan's suggestion (p. 174) that Tennyson had not come to Macmillan earlier because he wanted too much money is distinctly undercut

by the erroneous assertion that Macmillan guaranteed Tennyson £4,000 annually, the actual amount having been £1,500.

6. Hallam Tennyson, *Alfred Lord Tennyson: a memoir.* 2 vols (London: Macmillan, 1897), II, 383. For Tennyson's relations with Henry Samuel King see Hagen, pp. 131–44.
7. Hagen, pp. 100–18, 144–57.
8. A. Y. [i.e., 'Amos Yates', i.e., Alexander Macmillan], 'The *Quarterly Review* on Mr. Tennyson's *Maud*', *Macmillan's Magazine*, 1 (December 1859), 114–15.
9. He told Emily Tennyson in 1859 that it would 'be an inexpressible delight for me to be in any way connected as a publisher with Mr. Tennyson': *Letters of Alexander Macmillan*, edited by George A. Macmillan (Glasgow: private circulation, 1908), p. 24.
10. Letter of 16 January 1884 (Tennyson Research Centre, Lincoln; subsequently TRC). I take this opportunity to thank Sue Gates, Curator of the Centre, for her invaluably informed and active assistance with this chapter.
11. *Letters of Alexander Macmillan*, p. 324.
12. Charles L. Graves, *Life and Letters of Alexander Macmillan* (London: Macmillan, 1910), p. 281. I have not provided duplicate references to Graves's many reprintings of items first printed in *Letters of Alexander Macmillan.*
13. *Letters of Alexander Macmillan*, p. 38.
14. See for example, *Letters of Alexander Macmillan*, pp. xxx–xxxi, 20–5, 28–9, 173, 174, 184, 314; and Hagen, pp. 160, 163, 169. In Add.MS. 54980, f. 1, is a letter to Alexander Macmillan of 15 July 1868 written by Hallam Tennyson while still at school.
15. *The Letters of Lord Alfred Tennyson*, edited by Cecil Y. Lang and Edgar F. Shannon, Jr, 3 vols (Oxford: Clarendon Press, 1981–90), II, 242–3.
16. Emily Tennyson to Tennyson, 26 June 1864 (TRC). The letter appears, though incompletely transcribed, in *The Letters of Emily Lady Tennyson*, edited by James O. Hoge (University Park: Pennsylvania State University Press, 1974), p. 181. The title Emily Tennyson disliked, *Idylls of the Hearth*, was in fact replaced by the inelegant – and perhaps hastily chosen – *Enoch Arden, etc.* shortly before publication of the volume later in 1864.
17. *William Allingham's Diary*, introduction by Geoffrey Grigson (Carbondale: Southern Illinois University Press, 1967), p. 105; in effect, a reissue of the edition of 1907.
18. *Letters of Alfred Lord Tennyson*, II, 476 and n., 481 and n., 482–3; see also *The Poems of Tennyson*, edited by Christopher Ricks, second edition, 3 vols (Harlow: Longman, 1987), II, 707–8, and Edgar F. Shannon, Jr's richly documented article, 'The Publication of Tennyson's "Lucretius"', *Studies in Bibliography*, 34 (1981), 146–86.
19. *Letters of Alfred Lord Tennyson*, II, 476 n.
20. Macmillan & Co. to Arnold W. White, 27 September 1883 (solicitor's copy as sent to Tennyson, TRC). The contract was renegotiated in 1891, partly in response to the new United States copyright legislation, and made effective for ten years beyond that date, even should Tennyson himself die during the interim (Add.Ch. 75725).
21. Letter from George Lillie Craik to Hallam Tennyson (HT in subsequent notes), 13 January 1893 (TRC); yearly totals for 1892–1903 given in Craik to HT, 3 May 1904 (TRC; copy in Add.MS. 55844, f. 721).

22. Hagen, pp. 143–4, 161.
23. Add.MS. 54987–9.
24. These and other aspects of the marriage are richly evoked in Ann Thwaite, *Emily Tennyson: the poet's wife* (London: Faber, 1996).
25. *Letters of Alfred Lord Tennyson*, II, 477.
26. See for example, C. Tennyson, *Alfred Tennyson*, pp. 524, 529, 533.
27. See for example, *Letters of Emily Lady Tennyson*, pp. 345–6.
28. HT to Craik, 22 September 1890 (Add.MS. 54980, f. 186).
29. Undated letter annotated '1890', Add.MS. 54980, f. 193; letters of 23 April 1894, 28 June 1894, 7 August 1896 (Add.MS. 54982, ff. 11, 23, 93). Similar requests are occasionally addressed to Frederick Macmillan: for example, postcards of 30 August 1892 and 1 March 1893 (Add.MS. 54981, ff. 74, 139).
30. 'My father wd have hated it all': HT to Craik, 5 November 1893 (Add.MS. 54981, f. 66); see also letter to Craik of 1 February 1893 (Add.MS. 54981, f. 136).
31. For publications prior to the *Memoir* of his father, see *Testamentary Acts*, p. 49, and notes.
32. Will, Somerset House.
33. See Philip L. Elliott, *The Making of the Memoir* ([Greenville, SC]: Furman University, 1978; repr. by Tennyson Society, 1993), Millgate, *Testamentary Acts*, pp. 49–55, and (especially for Emily Tennyson's contribution) Thwaite, *Emily Tennyson*, pp. 19–37.
34. On this last point see, for example, HT to Craik 4 and 25 September 1897 (Add.MS. 54982, ff. 116, 132).
35. Add.MS. 54984, f. 82.
36. HT to Craik 8 February 1895 (Add.MS. 54982, f. 50). HT adds of Collins, evidently with reference to his *Illustrations of Tennyson* (London: Chatto & Windus, 1891): 'A man who has vilified my father's work now wishes to make money by cribbing what he can from it after accusing my father of plagiarism & all sorts.'
37. See Ricks, *Poems of Tennyson*, I, xv–xvi, and *Testamentary Acts*, pp. 65–6. Ricks suggests that if Tennyson had deeply objected to the publication of variant readings he would probably have destroyed his manuscripts instead of preserving them in such profusion.
38. In one instance (*Memoir*, I, 118) he cites his father as having given permission for the quotation.
39. *Memoir*, I, 118. Such retroactive tracing has now been greatly facilitated by the dedicated work of Christopher Ricks in *Poems of Tennyson*, as reinforced by the 31-volume series of manuscript facsimiles published as *The Tennyson Archive*, edited by Aidan Day and Christopher Ricks (New York: Garland Publishing, 1986–93). See also Susan Shatto and Marion Shaw's edition of *In Memoriam* (Oxford: Clarendon Press, 1982), Susan Shatto's edition of *Maud* (London: Athlone Press, 1986), John Pfordresher's *A Variorum Edition of Tennyson's 'Idylls of the King'* (New York: Columbia University Press, 1973), and the discussion of Tennyson's 'self-borrowing' in Ricks's Chatterton Lecture, 'Tennyson's Methods of Composition', in *Proceedings of the British Academy*, 52 (1966) [209]–230.
40. *Testamentary Acts*, pp. 60–4.

41. One set of the proofs (TRC) is annotated in HT's hand: 'The last proof my Father corrected October – 1892'.
42. Thomas J. Wise, *A Bibliography of the Writings of Alfred, Lord Tennyson.* 2 vols (1908; London: Dawsons, 1967), II, 40–2.
43. The chronology in *Memoir*, I, xxi, describes 'The New Single-Volume Edition of Works' of 1884 as 'Revised by the Author with corrections'. The additions included the privately printed 'Child-Songs' of 1880 and three early poems (one of them 'Supposed Confessions of a Second-rate Sensitive Mind'); in *The Works of Alfred Tennyson* (London: Kegan Paul, Trench, & Co., 1882) 'The Golden Supper' was present both as a separate poem on pp. 181–8 and as Part IV of 'The Lover's Tale' on pp. 687–95.
44. TRC; quoted in Hagen, p. 160.
45. These and other figures relating to copies actually printed have been obtained (with the generous co-operation of Robert Machesney, the Macmillan archivist) from the records – primarily the original Editions Book and its continuation as a series of file cards – still in the keeping of the Macmillan firm and here identified, in subsequent notes, as 'Macmillan records'. Dates and details of the orders initially placed with the printers can be obtained from the different set of Editions Books in the British Library Macmillan archive, although these begin, with Add.MS. 55909, only in March 1892.
46. The page, however, numbered 602 in 1884, was subsequently renumbered 499.
47. I have not been able to discover how many sets of duplicate plates were made, either when the one-volume edition of 1884 was originally electrotyped or later on; but that such plates must have existed seems clear from the fact that the Macmillan records make no mention of new plates until 1906, by which time well over 400,000 copies had been printed.
48. During this period 173,000 copies were printed, including 23,000 for the American market (Macmillan records).
49. Dr George Dabbs, Tennyson's personal physician, had attended his deathbed; the Island was and is the Isle of Wight, location of Farringford, one of the Tennysons' two homes.
50. Letter of 9 October 1894 (Add.MS. 54982, ff. 37–8, square brackets in the original). An agitated telegram sent to Craik earlier the same day is in TRC. For Emily Tennyson's request that the dedication to Hallam on his birthdate be added to 'De Profundis' see Thwaite, *Emily Tennyson*, pp. 20, 602. The actual letter, dated 24 September 1893, is in TRC.
51. Emily Tennyson seems on other occasions to have wanted her son to be more forceful and persistent. Writing to Craik, 20 January 1893 (Add.MS. 54981, ff. 130–1), about the forthcoming new edition of *Poems by Two Brothers*, HT added, 'NB You understand that my mother wd like Timbuctoo at the end of both editions (small and large).' She seems later to have reinforced this message by pencilling the note, '"Timbuctoo" must come <u>last</u> of all', at the end of HT's 7 March 1893 letter to Frederick Macmillan (Add.MS. 54981, f. 142).
52. TRC.
53. TRC.
54. Letter of 15 October 1894 (TRC).

55. Craik makes this suggestion in his 14 October 1894 letter to Emily Tennyson. The note as worded in HT's letter does, however, appear at the end of Volume XXII of the Macmillan 'People's Edition' of the *Poetical Works* (that is, excluding the plays), published in 1895–96. In Volume XX of the same edition the dedication to 'De Profundis' also appears (unusually, and perhaps uniquely) in precisely the form specified by HT.
56. See Ricks, *Poems of Tennyson*, I, xii.
57. See Ian Jack, 'A Choice of Orders: the arrangement of "The Poetical Works"', in *Textual Criticism and Literary Interpretation*, edited by Jerome J. McGann (Chicago: University of Chicago Press, 1985), pp. 127–43.
58. Macmillan records indicate that 242,700 copies were printed, including 3,500 copies for the United States. It appears from the same records that 520,200 copies of the various versions of the one-volume 'Collected' and 'Complete' editions were produced between 1884 and 1932, including 11,500 for the American market.
59. This figure includes 44,920 copies supplied to the Frederick Warne company for its 'Albion' edition (Macmillan records). The 'Globe' edition pagination is identical with that of '1895' through to the end of the *Tiresias* poems; it then continues, omitting the plays, with the renumbered but otherwise identical pages for the *Demeter* and *Death of Oenone* poems, and concludes with a short section of 'Songs from the Plays' (not present in '1895'), 'Crossing the Bar', and the usual indexes. 'Kate', the dedication to 'De Profundis', and the full dedication to 'June Bracken and Heather' are all present. Reporting to HT, 12 January 1906 (Add.MS. 55845, f. 74), his royalties for the previous year, Frederick Macmillan described the one-volume 'Complete' and 'Globe' editions as 'the backbone of the property'.
60. Macmillan had published an *In Memoriam* 'Annotated by the Author' in 1905.
61. Letter of 19 July 1908 (Add.MS. 54985, f. 62).
62. Information in this sentence from Macmillan records.
63. The same sequence was again adopted in the final volume of the independently set Edition de Luxe of 1898–99 (Wise, II, 48–9).
64. The Macmillan records show clearly that the 'New Library'plates were used to print most and perhaps all of the actual Eversley texts – as distinct from the notes and appendices – and in a letter of 9 November 1907 (New York Public Library) George A. Macmillan told the firm's New York branch that the Eversley would be printed from 'the plates of the existing Library Edition in 9 volumes' and that a duplicate set of such plates could be sent if needed. Renumbering and the addition of notes and appendices apart, seven of the Eversley volumes (I, II, III, IV, V, VI, and VIII) appear to correspond precisely to pre-existing 'New Library' volumes, and five of these (I, II, III, IV, and VIII) to still earlier 'New Collected' volumes also. The old plates, however, may not have been used throughout: the phrasing of George Macmillan's letter to HT of 25 May 1908 (Add.MS. 55490, f. 1733) seems to leave open the possibility that Eversley VII was being reset line-for-line from the relevant portions of 'New Library' volumes 8 and 9; if so, the same procedure would presumably have been followed with Eversley IX, similarly a composite of texts from 'New Library' 8 and 9.
65. HT to George A. Macmillan, 26 May 1908 (Add.MS. 54985, f. 57).

66. HT to George A. Macmillan, 7 July 1908 (Add.MS. 54985, f. 60).
67. HT to George A. Macmillan, 12 July 1908 (Add.MS. 54985, f. 61).
68. George A. Macmillan to HT, 25 May 1908 (Add.MS. 55490, f. 1733); HT to George A. Macmillan, 26 May 1908 (Add.MS. 54985, f. 57). See note 64 above.
69. For example, the reading 'That' (rather than 'And') at the beginning of line 261 of 'Lucretius' ('That numbs the Fury's ringlet-snake, ...') is inherited in Eversley, II, 208, from the 'New Collected' setting of 1884, but altered elsewhere.
70. Ricks, *Poems of Tennyson*, I, xii.
71. Macmillan records show only a single impression of 3,000 copies.
72. In *The Times Literary Supplement*, 23 October 1913, p. 470, it was listed among the 'Reprints' and given only a two-sentence notice.
73. HT to [George A.?] Macmillan, 13 July 1913 (Add.MS. 54985, f. 189); and see *Testamentary Acts*, pp. 56–8.
74. The 'great Sicilian' mentioned in 'Lucretius' is wrongly identified as 'Theocritus' in Eversley II, correctly as 'Empedocles' in 1913. HT mentioned the mistake in a letter to George A. Macmillan of 9 August 1908 (Add.MS. 54984, f. 100), but it was not altered in the October 1908 second impression of Eversley II.
75. The Macmillan record card indicates that the texts derive 'From plates of Complete Works 7/6'.
76. Information in this sentence from the Macmillan records.

7
Macmillan in India

A short account of the Company's trade with the sub-continent

Rimi B. Chatterjee

There is a street in Calcutta that links the oldest and most venerable of the city's educational institutions, running south–north next to the lake called Gol Dighi. On it you will find Alexander Duff's Free Church Institute, now called the Scottish Church College, Bethune College for Girls, Sanskrit College, Presidency College, the David Hare School and many more. This thoroughfare is called, predictably, College Street. Should you happen to take a walk down it, you will not be able to go ten feet without being accosted by the vendors of books. There are very few bookshops on College Street; instead, there are the kind of stalls that gave the world the term 'stationer'. Little more than handcarts, these stalls appear at first sight to be crammed to the rickety roofs with notebooks, crambooks, guidebooks, model testpapers and other instruments necessary for the delicate operation of passing an examination. But your first impression would be wrong. For the odds are high that, at the first stall you come to, a little digging at the back of the precarious piles might yield, say, a copy of Lindley Murray's *Grammar* published in 1810 by the Calcutta School Book Society, or a pirated edition of Shelley's works printed in Bombay, and dated 1855. For here the detritus of the Raj is bought and sold along with other useful titbits of later times. And everywhere is to be found the name of Macmillan.

Alexander Macmillan was selling to India long before he ever thought of actually publishing works especially for it. Some of these sales were made through wholesalers, and some through orders presented directly in London by the agents of Indian booksellers. In 1860 he declined the offer of one J. Sendall to set up an agency in Colombo,[1] and in 1864 he wrote to Messrs G. C. Hay & Co. in Calcutta to announce the publication of his pride and joy, the Globe Shakespeare.[2] Letters and remittances from booksellers throughout this period indicate that a brisk trade was going on.

This is probably what persuaded Alexander to embark on a series specially for India. As early as 1866 he was writing to Gordon Robb, a bookseller friend employed by Hay, asking for 'the same sort of information on the colleges of India as to the Professors, teachers, officers, courses of study etc. as is given by the Cambridge Calendar about the University', explaining that he wanted this for a friend, but would be glad of the information for himself also, 'for general purposes such as you can understand'.[3] He began to make use of his Cambridge connections, seeking information from former university friends, many of whom had gone out to man the various offices of the Raj. C.W. Alexander, now teaching in Madras, advised on the ongoing revision of Barnard Smith's *Arithmetic* for use in Indian schools;[4] C. B. Clarke of the Bengal Department of Public Instruction, appealed to in 1866, gave information on education in India, especially the names of those in positions of influence.[5] In 1869, Clarke, an amateur botanist of some repute, was again consulted, this time for his views on a botany textbook intended to form part of the proposed Indian series. His scathing comments on its inaccessibility to Indian students, despite having been prepared specially for India by the curator of Kew Gardens, were a great disappointment – for, as Alexander Macmillan remarked, '[w]e have experience that when books do get into use in Indian schools the demand is very considerable'.[6]

Alexander's plan came nearer fruition in 1873, when W. Hullett of the Raffles Institute, Singapore wrote to ask if he would be interested in a series of cheap reading books for the Orient. The suggestion did not appeal to Alexander, who preferred books he could also sell in England if they failed to find an overseas market, but, having poured cold water on the idea on various grounds, he continued somewhat surprisingly: 'We have now in preparation a series of Reading Books and it is not at all impossible that we might work your idea into our series. Will it not be desirable partially to familiarize the natives with western thought?'[7]

All became clear a month later when he wrote to Professor Lethbridge of Presidency College, Calcutta. Lethbridge had contacted Charles Kingsley and E. A. Freeman, asking permission to use extracts from their work in a revised edition of a successful series of reading books he had co-authored with Peary Charan Sircar. This request was passed on to Macmillan, who owned the copyrights and had already received a warning from J. A. Sutcliffe, Principal of Presidency College, that such a scheme was afoot. Alexander now proposed a partnership with Lethbridge, provided previous publication did not preclude Macmillan from becoming involved. Lethbridge replied enthusiastically, outlining a plan much grander than Alexander had envisaged. The Indian series was to be the definitive set of schoolbooks catering for every need of the Indian schoolchild. The best scholars in each field were to rewrite their own textbooks in simple language that children whose mother tongue was not English could understand, and they were to Indianise as much as possible, with Lethbridge as the final editor/interpreter.[8]

Despite reservations about Lethbridge's abilities, Alexander found the scheme attractive, especially when he heard that Clarke was to be co-editor of the series. Lethbridge travelled to England in the summer of 1874 to work out the details, but doubts began to resurface as the proposed royalty climbed from an initial 10 per cent to over 20. If there was one thing Alexander had figured out from his (admittedly limited) dealings with India, it was that all demand was ineradicably price-sensitive – that if the price put on goods was not right they would not sell, whatever the quality, and that the demand would then be met by other means, notably piracy. Clarke agreed in this, but Lethbridge swept aside all objections.

So R. & R. Clark of Edinburgh began printing the first run of Macmillan's Textbooks for Indian Schools, averaging 2,000 to 5,000 copies per title.[9] Lethbridge returned to India, to act both as editor of the books and unofficial agent, receiving a commission on all Indian sales. Orders began to arrive, but Lethbridge quickly proved disconcertingly mercurial in his methods. His letters alternated between vaunting optimism and the depths of gloom, and he showed an unsettling tendency to request more books, then cancel the order in his next letter, then behave as if the cancellation had never happened. All this proved too much for Alexander's nerves, and he handed over the correspondence to George Lillie Craik, who had no qualms about lecturing the unreceptive Lethbridge in sound business methods.[10] It soon became apparent that sales, while good, were not nearly as favourable as Lethbridge had led his publisher to believe. Of the whole series, the

Reading Books proved the most successful. When later series of Readers were buffeted by anti-British sentiments engendered by the partition of Bengal, Peary Sircar's Readers showed only a momentary dip in sales, and by 1938, when the records cease, the First Book alone had sold three and a half million copies.

The results of this experiment showed that both Lethbridge and Macmillan had been guilty of simplistic thinking in constructing an Indian series. The books were in fact a Bengal series, although the publishers failed to recognise this, and they were unsaleable outside the Bengal market. Moreover, the risk involved did not warrant the kind of investment Macmillan had provided. At the primary to secondary school level textbooks had to be low-cost and locale-specific; a pan-Indian series, as Maurice Macmillan came to realise, was only possible at high school level or above.

At the same time other plans were taking shape. Macmillan published *Govinda Samanta* by the Rev. Lal Behari Day, under the title *Bengal Peasant Life*,[11] and also his collection of folk tales, though neither of these did well till the next century.[12] Meanwhile, in Calcutta Clarke was arranging translations of a number of works intended for a parallel series of the textbooks in Bengali. The identity of his native partner in this venture is not known, but as two of the books were the famous *Bornoporichoy* (probably the most successful Bengali textbook of all time) and *Bodhodoy* (based on a volume in *Chambers's Educational Course*), it may be that their author, Ishwar Chandra Vidyasagar, was involved.[13] Craik, however, was not happy, especially as the firm Lethbridge had chosen to handle the distribution of the books proved inept, and in 1876 he was forced to have the agency shifted to Thacker, Spink & Co. of Calcutta.[14] There things remained until Maurice Macmillan took over management of Indian operations in 1884.

Maurice spent 1885–86 combining a marriage tour with a business inspection of Australia and India where he made a point of meeting many of the most influential men in the various education departments. Like his uncle, Alexander, he too was convinced of the potential for a successful series of school books, provided the right formula could be found. In 1885 he pulled off a minor coup in signing up H. S. Hall and his various partners to prepare mathematics textbooks for Macmillan. Although popular in Britain, these books really took off with their adoption by Calcutta University; in India they enjoyed a run almost as successful as the Sircar Readers, and they are, in fact, still used today in Bengal.[15] A more ambitious plan, which he began to put into practice immediately on his return to England in 1886, was to provide cheap annotated editions of the English classics for use in Indian schools, deliberately avoiding India-specific notes, but with careful explanations of those words and concepts which would be unfamiliar to Indian children. W. T. Webb and F. J. Rowe were appointed series editors, with assistance over the years from K. Deighton of Bareilly, F. G. Selby of Pune, Michael Macmillan (no relation) of Bombay, William Wordsworth, grandson of the poet, and G. H. Stuart of Madras.[16]

While Hall was an unmitigated triumph, the English Classics were not. They were very different from earlier textbooks, in that Maurice kept a tight hold on the editorial reins, but it soon became clear that the series was not well positioned to tap the fastest expanding sector of the Indian educational market – primary schools. Sales were respectable but not spectacular, and he soon resorted to Macmillan's favourite escape route of repatriating unsold stock to England. Paradoxically, as they had been more fully and considerately annotated than ordinary English textbooks, they became quite popular there.

Maurice could see the need for textbooks that addressed a younger level of student, and were more localised and tailored to the requirements of individual departments. He began to look for compilers outside Bengal – men such as Eric Robertson, working on a series of New Oriental Readers in Lahore,[17] and J. C. Nesfield, the acting Director of Public Instruction of the North West Provinces, who had had some preliminary correspondence with Macmillan about books for his department, and who was making a name for himself with his Anglo-Oriental Readers. Maurice had to bear in mind, however, that no matter how successful a book was in India, its profits would be eroded by piracy in direct proportion to its success. The courts were proving unsympathetic, especially in cases of unauthorised translation,[18] and the most audacious pirates were turning out to be in Madras, where even a few Englishmen were busy plundering other publishers' works.[19]

In 1891 Nesfield sent J. A. Stagg of the Methodist Publishing House, Lucknow, to negotiate terms for the Readers and his set of experimental grammars.[20] Stagg was an enterprising type, and Maurice saw fit to do a deal with him when he showed up in London. It was arranged that Stagg would represent Macmillan in India, travelling the country with samples of their wares in return for a commission on all sales.[21] Lethbridge was furious when he heard of this, rightly sensing that Stagg was being positioned to replace him. To placate him Maurice gave Lethbridge a 1 per cent commission on sales as well, and he too announced that he was setting out to promote his 'Indian books'.[22]

Shortly afterwards Stagg left the employ of the Methodist Publishing House to work full time for Macmillan. In 1892 he was able to negotiate on Macmillan's behalf a ten-year contract with the paper manufacturer and stationer, John Dickinson & Co., who already had depots in Calcutta and Bombay for the distribution of their wide range of school equipment and stationery. This had a double advantage for Macmillan. Not only did they now have the use of two depots that Stagg could use as his headquarters, they also had the advantage of bulk shipments for their books. Dickinson's blackboards, exercise and drawing books, pencils, ink and pens were exported in the hundred thousands, and it was far more economical to send the books, which occupied comparatively little space, with the stationery shipments.

Stagg was equally instrumental in securing Macmillan the agency for E. J. Arnold of Leeds, producers of a wide variety of stationery goods such as test cards, class charts, workbooks and maps, as well as the Bright Story Readers.[23] Around this time Macmillan also linked up with the mapmakers W. & A. K. Johnston of Edinburgh, to sell their schoolroom maps in India, and a little later with A. & C. Black, whose popular *Who's Who in India* sold in huge numbers – and was pirated with enthusiasm.

As the two sets of Readers neared completion, Maurice began writing round to his contacts in India, preparing the ground for their introduction. As usual, regional prejudices were pronounced: Nesfield's series, for example, was seen as a North West Provinces production, and hence unacceptable to Madras, Bombay and Bengal. It is interesting that even the sahibs showed a pronounced regional bias in their outlook, insisting like D. Duncan, Director of Public Instruction, Madras Presidency, that the books had to be revised by someone in Madras before they could be prescribed there.[24] This attitude was common in educational circles, and demanded a great deal of patient letter-writing on Maurice's part.

In 1893 Edmund Marsden of the Madras Department of Public Instruction, and official Reader in Persian to the government, visited Maurice in London. Marsden, like Nesfield, was a do-it-yourself textbook writer, and, like Nesfield, he had found that native publishers could be less than reliable. Much of the proceeds of his series of geographies of the Madras Presidency had been appropriated by the publisher, V. Kalyanaram Iyer, who eventually had to be forcibly detached from the leftover stock.[25] These geographies, arranged by district and translated into the four major south Indian languages, were just what Maurice had been looking for. Their prescription was guaranteed because the schools in a given district could use them to teach their students a kind of micro-geography, and, indeed, a good percentage of the district schools had already taken them on. Moreover, they were well printed by the Basel Mission Press of Bangalore, probably the only Indian press that could produce illustrations to Maurice's exacting standards.

Marsden proved to have Lethbridge's enthusiasm as well as Stagg's sound business sense, and quite early on it was evident that he would be willing to leave his government post and join the firm. Unlike Stagg, whose background was in printing, Marsden understood how to deal with the educational authorities on their terms, and was well-qualified to take editorial decisions on his own without reference to London. With Stagg due to retire in 1903, Marsden accordingly took over.[26] In 1902 the contract with Dickinson expired, and by mutual agreement Macmillan took over the management of the depots.[27] At the same time, Macmillan also built their own office in Bombay, at 44 Hornby Road, designed by the firm's architect John Cash and executed by local workmen.

As if to justify their optimism, in 1904 Macmillan won a contract with the Bombay government for the exclusive manufacture of the Education Department's vernacular readers. These were published in four languages – Marathi, Gujarati, Kannada and Sindhi – and were compulsory in all district government schools, with total sales of half a million copies. Not surprisingly, other British publishers were incensed by this deal, and Blackie's representative, a Mr Mawson, went so far as to write a defamatory letter to the Bengal Director of Public Instruction, which had significant repercussions at a time when the Bengal government was also thinking of awarding an exclusive contract for their district textbooks (the Agricultural Readers) to Macmillan.[28] This they eventually did, but the districts put up a stiff resistance to their introduction.

In 1907, after much negotiation, Macmillan secured the Indian agency for Cambridge University Press.[29] This was an important development at a time when the Senior Cambridge Board Examinations had just been extended to India: school-leavers in most of British India now had to follow the Cambridge syllabus, with significant implications for the sale of Cambridge's set texts. (Cambridge dons, however, were not always enthusiastic about this new market. The mathematician, Samuel Loney, objected violently to Indian printing of his books on the grounds that this would lower the price, and consequently his royalty per book; Maurice's argument that they might ultimately sell five times the present quantity cut no ice.[30])

By now Bombay and Calcutta had permanent branch managers – E. S. Gaspar[31] and F. E. Francis respectively. It was decided that Marsden's last task before his retirement would be to set up an office in Madras, and accordingly in 1913 C. A. Parkhurst was sent out to Madras as the first branch manager. T. C. Hyslop took over as traveller-in-chief for Macmillan in India.

In 1910 Macmillan had acquired the Calcutta School Book Society from the government.[32] This was a venerable institution, formed at the beginning of the nineteenth century by a group of prominent Calcutta citizens, both native and European, for the purpose of providing India with school books. Since 1857, however, the Society had been little more than an official agency for supplying books to district schools, and the government, eager to cut its losses, sold the establishment to Macmillan, on condition that its operation continue unchanged. Renamed the Indian School Supply Depot, by 1913 it was a *de facto* fourth branch, although Macmillan insisted that it was an independent operation, dedicated only to retailing. Its manager, M. Graham Brash, took his independence seriously, and began contracting with Macmillan's competitors, whereupon he was politely removed, to be succeeded by Isaac Bateson.

Meanwhile in Bombay, resentment over Macmillan's exclusive contract was coming to a head, and there was talk of calling for tenders. As relations with the Education Department worsened, Maurice complained to Selby, then Director of Public Instruction, 'I don't like being hauled over the coals by natives, and I am not sure whether it is very good for them to be allowed to do it.'[33] In 1913 Maurice sailed to India, where he spent several weeks conferring with the Bombay authorities, but to no avail. The government renewed the contract but decreased Macmillan's commission and allowed other firms to compete.

In 1913 Macmillan published Rabindranath Tagore in translation, largely at the instigation of the poet's friend, William Rothenstein.[34] The Indian Society had originally taken the initiative in issuing an edition of *Gitanjali*, but the logistics of selling the books soon proved too much, and Macmillan, who had overseen the printing, was persuaded by A. H. Fox-Strangways of the Society to take over the rights. The award of the Nobel Prize for Literature to Tagore in 1913 momentarily focused the world's attention on his work, and although the initial interest in Britain was rapidly quenched by the war, sales in India and America gave the publishers cause for satisfaction.

Perhaps taking their cue from Rabindranath's entourage, Macmillan was extremely cautious when granting translation rights. The poet was asked not to give permission to prospective translators without first consulting the firm. 'We quite appreciate the poet's desire to help his countrymen in the matter of such vernacular translations,' his publisher wrote, 'but we would submit that even apart from the quantity of money return it would be most unwise for him to give free permission to all and sundry without making any condition as to the translation being made by thoroughly competent scholars'.[35] Rabindranath's liberality, in fact, created difficulties for Macmillan on several occasions. The British copyright in the translations of *The King of the Dark Chamber* (*Raja*) and *The Post Office* (*Dak Ghar*), for example, was lost due to previous publication in an American journal during one of Rabindranath's tours of the United States. Macmillan wondered what to do, then decided to sit tight; hoping that no one would notice, they sternly admonished W. B. Yeats, 'We strongly urge that you should not write to Mr. Tagore and tell him or anybody else that the English copyright is lost ...'[36] But in the event, the First World War caused the bottom to drop out of the market as far as Tagore's poetry was concerned.[37] Like all the other large firms, Macmillan was now racing to stretch meagre paper reserves to meet the new demand for war books and political tracts.

The war brought paper rationing and communication difficulties, but Indian markets remained comparatively buoyant. If the firm could manage to get books to India, they sold well. G. J. Heath, London's experienced general manager, began to consider the option of printing in the sub-continent – an idea which had never appealed to Maurice Macmillan, who felt that Indian printing did not reach a standard to which he could put his imprint.[38] In the meantime, imports from South America through the Parsons Trading Company fed the paper hunger somewhat. The catalogue of scientific works flourished during these years, apparently stimulated by the war, with the inclusion of notable works such as Professor H. B. Dunnicliff's practical chemistry books in 1917,[39] and Wadia's *Geology of India* and B. L. Bhatia's *Zoology* in 1919.

Back at home Nesfield was busy editing books of Urdu folktales to feed the new-found demand for vernacular texts. Alexander's old experiment, the *Folk Tales Of Bengal* by Lal Behari Day, made another appearance as a Calcutta University textbook, along with Charles Kincaid's *Deccan Nursery Tales*.[40] The branches also individually commissioned texts by local writers. Mool Raj in Lahore and K. A. Viraraghavachariar in Madras were especially active in finding good native writers and translators, although Maurice sometimes grumbled to Marsden that these two gentlemen seemed far too interested in higher work to do much travelling.[41] Marsden himself was now living in London, and receiving a retainer from Macmillan to update his long list of books for India to meet the rapidly changing education scene in the sub-continent.

Meanwhile books were needed for the Princely States, which were showing a new interest in European education, although they were not always accommodating on issues of copyright. Admittedly, Osmania University of Hyderabad had been paying Macmillan a royalty from the start, but, as Maurice often complained, there was little relation between the amount of the royalty receipts and the quantity and nature of books printed.[42] A number of series had been created for Assam, and progress was being made also in Burma where W. G. Wedderspoon's geographies had carved out a niche for themselves. Samuel Cocks and Charles Morrison also wrote for Burma,[43] with Maung Shwe Kyu of the Burma Education Department usually providing the translation. It was standard practice in the manufacture of these books for the American Baptist Mission Press in Rangoon to print a Burmese script edition, from which stereotypes were made, and either the flongs or the plates themselves shipped to Britain, where Macmillan would arrange for subsequent editions to be printed to their satisfaction by C. J. Clay or R. & R. Clark.

Macmillan was making similar progress in Bihar and Orissa, and Heath hoped that success in these areas would offset the difficulty of getting into markets in Punjab, the United Provinces (formerly the North West Provinces) and the new North West Frontier Province – where, as Heath remarked, even the sahibs behaved like Indians. These hopes were kept alive while Lionel Tipping, headmaster of a school in Peshawar and author of several Reader series for Macmillan, was active. He retired to Italy in 1910, where he continued to serve Macmillan well by reading and commenting on manuscripts of textbooks sent from India.[44]

Trouble over Macmillan's contract with the Bombay government resumed after the war, when the prices of most materials and services connected with the book trade hit an all-time high. By 1919 the government was decidedly restive, threatening to terminate the arrangement on the grounds that the new price increases in Macmillan's texts were not provided for in the original agreement. In 1921 Maurice was forced to visit in person once again, in an attempt to delay matters until the end of the financial year to give the firm a chance to offload its stock. This concession was useful, but it is doubtful whether it was worth the trouble of a long sea voyage to an old man.

The inter-war period was difficult for everyone in India. Political agitation had been in abeyance during the war, partly because of a vague sense put about by the rulers that if everyone pulled together until the Kaiser was defeated, the colonies would be suitably rewarded afterwards. These rewards, which most Indians interpreted as an increased share in government, failed to materialise. Consequently agitation grew. Political considerations had not previously affected the prescription of books, where the micropolitics of particular Text Book Committees proved more significant than conditions in the wider world. Now education, which was one of the few elements of the ruling apparatus that Indians could influence, was oriented towards the ideas of swaraj (self-rule) and swadeshi (self-reliance). Eager to accommodate Indian aspirations where they did not directly conflict with the aims of the rulers, the European higher management of education departments sided with their native colleagues, and demanded a thorough Indianising of textbooks, especially at the primary level.

Macmillan was in a position to meet this new demand, as by now the company had an extensive network of contacts all over the subcontinent, and was able to commission appropriate books from a number of highly placed officials, both Indian and European. However, they could still make elementary mistakes, as was revealed when Maurice had to ask T. O. Hodges to change the lesson 'Dolly engaged and married' in his *Fifth Book of English* because his representatives in Madras reported that 'Indians do not seem to like references to kissing, and are shocked at the whiskey and soda mentioned on page 167.'[45]

The firm's disadvantages when compared with Indian producers lay in just those features they thought of as their assets, namely their means of securing economies of scale. The rapidly changing situation in India's education system made stereotyping of textbooks utterly futile, whereas in labour-scarce England the cost of composition was a major consideration. Indian firms could hand-compose very cheaply, and invariably set each edition anew – indeed, with the exception of the special arrangements for Burmese books mentioned earlier, stereotyping was practically unknown in India. On the other hand, Macmillan's editions were rarely under 2,000 copies, whereas the average print-run for a thriving Indian firm was 500. These factors, together with the cost and delay of shipping, pointed to the transfer of the printing of Indian books as the next step forward.[46]

Macmillan's list now began to acquire a large number of significant social science titles, such as *Indian Finance and Banking* by G. Findlay Shirras (a classic in Indian economics), Pramathanath Banerjee's *Study of Indian Economics and Public Administration in Ancient India*, and the economics books of Professor L. C. Jain of Lahore University. Also important at this time was *Food* by Colonel R. McCarrison of the Pasteur Institute, Coonoor. In 1923 *Men and Thought in Ancient India* was the first of many books by Radhakumud Mukherjee of Lucknow University to appear under Macmillan's imprint; in 1938 they undertook to publish his *Ancient Indian Education*, but the Second World War intervened and publication had to be postponed until 1947.

The 1930s saw an increase in publishers' awareness of the need to stand together to fight piracy and other hazards in India. As long ago as 1926 Godfrey Cumberlege, OUP's Bombay manager, had tried to persuade British Indian publishers to club together in their own version of the Publishers Association.[47] The idea had been shot down largely by Macmillan, but times had changed and control had passed from Maurice, who was now very unwell, to G. J. Heath, assisted intermittently by Harold Macmillan when his political fortunes permitted. British firms in India now combined to pressurise the authorities into cracking down on pirates; in instances where universities prescribed pirated texts (which happened with embarrassing frequency), further permissions were refused until the offending book was taken off the lists. The publishers also tried to block the intentions of Text Book Committees to charge fees for each book submitted to them. Ultimately, however, the publishers had very little leverage; hence Frederick Macmillan advised a defiant William Longman, 'By all means let us do what we can to persuade the Text Book Committees to act reasonably, but don't let us talk of "fighting" when we know that if we do so we shall get the worst of it.' In July 1934 Frederick proposed to the Publishers Association that they establish a subcommittee to deal with these problems, which became known as the India Group, presided over by Daniel Macmillan in Britain, and by R. E. Hawkins of OUP in India.

With the passing of the Government of India Act in 1935, local Indian government grew stronger. Local bodies could now make independent rulings on syllabus and prescription, and the situation on the ground became more and more inaccessible to the people in London. There was a sharp increase in Indian recruitment to the Civil Service, with the result that there were fewer sahibs retiring to Eastbourne who could be asked to edit a textbook or two. Just to make things more difficult, war was once more looming in Europe.

In 1938 Sir Richard Gregory was succeeded as editor of *Nature* by L. J. F. Brimble, who believed strongly in attracting Indian scientists to write for Macmillan. One of his first actions was to sign up K. N. Biswas, superintendent of the Lloyd Botanical Gardens, Darjeeling, to write a textbook of botany. Also in 1938 Macmillan published an English edition of *The Dark Room* by R. K. Narayan, brought to them by the literary agent David Higham.[48] Sadly the book did not do as well as expected, and Heath complained that the public had failed to respond because it was so different from Narayan's other books.

The war brought the usual rationing and loss of shipping, but this time Macmillan went straight into the matter of printing in India. In 1943 they obtained a licence from the India Office to export stereotype plates of their most popular books. The first batch of titles included Lock, Lewis & Sur's *Arithmetic for Indian Schools*, Tagore's *Crescent Moon* and Kipling's *Jungle Book*, followed by Rowe & Webb's *Hints on the Study of English*, Tipping's *Introduction to the Teaching of English* and *Rapid Reader 2*, Marsden's *History of India for Junior Classes* and J. H. Gense's *English History Part 2* (needed in Bombay).[49] Unfortunately, printing was severely curtailed by the desperate shortage of paper in India. One of Macmillan's regular wartime reports to the government ended a sustained complaint about paper shortages with the observation: 'It appears that our Indian business will now fall away and may even vanish altogether unless we are quickly allocated more paper either here or in India.' The Indian government, it was pointed out, had introduced a new ruling of the Paper Control Board that, according to Macmillan, would leave India practically without school books; as it was, in the past three years the firm's stocks in India had been reduced by over £50,000 worth of books.[50] By 1943, when import restrictions had been extended to India, Macmillan was also trying to persuade the India Office to provide a separate quota for the New York Company's publications, pointing out that the Indian house was the largest educational publisher in the country, with an annual turnover of almost £250,000.[51]

In 1944 Macmillan embarked on an ill-starred attempt to publish in India for the Ministry of Information when John Baker of HMSO contracted for the publication of *Fleet Air Arm*. Difficulties began almost immediately. Macmillan estimated the probable Indian demand and printed accordingly, only to find that the HMSO had supplied A. H. Wheeler and Co., a well-known bookseller of North India, with a large number of copies. 'How can they dismiss a breach of contract as a matter of so little importance?' Lovat Dickson of Macmillan asked John Baker. Nevertheless, Macmillan went on to publish *The Mediterranean Fleet, The Eighth Army, Combined Operations* and Wickham Steed's account of Hitler, *That Bad Man*. Publication in India was mistimed and sporadic because of communication problems, and it was found that the BBC, which was supposed to publicise the books in radio discussions, reached comparatively few people in India because its broadcasting schedules followed Greenwich Mean Time. 'We are sorry that the sales have not been better,' wrote Macmillan, 'and we are afraid that the answer is that there is not nearly the demand for this sort of book which we all expected, particularly at the prices we have had to put on the books'. As usual in the

Indian market, price had triumphed over patriotism: some months later it was discovered that the government had supplied the Army from London. 'On the whole we feel that your people have not kept to the original agreement between us', Macmillan protested.[52]

In the midst of all this, during the last days of the war in 1945, Brimble accepted an invitation from the Indian Army to tour North East India as an adviser to the troops.[53] He took the opportunity to visit Calcutta and meet scientists and academics there, especially Shyamaprasad Mukherjee, Charu Chandra Biswas and P. Mahalanobis, although his visit was cut short practically at the gates of the Bose Institute of Science when the Army ordered him out to the wilds of the North East Hill Tracts. Despite this inconvenience, and the discomforts of travelling at the height of the monsoon season, Brimble made many contacts which he followed up assiduously by letter on his return home.

Shortly afterwards Harold Macmillan, now on the Opposition benches, also visited the country as an observer during the last months of the transfer of power. He was deeply influenced by what he saw, and found much to admire in both Jawaharlal Nehru, leader of the Congress, and Mohammad Ali Jinnah, leader of the Muslim League. Harrowing accounts of communal riots witnessed by staff at the Calcutta branch did nothing to dispel his fears for the future.

Partition changed India profoundly. From it has come a long legacy of political turmoil, endless threats by separatists all along the borders, and sometimes within them. The truth that Macmillan discovered, and grumbled about in the nineteenth century, is still valid. For there is no such thing as a pan-Indian book, a set of Readers or a collection of texts that will teach every Indian everything he or she needs to know. Instead there are literatures and knowledges. There is still a long way to go, but the signs are that there will be a boom in Indian regional publishing – small firms publishing in both their local language and English, or in their local language alone, or firms that specialise in translation. We are no longer making books that will teach us to be good citizens of the Raj, but books that tell us who we are, and who our neighbours are.

Where will Macmillan stand in all this? How will it define itself against the glamour of HarperCollins, the solidity of OUP, the polymorphic output of Penguin? What will it learn from Kali and Katha and Ravi Dayal? The old successes – Hall and Stevens, Palgrave's *Golden Treasury*, Wren and Martin's *Grammar* – are dying, or their deaths are long overdue. Educational books are mainly regional or state-sponsored, with Frank Bros, Orient Longman and OUP splitting the remainder between them. It is not primarily as an educational publisher that Macmillan can succeed in this new India; like Marsden and his micro-geographies, it will have to remap its territories.

Notes

1. Alexander Macmillan to J. Sendall, 3 December 1860 (Add.MS. 55839, f. 52).
2. Add.MS. 55383, f. 492.
3. Alexander Macmillan to Gordon Robb, 3 May 1866 (Add.MS. 55386, f.16).
4. Alexander Macmillan to C. W. Alexander, 3 August 1865 (Add.MS. 55384, f. 730).
5. Alexander Macmillan to C. B. Clarke, 10 May 1866 (Add.MS. 55386, f. 39).
6. Add.MS. 55390, f. 411.
7. Alexander Macmillan to W. Hullett, 17 July 1873 (Add.MS. 55394, f. 162).
8. Alexander Macmillan to Lethbridge, 21 August and 29 November 1873 (Add.MS. 55394, ff. 295, 787).
9. Editions Book (Macmillan records, Basingstoke). In the British Library letterbooks (Add.MS. 55397, f. 733), however, the printing estimate is attributed to Eyre and Spottiswoode.
10. Alexander Macmillan to Lethbridge, 23 February 1876 (Add.MS. 55398, f. 944).
11. Alexander Macmillan to L. B. Day, 27 July 1874 (Add.MS. 55395, f. 957).
12. James Foster to Helen Day, 9 January 1919 (Add.MS. 55551, f. 541).
13. Alexander Macmillan to Clarke, 27 July 1874 (Add.MS. 55395, f. 969). Also Add.MS. 55396, f. 870.
14. G. L. Craik to Lethbridge, 25 July 1876 (Add.MS. 55399, f. 899); Craik to Thacker & Spink (Add.MS.55399, f. 900).
15. Add.MS. 55418, ff. 1240 and 1300, and passim.
16. See for example, Maurice Macmillan to Professor Michael Macmillan, Add.MS. 55421, ff. 669, 1089, 1174; Maurice Macmillan to F. J. Rowe, Add.MS. 55421, f. 674; Maurice Macmillan to K. Deighton, Add.MS. 55421, f. 1284.
17. Macmillan to Eric Robertson, 1 July 1887 (Add.MS. 55424, f. 765).
18. See for example, Government of Bombay, Annual Law Reports 1895. C. F. Farran in Macmillan v. Khan Bahadur Shamsul Ulama M. Zaka, February 1895.
19. Macmillan to John Bradshaw, July 1884 (Add.MS. 55418, f. 207). Also John Bradshaw, *An Anthology of English Poetry* (London: George Bell & Sons; Madras: V. Kalianaram [sic], 1891).
20. Maurice Macmillan to Nesfield, 25 November 1891 (Add.MS. 55435, f. 203).
21. Maurice Macmillan to Stagg, 26 May 1892 (Add.MS. 55436, f. 1370).
22. Lethbridge to G. L. Craik, 19 October 1891 (Add.MS. 55062, f. 30).
23. Maurice Macmillan to Stagg, 20 July 1892 (Add.MS. 55437, f. 716).
24. Macmillan to Robertson, 18 April 1893 (Add.MS. 55440, f. 492).
25. Marsden to Maurice Macmillan, 31 May 1899, University of Reading (subsequently Reading) 22/70.
26. Marsden to Maurice Macmillan, 20 July 1902. Reading 22/10. See also Maurice Macmillan to W. L. Warner, 27 January 1903 (Add.MS. 55472, f. 36).
27. Macmillan to Dickinson, 29 January 1901 (Add.MS. 55464, f. 1833); 25 July 1906 (Add.MS. 55483, f. 1885).

28. Maurice Macmillan to G. J. Heath, 15 August 1905 (Add.MS. 54789, f. 81).
29. Add.MS. 55489, f. 104; Add.MS. 55489 passim for evidence of six-monthly statements of sales to the Press.
30. Add.MS. 55575, f. 400.
31. Gaspar resigned rather dramatically in 1921, then apparently tried to persuade Marsden to intercede for him. See Maurice Macmillan to Marsden, 1 June 1921 (Add.MS. 55571, f. 103).
32. Macmillan to DPI Bengal, 28 April 1911 (Add.MS. 55502, f. 1545).
33. Maurice Macmillan to Selby, 19 February 1908 (Add.MS. 55489, f. 1602).
34. *Imperfect Encounter: letters of William Rothenstein to Rabindranath Tagore, 1911–1941*, edited by Mary Lago (Cambridge, Mass.: Harvard University Press, 1972).
35. Macmillan to C. F. Andrews, 16 August 1918 (Add.MS. 55549, f. 183).
36. Add.MS. 55522, f. 978. Also Macmillan to C. F. Andrews, 6 August 1914 (Add.MS. 55525, f. 530).
37. Macmillan to Rabindranath Tagore, 27 August 1914 (Add.MS. 55525, f. 894). Although demand contracted, there was no decline in interest, as was revealed by the continuing piracy of his work. In 1927 the Orient Film Company, Bombay made a film called *Sacrifice*, based on Tagore's work (Add.MS. 55665, f. 319).
38. On 2 January 1918 Macmillan wrote to the Secretary, War Trade Department, asking permission to export electrotype plates to India (Add.MS. 55545, f. 754).
39. Dunnicliff taught chemistry at the Khalsa College, Amritsar, and had been writing books on practical chemistry and laboratory techniques for Macmillan since 1917.
40. See for example, Macmillan to Kincaid, 17 October 1916 (Add.MS. 55539, f. 20).
41. Add.MS. 55581, f. 903.
42. See for example, Macmillan to C. F. Clay (CUP), 30 January 1918 (Add.MS. 55546, f. 193).
43. See for example, Macmillan to DPI, Rangoon, 13 June 1912 (Add.MS. 55507, f. 1217); Macmillan to Potter; Macmillan to Cocks, 1 May 1913 (Add.MS. 55513, ff. 53, 66).
44. See for example, Macmillan to Tipping, 10 December 1918 (Add.MS. 55551, ff. 102–3).
45. Maurice Macmillan to Hodges, 4 May 1921 (Add.MS. 55570, f. 423).
46. Heath to Clay, 7 May 1921 (Add.MS. 55554, f. 32).
47. Maurice Macmillan to H. S. Milford (OUP), 10 August 1926 (Add.MS. 55806, f. 443).
48. Macmillan to Higham, 21 March 1938 (Add.MS. 55806, f. 443).
49. Macmillan to F. Thomson, Economic and Overseas Department, India Office, 16 February 1943, 28 June 1943 (BL Macmillan archive, second part).
50. Macmillan to Baker, 14 July 1944 (BL Macmillan archive, second part).
51. Macmillan to the Secretary, Economic and Overseas Department, India Office, 18 August 1943 (BL Macmillan archive, second part). In 1941–42 Macmillan imported over 200 tons of books into India, with OUP, the next largest importer, at 142 tons.

52. These difficulties are discussed in letters to John Baker (HMSO), 6 April, 20 April, 10 August, 6 November 1944; 13 February 1945 (BL Macmillan archive, second part).
53. Brimble to K. Biswas, 31 May 1945 (BL Macmillan archive, second part).

8
Letters from America

The Bretts and the Macmillan Company of New York

Elizabeth James

> For the record, my grandfather was employed by Macmillan's of England as a salesman. He came to the United States with his family in the service of Macmillan's of England and built up a business of approximately $50,000 before he died. He was succeeded ... by my father, who eventually incorporated The Macmillan Company of New York and built up a business of about $9,000,000. I succeeded my father, and we are currently doing a business of approximately $12,000,000. So then, the name of Brett and the name of Macmillan have been and are synonymous in the United States.[1]

George Platt Brett Jr, like Daniel Macmillan to whom he is writing here in 1947, was the third generation of a family devoted to the publishing and selling of books, and to the Macmillan Company in particular. The Bretts – George Edward, his son George Platt, and grandson George Platt Jr – successively managed and directed the Macmillan business in America from its first days as a modest distribution agency through to its incorporation in 1896, and eventual sale in 1951. Excessively hard-working, tenacious and astute, they were a highly respected and enterprising force in the New York booktrade,[2] and, at the same time, formidable defendants of their position within the Macmillan organisation. Their detailed letters, often engagingly outspoken, survive in an almost unbroken sequence within the archive in the British Library; with London's replies (from 1891 preserved in a separate sequence of New York letterbooks), a small number of financial reports, and related correspondence in the Macmillan Company of New York archive in the New York Public Library, they provide a remarkable record of over 80 years of transatlantic publishing.

Macmillan was not the first British firm to open an American branch. Routledge, Nelson, and Strahan were amongst almost a dozen houses already well-established in New York when Alexander Macmillan, acting both on his own behalf and as Publisher to the University of Oxford,[3] set sail in the Scotia on 10 August 1867 'to gain a more accurate idea of what can be done'.[4] The Macmillan company itself had some experience of the transatlantic market through its existing distribution arrangements with J. B. Lippincott & Co., Scribner's and Pott & Amery, but Alexander returned from his visit convinced that a direct agency would be required if they were to 'do much' in the face of severe competition, high import duties and in the absence of an international copyright agreement between Britain and America. The decision, as explained to Amery in June 1869, was partly motivated by a reluctance to offend any of their established agents, but more especially by a wish that the Macmillan name 'should stand clear before the American public'. 'If we are to go into it at all,' Alexander wrote, 'we had better face it fully. If we fail – tho I have no fear – we cannot lose a great deal, and we can blame no one but ourselves.'[5] A month later he was able to report confidently to Professor Bartholomew Price, Secretary of the Delegates at Oxford, that the 'right man' had been found for their New York business.[6]

George Brett was born in 1829, near Rochester in Kent. As a young man he had been employed in the influential wholesale business of Simpkin Marshall & Co., where he rose gradually to a senior position in the counting-house before leaving to take up a post with Macmillan at the end of 1868. It is not clear whether this appointment was made with the New York agency in mind, but within a year Brett was established at 63 Bleecker Street, in premises formerly leased by Fields, Osgood & Co. at the heart of New York's publishing district. A packer was appointed, and a lad to 'look after the shop', and, following a weekend supervising the cleaning, it was announced to the trade on 16 August 1869 that Macmillan had 'opened an Agency in New York under the management of Mr. Geo. E. Brett, by whom all their Publications and those of the Oxford University Press ... will in future be supplied'.[7] Their first advertisement featured a new two-volume edition of Arthur Hugh Clough's works, an influential collection of essays, *Woman's Work and Woman's*

Culture, edited by the social reformer Josephine Butler, Gladstone's *Juventus Mundi* and John Bright's *Speeches on Questions of Public Policy*.

Brett was aided in his task by Messrs Pott & Amery, who acted, at Macmillan's request, as mentors and advisors, introducing him to other members of the trade and offering guidance on such sensitive matters as pricing and distribution rights. It was much-needed support at a time when American publishers regarded foreign editions – especially English – as a serious threat to their trade, with the value of imported books reported at over four times greater than the value of exports,[8] and respected journals like *Harper's Weekly* provoking acrimonious debate with headlines such as 'No more American books'.[9] 'It is abundantly clear,' Brett declared bitterly to London on 22 March 1870, 'that the American publishers look upon this market as solely their own, and if an English publisher chooses or dares to come and sell his own books every impediment must be placed in his way and every effort made to oust him'.[10]

A fundamental problem concerned the pricing of their stock in a market where, at this stage in the nineteenth century, books tended to be cheaper than was customary in Britain. American purchasers might be prepared to pay a premium for the superior quality of some imported publications, but in most cases it was necessary to aim for the lowest possible prices if these were not to be undercut by unauthorised reprints and cheap imitations. At the same time, the New York Custom House was relentless in dealing with English publishers who might be tempted to undervalue their consignments, and so reduce the 25 per cent tariff payable on the market value of their goods. Indeed, 'market value' was itself variously and unpredictably interpreted by Customs officials, who relied upon senior members of the local booktrade to appraise disputed shipments.

During the first critical months Brett was constantly torn between congratulating himself and Macmillan on having insisted on moderately cheap prices for their books, and warning the London house against invoicing the cases at too low a rate. It was a difficult balance to maintain. He emphasised repeatedly the absolute necessity of 'relaxing our terms', especially for the popular Globe series, which sold at 3s. 6d. in England but was initially priced at $2, before being reduced to $1.50 or $1.25 when faced with competition from American reprints. On the other hand, the Clough volumes included amongst their earliest shipment were only the first of many to be subjected to additional import duty – in this case for having been charged at 7s. 6d. for American sale at $6, when the English price was 21s. Amery advised fighting it out with the Custom House officials, but Brett observed shrewdly that 'we stand in a somewhat different position towards our books to that of the regular trade here', and urged London not to drop too far below half the sterling selling price ('which seems to be their guide') when making out its invoices. 'We must steer clear of Custom House difficulties,' he concluded on 10 September 1869, 'for they would put a stop to this venture at once'.[11]

Whatever they did, detention or delay at the Custom House seemed unavoidable, and this, in turn, added pressure to the notoriously precarious practice whereby Macmillan – along with many other British publishers – sought to overcome their lack of copyright by sending advance sheets to America for swift republication. With Fields, Osgood & Co., Hurd & Houghton and Van Nostrand all complaining that sheets they had paid for were not early at all, 'I need not point out to you, dear Sir,' Brett reported soon after his arrival in New York, 'how injuriously such an occurrence ... affects us or how easy it would be for them ... to refuse to pay the account when due'.[12] Brett hoped, of course, that such special arrangements would decline with the establishment of the Agency, but during the initial, difficult years he discovered that the conventional courtesy of the trade, which gave prior claim to the firm which first advertised its intention to publish a foreign work, was by no means so willingly conceded to British companies. Speed was always of the essence, as he learned to his cost in 1870, when Wiley ('such a third rate house') brought out a cheap edition of Ruskin's latest work just days before Macmillan could get theirs onto the market. Time after time he was compelled to remind his employers that, while they were powerless to stop the reprints, with 'timely' help from London he could at least 'make the practice an unprofitable one for the American publisher'.[13]

Yet, despite these significant difficulties and Brett's dismay at the cost of everything from telegrams to rents and labour, there were modest signs of success. Their magazines, especially *Macmillan's Magazine, The Practitioner* and the newly-established *Nature*, were much in demand, and served as useful advertisements for the Agency. H. E. Roscoe's *Lessons in Elementary Chemistry* was soon widely used, J. N. Lockyer's *Elementary Lessons in Astronomy* was, he reported, 'gradually but surely making its way', while Macmillan textbooks in general showed 'every promise' of a wide – and lucrative – circulation in the country's schools and colleges. In December 1870 two children's books (*When I was a Little Girl* and Lady Barker's *Stories About:-*) proved ideal for the Christmas market at $1.25 – and would have done even better 'if we had had them early in November'.

By May 1871, with a balance of £9,586 9s. 7d. for 1870 and good prospects for the increase to £15,062 2s. 10d. recorded for December 1871,[14] Brett was encouraged to raise the question of his own salary. 'When I had the honour of being appointed your agent ... I was entirely ignorant of the value of money in this country and thought that ... the means I received would enable me to place my family in comparative comfort.' Instead, his wife had been compelled to sink into a 'domestic drudge', he could barely afford to clothe his daughters, and they found themselves considerably worse off.[15] No reply is recorded in the firm's letterbooks, but London did address his other request for a traveller to promote their books in important centres such as Philadelphia, Boston and New Haven. In August 1871 Daniel Macmillan's eldest son, the 20-year-old Frederick, was dispatched to New York to work as Brett's assistant. It was a much appreciated expression of confidence which gradually enabled the Agency to establish its independence of the well-meaning Pott and Amery.

There are no surviving letters from New York between 1871 and 1885. By the time they resume Frederick and his American bride, Georgiana Warrin, had long since returned to London; George Brett's son had joined the New York office after a brief period as traveller for the Agency in 1874; the first of a network of branch offices had opened in Chicago; and the American house, now based in more spacious premises at 112 Fourth Street, was beginning to take an interest in publishing for the home market. Increasing numbers of manuscripts were being sent to London for consideration, in the hope that 'some day we may light upon a work that will achieve as great a success as Mr. James'.[16]

Henry James himself came to the New York branch in 1885, at the instigation of Frederick Macmillan when James found himself caught up in the failure of his Boston publisher, J. R. Osgood and Co.[17] It was a prestigious, but not particularly happy relationship, which began inauspiciously with *The Bostonians* – a novel Brett described as 'splendidly written' but 'so long' – and lasted off and on until James terminated the connection following publication of *The Soft Side* in 1900. Frederick Macmillan's proposal of a 15 per cent royalty on both the British and American editions of *The Bostonians* ignored Brett's reservations about James's popularity in his own country and the hostility towards this novel in particular, with the result that the New York house was reported to be besieged by 'daily' complaints and 'requests to take back unsold copies'. Although the arrangements were repeated in 1886 for *The Princess Casamassima*, London was tactfully but firmly given to understand that no more than 1,500 copies would be welcome at the agency, especially if they were bound in the same 'ugly' style as before.[18]

Altogether more satisfactory was the young George Platt's first visit to the London house in 1886, where his 'intelligence and capacity' made such a favourable impression that it was agreed he should undertake a tour of Australia to pursue contacts initiated by Maurice Macmillan in 1885.[19] George's letters from Sydney, Melbourne, Hobart and the many smaller towns on his itinerary were carefully studied in London, and although an Australian branch was not formally opened until 1904, following the federation of Australian states in 1901, pencilled annotations in these early reports show that his emphasis on the need for more effective distribution of their books did not go unnoticed.

Back at home, Brett and his son (now rewarded with an extra 5 per cent commission) had to steer their way through a particularly turbulent period in American industrial and economic history. Widespread labour problems translated into a steady demand for 'any thoughtful, sound, solid' book on the subject, such as W. T. Thornton's *On Labour* (1869; 2nd. ed. 1870) – which, they were greatly irritated to discover, had been allowed to fall out of print by London. The booktrade itself became increasingly competitive, with a continuing downward pressure on prices intensified by the spread of department store bookselling and the newspaper serialisation of new fiction. 'I am afraid you rather pooh poohed my notion of a 25 cent novel,' Brett wrote in August 1887, enclosing an advertisement for E.P. Roe's *He Fell in Love with his Wife* published by Dodd, Mead in 1886, ' ... it seems they have sold 100,000 copies on which there must ... be some profit'.[20] It was, he admitted, a 'beggar-my-neighbour mode of doing business', which nevertheless encouraged their discussion of a 50 cent edition of Kingsley's novels in 1888, although it also forced an unwelcome rise in expenditure on advertising, especially during the all-important Fall season.

Meanwhile, with the growing sophistication of American book manufacture they were having to pay more attention to the physical appearance of their publications. The blue cloth binding favoured by Macmillan was criticised on more than one occasion for its tendency to fade in the hot summer sun, and similar objections were levelled at the Dutch metal decoration on the Golden Treasury volumes, which gradually discoloured in the humid conditions. London was instructed that 'all novels for sale in this country should have cut edges', and increasing annoyance was expressed at the 'rubbed' condition of items which arrived damaged as a result of poor packing.[21]

Much of this painstakingly detailed correspondence was conducted by George Platt, as his father's health gradually deteriorated, despite periods of rest and convalescence in New England and in the southern warmth of Augusta, Georgia. Although he struggled to return to work at the end of 1889, the elder Brett, writing most movingly 'with only a measurable distance to travel between the present and the grave', was finally forced to offer his resignation on 1 May 1890. 'We have all been profoundly touched by your letter', Frederick Macmillan replied. ' ... It is a great achievement for a man to go through this life with a spotless reputation & to be successful in what he sets himself to do. You will have succeeded in both these aims, and whatever fortune may have in store for the New York Agency, we shall not forget who it was that brought it through troublous times.'[22] Brett died on 11 June, having lived scarcely long enough to acknowledge his pension of $2,000 per annum, but greatly comforted to see his son confirmed as his successor.

Despite this show of continuity there was now a marked change in relations between London and New York. These became at once less personal, more businesslike, and temporarily uncertain, as the Macmillan family debated the future of its increasingly buoyant American operation. In 1891, probably at George Platt's instigation,[23] the two houses separated, with George Craik, Alexander and Frederick Macmillan each retaining a 20 per cent share in the New York business, and George and Maurice Macmillan 15 per cent each. Brett was taken into partnership with a 10 per cent share, in addition to his annual salary of $3,000 for an initial term of six years.[24] Towards the end of this period, after a good deal of unsettling hesitation, and a brief flirtation with the Century Company,[25] the Macmillan Company was incorporated in 1896, with the 38-year-old George Platt Brett as its first President. Described by one of his directors, Harold Latham, as an 'autocrat' whose 'influence was felt everywhere throughout the building',[26] and remembered somewhat warily by the Macmillan family as 'a martinet, non co-operative', 'unreasonable', who 'never bothered to give the reason for his actions',[27] he was essentially a shy man, rather austere (a 'lone wolf' according to another of his contemporaries, George H. Doran), who now set about transforming the Agency into one of America's largest and most powerful publishing houses.

Publishing, rather than bookselling, was the obvious way forward with the passing of the Chace Act in 1891, which, for the first time, extended copyright protection to foreign books upon manufacture of an edition in the USA. Macmillan famously celebrated by offering £7,000 on Brett's behalf for the American rights in Mrs Humphry Ward's latest novel,

David Grieve – an enormous sum which incurred losses the New York house was still trying to recoup when her next work appeared in 1893. Although Francis Marion Crawford – another Macmillan author with an insatiable appetite for large payments – complained that advances paid to Mrs Ward were 'smothering' the work of others,[28] fiction was one of the new Company's early triumphs during the literary mania which swept America at the turn of the nineteenth century.

The market for the 'conventional English novel' was in decline, but Brett had little hesitation in accepting Joseph Conrad's first novel, *Almayer's Folly*, in 1895, despite its rejection by the London house, nor Maurice Hewlett's *The Forest Lovers*, which was an unexpected success in New York in 1898. At the same time, he was energetically pursuing contacts and scouring the literary magazines in an effort to 'increase the connection with American literary production'. Novelist Winston Churchill's historical romance, *Richard Carvel*, published on 1 June 1899, had a dramatic effect on the firm's fortunes: the first edition of 500,000 copies sold out at once, and was followed within weeks by second and third printings of 25,000 and 10,000 copies.[29] The 500 unsolicited advance copies sent to London ('it is the sort of book you will be glad to do something with'), were greeted with grudging approval ('of course it would never have been written had it not been for the existence of Thackeray's *The Virginians*'), an order of a further 500 copies, and, from Frederick Macmillan, 'surprise and envy' at 'the ease with which you seem to sell 10,000 copies of a new novel'.[30] Such outstanding success was quickly followed by others: Churchill's *The Third Generation* (1899), Owen Wister's *The Virginian*, Gertrude Atherton's *The Conqueror*, and Jack London's *The Children of the Frost* (1902). By 1904 the Macmillan Company was advertising American 'Fiction of the Highest Types' – Charles Major's *A Forest Hearth*, Mabel Wright's *The Woman Errant*, and Jack London's *The Call of the Wild*, a novel Brett sat up all night to read before telegraphing acceptance the next morning.

Independence also had a liberating effect on the firm's school and college publishing, which received immediate investment in the form of an extended educational department and additional agents to promote an increasingly home-grown list.[31] University professors were encouraged to offer new work, which resulted in a succession of influential texts: *The Standard Cyclopedia of Horticulture* (6 vols 1914–17) by L. H. Bailey, Professor of Horticulture at Cornell; G. W. Botsford's series on ancient history; Edward Channing's *A Student's History of the United States*, the precursor to his far-reaching *History of the United States* (6 vols 1915–25); the works of R. T. Ely, Professor of Political Economy and founder of the Institute for Economic Research; Robert W. Hegner's *College Zoology*; E. B. Titchener's psychology manuals, and many more. Only the 'best' books, such as T. C. Allbutt's exhaustive *System of Medicine*, were to be imported, and although there was a certain element of nationalism in all this which also led Brett to believe that it would be unwise to reveal the extent of foreign stock and control in the Company, by 1901 he was confidently predicting a time when 'all text-books used in undergraduate work on this side will be by Americans or will have American revision'.[32]

In 1903 he acquired the educational business of Messrs Richardson, Smith and Co., with its useful links to the New York City School,[33] and by 1905 he was able to use the Macmillan Company's pre-eminence as one of the four largest school-book publishing houses to persuade London to release stock for the purchase of other 'smaller concerns ... which find it impossible to work the market satisfactorily'. 'This school book trade,' he insisted, 'is becoming fast of much more importance to us than our general business, and success in this field means, without question, the future success of the Company as a whole'.[34] Just four years later he was able to report that approximately half of the net sales of $1,682,003.39 for the financial year 1908–09 had been in educational books.[35]

The Education Department was only one element in what became affectionately known as the 'department store of publishing'. The organisation, as described to London in a letter of 28 February 1907, consisted of a branch in Chicago (effectively a separate business), agencies in Boston, Atlanta (with particular responsibility for high school work in the southern states) and San Francisco, and nine separate divisions based in New York, each specialising in a different aspect of the business and designed to operate more-or-less autonomously.[36] The largest of these was the trade department, dealing with distribution, travelling, book orders and trade correspondence of all kinds; but the college department, founded in 1906 under A. H. Nelson, a former faculty member of Columbia University, was potentially the most important. These were joined by a medical department in 1913, a children's department under the imaginative direction of Louise Seaman in 1919, and a horticultural department under H. A. Stevenson in 1927 – which used a delightful letterhead depicting a group of suburban cottages, with the words 'Books for Better Gardens' printed in green. In 1907 the departments employed 133 staff, as well as a number of special travellers in some of the states not covered by the agencies – among them George Platt Brett Jr who began work in the firm's packing department in 1913, but joined the sales team following his discharge from the army in 1919.

Many of the authors who approached this large, well-organised operation, did so because the Macmillan imprint had a reputation for quality, but more especially because it offered unparalleled opportunities for simultaneous publication in Britain, with access to even larger markets in the English-speaking colonies through branch offices in Canada, Australia and India. Although London maintained that there was no demand for many of these books, from 1903 the English company's annual catalogues included substantial numbers of New York publications; by 1919, a year in which Brett complained that 45 out of 100 new titles had had no orders from London, they constituted almost 25 per cent of the entire list.[37] The majority were literary works (English and American in similar proportions), followed by scientific textbooks, and a surprising number of studies on the theory and history of education. Books on medicine, agriculture, economics and American history were represented in almost equal quantities, with a further, significant minority on Brett's personal interest, horticulture. The Macmillans in London were frankly astonished by the 'enormous' list of new books appearing every year, but they were less impressed by the relatively low profits achieved by many of these publications. In 1920, having calculated that the previous year's net sales of $3,741,680.56 had in fact produced a mere 5 per cent profit, Frederick Macmillan ventured to wonder 'whether there is not an inclination on the part of your publishing department to undertake books which are unable to justify their existence either from a literary or commercial point of view'.[38] This was to be a recurring complaint, particularly in relation to miscellaneous or 'trade' books.

As a result of Daniel Macmillan's visit to the now overcrowded New York offices in 1922, permission was given for the construction of an imposing new headquarters building, complete with library and bookshop, at 60 Fifth Avenue. In 1924 Brett's salary was raised to $50,000 in recognition of the 'great debt' owed for his outstanding conduct of the business. Yet tension between New York and London was never far from the surface as the 1920s progressed. Frederick Macmillan, in particular, was always sensitive to charges of over-caution; while Brett, impatiently brimming with ideas and enthusiasm, was frequently frustrated by London's restraining influence. In 1923, and again in 1927, he proposed setting up a manufacturing plant, only to be advised that he was 30 years too old for such a venture.[39] He was reprimanded for an initiative to reprint London's out-of-copyright titles, even though these were freely available to other publishers of cheap series, and taken to task for supplying London books to Bermuda, despite an arrangement which deliberately left open distribution rights in the West Indies.[40]

However, it was foreign trade in New York's own books which caused the most friction between the two companies. Matters came to a head in the spring and summer of 1927, when Brett reported 'constantly receiving complaints' from customers in many countries about the impossibility of obtaining 'publications of the New York house from your various branches'. 'If we are to continue to get the best books in most fields of literature and the most important American authors,' he went on, 'it is very necessary that we should find some way of marketing them ... in other parts of the world'.[41] At the heart of this bitter controversy was the growing Australian market, controlled (but scarcely exploited, according to Brett) by Macmillan's house in Melbourne. Eventually, after months – indeed years – of wrangling, and a brief visit to investigate the trading position for himself in the late summer of 1927, he was able to negotiate more favourable conditions on behalf of American authors, allowing the New York house to offer Australian booksellers discounts of a third, as against London's 20–25 per cent.[42]

Unfortunately, this truce was not achieved without a certain amount of personal ill-feeling which almost certainly influenced Macmillan's decision to seek a financial reconstruction of the company in 1928. The result was a serious struggle for supremacy,[43] which eventually led to a wider reorganisation, and to Brett's resignation from the Presidency at the annual meeting in September 1931 and his subsequent appointment as Chairman of the board – where, by all accounts, he remained a dominating force in the business. George Platt Jr, who had thoroughly charmed the Macmillan family with his bright humour and engaging manner during a recent visit to London, succeeded his father as President. His brother Richard, a graduate of Williams College and employee of the firm since 1926, was appointed Treasurer, and Harold Latham and A. H. Nelson were promoted to fill two posts of Vice-President. (George Jr and Latham, who had grown up in the business together, were to prove a useful partnership: George claimed to have little patience for delicate negotiations with sensitive authors, whereas Latham had a devoted following amongst 'the feminine variety ... both male and female'.)

In his own words, young Brett's first year was 'a lamentable showing'. During 1932, as the depression deepened in America, even the vast Macmillan Company found itself under pressure. School and college libraries, the bedrock of its customer base, suffered declining budgets; at the same time the price of books became a crucial issue at all market levels, with the trade struggling to protect itself against ruthless under-cutting and a rapid rise in remaindering. In this fiercely competitive climate, English books were once again seen to be especially vulnerable as jobbers took advantage of the poor rate of exchange to import new publications for sale at rock-bottom prices. Even 'libraries, college professors and college bookstores', it was reported to a sceptical Daniel Macmillan, were finding they could 'avoid the duty and our overhead' by dealing directly with long-established wholesalers such as Simpkin and Marshall.[44]

Despite his disappointment at these initial setbacks, Brett remained cheerfully confident that trade would improve – 'School books do not last forever,' he observed wryly, 'although we publishers think they last altogether too long'. Throughout the 1930s he regaled London with long letters full of entertaining anecdotes of 'privation in a land of plenty', including his own 'fearsome engagement' with 12 professors from New York University who threatened to boycott Macmillan books on account of the company's anti-union policy.[45] In return, London expressed every confidence in the 'essential soundness' of the New York business, even when faced with a drop in sales of almost 20 per cent for 1932. In fact the situation was grim on both sides of the Atlantic, but in 1936 (an otherwise devastating year which saw the deaths of George Platt Brett in New York, and George, Frederick and Maurice Macmillan in England) both companies were unexpectedly and overwhelmingly rewarded for their optimism.

'We send you a set of proofs of an important novel which we are to publish in May', Harold Latham wrote from New York on 26 February. 'It is entitled *Gone with the Wind* and the author is Margaret Mitchell.'[46] Four months before publication it was already obvious that the huge, unprepossessing and incomplete manuscript, reluctantly handed over to Latham during a scouting trip to the southern states and hastily bundled into the largest suitcase he could find, was going to set new records in American publishing. Throughout the spring of 1936 the publicity department quietly courted the prestigious Book of the Month Club nomination, negotiated film rights with Selznick-International, and repeatedly revised its printing orders to meet ever-increasing pre-publication sales. Meanwhile Latham and Brett waited for London to come to a decision about the English market. Sir John Squire, who had been asked to read the manuscript, was notoriously slow in submitting his reports, and by the time Macmillan cabled an enquiry for 1,000 copies on 2 April the author had vetoed sheet exportation, and at least two other English firms were actively interested in manufacturing the book. A revised offer of 17 April, proposing a 10 per cent royalty on the first 3,000 copies, 15 per cent thereafter, was promptly matched by Collins with the added attraction of a £150 advance, and it was in some desperation that Brett telegraphed Harold Macmillan on 23 April, advising him to respond immediately with a £200 advance on a 10 per cent royalty on the first 2,500 copies.[47] Agreement was finally reached on 27 April, at the revised terms with a further 10 per cent royalty on Colonial Library sales.

The novel was published in America on 30 June at the height of a meticulously planned, $10,000 publicity campaign. By 17 July sales had reached 117,000 copies, and by 7 August Brett was able to report that 326,000 copies had been printed, a figure which had risen to 526,000 by 28 September.[48] Priced at $3, it was an early pawn in the growing price war over books, and for a time copies were available in New York's major department stores for as little as 87 cents, until the courts reasserted the state's fair trade law in March 1937. In London it was selected as the *Daily Mail* book of the month and published on 1 October, with about 5,000 copies subscribed before publication and a further 30,000 ordered during the build-up to Christmas.[49] 'What a book!' Brett wrote gleefully at the beginning of December, 'I must confess it's been more fun, if also indeed harder work, than anything I have had to play with since I have been in the business. It has enabled us to experiment with new selling methods ... and I am afraid everyone in The Macmillan Company, your humble servant included, is feeling rather smug over our ability to put the book over as we have.'[50] Macmillan in London pencilled an exclamation mark in the margin, but cabled congratulations on the 'magnificent success' of 'a unique event'.

And *Gone with the Wind* went on selling, contributing to an estimated 25 per cent increase in profits for 1936, and exceeding all expectations with sales of 650,000 copies of the 69 cent movie edition between December 1939 and February 1940. Yet Brett was uncomfortably aware that, amidst this triumph, the crucially important college, educational and juvenile departments were no longer finding it quite so easy to maintain their pre-eminent positions. Moreover, the expense of branch offices, advertising and manufacturing costs were rising sharply, and all this was happening when the general prosperity of the country at last appeared to be improving. For the first time in his letters to London he suggested economies, such as closing the Atlanta and Dallas offices (which were no longer essential distribution points following a proposed reduction in postage rates for books), and began to worry about pension plans for his staff, too many of whom were old or in ill-health and liable to become a 'millstone around our necks if we don't do something about them'.

As it turned out, he was thankful for his experienced staff when the war in Europe spread to America and the rest of the world. From 1940 important letters were sent in duplicate, by regular mail and by clipper, as both companies struggled to maintain normal business in the face of import restrictions, censorship and shortages of all kinds. Some firms began to introduce a war clause in new contracts to protect their interests in the event of publication delays caused by restrictions or shortages, but this was not altogether approved of by the Authors' Guild, which pointed out that Macmillan's clause, in particular, was heavily weighted against the author.[51] There was no doubt, however, that American book publishers were seriously affected by the shortage of paper – all the more so, according to Brett, because they had to compete against the overwhelming demands of the powerful magazine and newspaper proprietors. By 1943, when paper was 'getting scarcer than hens' teeth', it was even doubtful whether they could afford to offset Charles Morgan's centenary study, *The House of Macmillan (1843–1943)* – until Morgan clinched the matter by offering to write a special preface for the American edition.

Wartime regulations prevented London from importing fiction and juvenile books, or, indeed, anything that had not been specifically ordered; but there were fewer comparable restrictions on trade in the opposite direction, and certainly no decline in the demand for reading material of all kinds in either Britain or America. Correspondence about books and authors, therefore, went on much as before – except that Brett and Latham, perhaps detecting a growing divergence in literary taste, were increasingly inclined to reject works they considered unsuited to the American market.

Amongst those which failed to find favour were Osbert Sitwell's *Escape with Me!* ('a pleasant and entertaining volume but ... it would seem a little on the less consequential side to American readers'); Lord Baden-Powell's *More Sketches of Kenya* (New York was embarrassed to discover that the sample copy had been inadvertently included amongst the books sent to orphanages for Christmas 1940); and C. S. Lewis's *The Screwtape Letters*, offered by London on behalf of the British publisher Geoffrey Bles, which was regretfully judged too clever and difficult for the market.[52] For a long time Doris Patee, the New York company's immensely able children's book editor, resisted Enid Blyton, much preferring to promote her own flourishing stable of popular children's authors. She finally gave in over *The Island of Adventure* (1944), a mystery story with a deliberately anonymous location which had been specifically written (at the suggestion of Blyton's London editor) with the American market in mind.

More welcome additions to the list during the early 1940s were Sean O'Casey's play *Purple Dust* (1940) and his second volume of autobiography in 1942, although Brett privately feared that the enthusiasm of communist sympathisers, for the former in particular, would do neither the book nor the Macmillan Company any good. Vera Brittain, encouraged and supported by her close relationship with Brett, whom she found 'always ... the frankest critic of my work',[53] completed a triumphant lecture tour of America following the publication of *Testament of Friendship* in 1940. Arthur Koestler, already a valued author of the New York company, consolidated the association with his novel *Arrival and Departure* (1943), published jointly with Macmillan in London. Towards the end of the war A. L. Rowse's *English Spirit* (1945), and *West-Country Stories* (1946) were perhaps surprising successes – especially the latter, which was so well received that it was decided to offset an American edition. One work, however, which Brett would have dearly liked to publish was a new edition of Grove's *Dictionary of Music and Musicians*, with a much greater emphasis on American subjects and scholarship, but London – understandably enough – felt unable to commit resources to such a major undertaking when the future seemed so uncertain.

The end of the war was greeted with a surge of optimism in the American publishing industry, and an unprecedented demand for books of all kinds. The New York company reported a huge increase in orders for their college books as students flooded back to the universities, and a growing demand in Latin America for textbooks – especially those stalwarts of the Macmillan educational list, Nesfield's English grammars and Hall's mathematics series. Over 16,000 titles were listed in the catalogue for 1946, and sales for the tax year 1946–47 were in excess of $12 million, representing a net profit of $514,000. By 1947–48 sales had risen to $13,193,401.97,[54] and in 1948–49 profits reached an estimated $925,000.[55]

Business was so brisk, in fact, that the company found itself struggling to fulfil orders: by July 1946 they were out of stock on 646 titles, despite having doubled their print-runs wherever possible, and unable to satisfy requests for almost 1½ million books. As Brett explained bluntly to Harold Macmillan, 'Father used to say that there was nothing to the publishing business. It was as simple as this – "You always had too many until you had too few." Well, we have had too few of practically everything for the last three or four years ... '[56] With no sign of improvement in the paper supply, and with printing and binding capacity in the area severely overstretched, he resorted to juggling his manufacturing schedules to meet seasonal demand, giving priority to college books between May and July, and trade books from August to October. When production costs rose, as was inevitable in these circumstances, he experimented further with price-cutting measures, and in April 1947 agreed to the printing of 50,000 copies of the $1.98 edition of *Gone with the Wind* on newsprint, despite London's remonstrance that it would turn yellow within six months.[57]

'Although business is good, [and] no downward trend in sales has yet put in an appearance,' Brett wrote on 13 November 1947, 'I am sure that the day of reckoning is coming, that the public is simply going to rebel at the high prices that we are having to put on our books'.[58] Predicting a shift from a sellers' to a buyers' market, he confided to Daniel Macmillan his ambitious aim to build their export business into a million-dollar operation, so that they were no longer so entirely dependent on domestic sales. 'This organization needs volume to keep it going', he emphasised in March 1948. 'We must have volume or start retrenching, which isn't good for an enterprise of this kind.'

From this point foreign sales once again became the focus of attention, as they had been during the 1920s. This time, though, the stakes were very much higher as the Macmillan Company found itself under threat, both at home and abroad, from the new powerhouses of American publishing such as the increasingly dynamic Doubleday. Particularly disturbing was the rise of competitors with strong science lists – McGraw-Hill, Wiley and Van Nostrand, for example – all 'bragging about tremendous increases in their business with Europe', made possible, Brett firmly believed, by their freedom to deal direct with overseas customers.

> Dear Dan,
>
> As I think you know by now the heads of the big publishing houses in America are a pretty friendly lot, violent competitors to be sure, but we do get together and talk things over and swop percentages. I have learned, for instance, that they are shipping books directly from here on an open market basis to territories traditionally handled by their London houses, and I have been feeling for a long time that we ought to modify our agreement with you because we just aren't getting the business that is to be had in the world markets.[59]

London, however, remained resolutely opposed to giving up the agency for the New York company's books, for reasons made very clear in Harold Macmillan's carefully considered letter of 16 September 1948: 'I think you scarcely realise how vital the export and re-export trade is to our business', he wrote. 'Exports represent to you, at the most, ten per cent addition to the enormous home market which you enjoy. <u>This</u> business is organised upon a basis of exporting in one form or another more than fifty per cent of its total turnover.'[60]

The difficulty was greatly complicated by economic and political circumstances in both Britain and America. In Britain post-war austerity measures imposed strict quotas on the value of books which might be imported from America, either for the home market or re-export. One by one London felt compelled to concede its agency for New York's books in India, Pakistan, China and Hong Kong, before agreeing, in 1949, to revised working arrangements aimed at making Macmillan London and Macmillan New York books, except in certain exclusive territories, available in either sterling or dollars throughout the world. The quota system was all the more crucial to Brett because the New York company, being substantially British owned, was not able to participate in the special arrangements for trade with Europe made under the auspices of the Economic Cooperation Administration (ECA), which were creating vital new export opportunities for American publishers, especially in Germany. As the combined effects of these developments struck home during the heatwave of August 1949, Brett was more than ever convinced of the importance of his family's long association with the company – not least in helping to quell underlying fears, fostered by rival publishers, that children were being exposed to foreign influences through Macmillan texts.

'Had I your experience in diplomacy,' he wrote to Harold Macmillan on 7 February 1950, 'perhaps I should find a way which would enable me to put over my point of view without appearing to be dogmatic and without offending'.[61] Although both sides struggled throughout the year to find a mutually acceptable solution there was no avoiding the fact that London's quota was too small even to satisfy the UK market for New York's books. What is more, with sales for 1950 of $13.2 million the New York company was considerably larger and more powerful than its parent in London, whose turnover for the same period was £1.89 million.[62] At last, with great reluctance, but reportedly spurred on by the threat of changes in UK law relating to capital gains tax, the Macmillan family agreed to surrender its majority shareholding in the New York company. Brett put enormous effort into preparations for the sale, which took place in January 1951 amidst all the uncertainty of the outbreak of the Korean War. With the help of some useful press speculation – including a rather vulgar piece in *Time* magazine, captioned 'Crofter's crop' – the outcome exceeded all expectations.

Returning to work in February after a much needed holiday, 'with a heavy coat of tan and a peeling nose', Brett was full of optimism for the future. 'I share your sentimental point of view,' he told Harold Macmillan, 'but it isn't as though we had parted company, as though we had quarrelled'.[63] It was fully intended that agency arrangements between the two companies should continue, but by November 1951 Brett was reporting that his departments were full of complaints about 'inadequate selling effort' and 'inadequate stocking procedure'. The latest figures showed that sales to Macmillan in London amounted to just over 6½ per cent of their total export business for the first five months of the fiscal year, despite an overall increase in exports of more than 70 per cent.[64] 'It can be no secret to you by now,' he continued, 'that our working agreement is wholly unsatisfactory from our point of view; and yet while saying all these things I am sure you must be dissatisfied too ... Well, there we are, we are both in the same boat. We are both unhappy.' Macmillan in London agreed that they should try other outlets, since it seemed obvious they were not selling each other's books properly; and in July 1952 all formal connection between the two companies came to an end.

Brett continued in charge of the independent Macmillan Company (which retained its name despite the separation) until 1958, when he became Chairman and handed over the Presidency to his son, Bruce, who had been working his way through the various departments and branches since joining the staff as a graduate trainee in 1949. As for the London Macmillan & Co., a new American outlet for its books was provided by the foundation of St Martin's Press (named after the firm's London address, despite objections from New York that it sounded like a religious publishing house), which continues as a highly successful company within Macmillan's international organisation.[65]

Correspondence between the two companies virtually ceased in 1952. Three generations of strong personalities had made for stimulating, but often difficult relationships, yet one small, revealing coda is provided in an exchange of letters between George Platt Brett, Jr and Harold Macmillan in 1955. Having sent his congratulations on Macmillan's appointment to the Foreign Office, and receiving an equally warm reply, Brett wrote again on 19 April,

Dear Harold,

Well you are a peach as always. I do appreciate your letter of April 13 ... So far as I am concerned – and I think you must know this – 'the changes that have taken place between our two companies' have in no way affected the deep friendship which I have developed over the years for you ... It seems to me as I look back over my many visits to London that not only were you my close ally but that you and your family ... exemplified the feeling of 'belonging' ... Well, the sum of all this is that I have always been your great admirer; and that through thick and thin – and sometimes from my point of view things were pretty grim – I looked upon you as I look upon you now as my friend.[66]

Notes

1. George Platt Brett, Jr to Daniel Macmillan, 23 January 1947 (BL Macmillan archive, second part).
2. George Platt Brett was particularly active in trade circles; he was a founder member in 1901 of the short-lived American Publishers' Association, and an authoritative – if sometimes controversial – commentator on subjects such as bookselling, royalty payments and advertising. (See for example, his contributions to the *New York Evening Post*, 26 June 1896, *The Outlook*, 27 February 1904, and *The Atlantic Monthly*, 111 (1913), 454–62.)
3. Macmillan's arrangement with the University lasted from 1863 to 1881, with the Delegates contributing £50 towards the expenses of this American visit. (See Peter Sutcliffe, *The Oxford University Press: an Informal History*. Oxford: Clarendon Press, 1978, p. 25.)
4. *Letters of Alexander Macmillan*, edited by G. A. Macmillan ([Glasgow]: private circulation, 1908), p. 230.
5. Add.MS. 55842, f. 161.
6. Add.MS. 55842, f. 164.
7. *American Literary Gazette and Publishers' Circular*, 16 August 1869, p. 238.
8. Figures for 1869 quoted in the *American Literary Gazette and Publishers' Circular*, 25 January 1872, and supported by records in the *Annual Report of the Deputy Special Commissioner of the Revenue in Charge of the Bureau of Statistics* (Washington: G.P.O., 1870), give the value of imports as $1,607,201, exports as $385,850. For 1870 these figures are $1,769,180 and $341,044 respectively.
9. *Harper's Weekly*, 20 January 1866, p. 35.
10. Add.MS. 54797, f. 38.
11. A particularly serious situation developed in March 1870, when Brett was called to appear before a merchants' appraisement and, despite explanatory letters from London, was surcharged $500. On that occasion, but only after a very anxious four months, he was able to agree a settlement of $284 (Add.MS. 54797, ff. 38, 40, 64).
12. Brett to G. L. Craik, 5 August 1869 (Add.MS. 54797, f. 2).

13. See for example, his letter of 17 June 1870 (Add.MS. 54797, f. 69).
14. Add.MS. 54878, ff. 1, 2.
15. Brett to Alexander Macmillan, 26 May 1871 (Add.MS. 54797, f. 111).
16. Brett to Frederick Macmillan, 29 January 1886 (Add.MS. 54798, f. 8).
17. James Osgood had a brilliant, but brief and somewhat infamous career in publishing, summarised in John Tebbel, *A History of Book Publishing in the United States*, Volume II, *The Expansion of an Industry 1865–1919* (New York: Bowker, 1975), pp. 262–70. His business failure in 1885, and death in London in 1892, ultimately gave Macmillan both Henry James and Thomas Hardy.
18. Brett to Macmillan, 6 September 1886 (Add.MS. 54798, f. 83).
19. Add.MS. 55843, f. 116.
20. Add.MS. 54798, f. 215.
21. Add.MS. 54798, ff. 97, 136, 169, 29. Simon Nowell-Smith, in his *International Copyright Law and the Publisher in the Reign of Queen Victoria* (Oxford: Clarendon Press, 1968), points out (p. 77) that it was in the context of fading bindings that Macmillan decided in 1891 to provide paper wrappers for all books sent to America.
22. Add.MS. 54843, f. 268.
23. According to George Platt Brett's obituary in *The Publishers' Weekly*, 26 September 1936, pp. 1331–2, he refused to take his father's place as manager in 1890, but offered to buy in as partner if the American business was reorganised as an independent concern.
24. Add.MS. 55843, f. 307; Add.MS. 54883, f. 1.
25. Negotiations during 1895 for the English agency in the *Century Magazine* prompted Frederick Macmillan to propose an amalgamation between the two companies, not least because London was uncomfortably aware that their entire American operation was solely dependent on Brett (Add.MS. 54805, f. 40).
26. Harold S. Latham, *My Life in Publishing* (New York: Dutton, 1965), pp. 77–9.
27. George Platt Brett, Jr to Daniel Macmillan, 14 February 1940 (BL Macmillan archive, second part).
28. F. Marion Crawford to Brett, Add.MS. 54806, f. 158.
29. Add.MS. 54809, f. 166.
30. Add.MS. 54809, f. 140; Add.MS. 55283, ff. 523, 516.
31. According to Brett, this expansion was partly responsible for the disappointingly small profit of $8,321.06 recorded in the first audit of the Macmillan Company in 1897, although he could not resist the suggestion that Mrs Ward's latest production, *Sir George Tressady*, was the major culprit (Add.MS. 54883, f. 106).
32. Add.MS. 54811, f. 116.
33. Add.MS. 55845, f. 51.
34. Add.MS. 54813, ff. 116, 125.
35. Add.MS. 54816, f. 68. Twenty years later Brett proudly reported that, despite increasing competition from firms such as McGraw-Hill, the National Education Association's list of the 60 best educational books for 1926 included no fewer than 16 Macmillan titles (Add.MS. 54840, f. 63).
36. Add.MS. 54814, f. 118.
37. George Platt Brett to Frederick Macmillan, 16 December 1919 (Add.MS. 54824, f. 144). As a result of this protest, London agreed to take 25 copies of

each of New York's new books, with the exception of fiction, juveniles and anything already copyrighted.

38. Macmillan to Brett, 1 September 1920 (BL Macmillan archive, second part).
39. Macmillan to Brett, 8 March 1923 and 1 April 1927 (BL Macmillan archive, second part).
40. Add.MS. 54840, ff. 14; 48, 59; Add.MS. 55300, ff. 88–91.
41. Add.MS. 54840, f. 63. Brett's argument was fuelled by London's meagre order for 36 copies of Charles A. Beard's *Rise of American Civilization*, 'one of the most important books that we have published for many years', compared with the 250 copies sold 'to another English publisher'.
42. London accepted the agreement on 20 September 1927 (Add.MS. 55300, f. 352).
43. This difficult period 'which nearly wrecked the organization' is recalled by George Platt Brett, Jr in a letter to Daniel Macmillan of 4 February 1947, and again on 16 March 1949, where it is mentioned in the context of his son Bruce's prospects within the Company (BL Macmillan archive, second part).
44. George Platt Brett, Jr to Daniel Macmillan, 13 May 1932 (Add.MS. 54853, f. 81).
45. The American publishing industry came under scrutiny as part of the unionisation movement of the 1930s, and in a Senate report on industrial espionage of 1937 Macmillan was one of a small group of firms alleged to have employed labour spies. (See John Tebbel, *A History of Book Publishing in the United States*. Volume III, *The Golden Age between Two Wars 1920–1940*. New York: Bowker, 1978. pp. 472–6.) Brett made no secret of his reluctance to accept union membership among his workforce, but prided himself on having persuaded the NYU delegation that his employees were 'better off as they are, than they would be under any union regime' (Add.MS. 54869, f. 177).
46. Add.MS. 54863, f. 101.
47. Add.MS. 54863, f. 201. Brett followed his telegram with a conciliatory letter, explaining that in Latham's absence, and uncertain how far things had gone with Collins, he had felt obliged to take this step, knowing that 'there was a great question in the author's mind as to whether she would let us have the world rights because ... she was afraid that we would not make any great effort in her behalf for the balance of the English speaking world' (Add.MS. 54863, f. 203). The implication, borne out by Harold Macmillan's report of a telephone conversation he had with Collins shortly afterwards (Add.MS. 55310, f. 79), is that in his anxiety to secure the novel and his impatience with London's dilatoriness, Latham had probably proceeded further than Brett would have wished in his negotiations with Collins.
48. These figures are given in Brett's letters, Add.MS. 54864, f. 199; Add.MS. 54865, ff. 15, 95.
49. These figures are taken from the Editions Book for this period, Add.MS. 55930.
50. Add.MS. 54866, f. 2.
51. Macmillan's war clause, which gave the publisher sole discretion in determining whether a book should be postponed, was the subject of much heated correspondence in the *Authors' League Bulletin* during the spring of

1943. See Brett's letter to Daniel Macmillan, 14 April 1943 (BL Macmillan archive, second part).

52. 17 February 1940; 17 October 1940, 6 January 1941; Brett to Daniel Macmillan, 16 April 1942 (BL Macmillan archive, second part).
53. Vera Brittain to Lovat Dickson, 3 October 1939 (BL Macmillan archive, second part).
54. George Platt Brett, Jr to Daniel Macmillan, 4 June 1948 (BL Macmillan archive, second part).
55. George Platt Brett, Jr to Daniel Macmillan, 2 June 1949 (BL Macmillan archive, second part).
56. George Platt Brett, Jr to Harold Macmillan, 23 July 1946 (BL Macmillan archive, second part).
57. George Platt Brett, Jr to Macmillan, 4 April 1947 (BL Macmillan archive, second part). These reservations did not prevent London from importing 25,000 copies for the UK market.
58. BL Macmillan archive, second part.
59. George Platt Brett, Jr to Daniel Macmillan, 30 March 1948 (BL Macmillan archive, second part).
60. Harold Macmillan to George Platt Brett, Jr, 16 September 1948 (BL Macmillan archive, second part).
61. BL Macmillan archive, second part.
62. These figures have been kindly provided by Robert Machesney, the Macmillan archivist, from the company archives at Basingstoke; following the devaluation of the pound in September 1949, the sterling exchange rate was $2.80.
63. 27 February 1951 (BL Macmillan archive, second part).
64. These figures are given in a letter to Daniel Macmillan of 13 November 1951 (BL Macmillan archive, second part).
65. In June 2000 Macmillan Press announced its merger with St Martin's Press Scholarly and Reference Division under the Palgrave imprint to operate, once more, as an integrated global company.
66. Correspondence of George Platt Brett, Jr with Harold Macmillan (Macmillan Company Records, Box 25. Manuscripts and Archives Division, NYPL. Reprinted with the permission of Simon & Schuster).

9
W. B. Yeats on the Road to St Martin's Street, 1900–17

Warwick Gould

1900 and all that

Yeats's arrival at Macmillan in 1916 marked no sudden romance between a poet at the top of his powers and a publisher accustomed to picking writers at the top of their reputations. An unshakeable sense of his own becoming had been a constant feature of Yeats's career. At 17 he had boasted that his 'pecularitys' would 'never be done justice to until they have become classics and are set for examinations'.[1] In 1895 when Yeats was just 30, a collected, revised *Poems* had been published by T. Fisher Unwin. Even by then, Yeats had wanted a *Collected Works*. The diffidence which characterised his personal and political lives in the 1890s was notably absent from his creative ambition. The moment of a *Collected Works* was not a far-off and once-in-a-lifetime chance to winnow and to rewrite, but a periodically felt necessity to reassemble a self, according to bibliographical opportunity.

Macmillan had spurned an approach from Yeats in 1900.[2] The context of that fiasco is unique; but its underlying textual ambitions confirm the recurrent pattern of Yeats's bibliographical occasions. Stephen Gwynn, who had been brought in as a reader by George Macmillan to sign up Irish writers, had urged Macmillan to take Yeats on. Lawrence & Bullen, who handled Yeats's prose, were breaking up. His other work was spread among too many publishers, including Elkin Mathews (who had produced the *Academy* prize-winning *The Wind Among the Reeds* in 1899), and T. Fisher Unwin, to whom he was accustomed to grant limited-term rights for particular books, and who tenaciously renewed rights to the popular *Poems* from 1895 to 1927.

Macmillan asked Mowbray Morris to report and John Morley to reconsider Yeats's books. Their responses betrayed an intense hostility to the author's Republican and anti-Boer activities, disguised as a failure of taste. As Charles Morgan (or rather, Thomas Mark) was to concede in 1943, neither Morris nor Morley had been capable of allowing Yeats's 'quality to penetrate their disliking';[3] they had reported 'with the dangerous vehemence of men who feel that their citadel is being undermined'. Mowbray Morris's opinions could be 'written with a violence that men do not use except subconsciously in defence of a closed mind', comments which exactly describe both Morris's and Morley's rejection of Yeats.[4] The 'chillingly impersonal' Morley managed a little warm-blooded, if oblique, personal revenge.[5] The former Chief Secretary for Ireland (1892–95) had lost his safe seat in Newcastle-on-Tyne in the election following the fall of Lord Rosebery's government after Maud Gonne had organised the local Irish vote for a socialist candidate, because Morley had reneged on promises of amnesty for Irish treason-felony prisoners.[6]

Macmillan were embarrassed by their advisers, and whether Yeats ever knew the reasons is very doubtful. A political rejection would not have surprised him, but, whatever he was told, he was not dismayed. A. H. Bullen was the only one of his publishers to share Yeats's confidence that his published works could be constituted as an order of self. Bullen however had no money, because divorce from his business partner H. W. Lawrence was proving expensive. After his rejection by Macmillan, Yeats took an agent, A. P. Watt ('Mr 10 per cent' himself), who at first tried to transfer him to Hodder and Stoughton. Yeats's next book, *The Shadowy Waters*, did not provide the kind of success that might have fostered such a relation, but, even with the good offices of William Robertson Nicoll, 'the most successful Christian in history', a nonconformist house was never going to be the right environment for Yeats.[7]

The Macmillan Company of New York

In 1901 Yeats gave Watt full responsibility to choose publishers for all his books except T. Fisher Unwin's one-volume *Poems*. Watt advised him to stay with A. H. Bullen as the best publisher he could expect to have.[8] As yet, however, he had no satisfactory publishing arrangement in America. Various co-publishing arrangements – with Cassells, Stone & Kimball, Roberts Bros, and Copeland & Day – had proved impermanent, although Lawrence & Bullen had managed to sell sheets of *The Celtic*

Twilight (1893) to the Macmillan Company of New York, who published it in 1894.

By 1895 Yeats knew that poetry rather than fiction or drama would define him. Poets need time: time is money. Poets (as Paul Verlaine had said) 'think of nothing else ... and with reason!'[9] Publishers exist to finance promise: some such thought underlies Yeats's knowingness in his handling of them. He turned from publisher to publisher, advance to advance, in the pivotal year of 1896. By 24 March the leading Fifth Avenue publishers' agent, Paul Revere Reynolds (1864–1944), was offering George P. Brett of the Macmillan Company the refusal of a 'new story by Mr Yeats of 75,000 words'. Reynolds claimed to be able to 'sell the American book rights for 100 pounds'.[10] He was a double agent who acted for English publishers and their American counterparts, a reputable man in what was then an inherently impure trade. While he had some English authors on his books (chiefly through J. B. Pinker, Curtis Brown, and the Literary Agency of London), it seems most unlikely that Yeats was one of them.[11]

Reynolds was hawking Yeats's idea for what became *The Speckled Bird,* on commission for a publisher, possibly T. Fisher Unwin. Brett did not want the book. Macmillan had probably found little success with *The Celtic Twilight*: they certainly left the sheets of *The Secret Rose* (1897) to Dodd, Mead, although they did take Bullen's sheets of the enlarged edition of *The Celtic Twilight* (1902). When Yeats could not finish *The Speckled Bird* Bullen kindly set the advance against *Ideas of Good and Evil* (1903), sheets of which were taken by Macmillan New York.

At the turn of the century, piracy of European authors in the United States remained rife as a result of the country's isolationist stance in respect of international copyright law following the ratification of the Berne Convention in 1887. The Chace Act of 1891 restricted US copyright to works set and printed in the United States. It had done nothing to stop the determined pirate from plundering foreign authors whose works did not meet the 'manufacturing' condition. European *fin-de-siècle* writing was popular, and US markets were hungry. Authors such as W. B. Yeats who were still making their names in North America were vulnerable if their London publishers sold sheets or bound stock of London editions to the American market: such texts were not protected by the Chace Act. Yet such was the way young writers got known, until that is, they were known well enough to be prized by pirates.

Yeats was aware that he was in this position. When pressed by John Lane (publishing from New York) to secure the printing of the entire edition of *The Wind Among the Reeds* (1899) for John Wilson & Sons of the University Press, Cambridge, Mass., he had agreed. In an atmosphere of profound and justified suspicion, Lane's former partner, Elkin Mathews, as publisher of the English edition, took and bound the imported sheets. But Yeats's American rights were, for once, secure.[12]

By agreeing to lecture across America in 1903–04, Yeats attracted enough publicity and created enough of an audience to rouse the attention of Thomas Mosher, the pirate of Portland, Maine, who issued *The Land of Heart's Desire* in time for the trip. George P. Brett of the Macmillan Company of New York was induced to see that Yeats's emerging difficulty with Mosher was Macmillan's opportunity. He began to print (and so to protect) Yeats in America, by publishing *Where There is Nothing: being Volume 1 of Plays for an Irish Theatre* in May 1903; *In the Seven Woods | Being Poems Chiefly of the Irish Heroic Age* in August 1903, a vilely printed misapprehension of the bibliographical codes of the Dun Emer volume of that year; and *The Hour-Glass and Other Plays | Being Volume 2 of Plays for an Irish Theatre* (1904).

After protracted negotiations, both in the United States and following his return to London, Yeats, with considerable reluctance, granted an exclusive licence to the Macmillan Company of New York to produce collected editions of his works in that market for the lifetime of his copyrights. In accepting these terms (he had always refused to give his London publishers more than a few years' rights in his books), he demonstrated his obsession with collected editions, and possibly some frustration with the necessarily slow progress towards the *Collected Works in Verse and Prose* which Bullen was promising him. Macmillan issued *The Poetical Works of William B. Yeats* in two volumes in 1906–07, even giving their author a recognisably American name.

The long-pondered eight-volume *Collected Works in Verse and Prose*, printed at the Shakespeare Head Press in Stratford-upon-Avon and sumptuously bound in quarter vellum by James Burn, appeared in 1908 with 1,000 of 1,060 printed sets for sale. Bullen was more printer than publisher. Obsessed with the quality of his work, he planned to put the names of a number of other publishers on the title-page. He tried Heinemann without success; Elkin Mathews refused to take copies for his Vigo Street shop; T. Fisher Unwin, Bullen's mortal enemy in the matter of Yeats, strung Bullen along until he was irrevocably committed to his print-run, and then refused to take copies. It was probably a calculated attempt to bankrupt Bullen, as Unwin reissued *Poems* in its fifth edition to ride on the publicity for the *Collected Works*.

Finally Chapman and Hall took just 250 sets of the *Collected Works*. Arthur Waugh remembered

> After he had set the press to work, it occurred to Bullen that he had hardly at his disposal the full machinery for planting out the edition in the provinces, and that it would be an advantage to get the co-operation of a general publishing house. So he suggested to Chapman & Hall that they might share the stock and the market, and any firm with the vestige of a literary sense would have been only too proud to see its imprint upon so fine a set of books. When to the public credit there was added the private privilege of conferring with Bullen from time to time upon details of the enterprise, and of sharing in those glowing talks, to which he himself contributed all the fire and the enthusiasm, it is not surprising that the connection has left behind it a trail of memory, rich in the golden qualities of friendship ...[13]

Sales of the edition were very disappointing, and by October 1912 Bullen still had 21 bound sets and 460 sets in quires. The implication of the 460 quires is that only 540–600 sets were bound in any form (the number of 'spoils' is uncertain). Allowing for Bullen's 150 plus 25 sets, and Chapman and Hall's 250, plus a further 50 sets in two lots of 25 late in 1910, a total of 475 sets were bound in full vellum by Bullen's binder, James Burn.[14] A further 65–125 sets are therefore unaccounted for. These may include up to 25 Irish sets, buckram-bound for Maunsel, but it is clear that by October 1912 Bullen had perhaps 100 extra sets, even though cheaply bound states from this period are not recorded by Yeats's bibliographer.[15] When Bullen computed the sums owed to Yeats on 17 November 1915, he indicated that 45 copies had been sold at half price before 30 September 1912.[16]

Bullen identified three causes for 'this poor result'. First, the Macmillan Company had refused to import copies into America, or to let another publisher handle the work, actions defended by legal justifications concerning a new restriction of US copyright law, which John Quinn, the ebullient New York lawyer and patron, exposed as a commercial decision. Their copyrights would not have been affected, but Macmillan New York, with its exclusive licence, had the legal right to decide as it did. Nothing could be done: Yeats had signed that licence (which that company and its heirs still exercise). Bullen found George Brett 'higheadedly obdurate'.[17] Moreover, the Macmillan Company had refused to publish plays in verse as plays, issuing them only as 'dramatical poems', in Volume 2 of the *Poetical Works of William B. Yeats*.[18] The exclusive licence granted to Macmillan almost immediately closed Yeats's options in the USA.[19] Second, the literary press had been booming Synge, Bullen thought, at Yeats's expense. Finally, Chapman and Hall had, in his view, been

> very inefficient allies. My sales would have been larger if I had not bought back copies from them, and handed over to them – for their encouragement – orders that I would have been glad to execute myself.[20]

In 1912 Bullen was still buying unsold Chapman and Hall stock. Later that year, Unwin proposed to Yeats a cheaper uniform set. Yeats inquired whether it could be printed by Bullen, who found it 'an intolerable proposal ... indeed insulting' because he, too, had a range of cheaper editions of Yeats in print.[21] Nothing came of the idea, but both Yeats and Bullen were stirred into thinking how the Collected Edition might be salvaged. Yeats wanted to incorporate newly revised texts into the remaining quire stock of *The Collected Works in Verse and Prose* (1908). Should Bullen augment the volumes with new texts, or should he substitute new sheets for old gatherings which could easily be removed? Bullen prevaricated on 6 and 10 February 1913.[22] Yeats responded in masterly fashion:

> Before finally deciding what we are to do with the 'Collected Edition' I wish you would tell me if it really is more expensive to substitute than to add. And if so, why? The place where substitution is most required is in the case of *Deirdre*. The alterations are small and continuous. Nothing of value is left out, and there is no reason, on literary grounds, for the old version remaining. I should prefer substitution throughout in the case of all the changes, but if there are solid reasons against this, most changes can be done by addition. I am convinced however that, if it can be avoided, it is a great practical mistake except in the case of *The Hour-Glass*, which is practically a different work of art. It changes the volumes from being a collection precisely [of] those things I wish to be my permanent self, into a collection of odds and ends, including some that should not have been published. However, give me an opportunity of judging by telling me your reasons against substitution. The one thing I do vehemently object to is substitution in smaller print. To consent to that would be to avow the inferiority of my final version ... I won't keep you waiting.[23]

Various models were tried, including the addition of an extra volume. For a time it seemed that Yeats had got his way as Bullen agreed to a 'refurbished edition' with 'all pages I have re-written replaced', and illustrations by Robert Gregory and Edward Gordon Craig. The books were to be rearranged, with 'all the *Samhains* and theatre essays in general making up one volume'. Yeats was even prepared to 'pay some of the money myself out of what Bullen owes – to get a free hand'. For once, Yeats seems more affluent than his publisher. Supporting his father in New York was becoming more and more difficult, yet in the same letter to Lady Gregory he asked her to '[d]o what you think right about my father. I have that £160 legacy installment and I leave you quite free within this limit – I would prefer not to pay more than £50 but I trust you entirely in the matter.'[24] By contrast, lack of capital, the closure of the American market, and a Balzacian accumulation of debt meant that Bullen could not proceed with this revision of *The Collected Works* in 1913. This stalemate became for Yeats the key factor in his eventual decision to seek another publisher.

Rabindranath Tagore

Rabindranath Tagore had arrived in England in the summer of 1912, and William Rothenstein had urged Yeats to take him up.[25] Tagore and Yeats met on 27 June 1912, and Yeats first encountered the translations that became *Gitanjali* on 7 July at Rothenstein's. He proposed a toast to Tagore and read three poems at a dinner at the Trocadero on 10 July. 'Within a week or so Yeats was at work selecting and arranging the poems and making pencilled corrections for Tagore to consider.'[26] *Gitanjali (Song Offerings)* appeared in a limited edition from the India Society late in 1912, with Yeats's beautiful introduction. *The Times Literary Supplement* thought the poems 'the Psalms of David of our own time'.[27] Rothenstein then urged Macmillan to publish a trade edition, which resulted in ten printings between March 1913 and the award of the Nobel Prize to Tagore in November of that year. Tagore was thus launched as an Eastern mystic in the West. Though Ezra Pound later regretted 'the cleverest boom of our times', he had pushed the bandwagon for the modern 'Dante' with his 'poetic piety' as vigorously as anyone.[28] It is now evident that, while Tagore's work was published as 'A Collection of Prose Translations made by the Author from the Original Bengali', it was Yeats who perfected the translations. He continued to carry out such work on Tagore's books (with some help from Thomas Sturge Moore) until 1917.

Tagore had moved Yeats to the discovery of himself: his Preface is at one with his essays of the time in discovering a 'supreme culture' which is 'as much the growth of the common soil as is the grass and the rushes'. Of *Gitanjali* Yeats wrote

> A whole people, a whole civilization, immeasurably strange to us, seems to have been taken up into the imagination; and yet we are not moved because of its strangeness but because we have met our own image, as though we had walked in Rossetti's willow wood, or heard, perhaps for the first time in literature, our voice as in a dream.[29]

It was as if Yeats had found another Mohini Chatterjee, the Indian sage who had come to Dublin at the behest of the Theosophists in April 1886.[30] In the midst of writing the 'Dying Lady' poems about Mabel Beardsley, Yeats exported his excitement about Tagore to Florence Farr in Ceylon.

> ... Tagore writes all his poems to music & is said to be a great musician. I cannot send you his poems yet as they went out of print in a few days, but when the new edition comes you will have a copy. Do you remember Mabel Beardsley? She is dying of cancer & showing a gay and beautiful courage ... I have been deeply moved by Tagore. It has given me a great desire to get away from controversies everything but to minds daily caprice. I have been free for two months or more from the theatre & have written lyrics – I am in the middle of the seventh about Mabel Beardsley who grows weaker but not less joyous ...[31]

There is controversy over how much of *Gitanjali* Yeats rewrote. Tagore himself immediately admitted that Yeats had selected the poems 'that required least alteration', 'rejecting others in spite of their merits', a selection from a mass of other material which proved unerring.[32] It is now clear, however, from the mysteriously overlooked Yeats side of the correspondence in the Macmillan archive that Yeats was effectively literary and theatrical agent, safeguarding Tagore's rights, guarding against error, remaining discreet about the extent to which he had reworked *Gitanjali* and the next three of Tagore's books. By 10 April 1916 Yeats, 'overwhelmed with work' and in the midst of mounting his play *At the Hawk's Well*, had 'two books of verse by Tagore to revise for Macmillan who has no notion of the job it is', as well as an introduction to write for the Cuala edition of *Certain Noble Plays of Japan* and his own poems to revise for Macmillan.[33] Tagore's reputation was now in urgent need of some critical assistance. Yeats proposed to Sir Frederick Macmillan that they might add to Tagore's next book a 'short essay on his prosody' to

> remind readers and reviewers that they were reading translations of poems, which in the original had very exact and difficult forms, & not the work of a facile mind, choosing the easiest form.

Unable to find a Hindu 'competent to comment' Yeats proposed Ezra Pound 'who made a study of Tagore's prosody, when Tagore was in London' as 'the best available man' but feared that it might be too late. So it proved.[34] On 9 July Yeats returned to the subject. Tagore was 'not a writer of facile English for English religious readers but a master of very arduous measures, whom they read in a tongue that is not his'. Moreover, sensing 'a re-action against his reputation' he stressed that 'we should feel once more that he belongs to a different civilization, & does not speak directly to us at all'.[35] Yeats then promised to work over the proofs of *Fruit-gathering*.

By 28 January 1917, however, he was addressing the decline in quality of Tagore's work in a private note to Sir Frederick. 'A Lover's Knot',[36] he confided, was 'rather an embarrassment'. He proposed to write to Tagore saying that Macmillan had asked him to make 'as few alterations as possible as American publication hurries us', and to suggest that, in any case, Tagore's English was 'now much more perfect'. The letter continued:

> You probably do not know how great my revisions have been in the past. William Rothenstein will tell you how much I did for *Gitanjali* and even his MS of 'The Gardener'. Of course all one wanted to do 'was to bring out the authors meaning' but that meant a continuous revision of vocabulary & even more of cadence. Tagore's English was a foreigner's English & as he wrote to me he 'could never tell the words that had lost their souls' from the rest. I left out sentence after sentence & probably putting one day with another spent some weeks on the task. It was a delight & I did not grudge the time, & at my request Tagore has made no acknowledgement. I know that if he did so his Indian enemies would exagerate what I did beyond all justice and use it to attack him. Now I had no great heart in my revision of his last book 'Fruit-gathering'. The book is a mere shadow. After 'Gitanjali' and 'The Gardener' and 'The Crescent Moon' (exaustively revised by Sturge Moore) as [?or and] a couple of plays and perhaps

'Sadhānā' nothing more should have been published except the long autobiography which has been printed in 'The Modern Review', a most valuable and rich book. He is an old man now & these later poems are drowning his reputation. I told this to Rothenstein & he said 'we must not tell him so for it would put him into the deepest depression'.

I am relieved at your letter though I would not like to tell Tagore so. I merely make ordinary press revisions for there is nothing between that and exaustive removal of all phrases and rhythms that 'have lost their soul' or have never had souls. Tagore's English has grown better, that is to say more simple & more correct but it is still often very flat.

Excuse my writing so much unasked criticism, but I have been deeply moved by Tagores best work & that must be my excuse.

I am still prepared to make the old exaustive revision if you wish it but it would take time & I shall hope that you do not wish it.[37]

Closing in on Bullen

Such, then, was the Yeats who was known to Macmillan when they took him on in 1916. This is not the place fully to chronicle the decline in Bullen's fortunes, nor to do more than register Yeats's sublime patience as his publisher's creditor. On the whole, Bullen has had a bad press as Yeats's publisher.[38] The unchecked assumption based on incomplete recovery of their correspondence and Bullen's archive has been that Bullen took liberties with Yeats's texts, but that view is radically false. It is also easy to start from the assumption that the Dun Emer and Cuala volumes should have, in the normal course of things, emerged in trade editions on both sides of the Atlantic, subsequently to be absorbed in larger collections from time to time, also published in both London and New York. Bullen has been blamed for not bringing out an English trade edition of *In the Seven Woods | Being Poems Chiefly of the Irish Heroic Age*, or of *The Green Helmet and other Poems* (as Brett had done), but the criticism is insubstantial and anachronistic.[39]

Yeats remained faithful to Bullen's enterprise for a very long time, and the material conditions of authorship on both sides of the Atlantic provide a rational explanation of the consequent difficulties. He had been relatively indifferent to Bullen's unwillingness to bring out a London trade edition of *In the Seven Woods | Being Poems Chiefly of the Irish Heroic Age* because by then Bullen had a larger volume in hand, one which had a much more important role in prospect, *Poems: 1899–1905*. Both Yeats and Bullen had intended that volume to include the poems from *The Wind Among the Reeds*, but protracted legal difficulties with John Lane, who had 'never sent an agreement, never furnished an account, never paid a penny, never answered a letter' spelled irritating delay.[40] In the end, those poems were omitted from *Poems: 1899–1905* as Yeats levered Lane into a position whereby he would concede that he had no remaining rights in *The Wind Among the Reeds*, so that they could be included in *The Poetical Works of William B. Yeats*. Second, absorbing and useful as the project of *The Poetical Works of William B. Yeats* had been, in allowing Yeats to see the virtues of a chronological array of his lyrical and narrative poems and of simplifying their notes for an Irish-American audience, the resultant volumes were slow sellers (especially the second volume, *Dramatical Poems*, 1907).

Relations with Macmillan New York were soon soured by their refusal to take Bullen's *Collected Works in Verse and Prose*. *The Poetical Works* had to do service in the United States for a number of other volumes never published there, including *Plays for an Irish Theatre* (1911).[41] A. H. Bullen and the Macmillan Company of New York were never co-ordinated, and until Yeats went over to Macmillan and Company, London, in 1916, America remained a potentially hazardous place to publish. Sales there were relatively unfulfilled during the lifetime of *The Poetical Works of William B. Yeats*. Many changes made for *The Collected Works in Verse and Prose* and carried into *Poems: Second Series* and *Plays for an Irish Theatre* effectively left the American texts of the first volume of *The Poetical Works of William B. Yeats* superseded and stranded, out of the line of textual descent. It was reprinted nine times until 1922, but without revision or enlargement.[42]

To make matters worse, *The Green Helmet and other Poems* must stand as the volume most reviled by its author for its cover design. Macmillan New York's first new collection of Yeats's poems since 1906 was issued on 23 October 1912, in tan paper boards with a green ornamental design which enclosed its title on the top board within a helmet absurdly reminiscent of contemporary diving suits. No doubt the designer thought he was paying a sincere tribute to the title play and perhaps to Yeats's half-forgotten helmets and crowns of the *Poems* (1895) period. Yeats loathed this 'hateful American copy decorated in my despite', as he told Robert Bridges, and inscribed Sturge Moore's copy 'The cover is the unaided work of the American publisher. He says it is he believes the kind of cover I like.' Taking private revenge upon the Macmillan Company, he pertinaciously branded other copies with similar sentiments.[43]

The origins of the Macmillan New York edition of *The Cutting of an Agate* lie in a letter to Edith Lister of the Shakespeare Head Press of 28 July (1911). The Abbey Players were to visit the United States in 1911. Before he departed on 13 September, Yeats wrote proposing that

> If Mr. Bullen does not think it would injure the collected edition I would get out *in America* while the company is there a volume of essays containing (1) *J. M. Synge and the Ireland of his Time* (just published by my sister) (2) *Discoveries* (3) *Literature and Tradition* (4) Essay from the *Mask* (5) *Edmund Spenser*. Let me [know] at once about this. I think it might have a large sale as the players would be there.[44]

Macmillan New York published *The Cutting of an Agate* on 13 November 1912, just in time for Lady Gregory's December tour there with the Abbey Players, and with its contents augmented to include 'Thoughts on Lady Gregory's Translations' (an essay compiled from Yeats's introductions to *Cuchulain of Muirthemne*, 1902 and *Gods and Fighting Men* 1904), the 'Preface to the First Edition of *The Well of the Saints*', 'Preface to the First Edition of John M. Synge's *Poems and Translations*', and 'John Shawe-Taylor', together with 'J. M. Synge and the Ireland of his Time', *Discoveries*, 'Poetry and Tradition', 'The Tragic Theatre' (first published in *The Mask* [Florence] 1910), and 'Edmund Spenser'. Yeats was thus able to issue a large section of his prose hitherto uncollected in the United States. A regretful preface implicitly castigated Macmillan (who had shown no interest in his prose since they had taken copies of *Idea of Good and Evil* from Bullen in 1903): the 'detailed defence of plays and players, published originally in *Samhain*, the occasional periodical of the theatre, and now making some three hundred pages of Mr. Bullen's collected edition of my writings, is not here' Yeats explained.[45] *The Cutting of an Agate* was a book Bullen could not afford to publish in Britain and the Commonwealth, and it remained unpublished in those markets until Macmillan brought it out in 1919.[46]

It can be seen, therefore, that in the United States Yeats had sacrificed a *Collected Works* to the need to copyright individual volumes, whereas in Britain, where copyright was not an issue, such trade editions as Bullen 'missed' were sacrificed by Yeats to his idea of a *Collected Works*. He also preferred to be edited well and printed beautifully than to be published lucratively. No doubt the Royal Literary Fund annual pension of £150 helped a good deal from 1910 onwards. No doubt, too, he had been for so long inured to poverty – from which he was somewhat isolated in his Coole Park summers – that it was difficult for Yeats to stir himself to do anything about Bullen.

Unwin again

Psycho-biographers and business historians might ponder the way in which Yeats's necessary foreconceit, his desire for a *Collected Works*, seems to have affected the trade cycle like sunspot activity. Whenever Yeats and a publisher began to talk about a new collected edition, an economic downturn was in full spate or on its way. In 1893, as the worst recession since 1812 hit, Yeats had begun pressing Unwin for a collected edition.[47] There had been a recession in 1907–08 when Bullen produced his great *Collected Works in Verse and Prose*.[48] By December 1915, when Yeats told his sister that he was 'transferr[ing] my works to Unwin', that publisher must have been very wary.[49] The primary issue was, of course, money: Bullen owed £143 11s. 6d. in royalties.[50] To have capitulated to Unwin at this stage would have been saddening for Yeats, and he would have been neither surprised nor disappointed when the move (as ever with Unwin) came to nothing. Evidence is scanty because Unwin's archives were largely destroyed, but the presumption must be that Unwin was as parsimonious to this established author as he had once been generous to young ones. Such was his usual pattern.

Money apart, there was another pressing reason. Although Bullen had a vast unsold stock of Yeats, his works were largely unavailable in Ireland. There were various reasons for this, including Yeats's unpopularity, his self-denying ordinance against sending his books for review in Ireland, and Bullen's lack of an effective agency either in that country or in the rest of the British Isles. The special Irish edition of his expensive *Collected Works* had failed.[51] The era in which Yeats could ignore his Irish audience and be published only for the few was however coming to an end. Even as he began writing plays such as *At the Hawk's Well* for coterie audiences,[52] he wanted to avoid the fate of Robert Bridges, known as a poet published only by coterie presses. The issue was focused for Yeats by the publication by Maunsel of Joseph Hone's *William Butler Yeats: the poet in contemporary Ireland* in 1916, when he decided to 'mak[e] some alterations in my publishing scheme' to make his work 'as a whole accessible. Up to this no young Irishman as poor as I was when I was twenty could afford to read me.' Hone's book allowed Yeats to reflect further. 'Your difficulties,' he told Hone, 'have come from my house being still unfinished, there are so many rooms and corridors that I am still building upon foundations laid long ago ...'.[53]

That old obsession of a completed *oeuvre*, or *Collected Works* now drove him to resolve the impasse with Bullen. Presumably at Yeats's request, and bearing in mind the added cachet of Yeats's role in Tagore's fame, as promoter, editor, handler and log-roller, A. P. Watt approached Macmillan. Three distinct aspects of the deal had to be put together by Watt: the transfer of stock and plates from the Shakespeare Head Press, securing the publication of new work, and – underlying the whole thing – a contract for a new *Collected Works.*

As early as 9 February 1916, Macmillan inspected some of Yeats's Unwin titles, but decided against taking them over.[54] On 14 March Macmillan took in and reviewed copies of the entire Shakespeare Head stock, some 13 titles, including all the in-print Theatre Editions.[55] Sent by Watt, the volumes were not despatched to readers, nor were they returned to the author, but by 18 April 1916, Watt had secured Yeats's agreement to 'the transfer of the existing stock of certain of his books from Mr A. H. Bullen' to Macmillan, on condition that Macmillan undertook 'the publication of a new edition of his collected works'. The volumes were listed as 'accepted' on 20 April.[56] Macmillan paid £210 for this stock (some 5,879 volumes) and plates from Bullen. 'All Yeats Works with the exception of 20 copies and spoils of each work and the whole of the [bound stock of the] Collected Edition were sent away to Burns on May 18 /1916', reads a mournful note in Bullen's stock book.[57] This remainder of the stock was in Macmillan's hands by 28 June or shortly after, and file copies are still in the Macmillan library. It was all rather different from the 1900 rejection.

The formal agreement with Macmillan calling for 'the publication of a Collected Edition in not less than six volumes' was concluded on 27 June 1916.[58] Yeats had to promise not to reprint or to add to Bullen's *Collected Works in Verse and Prose.* It is obvious from its depleted stock at November 1915 that Bullen had remaindered much of it in cheaper bindings some time before,[59] but after the transfer to Macmillan, he formally remaindered the *Collected Edition* in light brown paper boards with grey-green buckram spines.[60] Through various remainder merchants 186 sets were sold to pay Bullen's binder, James Burn, by the end of 1916, and a further 22 by October 1919.[61]

First fruits with Macmillan, London

By 10 April 1916 Yeats was revising *Responsibilities* 'for Macmillan', and soon sent the revised copy to Watt.[62] He was content to leave to Macmillan the date of publication, but wondered if the poems might not be published at the same time as *Reveries.* If Macmillan did 'not like the suggested title "New Poems" he can call it "Responsibilities" which runs with "Reveries". I have called it "New Poems" because it has sections from different books.'[63] He was in other ways prepared to accommodate Macmillan's textual preferences.[64]

The Macmillan Company then sent an advance copy of *Reveries over Childhood and Youth* (published in New York on 26 April 1916). Yeats's sisters had held back the Cuala issue of this book to 'suit the American publisher', and 'all kinds of copyright difficulties, the usual ones acentuated by wartime' had delayed Macmillan.[65] In order to render the edition less vulnerable to piracy, Yeats had to narrow the gap between Irish and American publication. The Cuala edition had been finished by All Souls' Day 1915, Emery Walker's block for the cover design of the American edition had been ready from the end of January, and the book was published on 20 March, with the New York edition published on 26 April 1916.[66] This was a book which had its problems. Yeats disliked the American placement of the legend to the frontispiece (his brother Jack's idyll of Sligo and Rosses' Point, 'Memory Harbour') on the tissue paper protecting the title-page from the frontispiece.

> I do not much like this plan, as the tissue paper should not be looked upon as a permanent part of the book. (I always tare it out when its purpose has been served.) Could you find a place for it? It could go at back of dedication, or title page or as a PS at end of preface? If the last I had better have a proof as I do not remember the wording & so cannot say how it will go with preface.[67]

It is unclear whether Yeats had ever seen a proof of the cover design. Unlike their London counterparts, the American editions of *Reveries* and *Responsibilities* are not bound in cloth, with gold blocking. Instead, the Sturge Moore designs were printed in black on blue-grey paper, glued to buff cloth in the case of *Reveries,* on blue-grey paper boards with a buff linen spine in the case of *Responsibilities*. Yeats asked Watt to request that Sturge Moore 'do a modified form of his "Reveries" design (this ~~American~~ design as it stands shows signs of haste) for the English edition of that book'.[68] Sturge Moore's design for the American edition borders on the allegorical, and is crowded with symbols (Plate 11). The tower, baby, female figure, mysterious sea and finger of God survive into the English design, but the whole thing is radically simplified and stylised (Plate 12). This is not the only work Sturge Moore was doing for Yeats at the time, and a new, multi-purpose symbolical design was already in progress, one which Yeats wanted the Macmillan Company of New York to use in future – a design of 'great beauty & better suited for my American books in general than the design for "Reveries"', Yeats wrote. He also expected Macmillan London to use it (though not for all of his books), and concluded that 'the block should be made in London & that the expense of this will not fall on me'.[69]

This was not the design worked up from the Irish boards of the Latin Gospels of St Willebrord (d. 739), which Sturge Moore had seen in Paris and adapted to 'illustrate' *At the Hawk's Well* in *Responsibilities*, but a wholly different design, and one which Yeats wanted to confer a more general significance.[70] The panelled design of the stylised rose and thorns (Plate 13) was to Yeats a 'fine grave design', first used upon both English and American editions of *Per Amica Silentia Lunae* (1918), and the American (but not the English) edition of *The Wild Swans at Coole* (1919), and upon one issue of the American *Selected Poems* (1921).[71] The cloth issue of *Selected Poems* uses the rejected Sturge Moore design made for the American edition of *Reveries.* Only the book title itself has been changed (Plate 14). Wade implies that the cloth issue came first, which might suggest that Yeats decided to restore the Rose design on the paper issue, but evidence is scanty.

The Rose emblem offered Yeats a way of forestalling American book designers and of presenting himself in a uniform livery for the American market, much as Althea Gyles's spines on *The Poetical Works of William B. Yeats* and *The Unicorn from the Stars and other Plays* had done for a number of years.[72] Sturge Moore had even provided for spines of different thicknesses, offering one spinal design of a single-thorned stem, and another of a pair of such stems. By contrast, his gold-blocked blue cloth covers on the English editions from *Reveries* through to *The Cutting of an Agate* and *The Wild Swans at Coole* allowed some unity but also individuality to the various volumes.

The deal with Macmillan London also allowed Yeats some way to lessen the worst effects of that resetting necessary under American copyright law. 'I think the American firm had better do my book of poems from the proofs of the English edition, – it is probably too late for the American season now in any case', he wrote to Watt.[73] *Reveries over Childhood and Youth* and *Responsibilities and Other Poems* were published in London on 10 October 1916, and the New York edition of *Responsibilities* followed on 1 November. There is no doubt that Yeats had long wanted such a publishing system, especially when volumes were initiated in London where he had easy access to publishers and their readers or editors. Such a system was established in 1916, and Macmillan in London did provide Macmillan New York with marked proofs from which to (re)set Yeats's new work.[74] The system was not really secure. He 'hate[d] correcting American proofs'.[75] The difficulty of working with editors on the other side of the Atlantic goes only some way to explaining why Yeats, despite Quinn's urging, continued to feel hostile to the processes of initiatory publishing in America. Ultimately, he resented the loss of control over the finish of his work which he felt the established relationship with Thomas Mark assured him. American publishers were just too far away.

By the time he was planning his *Collected Edition* in the 1920s, Yeats was also warning Macmillan of the possibility of 'no end of a row with that ill-tempered Unwin'.[76] Yeats remained the hostage of his successful publishing arrangement with Unwin (who had refused to deal with Watt), until *Poems* (1895) had run its course, and this did not happen until Ernest Benn took over Unwin's *Poems* and drove Yeats's sales down to nothing after 1927.[77]

Yeats's transfer was decided during Easter 1916, and on Sunday 30 April, the day after the remaining Volunteers of the Irish Republican Brotherhood surrendered, he wrote a rather anxious PS: 'I have been hoping to hear that the books have been transferred. Is Sir Frederick Macmillan back?'[78] It was in general an anxious time: he had refused a knighthood in late 1915, was in London but did not know quite where his future lay.[79] It is only faintly possible that his anxiety about being accepted by Macmillan echoes his political rejection in 1900.[80]

The news of the transfer was optimistically received by the Irish literary press. John S. Crone supplied the 'Editor's Gossip' in the *Irish Book Lover*:

> In the thirty years that have sped so swiftly since Mr. Yeats's maiden, and now much sought after, publishing venture, 'Mosada' – an off-print from the 'Dublin University Review', then edited by his friend Rolleston – issued from the house of Sealey, Bryers, he has had many publishers at home and abroad. Now, I am told, he has finally transferred all his copyrights to the great firm of Macmillan, who will henceforth be solely responsible for his future works. I should not be a bit surprised but that when normal conditions return the outcome might be an additional bay in the chaplet of our bard, viz., a Globe Edition of Yeats![81]

Conclusion

Other chapters in this volume confirm that on the whole Macmillan sought to publish authors at the height of their powers. Yeats was no exception. By the time he came to Macmillan in 1916 he had one great, multi-volume *Collected Works* behind him, and a continuing dream of new occasions for further such assemblages.

He had procrastinated in resolving the difficulty with his old friend A. H. Bullen until both were in an impossible position. This, surely, is the point. When we follow the working life of the poet from publisher to publisher we see something of great constancy. The first two volumes of Yeats's letters show that he had to be professional to survive even before he had begun to succeed. John Morley had been thus able to wrap up his revenge in the captious dismissal 'His work has been well before the public, and I do not observe that the publishers who have had it in hand, have clung to it.'[82]

If one pieces together fragments from the archives of Elkin Mathews, T. Fisher Unwin, A. H. Bullen, the Shakespeare Head Press, Sidgwick & Jackson, and Macmillan on both sides of the Atlantic, they give life to each other. The Yeats who would not let Bullen print 'one word I have not passed' in 1907 was the same man who demonstrated his concern for costs and technical processes in restructuring his *Collected Works* in 1913, and who brokered the runaway success of *Gitanjali* in the same period, before presenting himself to Macmillan as a formidably efficient and co-operative working writer in 1916. Yeats was magnanimous in not referring to how badly he had been treated in 1900.

The life of a revising author's texts is measured out in bibliographical occasions. This book-dependent contingency is every bit as important for the understanding of intention as is artistic preference. A transfigured awareness of authorial intentionality is of enormous importance to literary criticism, and, in the case of revising authors such as Yeats, to textual and to literary biography. It has become possible through close scrutiny of a number of publishers' archives to recover textual intention in the context of authorial expectation under specific and demonstrably well-understood conditions. Once the author/publisher's reader relation has been fully explored, a pattern of 'active' and 'latent' intentions can be descried in the realisation of long-standing projects and contracts, with the former, of course, contingent upon the latter.

In this way, the Macmillan archive has transformed what we know of the working life of W. B. Yeats and the lives of his texts. New texts have been prepared, and continue to be prepared, by Macmillan and a number of other publishers, based on interpretation of materials in the Macmillan archives and in collateral Yeats collections around the world. Understanding of these materials demands a full appreciation of the partnerships between Yeats and various editors in the firm from 1916, notably that with Thomas Mark who worked on his texts from 1929 to Yeats's death and after, right through until after his own retirement – Mark died in 1963 – with the more distant collaboration of George Yeats.

During the 1980s that archive initiated, fuelled and, finally, resolved the textual debate surrounding Yeats's last intentions for his poetic *oeuvre.* Initially very divergent views were taken of this author/publisher/in-house editor relationship, beginning with the extraordinary charge – that, after Yeats's death, Mrs Yeats and Thomas Mark engaged in a 'process ... of ... corrupting the texts which he had worked so hard to perfect'.[83] More recent work, and a greater understanding of the wider context of the Macmillan archive itself, and the archival field in which it is pre-eminent, has enabled scholars to see the eccentricity of that remark in the context of full examination of the archive from 1929 to 1949.[84]

Notes

1. *The Collected Letters of W. B. Yeats: Volume One, 1865–1895,* edited by John Kelly and Eric Domville (Oxford: Clarendon Press, 1986), p. 7. I am grateful to Professor Kelly and Oxford University Press for permission to cite copyright material.
2. See Warwick Gould, '"Playing at treason with Miss Maud Gonne": Yeats and his publishers in 1900' in *Modernist Writers and the Marketplace,* edited by Ian Willison, Warwick Gould and Warren Chernaik (London: Macmillan Press, 1996), pp. 36–80.
3. Charles Morgan, *The House of Macmillan, 1843–1943* (London: Macmillan, 1943), p. 222. On Thomas Mark's drafting of much of this book, see Warwick Gould, 'W. B. Yeats and the Resurrection of the Author', *The Library,* 16 (June 1994), 101–34 (p.115, nn. 59, 60).
4. Morgan, pp. 222, 144.
5. This is John Gross's judgement. Morley was 'a mid-Victorian ... a self important, watchful front-bench rhetorician'. See John Gross, *The Rise and Fall of the Man of Letters: Aspects of English Literary Life since 1800* (London: Weidenfeld and Nicolson, 1969), p. 112.
6. Gould, '"Playing at treason ..."', pp. 51–3.
7. The remark is Clement Shorter's. See Bernard Falk, *Five Years Dead* (London: The Book Club, 1938), p. 258.
8. *The Collected Letters of W. B. Yeats: Volume Three, 1901–1904,* edited by John Kelly and Ronald Schuchard (Oxford: Clarendon Press, 1994), pp. 67, 72, 81.
9. See Verlaine's 'My visit to London (November, 1893)', translated by Arthur Symons, *The Savoy* 2 (April 1896), 113–35 (p. 120).
10. His authority was a letter from a 'Mr. Marsden'. The implication is that Marsden – known to Brett – had declined the book. Reynolds, in establishing his own *bona fides,* was unwilling to reveal Marsden's reasons (Macmillan papers, NYPL).
11. Reynolds was agent for the Cassell Publishing Company, Heinemann, Sampson Low and Marston, Unwin and Constable. See Frederick Lewis Allen, *Paul Revere Reynolds* (New York, 1944), and James Hepburn, *The Author's*

Empty Purse and the Rise of the Literary Agent (London: Oxford University Press, 1968), pp. 67–75.

12. *The Collected Letters of W. B. Yeats: Volume Two, 1896–1900*, edited by Warwick Gould, John Kelly and Deirdre Toomey (Oxford: Clarendon Press, 1997), pp. 156–8, 199.
13. Arthur Waugh, *A Hundred Years of Publishing, being the Story of Chapman and Hall, Ltd* (London: Chapman and Hall, 1930), pp. 262–3.
14. Shakespeare Head Press papers, Stratford Record Centre, ER 136/5, ff. 25–8. The initial binding order for 'Shakespeare Head Press' sets was 150. Twenty-five sets separately ordered in late 1908 could have been an Irish set, but (to judge by their price) were evidently also vellum-bound. Fifty-eight copies of Wade's *A Bibliography of the Writings of W. B. Yeats* (contained in Vol. 8) were separately bound, perhaps from 'overs' of Volume 8.
15. The number of 'spoils' (Bullen had allowed for up to 60) is uncertain. The Harry Ransom Center, University of Texas at Austin, has a Shakespeare Head Press set bound in full buckram (dark brown), stamped on each spine in gold with identical decoration, lettering, and so on, to that seen on the vellum sets, but there is no indication in Bullen's records that they were bound by Burn. The top and bottom (bevelled) boards are blank (PR5900 A1 1908b Copy 1 HRC). This state is not recorded in Allan Wade, *A Bibliography of the Writings of W. B. Yeats*, third edition, revised by Russell K. Alspach (London: Rupert Hart-Davis, 1968, hereafter Wade plus item number).
16. Stratford Record Centre, ER 136/8, f.6. £56 5s. 10d. had been due to Yeats on the *Collected Edition* alone by 30 September 1912, and a further £35 16s. 2d. by 30 November 1915. Yeats received a 17½ per cent royalty on the four-guinea issue, and 10 per cent on the cheaper issue. Of the 103 sets sold in the period 1912–15, 76 were of the cheaper issue (SRC. ER 136/8a).
17. *Letters to W. B. Yeats*, edited by Richard J. Finneran, George Mills Harper and William M. Murphy, with the assistance of Alan B. Himber (London: Macmillan; New York: Columbia University Press, 1977), pp. 256–7. Macmillan New York rigidly adhered to this policy, even cancelling its commitment to take copies of the 1927 *Stories of Red Hanrahan and The Secret Rose*, decorated by Norah McGuinness, because the works it contained were in copyright in the United States, and 'the copyright would, of course, be vitiated if we imported copies of your edition' (Brett to Frederick Macmillan, 28 October 1927, NYPL).
18. Macmillan did, however, allow the word 'Plays' – on the spine only – of volume 2.
19. Under the 1998 Copyright Term Extension Act, this licence will continue to dictate his reception there until 2009.
20. *Letters to W. B. Yeats*, pp. 256–7.
21. *Letters to W. B. Yeats*, pp. 256–7.
22. *Letters to W. B. Yeats*, pp. 262–3.
23. *Letters to W. B. Yeats*, pp. 256, 263–4 and *The Letters of W. B. Yeats*, edited by Allan Wade (London: Rupert Hart-Davis, 1954), p. 576. Yeats explained that an updated edition would 'drive out' unrevised sets which could be 'sold off'. Twenty-four sets would have to be sacrificed in this way but it 'would be a mistake ... to spoil a large number of unbound copies for the sake of so few' (*ibid.*).

24. *The Letters of W. B. Yeats*, p. 578. He had taken 30 French lessons, and 'just paid for 50 more'.
25. See Krishna Dutta and Andrew Robinson, *Rabindranath Tagore: the Myriad Minded Man* (London: Bloomsbury, 1995), pp. 163 and ff.
26. Dutta and Robinson, p. 165.
27. See Ezra Pound, 'Rabindranath Tagore', *Fortnightly Review,* March 1913, p. 576. In January 1917, Pound claimed that the 'boom' originated in 'the fiat of the omnipotent literati of distinction'. Tagore had then 'lapsed into religion and optimism and was boomed by the pious non-conformists. Also because it got the Swedish Academy out of the difficulty of deciding between European writers whose claims appeared to conflict. Sic. Hardy or Henry James? Tagore obviously was unique in the known modern Orient. And then, the right people suggested him. AND Sweeden is Sweeden. It was also a damn good smack for the British Academic Committee, who had turned down Tagore (on account of his biscuit complexion) and who elected in his stead to their august corpse, Alice Meynell and Dean Inge. Therefore his Nobel Prize gave pleasure unto the elect.' (*The Letters of Ezra Pound 1907–1941*, edited by D. D. Paige [London: Faber, 1951], pp. 159–60. Sturge Moore and the Royal Society of Literature had lobbied for Tagore.
29. Rabindranath Tagore, *Gitanjali (Song Offerings)* (London: Macmillan, 1913), pp. xiii–xiv, xvi–xvii. For Dante Gabriel Rossetti's sonnets 'Willowwood' and the drawing, 'How they Met Themselves', see *The Collected Works of Dante Gabriel Rossetti*, edited by William Rossetti (London: Ellis and Elvey, 1897), I, 201–2; and plate 3 of *Yeats and the Nineties: Yeats Annual* 14, edited by Warwick Gould (London: Macmillan Press, 2000).
30. Mohini Mohun Chatterji (1858–1936), a brilliant young Hindu member of the Theosophical Society, was related to Debendra Nath Tagore, father of Rabindranath Tagore. See P. S. Sri, 'Yeats and Mohini Chatterjee', *Yeats Annual* 11 (London: Macmillan Press, 1994), pp. 61–76.
31. 18 February 1913. The letter was sold at Sotheby's 15–16 July 1998, lot 158. It carries on, immediately quoting verses beginning 'She has not grown uncivil' (cf., *The Variorum Edition of the Poems of W. B. Yeats*, edited by Peter Allt and Russell K. Alspach [New York: Macmillan, 1957], p. 365). See also *Yeats & Women*, edited by Deirdre Toomey (London: Macmillan Press, 1997), pp. 294–5, and cf., the confident claim of Richard Finneran that Yeats would not have divulged the identity of Mabel Beardsley as the subject of this group of poems, but would have said 'in effect, that although the poem may have been "about" Mabel Beardsley, he preferred to present it as a universal statement on death and dying'. See *The Poems: Second Edition* (New York: Scribner, 1997), edited by Richard J. Finneran, p. 623.
32. Dutta and Robinson, p. 184.
33. *The Letters of W. B. Yeats*, pp. 611–12.
34. 1 July [1916]. Add.MS. 55003, f. 28.
35. Add.MS. 55003, f. 29. In the same letter Yeats wondered if he were not 'over-anxious' and hoped the reaction might 'not go very far'.
36. Published as *Lover's Gift; and Crossing* by Sir Rabindranath Tagore (London: Macmillan, 1918).
37. Received by George Macmillan, 29 January 1917. Add.MS. 55003, ff. 43–4.

38. See for example, David Holdeman, *Much Labouring: the Texts and Authors of Yeats's First Modernist Books* (Ann Arbor: University of Michigan Press, 1997), pp. 133 & ff.
39. Holdeman (p. 134) blames Bullen for the non-appearance of 'new volumes of poetry on their own' in Britain, as though such collections as *Poems 1899–1905*, the *Collected Works* itself, and *Poems: Second Series* were not 'new volumes' produced to Yeats's specifications and for his purposes.
40. Letters to George P. Brett, 31 March 1905, dict. Lady Gregory; 5 June 1905, dict. Annie Horniman (NYPL).
41. The Cuala Press edition of *The Green Helmet and Other Poems* had been published in Dundrum in December 1910, and a copyright edition published in New York by R. Harold Paget and entered at the Library of Congress on 16 January 1911. The Macmillan Company's edition added a group of new poems which were later to go into *Responsibilities: Poems and a Play* (Dundrum: Cuala Press, 1914). See Wade 84–5, 101, 110.
42. The second volume, *Dramatical Poems* was reprinted in 1909 and 1911, revised and resubtitled *Dramatic Poems* in 1912 to incorporate new texts of *The Countess Cathleen* and *The Land of Heart's Desire*, and reprinted five times until 1921 (Wade 98).
43. *The Letters of W. B. Yeats*, p. 596. The presentation copy to T. Sturge Moore, in the Sterling Library, University of London, is inscribed 'December 1912'. Similar inscriptions can be found in other presentation copies. Allan Wade's copy, inscribed by Yeats in December 1912 has a similar annotation (Lilly Library).
44. *The Letters of W. B. Yeats*, p. 561.
45. *The Cutting of an Agate* (New York: Macmillan, 1912), p. v.
46. Wade 126. 'Certain Noble Plays of Japan' replaced 'Thoughts on Lady Gregory's Translations', and the Preface was revised.
47. From 1870 to 1900 prices in Britain fell by a third as free trade and technological advance coincided with falling unit costs and rising wages.
48. As Macmillan signed Yeats's agreement for a *Collected Works* in 1916 their letters to authors tended to begin 'In view of the very unsatisfactory state of the book market we are not at all disposed ...' (Add.MS. 55534, f. 859). Yeats's modest plan for a uniform edition was made on 23 December 1920. A crash followed in 1921, and between 1921 and 1938 prices fell again by one-third. Thomas Mark first worked on *Selected Poems* in the infamous year of 1929, and while Macmillan began preparing for the *Edition de Luxe* in 1930 (Add.MS. 55704, f. 195), conditions in publishing deteriorated in 1931–33, his *Edition de Luxe* went into abeyance, the stopgap *Collected Poems* appeared (Add.MS. 55731, ff. 405–7), and so on, throughout the Thirties, the War, the later Forties, the Fifties.
49. *The Letters of W. B. Yeats*, p. 604.
50. Stratford Record Centre, ER 136/8a.
51. Bullen had expected Maunsel and Co. (Dublin) to take 50 sets. Maunsel originally advertised the vellum-bound set. P. S. O'Hegarty saw a set bound for the Irish market in dark green buckram, and thought that a 'maximum of 20' sets had been issued in this way (Wade, p. 94). The implication of the Shakespeare Head Press account books is that these sets were not bound by Burn.

52. 'I hope to create a form of drama which may delight the best minds of my time, and all the more because it can pay its expenses without the others. If when the play is perfectly performed (musicians are the devil) Balfour and Sargent and Ricketts and Sturge Moore and John and the Prime Minister and a few pretty ladies will come to see it, I shall have a success that would have pleased Sophocles. No press, no photographs in the papers, no crowd. I shall be happier than Sophocles. I shall be as lucky as a Japanese dramatic poet at the Court of the Shogun' (*The Letters of W. B. Yeats*, p. 610).
53. *The Letters of W. B. Yeats*, p. 605.
54. Copies of *The Land of Heart's Desire* and *The Countess Cathleen*, forwarded to Macmillan by Gladys M. Riley, arrived on 9 February 1916 and were returned the same day (Add.MS. 56008, f. 139). They played no part in the negotiations, but allowed Macmillan to gauge the opposition.
55. The titles of the volumes in Macmillan's records are abbreviated and far from accurate. The copies include *Stories of Red Hanrahan: The Secret Rose: Rosa Alchemica* (1913); *The Shadowy Waters* (edition unknown, but probably the 1906 A. H. Bullen 'Theatre Edition'); *The Tables of the Law; & The Adoration of the Magi* (almost certainly the 1914 Shakespeare Head Press edition); a volume called *Poems* (possibly Unwin's seventh edition, 1913, but also possibly A. H. Bullen's *Poems: second series* of 1909 in the 1913 reissue, the remainder of which was transferred to Macmillan, Wade 83); *The King's Threshold* (presumably the second of the two Shakespeare Head Press 'Theatre Editions' of 1915, the remainder of which was transferred to Macmillan after 28 June 1916, Wade 91); *The Pot of Broth* (probably the Bullen second 'Theatre Edition' 1911, the remainder of which was subsequently transferred to Macmillan, Wade 61); *Deirdre* (probably the Shakespeare Head Press second 'Theatre Edition' of 1914, the remainder of which was transferred to Macmillan, Wade 87); *The Hour Glass* (probably one of 50 copies of the 1914 Cuala edition, Wade 108); *Cathleen ni Houlihan* (probably the third 'Theatre Edition' of the Shakespeare Head Press, 1911, the remainder of which was transferred to Macmillan, Wade 63); *On Baile's Strand* (probably the A. H. Bullen 'Theatre Edition' of 1907, the remainder of which was transferred to Macmillan, Wade 68); *Ideas of Good and Evil* (probably the 1914 Shakespeare Head Press fourth edition, the remainder of which was transferred to Macmillan, Wade 46); *The Celtic Twilight* (probably the 1912 A. H. Bullen edition, the remainder of which was transferred to Macmillan, Wade 38); *Plays for an Irish Theatre* (probably the second [1913] impression of the 1911 A. H. Bullen edition, the remainder of which was transferred to Macmillan, Wade 92). All of these volumes have been identified from Add.MS. 56008, f. 181, and Macmillan's file copies.
56. Add.MS. 55003, f. 64; 54897, f. 193, and 56021. See also *The Secret Rose: Stories by W. B. Yeats: a variorum edition*, edited by Warwick Gould, Philip L. Marcus and Michael J. Sidnell (London: Macmillan, 1992), p. xxi.
57. Stratford Record Centre, ER 136/8, f.6.
58. Add.MS. 54898, f. 138. The volumes were to be issued at 7s. 6d. net, and a royalty of 20 per cent paid to Yeats in the home market. Yeats kept all rights of translation and dramatisation, and the copyright was to revert to him after five years, at which point he would purchase plates and stock.

59. By 17 November 1915 he had just 345 quires and 12 bound sets at Stratford, and a further 6 bound sets at the remainder merchants W. W. Gibbings in Bloomsbury. There was one further set on the premises, making a total of 364 bound and unbound sets, contrasting with previously reported stock of 450 quires and 22 bound sets, a total of 472 on 30 September 1912 (ER 136/8, f. 6).
60. These bindings are virtually identical with those on such titles as *The Celtic Twilight* (1912), and were done in Stratford. Bullen had temporarily closed his own bindery in 1907, but seems still to have it in May 1913 (Sidgwick and Jackson papers, Bodleian Library, 279, ff. 83–4).
61. Stratford Record Centre, ER 136/8, ff. 58–9. Wade states (p. 94) that 'Later Bullen issued a "remainder" of the unsold copies ... bound in light brown paper boards with grey-green linen spine', but does not say when this was done. Bullen still had 140 bound sets in January 1917, but only 52 sets by 26 January 1921 (Stratford Record Centre, ER 136/9\2, 9\3).
62. *The Letters of W. B. Yeats*, p. 612. 'I send under a separate cover the contents of my new book of verse. It contains one book published by my sister "Responsibilities" ~~with a play~~ & part of the contents of another. Neither of the books has ever been sent for review. I have much more verse written since but am keeping this book to make a small book for my sister sometime next winter' (Add.MS. 55003, f. 26). The letter was sent on by Watt to Frederick Macmillan and is stamped F. M., Sunday, April 30 [1916].
63. *The Letters of W. B. Yeats*, p. 612. The title *New Poems* was provisional. Late in life Yeats used it for a 1938 Cuala volume, but almost every volume Yeats published after 1933 was in effect unfinished. Yeats offered 'a preface or prefatory note' to 'explain ... the previous publication at Cuala Press'.
64. While *Responsibilities* was in production, Yeats rewrote 'The Witch' as 'The Bitch' on the proof, but acquiesced when Sir Frederick requested the original text and title to be restored (Add.MS. 55537, f. 498). '... much as I desire to see the vocabulary of the seventeenth century restored I prefer to leave martyrdom to the young who desire it', Yeats wrote (Add.MS. 55003, f. 29). Pound was furious that the poem had been 'castrated by the greasy Macmillan' but Yeats had been similarly accommodating to Bullen's suggestions. See Warwick Gould, '"Witch" or "Bitch" – Which? Yeats, Archives and the Profession of Authorship' in *Writing the Lives of Writers*, edited by Warwick Gould and Thomas F. Staley (London: Macmillan, 1998), pp. 173–90.
65. *The Letters of W. B. Yeats*, pp. 602, 607.
66. See *W. B. Yeats and T. Sturge Moore: their correspondence, 1901–1937*, edited by Ursula Bridge (London: Routledge; New York: Oxford University Press, 1953), p. 24; Wade 111, 112.
67. 18 July [1916] (Add.MS. 55003, f. 30), quoted in Warwick Gould, 'Singular Pluralities: Titles of Yeats's *Autobiographies*', *Yeats Annual* 11 (London: Macmillan, 1994), pp. 205–18 (pp. 210–11). The legend was placed in the list of illustrations in the London edition (Add.MS. 55537, f. 752).
68. Add.MS. 55003, f. 26.
69. Add.MS. 55003, f. 26.
70. See Warwick Gould, *Yeats Annual* 4 (London Macmillan, 1986), plates 9–11.
71. Wade 120–1, 130, 128.

72. Wade 65, 71, 73. Gyles's designs for the Unwin editions of *Poems*, and Bullen's *The Secret Rose, The Celtic Twilight* (1902), *Poems, 1899–1905* and *Poems: second series* had performed a similar function in the British market.
73. 30 April [1916] Add.MS. 55003, ff. 26–7. A 'complete set' of proofs of *Responsibilities* was sent from Macmillan in London to New York in August (*W. B. Yeats and T. Sturge Moore: their correspondence, 1901–1937*, p. 25).
74. Macmillan London also 'caught up' with *The Cutting of an Agate* (1918), first published in New York in 1912.
75. Draft undated letter to Watt, National Library of Ireland MS. 301018. See also *The Secret Rose, Stories by W. B. Yeats: a variorum edition*, p. xxv. Some resetting necessary under American copyright law was done from duplicate sets of uncorrected English proofs, and American printings of the Macmillan *Uniform Edition* of the 1920s contain many unauthorised departures from the English texts. On his insistence that Scribner's Sons 'must print from the latest London text of my work' for their *Dublin Edition* in the late 1930s because the 'American editions of my writings are full of misprints' see *Yeats's Poems*, edited by A. Norman Jeffares, with an appendix by Warwick Gould (London: Macmillan, 1989; third, revised edition 1996), p. 720.
76. Add.MS. 54898, f. 55. See also Gould 'Singular Pluralities', pp. 211–12.
77. 'This book for about thirty years brought me twenty or thirty times as much money as any other book of mine – no twenty or thirty times as much as all my other books put together ['about thirty-five pounds a year' in 1905: see *The Letters of W. B. Yeats*, p. 470]. This success was pure accident. 'Five or six years ago "T. Fisher Unwin" ceased to exist and it passed to the firm of "Benn" & within twelve months the sales were halved, & another twelve months fallen to one tenth of what they had been.' So Yeats wrote in a copy in his own library. See Edward O'Shea, *A Descriptive Catalog of W. B. Yeats's Library* (New York and London: Garland Publishing, 1985), no. 2404 and Wade 153,154.
78. Add.MS. 55003, ff. 26–7.
79. 'The Dublin tragedy has been a great sorrow and anxiety', he was to write to Lady Gregory on 11 May. In the 'great grief' he felt 'We have lost the ablest and most fine-natured of our young men.' See *The Letters of W. B. Yeats*, pp. 612, 604.
80. 'Easter 1916' was finished on 25 September 1916. It was privately printed by Clement Shorter in an edition of 25 copies 'for distribution among his friends' (Wade 117), but it was not accessioned by the British Museum until 9 June 1917. It was probably not available for distribution until Spring 1917 (Lady Gregory's copy was not inscribed until 31 May. See Conrad A. Balliet, with the assistance of Christine Mawhinney, *W. B. Yeats: a census of the manuscripts* [New York and London: Garland Publishing, 1990], p. 16). The poem was omitted from the Macmillan edition of *The Wild Swans at Coole* (1919) where Yeats might have been expected to collect the poem, and appeared in *The New Statesman*, 23 October 1920, and in the New York *Dial* in November 1920, and was collected in *Michael Robartes and the Dancer* (Dundrum: Cuala, February 1921). Macmillan did not give this book a trade edition because by 23 December 1920 Yeats had begun pressing them for some action on a new 'Collected Works' (Add.MS. 55003, f. 64). The resultant uniform edition began with *Later Poems*, published on 3 November 1922 and

containing the *Michael Robartes* poems. Tom Paulin has argued that Yeats suppressed the poem only to issue it in 1920 when Terence MacSwiney was on the point of death in Brixton prison. He offers evidence of a copy of *Easter 1916* signed for Henry Maggs in April 1917, and shows that Yeats was uncertain of publication because the poem was one of a group on the Irish Rebellion. See 'Yeats's Hunger-strike Poem' in Paulin's *Minotaur* (London: Faber, 1992), pp. 133–50.

81. *Irish Book Lover* VIII (1917), p. 13.
82. Add.MS. 55961, ff. 181–3.
83. See Richard J. Finneran, *Editing Yeats's Poems* (London: Macmillan, 1984), p. 30. The same author's *Editing Yeats's Poems: a reconsideration* (London: Macmillan, 1990) showed that he preferred not to reconsider this charge (p. 39).
84. See Gould, 'W. B. Yeats and the Resurrection of the Author', pp. 101–34; 'Appendix Six: the Definitive Edition: a History of the Final Arrangement of Yeats's Work' in *Yeats's Poems*, edited by A. Norman Jeffares, pp. 706–49; 'Predators and Editors: Yeats in the pre- and post-Copyright Era' in *Textual Monopolies*, edited by Patrick Parrinder and Warren Chernaik (London: Office for Humanities Communication/Centre for English Studies, 1997), pp. 69–82. More work on the period 1916–29 awaits the publication of Yeats's letters of the period, see, however, *The Secret Rose, Stories by W. B. Yeats: a variorum edition*, pp. xx–xliii.

10
A Risk-bearing Author
Maynard Keynes and his publishers[1]

D. E. Moggridge

For historians of economics, the Macmillan archive is a relatively unexploited treasure. It is a treasure because Macmillan published most of the leading English economists writing during the period of the initial archive: Henry Fawcett, William Stanley Jevons, Herbert Somerton Foxwell, Henry Sidgwick, Alfred Marshall, John Neville Keynes, John Shield Nicholson, J. A. Hobson, A. C. Pigou and John Maynard Keynes.[2] It is relatively unexploited in that, except for some studies of Jevons, Marshall and Maynard Keynes, historians of economics have not used it.[3]

John Maynard Keynes's relationship with Macmillan was unusual in several respects, and certainly very different from those of both his predecessors and contemporaries. For his own work, he dealt with five English-language publishers during his career: Cambridge University Press, Harcourt Brace, the Hogarth Press, Macmillan, and the New Republic.[4] He signed his first contract with Cambridge, but, in the end, published only his last book with them – an edition of *An Abstract of a Treatise on Human Nature 1740: a pamphlet hitherto unknown by David Hume* (1938), which he edited with Piero Sraffa. He published three pamphlets with the Hogarth Press: *The Economic Consequences of Mr Churchill* (1925), *A Short View of Russia* (1925) and *The End of Laissez Faire* (1926). Only the first of these, whose 10,000 copies at short notice obviously disrupted her life, is recorded in Virginia Woolf's *Diary*, but both the first and last received brief mention in her letters.[5] The New Republic published a combined American edition of the last two pamphlets under the title *Laissez Faire and Communism*; otherwise, with the exception of *A Treatise on Probability* (1921), handled by Macmillan's American house, Harcourt Brace acted as his American publisher.[6] In Britain, except for his 1929 pamphlet (with Hubert Henderson) *Can Lloyd George Do It?*, Keynes channelled all his remaining publications through Macmillan – who also published the *Economic Journal* which Keynes edited from 1912 to 1945, and various other publications of the Royal Economic Society of which he was secretary from 1913 to 1945.

Keynes's first contacts with the Macmillans came while he was at Eton, where Daniel Macmillan was in the Election behind Maynard and a close friend (indeed, if we are to believe Keynes's record of his sexual activity, they were experimental lovers in Keynes's final year[7]). They remained friends, regularly exchanging visits, after Keynes left Eton for King's College, Cambridge, and Dan went on to Balliol College, Oxford. Thus it was not surprising that in August 1910 he began reviewing manuscripts for the firm, nor that Macmillan suggested he try his hand at an economics textbook. Keynes replied somewhat cautiously:

> Many thanks for your suggestion that I should write some day an economic textbook. Eventually I hope I may:- but an elementary book is almost entirely a matter of exposition, and I feel that I want much more experience in teaching over the whole field of the subject before I can know what the right matter of exposition is.
>
> I am delivering some lectures next year, both in Cambridge and London, on Indian Trade and Finance; and I have some thought of making them into a small book, if they turn out well. But they would not be elementary.
>
> Perhaps I might write you about them at some future time, if I find them, when they are written, worth publishing.[8]

There matters rested for the moment.

Earlier that year Cambridge University Press had agreed to publish Keynes's revised fellowship dissertation for King's College, Cambridge, *A Treatise on Probability*.[9] In September 1912, with a substantial amount of manuscript in hand and a request from Keynes to provide proofs for what existed, the Press realised that the book would be much longer (420 rather than 320 pages) than envisaged. As it anticipated a larger loss (£110 rather than £80) the Press asked the author to advance £30 towards the costs of the book on publication – that £30 being the first charge on any profits. It also asked for the whole copy before sending any of it to the printer.[10] Faced with these demands, Keynes wrote to

M. R. James, the Provost of King's and chair of the Syndics, complaining that he was expected 'to put myself in a position of greater risk than the Press of losing money on the book, but am refused all information by which I can judge of the risk I am asked to run', and requesting, finally, to be released from his contract with the Press.[11]

Once freed, he took both *Probability* and a project tentatively entitled 'Monetary Affairs of India' to Macmillan on a half-profits basis.[12] *Indian Currency and Finance* – the title eventually chosen for this, his first book – appeared on 6 June 1913, the day after Keynes's thirtieth birthday and a month after he had attended his first meeting as a member of the Royal Commission on Indian Finance and Currency. It was followed by the anonymously edited *England's Financial Supremacy* (1917), a translation of German articles on British finance prepared jointly with Dudley Ward. However, Keynes's relationship with the firm changed significantly with the publication in 1919 of the work that made him a household name, *The Economic Consequences of the Peace.*

Keynes had resigned from the Treasury over the Treaty of Versailles on 5 June 1919. At the urging of General Smuts that he write a 'clear connected account of what the financial and economic clauses of the Treaty actually are and mean and what their probable results will be',[13] Keynes began his book at Vanessa Bell's and Duncan Grant's Sussex farmhouse, Charleston, on 23 June. He offered the work on 26 July to Daniel Macmillan, who accepted on the firm's 'usual terms' two days later, also agreeing to ask the New York office how many copies they would take. Macmillan was clearly thinking in terms of a print-run of 1,000 copies, whereas Keynes had a much more substantial figure of 5,000 in mind. It was George Macmillan, standing in for the holidaying Dan, who agreed to obtain an estimate for 5,000, while expressing the opinion that it was still probably not worth printing an American edition, and briskly reminding Keynes that if he didn't like Macmillan's American arrangements he could go elsewhere.[14] With George Macmillan's estimate of 18 August to hand, Keynes calculated the available profits on a printing of 5,000 in various bindings and at various prices.[15] As a result, the basis of the author–publisher relationship was transformed. Keynes would hereafter publish on commission: he would pay the costs of production; Macmillan would receive a commission of 10 per cent on those costs (printing, paper, binding, advertising and so on), as well as 10 per cent on the net amount received from sales. Keynes would keep any remaining profits.[16] Desultory discussions on an American edition continued for a time with William Macmillan,[17] but there the position was also transformed through the intervention of Felix

Frankfurter, Professor of Law at Harvard (with whom Keynes dined on 25 August) and the influential American journalist, Walter Lippmann: on 2 October 1919 Harcourt Brace agreed to produce and publish the book in the United States on a royalty basis.[18] The rest, as they say, was 'history': the book was an outstanding publishing success, selling 60,000 copies in Britain and the United States in its first two months. Furthermore, he also received $6,947.37 from Harcourt Brace in March and $5,025 in September.[19] It was just as well, as Keynes needed *advances* on his profits to help bail himself out of the disastrous consequences of his currency speculations in May 1920.[20]

Keynes's post-1919 arrangement with Macmillan meant that he had much more control over all aspects of production, pricing and publicity. For example, in August 1920 he and Harold Macmillan argued over the production costs and possible returns from a cheap edition of *Economic Consequences* 'on inferior paper and with paper-board binding'.[21] At the same time, he tried on the idea of 'a definitive, revised library edition' which would include 'any corrections which the passage of time has made necessary and also probably a postscript giving my views on what has happened since I wrote'.[22] On 15 June 1921, in connection with the forthcoming publication of *A Treatise on Probability* (1921), he asked for a list of review copies so that 'he could then make additions & omissions'.[23] Three months earlier he had revised the 1912 arrangement with Macmillan covering *Probability*, partly because he wanted a price lower than the profit maximising one, and partly because he wanted to circulate galley proofs (and correct them without worrying about the allocation of costs), the way other authors circulated typescripts or (later) photocopies.[24] In 1936, Keynes's arrangement with Macmillan meant that his most significant work, *The General Theory of Employment, Interest and Money*, could appear at a price of five shillings, well below the price of similarly sized books, such as Joan Robinson's *Economics of Imperfect Competition* (1933) which appeared at 12s.6d. for 352 pages, or Lionel Robbins's *The Great Depression* (1934) which cost 8s. 6d. for 238 pages. It also gave him freedom in disposing of his books: Macmillan would have found it difficult to offer copies of *A Revision of the Treaty* (1921), his sequel to *Economic Consequences*, where there were large unsold stocks,[25] or *Economic Consequences* itself, to those taking out one-year subscriptions to the *Nation and Athenaeum*, a weekly that Keynes and his friends had recently acquired.[26] It also had unintended consequences: during the Second World War, it meant that he had to insure stocks of his books against war risks.[27]

On the one occasion after 1919 when he did publish with Macmillan on a royalty basis – his influential essay *How to Pay for the War* (1940) – Macmillan's timidity soon made him long for his usual terms:

> The main question, however, which arises out of your letter of the 16th February is your printing order. I am sure that so small an order as 5,000 copies is a serious risk. I shall reckon the pamphlet a failure if less than 20,000 copies are sold, and am hoping for something well in excess of that. I have never written any book on economics, however highbrow, which has sold less than 5,000 [ms. alteration from typescript 10,000] copies, nor any pamphlet which has sold less than 12,000 [ms. alteration from typescript 14,000]; though these have had vastly less advance publicity than this one ... I should be prepared, if necessary to give away 5,000 copies myself rather than have so little circulation for it ... The suggestion at one time was that I should have this printed as a *New Statesman* pamphlet. We should never have dreamed, in such a case, of an initial order of only 5,000 copies; and, in the case of a Penguin Special, which was another suggestion which had been made the initial printing would, I think, have been 50,000 ...
>
> All of the above brings to a head still more definitely than before the question of terms. Obviously I cannot ask your firm to run risks or spend money on the above scale. It looks to me as though it would be wise, after all, for us to return to the arrangement which I originally discussed with Mr. Harold Macmillan, by which you publish on my behalf on commission. I am quite prepared to lose £500 on the book rather than jeopardise its free and prompt circulation or cut down unduly the amount spent on publicity. I was always a little anxious that any other arrangement might stand in the way of my, as I am afraid, excessively uncommercial ideas.[28]

Macmillan held to the original terms, but raised its printing order to 11,500. This was followed by a reprint of 15,000 copies on publication and, later, with what was virtually a second edition, even though it was not so described.[29]

Keynes's post-1919 arrangement with Macmillan also had implications for his American publishing. Under American law, in order to obtain copyright for a British author, a complete copy of the British edition had to be deposited in Washington within 30 days of publication in England, and an American edition printed from type set in the United States to be on the market within 30 days of that deposit. If, however, an author was willing to violate the manufacturing condition of the American copyright law, and thus forgo copyright protection, the initial British print run could be increased – and average per copy costs of production reduced – by shipping sheets or bound volumes to the American publisher. Keynes's first initiative, and only connection with Macmillan's American house, involved sending bound volumes of *A Treatise on Probability* to New York, an experience which he clearly found unsatisfactory.[30] With *A Treatise on Money* (1930) he began to ship sheets to Harcourt Brace, a practice he continued for *Essays in Persuasion* (1931), *Essays in Biography* (1933) and *The General Theory*.[31] He was aware that he would not have copyright protection, but, as he told Alfred Harcourt over *A Treatise on Money*, 'I should imagine that the chances of a pirated edition for a big book of this kind would be very remote indeed, in which case it seems rather wasteful to set up the whole thing twice, let alone the chances of misprints creeping in.'[32] The book, which has never been pirated, eventually ran to over 750 pages and appeared in two volumes.

Although Keynes had copyright for almost all the individual items in *Essays in Persuasion*, Alfred Harcourt warned him that, while the question could be regarded as 'academic', violating the manufacturing condition would probably result in the loss of copyright even in those 'protected' items. Keynes, in reply, could not resist a sidelong attack on American law:

> I am interested to hear what you report about copyright. It sounds to me a most peculiar state of law. But I know there is no form of rapine which the American law and American courts are not prepared to ensue towards foreign authors. However you are right as to my final decision. I do not rate high the risk of a pirated edition and consider the economies of joint production outweigh this risk.[33]

One result of this arrangement was that, as Harcourt Brace normally reprinted photographically, later American issues of these books did not always carry the corrections Keynes inserted in subsequent English printings.[34] Another was that an American publisher's proposal to produce a special edition of *The General Theory* for sale in a collection of 'influential' books of the twentieth century came to grief because of the absence of copyright protection.

Thus far, I have concentrated on Keynes's publishing arrangements as revealed in his correspondence with his publishers. Their letters also throw light on other matters. For example, before the availability of his extensive correspondence with the Russian ballerina, Lydia Lopokova, whom Keynes married in 1925,[35] the editors of *The Collected Writings of John Maynard Keynes* regularly used the publishers' files to help trace the evolution of preparations for particular volumes.

More unusually, the correspondence with Macmillan reveals most sharply Keynes's views on the work of many of his fellow economists that is not often recorded elsewhere in his papers. For nearly 30 years between 1913 and 1940 he was regularly invited to appraise manuscripts or proposals submitted to the firm for publication. His confidential reports, submitted in the form of typed or manuscript letters, provide discussions of over 50 texts, including works by D. H. Robertson, G. D. H. Cole, Paul Einzig and Joan Robinson.[36] Indeed, his referee's reports on two famous Macmillan books – J. R. Hicks's *Theory of Wages* (1932) and Joan Robinson's *The Economics of Imperfect Competition* (1933) – and one book Macmillan didn't take – Wicksell's *Lectures on Political Economy* (1935) have appeared in *The Collected Writings* (*JMK*. xii, 861–8).

From the beginning, his opinions were forthright. 'I do not know whether you will think I am taking too high a standard for your purposes,' he wrote to Maurice Macmillan in 1913, 'but it is very difficult to say anything about a 'hack' book except that it is a 'hack' book. My line on reporting on books for you is to write rather discouragingly, unless I am *quite* clear that you would be wise to publish it; and in reading my reports this standard should be borne in mind.'[37] Later that year he wrote to Dan Macmillan:

> Before opening the parcel which contains Hobson's book I ought to say that I am doubtful if I am the right person to report on it for you.
>
> Hobson has his public and his admirers. But personally I take, on the whole, a very unfavourable view of his books. See, for example, my review of his latest work in the Economic Journal for September.
>
> If you want to know whether the book is likely to pay, I can say without looking at it, that a work by Hobson, entitled *Work and Welfare*, is certain to have a respectable circulation. But I have so much prejudice against what I regard as his sophistries that it is scarcely fair that I should report on his work for a publisher. Shall I return you the package unopened?[38]

He returned the package on 29 October.

He also provided introductions to the firm. Colin Clark's, with his *National Income and Outlay*, ran as follows:

> My own judgement is that Clark's work on this and allied subjects, is quite outstanding, and that he is likely to become the recognised authority, in course of time, though it may be long before his name carries the same weight as that of Bowley or Stamp.
>
> Indeed, Clark is, I think, a bit of a genius:– almost the only economic statistician I have met who seems to me quite first class ... I think he is the sort of person whom you would not be sorry to have taken into your fold from his youth up.[39]

James Meade was 'one of the most promising of the very young but interesting school of Oxford economists', although Keynes thought his first book, *The Rate of Interest in a Progressive State*, 'probably half-baked', and believed it wouldn't be profitable. He continued:

> I am only afraid that you may have had too many of this type coming along. The fact is that the subject is in a state of violent upheaval. Everyone wants to write something, and most of what is written is incomplete, partly wrong, likely to be superseded in a few months, and quite incapable of becoming a text-book.[40]

Macmillan published the book in 1933. On the other hand, Keynes was dismissive of Richard Sayers, who was never a Macmillan author but became the doyen of monetary historians of his generation: 'I consider him quite a sound man, but of the second class rather than of the first class. I should not expect him to do work at any time of the first importance.'[41]

In contrast he warmly advised Harold Macmillan to establish contact with Roy Harrod, his future biographer, 'the best man at Oxford, both as pure economist and publicist', although he warned that Harrod was a little inclined to 'over-write', or at any rate to publish a little too hastily, 'once he has got a thing off his chest, he is a little disposed, I think, to rush into publication before he has chewed it over sufficiently and got it quite as good as it can be made'.[42] But then, as editor of the *Economic Journal*, Keynes had recently been trying to knock Harrod's 'An essay in dynamic theory' into shape for the March 1939 issue (*JMK*, xiv, 320–50). As he told A. C. Pigou, who thought that the article should have been rejected:

> I don't think there has ever been an article about which I corresponded with the author at such enormous length in the effort to make him clear up doubtful and obscure points and reduce its length. I

produced a little effect but not perhaps very much in proportion to the effort.[43]

In summary, Keynes's relationship with his publishers was unusual in many dimensions, and especially in his departure from the customary half-profits, or more modern royalty, arrangement.[44] Once beyond that basis, with the author bearing the risk, many other aspects of the author–publisher relationship change: with no need to allocate the costs of proof corrections, in Keynes's far off, pre-xerox days, galley proofs could circulate as drafts subject to revision;[45] the author could control the price and, if he believed that demand was price-elastic, reduce it significantly to increase sales. Finally, the author could, in the interest of deliberately reducing unit costs, deliberately forgo copyright protection in cases where print-runs were long enough for most publishers to meet the American manufacturing condition. Of course, one has to be a best-selling author willing to bear the risks and to take the time to see to all the details. But then, whether it was raising pigs, managing his Cambridge theatre,[46] or dealing with his intellectual property, Keynes revelled in the details.

Notes

1. I should like to thank the Provost and Fellows of King's College, Cambridge for permission to cite material from the Keynes Papers in the Modern Archive Centre in the College, and from Keynes's writings generally; and Christopher Johnson for permission to cite one letter from the Robbins Papers which will eventually reside in the British Library of Political and Economic Science. Unpublished writings of J. M. Keynes copyright The Provost and Scholars of King's College, Cambridge 1998.
2. A second instalment of the archive, received in 1990, continues this tradition by including the letters of Roy Harrod; the correspondence of others, such as Joan Robinson, is still with Macmillan. The archive might also have included Dennis Robertson, but, in his haste to arrange publication before he anticipated going off to the Dardanelles, he was unwilling to undertake the revisions to his *A Study of Industrial Fluctuation* (1915) demanded by Macmillan, with the result that the book (and its successors) went to P. S. King. (See Robertson to Keynes, 6 June 1915, King's College, Cambridge, Keynes Papers, subsequently KCKP, L/R; Robertson to Henderson, 22 April and 12 July 1915, Nuffield College, Oxford, Henderson Papers Box 20.)
3. Marshall's most recent biographer, Peter Groenewegen (*A Soaring Eagle: Alfred Marshall, 1842–1924.* Aldershot: Edward Elgar, 1992), does not seem to have been aware of the archive's existence.
4. Of course, he also dealt with Nisbet and Cambridge University Press over the Cambridge Economic Handbooks, but, except for editorial introductions, did not contribute to the series.

5. *The Diary of Virginia Woolf. Volume III: 1925–1930,* edited by Anne Olivier Bell (London: Hogarth Press, 1980), pp. 35, 38; *A Change of Perspective: the letters of Virginia Woolf. Volume III: 1923–1928*, edited by Nigel Nicolson (London: Hogarth Press, 1977), pp. 194–5, 282.
6. Keynes was not consistent in disposing of his Canadian rights. He used Macmillan's subsidiary in Toronto for *Economic Consequences of the Peace, Essays in Biography* and *The General Theory*, but Harcourt Brace for *A Revision of the Treaty, A Treatise on Money* and *Essays in Persuasion.*
7. D. E. Moggridge, *Maynard Keynes: an Economist's Biography* (London: Routledge, 1992), pp. 40, 838, plate 9.
8. Add.MS. 55201, f. 2. Keynes's first reviewer's report was dated 1 August 1910.
9. R. Wright to Keynes, 11 March 1910 (KCKP, $TP1_2$).
10. Weller to Keynes, 4 and 25 September 1912 (KCKP, $TP1_2$).
11. Keynes to James, 22 October 1912 (KCKP, $TP1_2$).
12. Keynes to Daniel Macmillan, 11 December 1912 (Add.MS. 55201, f. 14).
13. *The Collected Writings of John Maynard Keynes*, edited by E. Johnson and D. Moggridge, 30 vols (London: Macmillan, 1971–89), XVII, 3.
14. Dan Macmillan to Keynes, 28 July 1919; George Macmillan to Keynes, 8, 12 and 15 August 1919. (KCKP, EC3. Copies of these letters are also in the firm's letterbooks, Add.MS. 55556, ff. 68, 144–5, 228–9.)
15. Charging 7s. 6d. for a full cloth-bound volume and selling 4,800 copies would, Keynes estimated, net him £765; a stiff paper-bound volume selling at 6s. would net £600.
16. This form of contract continued long after Keynes's death, for Macmillan published *The Collected Writings of John Maynard Keynes* on a commission basis for the Royal Economic Society – a decision that, when coupled with a heavy publishing programme, a collapse of prices on the London Stock Exchange, and an explosion of printing costs, would have traumatic effects on the financial condition of the Royal Economic Society in the early 1970s.
17. William Macmillan to Keynes, 21 and 25 August 1919 (KCKP, EC3).
18. KCKP, $EC5_1$.
19. Alfred Harcourt to Keynes, 12 March 1920; royalty statement, September 1920 (KCKP, $EC5_1$).
20. Keynes to Dan Macmillan, 29 May 1920 (Add.MS. 55201, ff. 92–3). At one point, the speculation left Keynes technically bankrupt (*JMK*, xii, 5–6). In addition to £1,500 resulting from the letter of 29 May, Macmillan had paid Keynes £1,000 in April. Keynes asked Dan for a further £500 on 19 November (Add.MS. 55201, f. 109), but was refused by Maurice Macmillan even though the amount to his credit was £486 9s. 7d. (note to file, 22 November 1920, Add.MS. 55201, f. 110; Maurice Macmillan to Keynes, 22 November 1920, KCKP, EC3).
21. Keynes to Harold Macmillan, 4 and 19 August 1920 (Add.MS. 55201, ff. 99–100). He revived the idea with his *Tract on Monetary Reform* (Keynes to Dan Macmillan, 14 February 1923, KCKP, BP).
22. Add.MS. 55201, f. 99.
23. Add.MS. 55201, f. 131.
24. Keynes to Dan Macmillan, 19 March 1921 (KCKP, $TP1_2$). Contemporary authors might be interested to know that, in Keynes's case, Macmillan (or

more accurately, R. & R. Clark for books, and Richard Clay for *The Economic Journal*) would set type from pencil.

25. The book was published in January 1922. When the first printing of 10,000 copies seemed likely to be exhausted, Keynes reprinted in February 1922: six months later total sales were less than 7,000.
26. New subscribers were offered either book, together with a copy of Virginia Woolf's *Jacob's Room*. Keynes to Dan Macmillan, 16 September and 10 November 1923 (Add.MS. 55201, ff. 186–7, 196).
27. Macmillan to Keynes, 8 December 1939 (KCKP, BP_1).
28. Keynes to Roland Heath, 18 February 1940 (Add.MS. 55204, ff. 90–1).
29. Roland Heath to Keynes, 19 February and 4 March 1940; Harold Macmillan to Keynes, 19 March 1940 (KCKP, HP7). Keynes's remarks to Roland Heath on the 'second' edition are of some interest: 'I notice, however, that although the various misprints have been corrected, there is no indication that the text is a second edition, a reprint or in any way revised. This seems to me rather troublesome, as there is no means of discovering whether a copy in anyone's hands is the corrected or uncorrected version. Also I am a bit shocked *bibliographically* at this action! Surely when a revised text is issued, there should be some indication that this is so. I know there are cases to the contrary. Locke played the same trick in respect of the second edition of his pamphlet on Education, and was only caught out by bibliographers two or three years ago. But this is not a practice to be encouraged' (4 April 1940, Add.MS. 55204, f. 132). One result is that the rarer, red covered, corrected version of *How to Pay for the War* consistently sells for less than the more common, green covered, uncorrected version.
30. Keynes to Dan Macmillan, 16 April, 17 and 22 May, and 1 June 1921; Dan Macmillan to Keynes, 12 April, 12, 20 and 25 May 1921 (KCKP, $TP1_2$); Keynes to Dan Macmillan, 5 October 1927 (Add.MS. 55202, f. 41). The arrangement saw the Macmillan Co. of New York taking 400 bound copies at half the UK published price.
31. In the case of *A Treatise on Money* this took his total first print-run to 8,000 copies, of which 3,000 were dispatched to the United States (Keynes to Harold Macmillan, 22 June 1929, Add.MS. 55202, f. 70). With *The General Theory*, the print-run was 12,000, including 5,000 for the United States (Keynes to Dan Macmillan, 6 November 1935, Add.MS. 55203, f. 150).
32. 26 September 1928 (KCKP, TM3).
33. Keynes to Alfred Harcourt, 8 and 31 October 1931; Alfred Harcourt to Keynes, 20 October 1931 (KCKP, P1).
34. With *The General Theory* the case is more confused: Keynes supplied Harcourt Brace with English-printed sheets until the outbreak of the Second World War, but ceased to do so when paper became unavailable. Once Harcourt Brace began reprinting they used a copy of the first printing as the basis of their text – a practice that has persisted.
35. Lydia and Maynard exchanged letters daily when they were apart, which, given his Cambridge commitments, meant at least four days a week during term time. A selection of letters written before their marriage was published as *Lydia and Maynard: Letters between Lydia Lopokova and John Maynard Keynes*, edited by Polly Hill and Richard Keynes (London: André Deutsch, 1989).
36. BL Macmillan archive, second part.

37. Keynes to Maurice Macmillan, 16 June 1913 (Add.MS. 55201, f. 22).
38. Keynes to Dan Macmillan, 25 October 1913 (Add.MS. 55201, f. 28). Keynes's review of J. A. Hobson's *Gold, Prices and Wages* (1913), published in the *Economic Journal*, September 1913, concluded: 'Belonging to no one race or age more than another, there lives an intellectually solitary race of beings who by some natural prompting of the soul think about monetary theory in certain specific, definite ways, superstitious or delusive, mystically, not materially, true, if true at all. All of these will find their natural instincts expressed here in forms more plausible-topical than they can usually shape themselves. Mr. Hobson has given us the Mythology of Money, – intellectualised, brought up to journalistic date, most subtly interlarded (and this is how it differs from the rest) with temporary concessions to reason' (*JMK*, xi, 388).
39. Keynes to Dan Macmillan, 2 December 1931 (Add.MS. 55202, ff. 150–1).
40. Keynes to Dan Macmillan, 10 January 1932 (Add.MS. 55203, f. 4).
41. Keynes to Dan Macmillan, 16 October 1935 (Add.MS. 55203, f. 146).
42. 21 February 1939 (Add.MS. 55204, f. 18).
43. *JMK*, xiv, 320.
44. There are at least two exceptions – the French economist Leon Walras, and the English economist Philip Wicksteed. For all Walras's books from 1874 onwards, the name of L. Corbaz et Cie of Geneva appeared on the title-page, along with those of one or two booksellers such as Guillumin et Cie of Paris and H. Georg of Basel. However, Corbaz, a commercial printer and stationer, merely acted as banker and business agent. Walras paid all the expenses and supplied the books to the booksellers on a sale or return basis at a 50 per cent profit margin. Unlike Keynes's, it was not an arrangement of choice. Nor was it a profitable arrangement for Walras: in 1891, when he closed his accounts on a number of publications, including the first edition of his *Eléments d'économie politique pure*, he *owed* Corbaz 1803 francs (William Jaffé, *William Jaffé's Essays on Walras*, edited by D. A. Walker. Cambridge: Cambridge University Press, 1983, pp. 84–5). In the case of Wicksteed's *The Co-ordination of the Laws of Distribution* (1894), the publisher was Macmillan. Sales were few: his daughter remembered him giving most of his copies away, and saying that 'only four copies had been sold – two of them to his prospective sons-in-law' (Rebecca Wicksteed to Lionel Robbins, 7 September 1930, Robbins Papers).
45. Revisions to *A Treatise on Money* meant an expansion from one to two volumes with an extensive rewriting and reorganisation of the earlier chapters.
46. In the case of the Cambridge Arts Theatre, which Keynes built and got onto its feet before handing over to the City and the University, this meant running the box office, pricing wine in the restaurant, reading plays such as Auden and Isherwood's *The Ascent of F6* and *On the Frontier* in manuscript and seeing them through to production, sometimes in London.

11
'Not a Tear or a Prayer in It'
Gwen Raverat's illustrated edition of *The Runaway*

Frances Spalding

Gwen Raverat is best known as a wood-engraver, and as the author of *Period Piece: a Cambridge Childhood*, which, since it first appeared in 1952, has entertained generations of readers with its account of, among other things, her Darwin relatives. Like her grandfather Charles Darwin, who once observed that 'without speculation there is no good and original observation',[1] Gwen Raverat was intensely interested in facts and in the way in which they feed into the imagination. Whether illustrating a novel, children's verse or a play, she pounced deftly on period costumes or farm implements, poses or facial expressions, her keen attention making vivid her subject. She was also alert to the drama inherent in a scene and had a good eye for comic situations. In *Period Piece* there is a drawing of Aunt Etty wearing an anti-cold mask, which, made out of a kitchen strainer filled with antiseptic cotton wool, she tied on to her face like a snout. Her furious battle against household germs and draughts involved her husband, Uncle Richard, in a charade of delicacy. Following his wife's instructions, he meekly sat behind a screen, covered from head to foot in a dust sheet, while the room was aired, as Gwen Raverat shows, in another unforgettable vignette which touches affectionately on the absurd.

But anyone who treasures Gwen Raverat's work must recognise a marked difference between those of her illustrations which are drawn, as in *Period Piece*, and those which are the product of wood-engraving. This latter medium drew from her greater subtlety of invention and a broader emotional range. But in addition she brought to her wood-engraved illustrations an enthusiastic and intelligent grasp of the whole process of book production. Nowhere is this more evident than in her work for Macmillan on the Victorian novel, *The Runaway*, which was reprinted at her own suggestion in 1936. By this date she was very experienced at working with commercial publishers and, among other commissions, had earlier this decade produced three major books with wood-engraved illustrations for Cambridge University Press: *The Cambridge Book of Poetry for Children*, Frances Cornford's *Mountains and Molehills* and *Four Tales from Hans Andersen*. In the last two of these, she had pioneered the use of the double-page spread which was also to be a feature of *The Runaway*. Throughout, the illustrations, which vary in sizes and shape, punctuate the text with enlivening irregularity, showing her mastery of the *mise en page*.

Wood-engraving, a severe and necessarily disciplined medium, tautened her grasp of the overall design and released a more intense poetry than is found in her line drawings. The patterning in her work is important as it freed her illustrations from the finicky literalism that sometimes mars the work of Dickens's illustrators. She had first acquired the technique of wood-engraving while studying painting at the Slade, and by the outbreak of the First World War she had completed 60 prints. Her work at this stage was seen to be novel and inspiring. She was championed in the *Studio* by Malcolm Salaman in 1919, the year after Herbert Furst chose to inaugurate his *Modern Woodcutters* series with a monograph on her work. 1920 also saw her first solo exhibition, at the Adelphi Gallery, which contained 92 wood-engravings. This same year she became a founder member of the Society of Wood-Engravers which sought to raise the professional status of its practitioners. Simultaneously, there was renewed interest in the work of Thomas Bewick whose tailpieces Gwen Raverat had first discovered as a child, while reading alone at her Aunt Etty's house in Kensington. Her sense of affinity with this artist left her, as a child, wishing passionately that she had been Mrs Bewick. 'O happy, happy Mrs. Bewick! thought I, as I kicked my heels on the blue sofa.'[2]

As a child, part of a large tribe of Darwin cousins growing up in Cambridge in the 1890s, Gwen had read avidly. Her mother recorded the development of her four children in leather-bound books, devoting a separate volume to each child. Inside the one entitled 'Gwendolen Mary Darwin', she noted that Gwen absorbed many of the classic children's tales – the Brothers Grimm, Hans Andersen, Kingsley's *Water Babies*, among others – and developed a passionate love of books. 'Gwen remains intensely fond of reading,' reads the entry dated 25 March 1894, by which time she was nine years of age, 'and would read all day long if allowed to do. She gallops through a book very quickly and then often begins it again at once. She seems to find a great amusement from her drawings and they often show a good deal of imagination.'[3] That her interest in drawing was stirred by her reading is evident from certain illustrated essays and other pieces of juvenilia that exist. Her love of drawing became still more pronounced when the following year she started taking drawing classes, along with several of her cousins, with the Cambridge artist, Mary Greene (the aunt of the novelist Graham Greene), and there were tears if for some reason she had to miss a lesson. But her love of reading did not lessen. 'In every room she has a book ready to read if she has a few spare moments', her mother records. 'When she goes to wash her hands in the night nursery, she has a book open on the washstand, then to the day nursery to put on her boots and first a book is opened and put on the floor to read while she is buttoning them.'[4]

Many visits were made to Down House, the home of her grandmother, Emma, Charles Darwin's widow. As novel reading had been an important part of Charles Darwin's life, the house contained many fictional opportunities and it was here that Gwen and her siblings discovered *The Runaway*, which had first been published in 1872. Also memorable at Down House were the great four-poster beds, 'with ceilings and curtains of stiff shiny chintz hanging all round them',[5] very like those which figure so prominently in Gwen Raverat's several illustrations of beds in the later edition of *The Runaway*. 'Of course,' she recalled, 'I cannot expect anyone else to feel such romance and excitement about it [*The Runaway*] as I used to do, when I climbed into the great curtained bed ... to have it read aloud to me by a sick aunt'.[6] But she certainly shared it with her peers (and later with her own children), and when she went away to Levana, a school run by the Misses Young near Wimbledon Common, she scripted a play based on the novel.[7] As an identical version of this script also exists in her cousin Frances Darwin's hand, it is possible that it was a collaboration, in connection with the Darwin family tradition that each Christmas the children would perform a play for the adults.

'It is ... a gay, rather farcical book,' Gwen Raverat wrote in 1935, when attempting to persuade Macmillan to republish *The Runaway*, 'which was the delight of my own childhood (& I suppose of the generation before as well) & has been very much loved by my own children, & by many others'.[8] That which may have particularly appealed to Gwen Raverat was its dry humour and a style in places reminiscent of Jane Austen. Miss Simmonds, the governess, is described as 'an excellent sensible woman whom it was easier to respect than love, as she had few original ideas, no fancies, a reserved manner, and a well-regulated mind';[9] and the two children, Clarice and Olga (the Runaway) find themselves in agreement that they like irregular proceedings. (When Olga insists, 'I like old people to be irregular, don't you?, Clarice replies: 'Yes, of course I do, everybody must; but they so seldom are.'[10]) In addition, it is a tale of concealment, of a child from adults, with all the thrilling tension caused by the possibility of discovery. There is enough incident to maintain the narrative at a good pace and an engagingly tender bond between the two girls. If it is not a tale that has entered the canon of classic children's stories, it nevertheless has an undeniable capacity to hold and entertain a child's imagination.

The original edition had six illustrations by J. Lawson which, in Gwen Raverat's opinion, were 'very bad'. Would Macmillan consider republishing it 'with woodcuts by me, as a venture of my own?' she enquired. Her letter continues:

> The book is short, very amusing; not a tear or a prayer in it; I believe it might have some success; and it would be amusing to illustrate it with pictures in the dresses of the sixties ... Will you consider this at your leisure, and let me have some answer some time?[11]

Gwen Raverat's reputation as an artist and illustrator was well enough established by this date for Macmillan to express immediate interest. But her question as to who owned the copyright was at first difficult to answer. It would appear that Macmillan, the original publisher, had no record of the name of the author, and it was Gwen Raverat who informed them that, according to her sister, the author's name was Menella Smedley. But she added that her sister could neither explain how she knew this fact, nor did she know anything more about her. A further hunt was made in the publisher's archives. 'Our records do not enable us to trace any personal particulars regarding the author, Mrs. Smedley,' Harold Macmillan wrote, adding diplomatically, 'and my own feeling is that it would be much better to describe it merely as "By the author of *Mrs. Jerningham's Journal*", and it would probably stimulate curiosity as to whether it was a genuine Victorian production or a pastiche'.[12] However, by the time the book was published it had been discovered that the true author was Menella Smedley's sister, Mrs

Elizabeth Anna Hart. Copyright was not an issue as the book had originally been bought outright.

Macmillan proposed to sell the book at six shillings, and offered Gwen Raverat a royalty of one shilling on each copy sold. 'If you are willing to supply illustrations on these terms,' wrote Harold Macmillan, 'we shall be pleased to receive the suggestions you mention regarding the format, type, etc.'.[13] She had particularly requested the right to have a say in the choice of type and size of page. She had also suggested that it would be extremely convenient for her if it could be printed in Cambridge at the University Press. 'They are used to printing from wood blocks, which is a great advantage as far as I am concerned; and are most excellent printers, and are no dearer than other printers I think.'[14] To this, too, Macmillan agreed, adding: 'We are naturally very pleased to have the opportunity of co-operating with you in this interesting undertaking.'[15]

As mentioned, Gwen Raverat had recently finished a book with Cambridge University Press in which she had rehearsed some of the ideas which she was to develop in *The Runaway*. *Four Tales from Hans Andersen*, in a translation by R. P. Keigwin, had established, to her thinking, a very satisfying balance between text and image, using considerable variety in the size of illustrations and in their positioning on the page. But if *The Runaway* is compared with the *Four Tales* it can be seen that she refined on the formula at which she had arrived: firstly by changing from Bodoni to a larger, more modern choice of type; and secondly by allowing herself more space for the illustrations and at the same time greater density and richness in their construction.

She toyed also with the idea of colour, though in the final product, probably for reasons of cost, none appears. But it is hard to imagine how colour could have improved on the existing illustrations which are full of interest and character. The only means at the wood-engraver's disposal are the white ground created by cutting away the surface of the wood, the blackness of the ink left on the surface, and the outlines and hatching that mediate between these two extremes. Each scene has to be envisaged in terms of degrees of light and dark. Often Gwen Raverat further enriches the texture of the whole by use of patterning, in curtains, wallpapers, quilts and rugs, her careful shadows and pulsing light drawing the viewer in as the scene gradually unfolds in the mind. The generosity of scale, as in the headpiece to Chapter II, showing Clarice taking tea with her father, the portly Mr Clavering, amply conveys a sense of mid-Victorian comfort. When Clarice and Olga spend the morning in a green-canopied glade, Raverat allows a tree in one illustration to extend its branch across the opposite page (Fig. 11.2). Later, when the police are about to search the house, and the two girls are plotting a new hiding place for Olga, they scamper across a landing on one side of the page, while on the other we see the back of the maid descending the staircase, a detail not mentioned in the story but which heightens the sense of danger (Fig 11.3).

Figure 11.1 *The Runaway,* headpiece to Chapter II

Inevitably, such intricate work took longer than Gwen Raverat had predicted and she had to ask for a little more time than was contracted. She worked always with the text near to hand and, at her own suggestion but with the publisher's permission, she shortened the first three pages of the book ('I can always read Victorian books, but I was afraid other people couldn't be bothered to do so, if the beginning was at all long-winded.'[16]) She also cut one verse at the end of Chapter III, for reasons of space and because she felt it had little interest. One nice touch, which she later repeated in her illustrations to Walter de la Mare's *Crossings, A Fairy Play* (published by Faber in 1952), was the use of small vignettes of single figures as and when each character first appeared in the text. Together with short captions, a group of these figures combine to form front and back endpapers in *The Runaway* (Fig. 11.4), as they do both fore and aft in *Crossings.*

Figure 11.2 *The Runaway*, pp. 52–3

which,
peeping out at her,
looked like the bodiless angel heads in old pictures, wanting only the wings instead of a neck to be the angel-head complete. "I can imitate animals just as well as birds," cried a gay sparkling voice, "so that they all come flocking round me, only I dare not do it here, you know, as cows and horses cannot be supposed to live in this glade."

"Come down, naughty child," said Clarice quite fondly, and down ran Olga like a squirrel, and nestled by her side.

"I have found my bag," cried she, "and only think, the mouth was open, and half the things had tumbled out, but I hope I have collected them all; and Oh, Clarice! as I was picking them up, only just fancy, I saw a man looking at me over the hedge—he was in the lane outside you know; but wasn't it rude?"

"I don't know," answered Clarice; "he must

"People," whispered Olga to her terrified companion, who dragged her breathlessly along when she found her beginning to talk—"people, *not*

Figure 11.3a *The Runaway*, p. 154

As the work neared completion in the autumn of 1936 Gwen Raverat was concerned that her carefully crafted illustrations might, at first glance, be misunderstood by young readers of the book. 'I should be very glad if in the description on the flaps, or any other advertisement,' she wrote to her publisher, 'you could emphasise the fact that the book is not at all frightening, but very gay? I am afraid some people may think the pictures look alarming though they really cannot frighten anyone, as the reader is always in the secret beforehand.'[17] Finally, with the jacket layout agreed, the paper quality settled, and the light blue cloth binding with its gilt-blocked decorations warmly approved, the book was ready for publication at the end of October, in an edition of 3,000 copies.[18]

Gwen Raverat was anxious that advance copies of the book should be sent to her cousin Bernard Raverat, in the hope that he would review it in *Country Life*, and to Walter de la Mare. The latter's pronouncement – that it was 'a vivid and enchanting little story – fresh, unexpected and full of insight' – was passed on to the Macmillan Company in New York, in the hope that they would order a good number of copies for the American market.[19]

Figure 11.3b *The Runaway*, p. 155

Ten years later, when the book was again out of print, Gwen Raverat was surprised to hear on the radio a broadcast of *The Runaway* in the children's hour. It caused her to write again to Macmillan: 'I am constantly being asked if *The Runaway* is still obtainable. I wonder if you would think of reprinting it some time?'[20] The publisher's notes appended to her letter record that the book had gone out of print in July 1942. But no reprint had so far appeared, and in 1952 Gwen Raverat wrote again:

> Some years ago you published *The Runaway* with engravings by me. As I imagine you have no thought of reprinting (though I should be delighted if you would do so) I should be so glad if you could let me have the wood engravings again? I think they must really belong to me.[21]

Macmillan replied promptly: the moulds made from the original blocks for the wood-engravings were still at Cambridge University Press, and Macmillan relinquished all rights to them. In her reply, thanking them,

Figure 11.4 *The Runaway,* right front endpaper

she mentioned that she was trying to get some other firm to take up the book, and in March 1953 Cambridge University Press was instructed to transfer all the moulds, together with the blocks for the text, endpapers and jacket to Duckworth, who republished *The Runaway* later that year. Nowadays, however, the book, becoming ever rarer, is less a children's book than a collector's item. Which is perhaps a pity, for as Walter de la Mare wrote: 'Of its merits – its liveliness, limpidity, understanding of childhood and quiet art – there could hardly be two opinions.'[22]

Notes

1. *The Correspondence of Charles Darwin*, edited by Frederick Burkhardt and Sydney Smith, Volume VI (Cambridge: Cambridge University Press, 1990), p. 514.
2. Gwen Raverat, *Period Piece: a Cambridge Childhood* (London: Faber, 1952), p. 129.
3. 'Gwendolen Mary Darwin', unpublished biography of Gwen Raverat's early life, written alternately by Sir George and Lady Darwin. Manuscript Room, Cambridge University Library (subsequently CUL). These extracts, and quotations from Gwen Raverat's letters to Macmillan and her illustrations to *The Runaway* are reproduced here with the kind permission of Mrs Sophie Gurney.
4. Ibid.
5. *Period Piece*, p. 162.
6. Gwen Raverat, in the Preface to *The Runaway* (London: Macmillan, 1936).
7. The manuscript of the play can be found among Gwen Raverat's papers in Cambridge University Library's Manuscript Room, Add.MS. 9209.
8. Gwen Raverat to Macmillan, no date [late summer/autumn 1935]. Add.MS. 55233, f. 168.
9. *The Runaway*, p. 3.
10. *The Runaway*, p. 35.
11. Add.MS. 55233, f. 168.
12. Harold Macmillan to Gwen Raverat, 30 January 1936. Add.MS. 9209.1.1041 (CUL).
13. Harold Macmillan to Gwen Raverat, 24 October 1935. Add.MS. 9209.1.1039 (CUL).
14. Gwen Raverat to Macmillan, 15 October [1935]. Add.MS. 55233, f. 179.
15. Add.MS. 9209.1.1039 (CUL).
16. Gwen Raverat to Macmillan, no date [received 18 June 1936]. Add.MS. 55233, f. 196.
17. Add.MS. 55233, ff. 197–8.
18. Add.MS. 55930, f. 37.
19. De la Mare's remarks are quoted in the Macmillan correspondence with the Macmillan Company, New York, 26 May 1936. Add.MS. 55310, f. 74.
20. Gwen Raverat to Macmillan, 17 December [1946] (BL Macmillan archive, second part).
21. Gwen Raverat to Macmillan, 14 November 1952 (BL Macmillan archive, second part).
22. Add.MS. 55310, f. 74.

12
From Carroll to Crompton
The work of a children's publisher

Michael Wace

In this contribution I shall try to give some account of the role of children's editor and of children's publishing since Macmillan's first books of this kind were published in the 1850s. In recent times, thanks to the foundations laid by my predecessors, including Marni Hodgkin, the list has had – and still has – some major figures: from the novels and stories of Rumer Godden, Geoffrey Trease, Robert Westall and Jill Paton Walsh, to the picture books of Jill Murphy, Mary Rayner and Graham Oakley, and the poetry of Charles Causley. Throughout British publishing, the decades since the 1960s have seen a great flowering of talent in the writing and illustration of children's books and, as a recently retired editor, I have found it illuminating to look back to the trends and events of earlier days.

There is not time to examine in detail the various genres of which children's literature is composed, but I thought I would remind us of the two forces which have lain behind so much of what has been, and still is, offered to children: the drive to mould, educate and improve, and the drive to please and entertain. I turn to Richmal Crompton's William Brown, Just William, to give us his opinion on the perils inherent in unskilfully attempting the former:

> [Aunt Ellen] gave him a book called *Little Peter, the Sunshine of the Home* and put a chair out for him in the garden. 'It's a beautiful book, William,' she said, 'and I think will do you good. It's a true book,

written by the boy's mother ... He is a beautiful character ... We'll have a nice little talk about it when you've read it. It might prove the turning-point in your life. I'm sure you'll wish you knew Peter and his dear mother.'

William, after reading a few pages, began, as she had predicted, to wish he knew Peter and his mother. He wished he knew Peter in order to take the curl out of that butter-coloured hair and the fatuous smile from the complacent little mouth that stared at him from every illustration. Driven at last to fury, he dropped Peter down the well and began to look for more congenial occupations.[1]

And William himself, author and playwright *extraordinaire*, has given us a sample of what *he* would find really gripping:

'Ho!'sez Dick Savage,' he wrote. 'Ho! Gadzooks! Rol in the bottles of beer up in the beech. Fill your pockets with the baccy from the bote. Quick, now! Gadzooks! Methinks we are observed!' He glared round in the darkness. In less time than wot it takes to rite this he was srounded by pleesmen and stood, proud and defiant, in the light of there electrick torches wot they had wipped quick as litening from their busums.

'Surrender!' cried one, holding a gun at his brain and a drorn sord at his hart, 'Surrender or die!'

'Never,' said Dick Savage, throwing back his head, proud and defiant, 'Never. Do to me wot you will. I die.'

One crule brute hit him a blo on the lips and he sprang back, snarling with rage. In less time than wot it takes to rite this he had sprang at his torturer's throte and his teeth met in one mighty bite. His torturer dropped ded and lifless at his feet.[2]

Steering a passage between these two extremes has ever been the task of the editor of children's books.

You will understand if I cannot maintain the level of excitement set by William but I can begin by describing what for me was also a breathtaking moment.

A dozen or so years ago, I received a phone call in my office from Paul Trotman, the company secretary, who was speaking from the firm's bank, the National Westminster in Covent Garden, to say that he had come across two deed boxes among the items Macmillan had deposited there, which were labelled 'Alice – keys in accounts department' in faded ink, and would I like to come to look at them. Faster than Bill the Lizard popping out of the chimney in the White Rabbit's house, I rushed over to Henrietta Street where Paul, with the aid of a crowbar kindly provided by the bank's management, had already forced open the boxes (it seemed that the keys had long since departed from the accounts department). There, neatly wrapped and packed, were the original engraved wood blocks of Sir John Tenniel's illustrations for *Alice's Adventures in Wonderland* and *Through the Looking-Glass*. It was an extraordinary discovery. I, and others in the firm, had unthinkingly assumed that the blocks had long since departed to some North American university or museum (as, for example, had those for *The Hunting of the Snark* in the 1950s) but here they were, under our very eyes.

In the days of letterpress printing – which was the preferred method for printing books until well after the Second World War – the wood blocks had been used as masters for the making of electros (metal electrotype plates) and never for direct printing of the books. That was why they were left in the bank and only taken out when Richard Clay, the printer, needed to make fresh plates. ('A more painstaking, conscientious printer never lived', Alexander Macmillan wrote in 1865, and Clay continued to print the letterpress editions.) As photolitho gradually took over from letterpress, the wood blocks stayed in the bank and were quietly forgotten.

The first thing to do was to get an assessment of their condition from an expert, and I was fortunate in obtaining the help of Iain Bain who has done so much for the preservation of Thomas Bewick's blocks, and for wood-engraving in general. Iain pronounced the blocks as being in good condition and, with proper handling, they could be used for printing. So, for the very first time, and with the approval of the C. L. Dodgson estate, it was decided to print from the blocks; the edition was limited to 250 sets of prints. I am glad to say that the blocks themselves now rest in the British Library, alongside the manuscript of *Alice's Adventures Underground*, the nine volumes of Lewis Carroll's diaries and a copy of the first, rejected, edition of *Alice*.

The first 'Alice' book was published in 1865, 22 years after the booksellers-turned-publishers, Daniel and Alexander Macmillan, began to publish. The story of the steady success and growth of that business is well-known to students of publishing – by 1865 they were issuing more than 80 new books a year. Children's books were a small part of that output and it seems unlikely that there was ever a deliberate plan to publish such books: there was only one other new children's title in the year of *Alice's* publication. Macmillan's first book in this field was Charles Kingsley's *Westward Ho!* in 1855, and, in the ten years which followed, one or two children's books were published each year. But what books they were! Among the 14 published in those 11 years were Thomas Hughes' *Tom Brown's School Days* (an early example of that genre of school tales which would encompass Angela Brazil's girls and Billy Bunter, Grange Hill and Sweet Valley High), *Tom Brown at Oxford*, Carroll's *Alice*, two more best-sellers from Kingsley – *The Heroes* (the stories of Perseus, Theseus and the Argonauts) and *The Water-Babies* – and two by authors who were increasingly important to Macmillan, *The Fairy Book* by Mrs Craik and *A Book of Golden Deeds of all Times and of all Lands* by Charlotte Yonge (the two books were reprinted 12 and 20 times respectively in the following 20 years). Eight big sellers out of 14 published is an enviable – not to say, astonishing – record, and I doubt whether it has ever been matched.

Thanks to the admirable bibliographical catalogue which Macmillan published in 1891 (incidentally, the only publisher's catalogue I've come across which includes blurbs in Latin) we know that from 1843 to 1865 the firm published some 772 titles.[3] However, this figure includes over 230 pamphlets (which I have defined as a publication with 50 or fewer pages of text) as well as books which were 'first published elsewhere'. That leaves around 500 titles as the core of the publishing business and which were generating the turnover. So the 14 children's books – which between them, had a total of 42 (Carrollians will note) printings within the 11 years 1855–65 – represented less than 3 per cent of the output even on the revised, lower, total but certainly a substantially higher proportion of the sales overall.

On the face of it, children's books would seem to be an unlikely element – small though it was – in a list that developed from a university bookshop. Far more typical of those early years, for example, were such titles as *The Fitness of Holy Scripture for Unfolding the Spiritual Life of Men* and *An Outline of the Theory of Conditional Sentences in Greek and Latin*. Daniel and Alexander ran the business and *they* decided what books should be published. Overwhelmingly, they made it a religious and academic list. Their Cambridge bookshop was much used by members of the university, and the two hard-working, self-educated brothers, earnest and determined on success in the best Victorian manner, soon found that bookselling, and their own religious interests, gave them an introduction to those in the forefront of religious and intellectual debate and their circles, as well as to university teachers from many disciplines. Daniel himself wrote in 1852, 'I am convinced that we shall gradually, in a few years, have a first-rate and capital paying publisher's trade – our retail trade will chiefly be valuable as bringing about us men who will grow into authors.'[4]

But how was it that, out of a modest number of children's books, so many were so successful? And this was well before the job of a children's editor was common in publishing houses. It seems unlikely that such books were accepted solely on the judgement of either Daniel or Alexander – their interests lay elsewhere, as I have indicated – but rather that they received significant help from writers who were much closer to the market-place for children's stories than they were.

From the 1850s onwards a number of magazines, aimed specifically at children, were launched. They included *The Monthly Packet* (edited by Charlotte Yonge), *Aunt Judy's Magazine* (edited first by Mrs Gatty and then by her daughter, Mrs Ewing) and *Good Words for the Young* (edited by George Macdonald): magazines produced by established authors, commissioning work from other published writers and whose editors assessed the many unsolicited manuscripts they received. These were the people who knew what parents wanted their children to read (or would at least find acceptable), so what better source of expertise for a young publishing house – busy with books with a loftier content – on what children's books to publish? Furthermore, when in 1865 Alexander, eight years after his brother's death, took the important step of taking on a partner, the man he chose was the reliable Scot, George Lillie Craik, who had recently married Dinah Mulock, a friend of Alexander's and already established as a children's writer. Under her married name of Mrs Craik she continued to contribute to the magazines as well as to publish children's books and adult novels – many with Macmillan. With the wife of a partner actively and successfully involved in writing for children, the appropriate knowledge was already to hand. Alexander was never slow to grasp a publishing opportunity: in C. L. Graves' biography he is quoted as writing of Mrs Craik, 'She has become a great ally and will be very useful to us.'[5]

Macmillan's children's list continued steadily in the years following the publication of *Alice*, with a particularly busy period in the early 1870s when 32 books were published in five years, of which no fewer than 9 were by Charlotte Yonge. In later years it was Mrs Molesworth who dominated the list with at least one book a year and sometimes several. From 1855 to 1889 (the last year covered by the bibliographical catalogue) nearly half the total children's book output of 86 titles was contributed by three authors – Mrs Craik, Charlotte Yonge and Mrs Molesworth. I think it would be safe to assume that Mrs Craik continued to be 'very useful' to Macmillan and that her presence must have reduced the need to have someone in the firm who was concerned with acquiring children's books.

This was not necessarily the case with other publishing houses: Frederick Warne and Company (established in 1865) published more children's books than Macmillan (Lear, Caldecott, Greenaway among others) and although, according to Warne's centenary history, there were three principals, there was also a Mrs Valentine, the only female member of staff and, as the history puts it, the 'editress' for the children's list. Part of Mrs Valentine's duties was probably akin to those of Thomas Bowdler, as Warne's first catalogue reported that, for their edition of *The Arabian Nights* 'the editor has been able to expurgate entirely the parts that parents consider objectionable for their children to read' – compare political correctness today. No doubt other companies which published the many series, both secular and religious, toy books, rag books and the like (Routledge, Ward Lock, Dean and Co. come to mind) would need the help of an 'editress'. However, it seems that Macmillan did not feel this need until about 1950, when they appointed their first children's editor.

It was in this immediate post-war period that today's job has its origins: in the 1950s and 1960s, editors specialising in children's books were first generally recognised as a separate species (although there are one or two earlier instances which I shall refer to later). It was a period when the importance of school libraries (and the dreadful inadequacy of many of them) for developing literacy was recognised, when the Plowden report on primary school education was stressing the importance of the teaching of reading and of books, and when the US government perceived school education as a key element of their response to Soviet Russia's success in sending a man into space: the market for all kinds of books for children was beginning to grow. As we moved into the 1970s the demand for non-fiction information books increased – children needed them for their school projects, local authorities set up inter-school library loan services and parents looked for them in the bookshops. Parallel with these developments, there were significant improvements in printing technology. The reproduction and printing of colour work became better and relatively cheaper, which led to a substantial increase in what is known as the co-edition market: children's reference books were planned for an international market, enabling publishers to share initial costs and to benefit from longer print-runs. Costs for young children's picture books could be reduced in the same way.

British publishers had some endemic advantages: they were accustomed to exporting; they had good designers available to them, and – particularly important – we were entering a golden age for British illustration. American publishers, on the other hand, at this period looked only to domestic sales; the design and illustration of their children's books was dull and unadventurous in a market dominated by conservative school and library interests.

By the late 1970s and early 1980s a definite boom could be discerned. The number of children's paperback lists increased, companies which specialised in non-fiction co-editions grew, as did the more traditional areas of fiction and picture books in order to feed the library and paperback markets and, for the general trade, pop-up and 'moveable' books which made a comeback, having almost disappeared after their German-inspired late nineteenth-century heyday.

As output increased, so did staff: more people were needed for design, promotion and publicity, desk editing and production. Children's editors (by this time themselves becoming specialists in some branch of children's books) were competing for authors and illustrators. The late Sebastian Walker, the founder of Walker Books, a company which raised the tempo of children's publishing by single-mindedly concentrating on well-illustrated, well-designed books for young children and selling them with style and vigour, tempted a number of established writers and illustrators to his lists. Agents were looking for bigger advances, and the larger American houses and media conglomerates with book publishing interests, were thinking that they might as well publish children's, as well as adult, books as they glomerated (*Chambers Dictionary* allows that) many of our better-known publishing houses. And perhaps that is where things began to go wrong for children's publishing.

We editors were busy encouraging writing and illustrating talent, hoping that agents would bring us their best authors, and cajoling our existing authors to produce more. We were expected by our bosses, *urged* by them, to publish more, but few of us paused to consider where all these books were going to go – the market is a finite one, and children soon move on from one level of book to another, computer and video games may become a new interest, as can grown-up books, and, of course, after a while they cease to be children. The result has been an absurd overproduction of titles, increasing from just under 2,500 in 1965, to 4,500 in 1986, and a staggering 8,000 in 1996. Even though the past 10 or 15 years have seen an increase in the number of good dedicated bookshops, one result – and perhaps it is a good thing – is that publishers increasingly look to other, non-traditional outlets for additional sales: supermarkets, Woolworth's stores, garden centres, theme parks, direct catalogue sales to parents and to children via the schools, children's bookclubs, and so on. Another result of this pressure to maximise sales has been a marked increase in ephemeral titles – for example, paperback series with a theme or a common setting, TV tie-ins – and in the exploitation of 'characters': those of Beatrix Potter and of the Reverend Awdry's Thomas the Tank Engine books come to mind, from Peter Rabbit egg cups to Thomas duvet covers. Of course, such exploitation is not just a contemporary phenomenon: Lewis Carroll himself was not averse to merchandising Alice – there was not only the Wonderland Postage Stamp Case he devised in 1888 and the famous biscuit tin of 1892 which reproduced drawings from *Looking-Glass* to which he gave his blessing (until he discovered that he had to buy the biscuits as well as the tin when he wanted some for his friends), but also umbrella and parasol handles carved with likenesses of Tweedledum and Tweedledee.[6]

So, in recent times, publishers have had to grapple with the problems of overproduction: lip service is paid to restraint but the intention is belied by the figures. Children's books of quality and originality do still get published, but (and I have to say it was ever thus) with difficulty if they do not fit neatly into a known category or are perceived as 'difficult' for the child. The potential for success in the long term has to be weighed against the need for profit in the short term.

I would like now to return to the story of the development of the modern children's editor: John Rowe Townsend, in *Written for Children*, says that the first children's editor in the USA was appointed by Macmillan New York in 1919.[7] However, there was a notable instance in this country some 13 years earlier, in 1906, when a joint venture was established by Oxford University Press and Hodder & Stoughton (they had neighbouring offices in Warwick Square). The imprint was Henry Frowde/Hodder and Stoughton, and the brief was to publish both children's and educational books.

Two men were appointed to run it, Herbert Ely and Charles James L'Estrange. Together they wrote and commissioned children's books and educational readers (hundreds of them, according to Sutcliffe's history of the Press[8]). For the children's books, Messrs Ely and L'Estrange called themselves Herbert Strang (and also Mrs Herbert Strang when it seemed appropriate). Under these names they wrote and edited children's books which were aimed at a truly popular market: they had no inhibitions about competing with the likes of Blackie and Collins – the latter was a major publisher in the field with 500 colour books published between 1903 and 1914. *Herbert Strang's Annual* was a staple of the list, as was *Mrs Strang's Annual* (for girls). There was also *The Red Book for Boys, The Great Book for Children*, a post-Jules Verne title *Round the World in 7 Days*

(1908), *The Air Patrol: a Story of the North-West Frontier* (1913), and a 1911 tale of an amphibious vehicle, *The Cruise of the Gyro-Car*. On the educational side, the editors were equally uninhibited by the aura of a university press with, for example, *Jolly Steps for Tiny Folks*, a series of readers with such titles as Fred Frog, Jolly Jumbo and Tish Fish.

Hodders were pleased with the venture as OUP brought much-needed capital to fund the publishing, and for Oxford it enabled them to get into a lucrative, popular market. The arrangement lasted for ten years, although the two elements of Herbert Strang stayed with the Press until they retired in 1938. Indeed, a 1930s OUP title, *The Book of Happy Gnomes*, suggests that Herbert Strang was still at work. But in the 1940s it seems the Press became more sensitive about the children's books it published; the story goes that the Delegates were embarrassed to discover that Capt. W. E. Johns's 'Biggles' books (no doubt taken on by Ely and L'Estrange) were on their list and sold them off at a knockdown price to their former partners, Hodder & Stoughton, who published the books from 1943.

Macmillan's children's publishing, in the ten years or so before 1906, was dominated by seven of Kipling's most popular books: the two Jungle Books, the *Just So Stories*, *Kim*, *Stalky & Co.*, *Puck of Pook's Hill*, and *Captains Courageous*. Even if Kipling hadn't been well established with Macmillan by this time, he was not the author to need coaxing (or, indeed, editing) by a children's editor. His professional relationship with Macmillan was, anyway, conducted at arm's length via his wife and his agent, A. P. Watt.[9] The same period saw the publication of Lewis Carroll's last, almost unreadable, children's book *Sylvie and Bruno*, also *The Nursery Alice* (*Wonderland* rewritten for younger children), and several more books from the prolific Mrs Molesworth. Apart from these, most of the publishing was concentrated on series related to the school market – notably 'English Men of Action' (Nelson, Drake, General Wolfe, Captain Cook and so on), and the Prize Library. The great expansion of education which followed the 1870 Education Acts had brought, among other benefits to publishers, a substantially increased market for school and form prizes: the London School Board, for example, maintained a list of about 600 titles suitable for prizes from which schools could choose, and it was not unknown for a single title to sell over a thousand copies through this one Board.[10]

In these years at the turn of the century, when few publishers took a direct personal interest in children's books, the recommendation of either the editor of a periodical or of that special sort of literary gent, the publisher's reader, was often enough to persuade a publisher to take a book on. For example, the 'vivid' and 'stimulating' (Kenneth Grahame's words) W. E. Henley in the case of Grahame himself, R. L. Stevenson and others, or that doyen of readers, Edward Garnett, in the case of Edith Nesbit and her first major children's book *The Story of the Treasure Seekers*. Beatrix Potter, however, was an exception: not only did she have considerable professional attention from her publishers, Norman Warne, but also his love and affection, as they became engaged to be married.

Few children's books of note were published during the First World War or immediately after; apart from the first 'Dr Dolittle' book (1922), brought in from the USA by Jonathan Cape, and some Walter de la Mare titles, little that is of interest today has survived from that period. It was A. A. Milne's *When We Were Very Young* in 1924, and *Winnie-the-Pooh* two years later, which were the first post-war children's books to find a big readership. Milne, already a successful playwright, had a close relationship with his publisher Methuen – he was one of their principal advisers. Although an educational department under E. V. Rieu had been established in 1923, I do not believe there was a children's editor there until Eleanor Graham arrived in 1943.

For the publishers who were catering for the more popular market, the Twenties was a period of fierce competition: it was the time of the low-cost bumper book (which often repeated text and pictures from other books) and was printed on a cheap and nasty paper called Featherweight Antique – it had an unpleasant crumbly surface, was full of air and consequently bulked splendidly. The publishers loved it because it made a 100-page book look like two hundred, and printers hated it because its loose composition meant that fluff and dust constantly clogged their machines, which necessitated slower running and additional washing-up.

It was also a period when children's comics and family and women's magazines flourished; it was these publications which carried much of the contemporary writing for children. Indeed, in the article 'Writing for the Juvenile Market' in the 1930 edition of *The Writers' and Artists' Year Book*, the author does not bother to mention traditional book publishers – only comics, magazines and annuals.

It was in just such a publication (*The Home Magazine* published by George Newnes) that Richmal Crompton's very first William story, 'Rice Mould', appeared in 1919. From Kay Williams' biography we know that it was a Mrs Constance Hall, the magazine's assistant editor, who recognised the quality of this story which appeared on the slush pile – the ever-growing heap of unsolicited manuscripts to be found in every publisher's office – and persuaded the editor to publish it.[11] Richmal received £3 and, naively, signed away all rights. More stories quickly followed, the magazine's circulation went up and, three years later, Newnes put 12 of the early stories into a book – *Just William* – though without troubling to tell the author (they had all the rights, after all!). Fortunately, by this time, Richmal had taken on an agent who organised proper royalty arrangements for her.

Thus there was little need for the services of a children's editor for the William books: if the stories were right for the magazine – and they were – then all the publisher had to do was to wait until there were enough stories to put between hard covers. For more than 30 years, until 1954, this was how the William books came to be published.

Although Eleanor Graham, the first Puffin editor, wrote of the late 1930s that there was 'an amazing burgeoning of the quality of children's books ... a burgeoning of talent, originality and freshness of writing' she was, perhaps, contrasting it with the fallow period that preceded it.[12] If you look at the company histories of the period it is noticeable that little attention is given to children's books: they just weren't important enough for the traditional publisher. It was the era of the comic, the bumper book, the annual, and these were not (*pace* Herbert Strang) the areas that most publishers could – or wanted to – enter, particularly at a time of recession. But as the Depression years faded, a few houses were appointing children's editors – Dent and Heinemann among them – and, in 1940, Allen Lane of Penguin had the vision to launch the Puffin Story Books, with Eleanor Graham – successful children's bookseller and a regular reviewer in the national press – as editor.

In Macmillan's case, the company almost stopped publishing new children's books from 1914 until the early 1940s – there was no Mrs Craik and no children's editor. It was not until – I think – 1952 that an editor *was* appointed. (The evidence for this is in the company's staff record books which, interestingly, record salaries in ink but job descriptions in pencil. One can only speculate on the significance.) However, before that appointment, Macmillan was already publishing some of the extraordinarily prolific Enid Blyton's educational books (she was a Froebel-trained kindergarten teacher) and, in 1944, the first book of her Adventure series – *The Island of Adventure*. Macmillan folklore has it that Miss Blyton (as she was always called) came to the list almost by chance. It seems that she chose Macmillan as one of her 17 publishers because she and Roland Heath, a director of the company, were members of the same golf club. For some years, Miss Blyton's books were to remain an important part of both the school and the children's lists; in the case of the former, at least until teachers would no longer accept the author's somewhat saccharine treatment of such subjects as RE and Nature Study in *Enid Blyton's Bible Stories* and *Nature Readers*. The Adventure series, on the other hand, together with Noddy, the Famous Five, and the Secret Seven (what Naomi Lewis has called 'the sliced white bread of reading') still flourish today.

Finally, I would like to reassure you that children's editors *are* necessary, since my references to Kipling, Crompton and Blyton, for example, may have suggested otherwise. Carroll, of course, needed – and demanded – constant attention from his publisher on every aspect of his books. Morton Cohen and Anita Gandolfo's excellent edition of Carroll's letters to Macmillan provides numerous examples of how extraordinarily demanding an author can be,[13] whether it is a matter of margins being amiss by a fraction, or an order for varying small quantities of a book to be bound in different colours, or questioning not only the details of an account but often the basis on which it was prepared, or – frequently – a request for theatre tickets – and I quote a typical letter to Alexander:

Christ Church, Oxford
March 2, 1877

Dear Mr. Macmillan,

I hope I'm not making a troublesome request in asking you to get me 4 tickets for the Adelphi Pantomime for Saturday afternoon (the 10th).

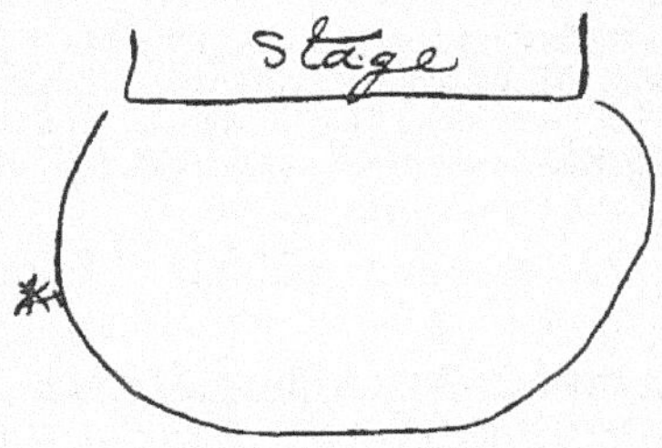

I want them dress-circle, front seats, about the place I have put a *. Two of them are for children under 12 (I mention in case children may be 'half-price').

Very truly yours
C. L. Dodgson

> PS We cannot arrive much before the thing begins – so, unless such seats are *numbered and reserved*, it would be better to get stalls (near the middle of 2nd. or 3rd. row), but I'm afraid little children wouldn't see so well from the stalls.

The tickets were procured. His letters were invariably answered promptly and courteously by one of the Macmillans or by Mr Craik.

The editor is there to build a list and that must always be in the forefront of his (or, more likely, her) mind. Sometimes contemporary editors may have to deal with a demanding or difficult author, but it is much more likely that the relationship will be a co-operative one. Take, for example, a children's picture book where, typically, words and pictures are by the same person. Dummies (or maquettes) have to be prepared, the design and layout – probably involving the house designer – approved, rough cover designs prepared for the sales people to comment on, plans for promoting and selling have to be considered – all this means discussion and collaboration between author, editor and other members of staff. If that goes well, then one will almost certainly have a better book and, one hopes, a happy author who will want to publish with you again.

It can also be the case that an editor is publishing the work of an author who is neither difficult nor cooperative – just dead. One might be tempted to think that this is an ideal situation: no one to chase for an overdue manuscript, no one to demand expensive and inappropriate promotion, no one to complain about sales. But, in practice, my experience with the books of both Lewis Carroll and Richmal Crompton is that a dead author can impose obligations, that you are not necessarily free to do as you – or what you think contemporary readers – may want. In the case of Lewis Carroll's *Alice* books (long out of copyright, of course) I felt, for example, that Macmillan had an obligation to use Carroll's final approved text, to stay with Tenniel's illustrations, and certainly to avoid the thoughtless crudities of some editions. In the case of Richmal Crompton's 'William' books (which remain in copyright, but came to Macmillan only in 1983) it was a matter of restoring Thomas Henry's inimitable illustrations to the stories (omitted from the previous publisher's edition) and which – like Tenniel and *Alice* – are forever associated with them, and to bring back into print the titles from the 1950s and 1960s which had never been reprinted.

Miles Kington, himself one of our funniest writers, has called the William books 'the funniest books ever written' and Harvey Darton, in his classic 1932 work, *Children's Books in England*, said of *Alice*, 'It was the coming to the surface, powerfully and permanently, the first unapologetic, undocumented appearance in print, for readers who sorely needed it, of liberty of thought in children's books.'[14] To promote such liberty is surely a prime purpose of literature designed for children, and I can think of no better reason for respecting the work of these authors and for continuing to search for others who may, one day, achieve similar status.

Notes

1. 'Just William's Luck', in *William Again* (London, 1923; repr. Macmillan, 1983).
2. 'William and the Smuggler', in *More William* (London, 1922; repr. Macmillan, 1983).
3. *A Bibliographical Catalogue of Macmillan and Co.'s Publications from 1843 to 1889* (London: Macmillan, 1891).
4. Thomas Hughes, *A Memoir of Daniel Macmillan* (London: Macmillan, 1882), p. 246.
5. Charles L. Graves, *Life and Letters of Alexander Macmillan* (London: Macmillan, 1910), p.146.
6. The problem with the biscuits, and the carving of the umbrella and parasol handles are raised in Carroll's letters. (*The Letters of Lewis Carroll*, edited by Morton N. Cohen, 2 vols. London: Macmillan, 1979. II, 938, 883.)
7. John Rowe Townsend, *Written for Children*, revised edition (Harmondsworth: Penguin, 1974), p. 163.
8. Peter Sutcliffe, *The Oxford University Press: an informal history* (Oxford: Clarendon Press, 1978), pp. 146–7. See also John Attenborough, *A Living Memory* (London: Hodder & Stoughton, 1975), pp. 51–2 for more information on the joint venture.
9. Perhaps the first literary agent, he was thought to have represented George Macdonald in 1875. See James Hepburn, *The Author's Empty Purse and the Rise of the Literary Agent* (Oxford: OUP, 1968).
10. J. S. Bratton, *The Impact of Victorian Children's Fiction* (London: Croom Helm, 1981).
11. *Just Richmal* (London, 1986).
12. 'The Puffin Years', in *The Signal Approach to Children's Books*, edited by Nancy Chambers (Harmondsworth: Penguin, 1980).
13. *Lewis Carroll and the House of Macmillan*, edited by Morton N. Cohen and Anita Gandolfo (Cambridge: Cambridge University Press, 1987), p. 135. Quoted by kind permission of A. P. Watt Ltd on behalf of The Trustees of the C. L. Dodgson Estate.
14. Harvey Darton, *Children's Books in England*, 2nd edition (Cambridge: Cambridge University Press, 1958), p. 268.

13
Macmillan: Or, 'Tis Sixty Years Since

Nicolas Barker

It is hard now, if you walk down the elegant pathway that leads to the bridge joining the Sainsbury Wing to the main body of the National Gallery, to imagine St Martin's Street as it was when Macmillan's building still stood there. It was a fine Italianate palazzo; to enter, ascend the grand staircase and reach the panelled chamber off which the main offices opened, dominated by the great portrait-drawings of the founders, was an unforgettable experience. The building was designed by John Cash, but the real architect, of the building, of the Net Book Agreement of 1899 that gave the booktrade its still surviving ethos, and of the business as I knew it, was Sir Frederick Macmillan. It was a measure of his greatness that he directed a business in which his brother Maurice and cousin George were also partners. Any suggestion of oligarchy had long since departed by the time I arrived in 1965. The Macmillan, who had only handed over the reins to his younger brother, Harold, two years earlier, was Daniel Macmillan. He was 'Mr Dan' within the firm, reflecting a time when he had been junior to Sir Frederick (*d.* 1936). This reflected a protocol that he himself observed. Once his brother's secretary rang him up with some message: 'Mr Macmillan has asked', she began, only to be cut short; 'I'm Mr Macmillan; you mean Mr Harold'. To him, younger brothers were best kept out of harm's way, and politics was as harmless an occupation as could be devised for them. One day in 1963, when Cuba was all the news, I was having lunch with him at the Garrick, when the Club bore came over and said to him in portentous tones, 'It says on the wireless that President Kennedy is on the telephone to your brother every hour.'

'Really', said Dan, with the unaffected surprise of one who had paid good money over the years to be spared that privilege, 'what on *earth* would he want to do that for?'

But Dan had gone before I entered the portal of St Martin's Street for the first time. It was said that when he heard (on the wireless, perhaps) that his brother, leaving office, intended to 'return' to the family business, he came into his office the same morning, summoned his *homme d'affaires*, and said, 'I'm retiring today. There are the cards, you know what to do', and walked out. That may not be true, but it does make clear the importance of Mr Dan's cards, which in their entirety were the nerve-centre of a system that he had devised to run the firm with a minimum of bother and a maximum of efficiency. But to explain that you have to go back to the Victorian heyday of the firm, the edifice that preceded the Victorian palazzo of 1897, and centred on the busy booktrade in Bedford Street. It had been created by the first Daniel, who died young in 1857 but was nonetheless given his place in that Victorian pantheon, *The Dictionary of National Biography*, no doubt on the strength of the memoir that Thomas Hughes wrote of him. Yet it was really the work of his younger brother Alexander, dismissed in the *D.N.B.* within a bracket after the words 'Macmillan & Co.' as 'the Co. being represented by Daniel's brother Alexander, *d.*1896, aged 78'. Which reminds me that within the firm, as the principal was called 'Mr Dan', so the firm itself was 'M. & Co.', never Macmillan or Macmillan's.

Alexander made M. & Co. great by application of a new invention, new that is to the British booktrade, the 'adviser' principle. This can be properly attributed to the founder, or rather to his reading that Victorian classic, *Guesses at truth, by Two Brothers*. Greatly daring, he wrote to one of its authors, Archdeacon Hare. Through Hare he met Frederick Denison Maurice, Richard Chenevix Trench, George Boole, Charles Kingsley and Thomas Hughes. *The Mathematical Analysis of Logic* (1847), *Westward Ho!* (1855), *The Water Babies* (1863), and *Tom Brown's School Days* (1857) all entered the list, but these successes were less important than the principle that lay behind them. Neither Daniel nor Alexander had been given much of an education, but they discovered how to borrow it. Up till then, a publisher had dealt with a book offered for publication in one of two ways. If he knew what it was about and could guess the market for it, he might publish it at his own risk. If he knew neither, he would publish it on commission for the author: that is, he would arrange for the printing, taking a commission on the bill, paid by the author, and he would remit the revenue from sales to the author, again taking a commission. The Macmillans realised that there were many authors, too poor (as they were) to pay for publication in this way, who might write or be persuaded to write books on subjects about which they (the brothers) knew nothing, but which would yet command a ready sale. They took advice from their influential friends, took a risk on their judgement, and found their faith justified.

In the latter part of the century, Lord Morley became the centre of a regular coterie that met in Bedford Street for Alexander's 'tobacco parliaments' which were a regular feature of Macmillan life from 1858 to 1907. Palgrave's *The Golden Treasury* (1861), the 'Globe Shakespeare' (1864), the 'Classical' and 'English Men of Letters' series, Grove's *Dictionary of Music* (1878–90), Tennyson (from 1884) and Henry James (from *The Europeans,* 1878), Jevons's *Political Economy* (1871), Freeman's *History of Europe* (1876), and Hall and Knight's *Elementary Algebra for Schools*, all these stemmed from the idea that a group of well-chosen advisers would know what was best, pick out the good offers from the bad, prompt a letter to a still unknown author, or at least know someone who would know and be able to advise on any book offered, no matter how obscure its subject. This outer ring grew and grew, and with it the 'adviser's report' came to be a regular part of the publishing routine. A considered estimate of the worth of each work under consideration, of the market it might reach, above all of its place in the Macmillan list, thus became the first step towards the publication of a book. The rest of its progress was planned with equal thoroughness; this was summed up on Mr Dan's cards, although the system itself long predated that ultimate refinement.

For a book to be published, it had previously to be printed, and M. & Co. entrusted printing in all its aspects to the people who knew how to do it, printers. The firm did not play around with many printers, still less play one off against another. To begin with there was only one, Robert MacLehose & Co. (cousin James MacLehose had been the confidant of the first Daniel's earliest endeavours) of Glasgow. As the business grew MacLehose was joined by R. & R. Clark of Edinburgh, and later by Richard Clay, at first conveniently close at Bread Street in London, later at Bungay in Suffolk. MacLehose always had the lion's share of the work, in particular the educational books, a humdrum business, but one that grew and grew in the second half of the nineteenth century. M. & Co. laid down educational books and series, particularly in the classics and mathematics, like port: the initial outlay might be considerable, but repaid itself in profits enjoyed over many years. As the literary side of the business took off too – as when the Globe

Shakespeare became a national, even international bestseller in 1864 – R. & R. Clark came in, under the formidable Robert Clark. He made a habit of reading the books sent to him to print, and once took exception to the printing order sent him for J. H. Shorthouse's *John Inglesant.* Too small, he thought, and, remonstration failing, doubled the number on his own account. Sure enough, a telegram for an urgent reprint arrived, requesting the best possible date for delivery – a fortnight, perhaps? Clark put the sheets on the next boat from Leith and two days later they were in London. In parenthesis, note that access to water transport was still vital for the transport of large consignments of printed paper; Richard Clay, when they moved from London, chose a place on the Waveney, convenient to the port of Lowestoft.

These were the reliable firms who took on the manufacture of M. & Co.'s books, together with two other necessary partners, the Carrongrove paper mill, convenient to the Forth, and James Burn & Co., the binders, at Saffron Hill, above what had once been the Fleet river, where Gerard had once gathered its eponymous herb. All five had been chosen because they knew their business, and could be trusted to get on with it, without 'progress-chasing', a concept then unknown. So, when the adviser's report had been duly considered and the decision to publish taken, the manuscript would be sent off to the printer selected. With it went a request for a specimen page-setting; the format, referred to by the relevant paper size, pott, post, crown, demy, or – M. & Co.'s special – globe, would be specified, nothing more, since the printer knew without being told what type, size and margins were appropriate. The specimen page would arrive and was rarely altered; it was then returned with a composition order. Order forms were made up in books with a flimsy after each form on which the details were preserved by an intervening carbon-paper. The layout of the forms had not been altered since an earlier stage of copying, when such documents were written out in special ink and pressed when still wet in a copying press (the evanescent script in such 'wet copy books' is the bane of the modern archivist's life). The form contained two important instructions: the words 'Please set up, using high/low spaces' (the significance of this delphic alternative will emerge later), and the author's address to which proofs were to be directed.

After that, the printer and the author were left to get on with it. The author knew his part of the business, and the printer, in the shape of that long-lost and sadly-missed hero, the printer's reader, was his opposite – often, when it came to accuracy, more than a match for the author. Galley-proofs would go out and come back, succeeded by page-proofs. These were returned with his last corrections by the author (plus the index, if any), but the printer's reader might himself call for a press-revise, a sheet taken from the press, always read by the reader, and if need be sent to the author for final clarification. There was no sense of hurry about this process. Both author and printer had a higher goal, accuracy. Nor were M. & Co. concerned by speed; a good book would find its market whenever it appeared. The cost of composition was not great, and was treated as an overhead expense, not attributed to the book concerned. If the author's share of the cost of correction exceeded 10 per cent, the balance was nominally charged to him; the printer bore the cost of his errors, scrupulously recorded by the reader. The progress of all this, galley by galley, page by page, was reported to M. & Co. by the printer on 'statements'. These were sent every week, detailing every book currently with the printer and showing how much further it had gone since the previous week. When author and reader had finally concluded their work, the book was recorded as 'passed for press'.

At this point, if not before, the crucial decision, how many copies to print, would be taken and recorded in the 'Editions Book', a quarto ledger bound in half-calf, at once the authority and the record for such a decision. At this point, the actual cost of the book began to be taken into consideration. Paper was the most substantial part of the whole bill, apart from the binding, which, unlike the rest, could be paid for piecemeal, as and when incurred, and did not involve the whole edition. A price for different qualities of paper, ranging in substance from feather-weight to antique, antique to 'm.f.' (machine-finished), m.f. to 's.c.' (super-calendered), with the final luxury of 'chart-paper', made with special care on a slow-running machine and used for folding maps or tables where strength was important, was agreed annually on the basis of weight, calculated indifferently by the ton or the pound. The particular size or finish for any book was irrelevant, too; Carrongrove and the printers could be relied on to make sure that adequate supplies were maintained; the printing order, when it came, rarely took them by surprise.

The cost of composition per page and of printing, calculated per 1,000 sheets of 32, 64 or 128 pages in each of the different paper sizes, was pre-determined by the 'Edinburgh scale'. This may well have been developed to meet M. & Co.'s needs, although 60 years ago it was in general use in the trade. Its original purpose was clear enough. The Scottish printers were at a disadvantage compared with their rivals in London, who enjoyed proximity to their customers. The London printers could be sent for, negotiated with and beaten down to an acceptable price. Four hundred miles away, MacLehose and Clark relied on cheaper prices, cheap because they had a comfortable cushion of M. & Co.'s work beneath them, so cheap that they were prepared to divulge, even advertise them. 'Just beat us', the Edinburgh scale seemed to say, and the London printers were hard put to do so. Once a month, the current MacLehose or Clark representative would descend to the metropolis and call on their customers, putting up for two or three days at the same club, the Caledonian. In public they made a point of solidarity, but privately were not above rivalry. Once, William Maxwell of Clark's returned from dining out, racked by a bad oyster. James MacLehose, who had dined in, took one look at him and hurried him up to bed, all solicitude. Next morning, he went back to the bedroom. 'It's the day in bed for you, Willie,' he said, 'just a little beef-tea if you feel strong enough. Tell me who you were going to see and I'll go and make your apologies.' Gratefully, the unsuspecting Maxwell gave him the list. James called on them all. 'Sad business about poor Willie', he would say, lifting his elbow suggestively.

'Passed for press' did not mean that it would be printed forthwith. Other processes might precede that. M. & Co. books might sometimes enjoy a large immediate sale; more often, there was a smaller but continuous demand, predictable to a firm that knew its market so well. If sales, though adequate, were likely to be of short duration, the book was printed from the type it was set in. If it had a longer life, stereotype plates were made from the type by moulding it in papier-mâché and casting hard metal in them; the plates could be faced with nickel for extra strength. If it enjoyed both large sales and a long life, the extra expense of electrotype plates was called for. Pages placed in an acid bath were covered in copper by electrolytic action, and the copper 'shells' filled with hard metal. Roughly speaking, type was good for a run of 20–25,000, stereos for 50,000 and electros for anything up to 300,000; in practice, these figures were often exceeded. M. & Co. did not invent this routine, but it was a large factor in the firm's success. This is recorded in a work still unique among publishers' annals, *A Bibliographical Catalogue of Macmillan and Co.'s Publications from 1843 to 1889*, published in 1891.

> ... The system adopted has been to give the publications of each year in alphabetical order; no title appears more than once, as subsequent editions and reprints are noted under the original entry [with their dates]. The titles and collations have been taken from copies of the first edition of every book, except in a few instances, in which the deviation from this rule has always been noted. A complete Index will be found at the end of the volume.

> One of the first things to be settled when this catalogue was undertaken was a definition of the word *Edition*, and after careful consideration the Publishers decided to describe as an *Edition* an impression from type set up afresh either with or without alteration and read for press by a proof-reader [sc. printer's reader]. An impression from standing type or from Stereotype or Electrotype plates is described as a *Reprint*. The letter **S** or **E** implies that Stereotype or Electrotype plates were taken. **M** means that paper moulds were made from which, if required, Stereotype plates could afterwards be cast.
>
> It need hardly be said that the numbers of Editions or reprints of any given book is no accurate guide as to its sale. An *Edition* may consist of 250 or 100,000 copies.

If understandably secretive about numbers which appear in the Editions Books, the *Bibliographical Catalogue* gives a very vivid picture of a number of special features of M. & Co.'s methods. The importance of the distinction of different kinds of printing surface, the critical intervention of the printer's reader, above all, the distinction between '*Edition*' and '*Reprint*', are all made clear. It was not, then, until the printing surface had been determined and made that it was possible for the printers to proceed. They had not been left wholly in the dark, however, for the composition order, with its specific instruction about the height of the spaces, had let them know which way the wind was blowing. 'Low spaces' were adequate for printing or stereotyping: 'high spaces' were needed if the type was to be electrotyped, otherwise the shell might sag and crack; they would not do for printing, since they might rise and catch the ink. High or low, there came a day when the printers' statements noted 'on machine next week'. This was the signal for a final order to print to be sent, with the further instruction that six (or for reprints two) early sets of sheets were to be sent to the binders. At this point, an entry was made in the 'Quire Book', another quarto ledger in which not merely 'Editions' but also 'Reprints' were recorded. It was the official record of all printing undertaken, to be reconciled with the record of paper used by the printers, and, most important of all, a forewarning to the binders.

James Burn did all the binding. There was no Burn by now, but Lionel Darley, the courteous and learned author of *Bookbinding Then and Now*, who worked for Burn from 1911 to 1963, used to call daily on Mr Dan, to whom he was better known than the MacLehose cousins. This daily visit was an interpretative mission, and an essential part of the system. But it had an agenda. This was created by the arrival of the 'early sheets' from the printer. Mr Darley would examine them and prepare six specimen binding cases, in two different shades each of green, blue or red cloth; the lettering, usually gilt (except for educational books), was deduced from the title-page, and the brasses for it cut by hand by Mr Avison (photographic reproduction was unheard of). The six sets of sheets would be bound in the six cases, and Mr Darley would take them for approval on his next daily visit. Sometimes this was a formality, sometimes there would be a delay before approval was granted, but eventually one of them was selected, and this became the model for Burn. Unlike printing and paper-making, binding was not a fully mechanised process. There was a Y-shaped sequence: the printed sheets would start down one arm, first to be folded and collated, then sewn, fitted with endpapers and trimmed; down the other, cloth (which Burn kept in stock) would be cut to size, made up with boards into cases, and blocked with the lettering in gold or ink; at this point, case and book would join each other, to be rounded and backed and then pressed, hundreds deep, in tall standing presses. Finally, the jacket, if there was one, would be wrapped round each finished book.

This process was determined by the binding order that Mr Darley would pick up with the approved early copy. By no means all the sheets printed would be bound at once, perhaps two-thirds or only a half of the full number. The rest would be held by Burn, nominally flat, although Burn might, to suit their own convenience, fold all. Nor were all the books bound delivered at once: to do so would have filled St Martin's Street to overflowing. Bind *x* copies, the binding order would say, and deliver *y*, *y* being always less than *x*. This was an operating necessity both for Burn and M. & Co., while both were limited by their London premises; neither could afford to waste space on books not immediately wanted. Both were eventually forced to find space further afield, Burn in the Royal Mills at Esher, Macmillan at Basingstoke, but this did not alter the system, a system that survived even the disasters of the Second World War and went back to medieval times, when the whole trade lived cheek-by-jowl within a stone's throw of St Paul's. The main façade of M. & Co.'s palazzo in St Martin's Street faced the Royal Watercolour Society's premises between it and the National Gallery, but the building stretched back the full width of the block bounded on its west side by Whitcomb Street. There, in Whitcomb Street, was the trade entrance, an archway closed by a pair of heavy iron gates. Burn's dray (later van) just fitted the archway, and the one-way system – in from St Martin's Street and out via Whitcomb Street – helped to prevent traffic jams. The books, wrapped in packets of 12 to 40 depending on size, were delivered to the loading bay, whence they were transferred to the shelves built to store them, until ordered and despatched.

The stock-manager was responsible for calculating the quantities of books delivered, against those that went out. This required a very nice judgement, based on long experience; there was no room, quite literally, for error. Daily contact with his opposite number at Saffron Hill ensured the volume of incoming deliveries. Although the M. & Co. 'travellers', whose job was to solicit booksellers' orders for each title, saw to it that there was a comfortable number in hand before the first consignment of a book was sent out, a great deal of the daily outward traffic went through the 'trade counter' into the hands, or rather capacious leather bags, of the 'collectors'. Every bookshop of any size and most publishers (for many publishers were still also retail booksellers, in fact if not in name) had its own collector, whose daily routine was to go from trade counter to trade counter, picking up books ordered. There were also independent collectors, who served the smaller bookshops and could be summoned in emergency by the larger if their own collector was fully occupied. All this required hourly vigilance; quick response by all concerned was essential. A bookshop, if out of stock of any book, was expected to get it the same day and, if need be, deliver it to a customer. Publishers met booksellers' orders in the same way. The publisher depended on an equally prompt and agile response from binders. If binding, unlike printing, was an only partially mechanised industry, it could also be regarded as the first step in a distribution process that was essentially human, not mechanical. Depending on demand, two, three, even six separate binding orders might cover a single printing (hence the multiple 'binding states' that bemuse bibliographers of the nineteenth century), and anything from one to a dozen 'call orders' for stock be issued against a single binding order.

All those involved in this process required access to a single uniform source of information on M. & Co.'s wares, and this was provided by the 'Folio Catalogue'. In this, every single item was listed, one item to a line, its author and title conveniently abbreviated, printed on folio sheets of squared paper, vertically ruled in red, and bound in 'Kraft', standard brown wrapping paper. Even so, Hall & Stevens's *School Geometry*, its six parts available singly or in a single volume or any combination of the same, every one of them with or without answers or 'answers separately', in imperial or metric measures, and all these combinations also available in Bengali, took several pages. Sometimes the abbreviated titles were odd: Professor Stanley Eugene Fish's first book, *Surprised by Sin: the reader in* Paradise Lost (1967), in which he ingeniously demonstrated how Milton beguiles the reader into sympathy with Satan only to confront him with the enormity of his offence, ended up as 'Fish Surprised by Sin'. But the lines and squares of blank paper that followed were filled by each user with vital information: dates of stock ordered and delivered, daily notes of numbers in and out, invoices sent and paid, and so on. It was the bible, with uniform chapter and verse, that enabled every member of the staff to communicate with any other about the current state of every item on the list. It was updated and reprinted annually, and the passage of the year was marked by the arrival of a new folio catalogue in its shiny new brown cover, just in time to supersede its now dog-eared predecessor.

But the key to all these documents and to the system of which they were part lay in Mr Dan's cards. I suspect that they were not the foundation of the system (which itself must have predated him), but rather its ultimate refinement, the sort of *reductio ad quintessentiam* to which his penetrating intelligence may have reduced it. The cards were ordinary ruled 6" x 4" index cards, one for every book in the list. The author's name and the title (in the same short-hand form) were written in the margin at the top, with the price and royalty and trade terms. Below, the card was divided into two by a vertical line. On the left, the number of copies first and subsequently printed was recorded, with the dates of each successive reprint. On the right, the annual sales were written in. An informed eye could tell at a glance whether the book had paid its way, and, as was so often the case, how much its continuing existence contributed to maintaining M. & Co. It is hard to imagine a neater and more succinct way of watching over a large and heterogeneous business. There was no need for estimates; all the cash figures that supplemented the cards were safely embedded in the Edinburgh scale and an even more complicated schedule of every combination and permutation of binding costs maintained by Burn. But like many another hieratic text, the information in the cards seemed less important than the daily liturgy of maintaining them. I suspect that Mr Dan knew most of them, certainly all the important ones, by heart. When he left, the ritual lost its meaning. Each time that Tarquin refused to buy the Sibyl's books, she burnt three of them; only when three were left did he relent. Dan's cards are all gone now, and in modern publishing firms a vast battery of computer-generated information on costs and revenue, numbers printed and sold, is available at a keystroke. I wonder if it tells them any more clearly where they are or what lies ahead of them.

Index

Lightning Source UK Ltd.
Milton Keynes UK
UKHW022145020921
389932UK00002B/179